IDEAS AND POLITICS
The American Experience

THE DORSEY SERIES IN POLITICAL SCIENCE

EDITOR   NORTON E. LONG   *Brandeis University*

MACRIDIS & BROWN   *The De Gaulle Republic*

MACRIDIS & BROWN (eds.)   *Comparative Politics: Notes and Readings,* rev. ed.

DRAGNICH   *Major European Governments, rev. ed.*

ROBINSON   *Congress and Foreign Policy-Making: A Study in Legislative Influence and Initiative*

JACOBINI   *International Law: A Text*

MANGONE   *The Elements of International Law: A Casebook*

GRIPP   *Patterns of Soviet Politics*

MINAR   *Ideas and Politics: The American Experience*

MEEHAN   *The Theory and Method of Political Analysis*

EDELMANN   *Latin American Government and Politics: The Dynamics of a Revolutionary Society*

JACOB & ATHERTON   *The Dynamics of International Organization: The Making of World Order*

IDEAS AND POLITICS

The American Experience

BY

DAVID W. MINAR
NORTHWESTERN UNIVERSITY

1964

THE DORSEY PRESS • Homewood, Illinois

First Printing, September, 1964

Second Printing, June, 1966

Library of Congress Catalog Card No. 64–24702

To Carola

PREFACE

This book grew out of the conviction that there is a serious place for the study of political thought in a systematic political science. Sometimes analysis of the ideas of the past is treated, even by its devotees, as though it were a kind of aesthetic criticism whose purpose is to expound questions of beauty and points of form. There is, to be sure, nothing wrong with criticism for its own sake. But insofar as political ideas are handled exclusively in this fashion, the entire enterprise of political science is the poorer. For, as the first chapter tries to show, there are uses to which contemporary political science, including those parts with positive or quantitative orientations, should be putting yesterday's political thought. Political ideas are themselves variables in the working out of political relationships, and they are also heuristic tools for the analyst. It seems important that students of political theory take these potentials seriously.

To put the case in a general way, the premise of the book is that political thought should be seen in terms of its relationship to other variables of political life: behavior, action, institutions, policy, etc. There is nothing very startling about this thesis, but to demonstrate it effectively, and thereby establish it as a worthwhile goal for political science is not a simple task. There are several ways in which it might be tried, and indeed some in which it has been. The methodological points involved might be discussed at length, or the materials of political theory might be sliced in some different fashion, for example by functions or topics. What follows is the product of a split scholarly personality, with feet in the past, perhaps, and head in the present. Therefore, the materials of the book are largely the traditional ones, the arrangement is traditional, and presentation traditional. The intent and execution, however, are not, and it is hoped that the overall effect can be regarded as some contribution to the renewal of a worthy subject.

This decision to rework the field of American political thought from the standpoint of its relation to action and institutions was influenced chiefly by personal interest and stimulating teaching experiences. Also relevant, however, were some convictions about the meaning of the American political experience. It may be trite to dwell on the point that the United States too was once young, once had a revolution, once underwent pangs of economic development. But whether or not the observation is getting old-hat, it remains worth keeping in mind as one ponders such questions as the role ideas play in stimulating and channeling political change. Surely no nation has had a more impressive exposure to social change, and few have responded more intriguingly either in economics or politics. This suggests that there may be a great deal of sense in returning now and then to the experience of our own culture with the interplay of ideas and politics. For this reason as well as others having to do with understanding the political world in general and the American political culture in particular, the study of American political thought seems eminently worthwhile.

If apologies are to be made for this book, they should probably be made for failing to innovate enough, for staying too close to customary usages and interpretations. Yet perhaps there is something to be said for working out from the customary and into the new, and it is hoped that this volume represents a step along the path. It is certainly not presented as an effort to do the whole job. This disclaimer may create some obligation to suggest where the study of political ideas should go next. Three kinds of work come to mind, all of them objects of some attention in current research. One is the statement of systematic and general propositions about the relationship of ideas to politics; these might particularly be propositions about the form of ideas as distinct from their substance and propositions suitable for testing in comparative cross-cultural studies. A second is concurrent testing of such propositions on various levels of political life: nation-state, community, organization, small group. Even experimental studies in this field do not seem impossible. Finally, there is need for specific attention to the linkages between ideas and action. These linkages, open to investigation at both individual and organizational levels, constitute the key element in efforts to present an orderly picture of a political world that includes widely shared and presumably influential ideas and the systems of behavior upon which they are presumably influential. We know little about the way these terms co-vary and even less about why they are connected as they are. But these, as indicated, are not the central problems of the present book.

Explanation of one or two procedural choices at this point might help clarify what follows in the substantive chapters. It should be perfectly clear that this book is not intended as an encyclopedia of American ideas. Many thinkers about politics, some of great importance, have been omitted from our account altogether. This is as it must be for two reasons: coverage is clearly impossible; and even if it were possible, it would be unnecessary in terms of the purpose of the book. In effect, we treat political thought as a set of clues to the political culture; to understand the culture it is not necessary to have read all the clues. A principle of parsimony is involved. The choice of clues is essentially arbitrary, though something about the "test of time" might be thrown in for purposes of validation.

In this light the main problems of the book can be seen as these: given this kind of political culture reflected in this political thought, what are the consequences for political action and institutions; and, given this kind and magnitude of change in political culture, what changes in political institutions can be expected to ensue. It is partly to facilitate this latter interest that the analysis in the chapters that follow moves along in essentially chronological order.

Many people have done many things to help make this book a reality. It is quite impossible to thank them all, but several must be mentioned for particular reasons. Norman Jacobson, as teacher and friend, had a great deal to do with shaping my interest in political theory in general and American thought in particular. Norton Long, colleague, friend, and series editor, did much to stimulate my early interest in this project and has provided continual critique and patient encouragement. Richard C. Snyder, as friend and department chairman, has facilitated my work in both intellectual and practical ways. Victor G. Rosenblum, colleague and friend, has listened and challenged in many settings over many years.

I also owe much to Northwestern students, graduate and undergraduate, who listened to these ideas, discussed them with me, and wittingly and unwittingly helped me sift and rethink them. Some particularly have read portions of the manuscript and given me the benefit of valuable advice: Craig Brown, Sandra S. Powell, Thomas M. Scott.

Most importantly, my thanks must go to my family: to my wife, who has edited and re-edited, typed and retyped, encouraged, reinforced, revivified; those who know her will appreciate how much she has done to see the job through; to an older son whose interest and sage advice have been spurs to effort; to a younger son who in his first year has been a helpless but cheerful victim of the process of preparing this book.

All responsibilities must of course remain mine.

DAVID W. MINAR

WILMETTE, ILLINOIS
June, 1964

TABLE OF CONTENTS

IDEAS AND POLITICS

This is a social science book about American political thought. If to some people political thought is the very core of political science, to others the two seem hardly related at all. Hence, this chapter is devoted to an exploration of their relationship, for the premise on which the following chapters are written is that the traditional study of political theory and the contemporary study of political behavior are mutually complementary pursuits.

The point is not that the study of political ideas needs any particular justification; indeed, it has long had a status both prestigious and self-validating. Furthermore, several qualities about political thought make it an important intellectual object intrinsically worth the attention of serious people. It has, for one thing, aesthetic values, for it is often set down in what must surely be considered great literature. For this reason if for no other, the preservation and study of the masterpieces of political writing seem defensible things to do. Reflection also suggests that political ideas have a generally stimulative effect on the mind. Thus, perhaps the mere process of handling the concepts and formulas of political thought is educational in the sense that learning mathematics or foreign languages equips one for better thinking.

But however these things may be, none of them explains the importance of the storehouse of political thought to a social science engaged in developing a clear and systematic interpretation of the world of interactions among men and groups of men. This question is not self-answering. The human meaning of both political ideas and political science may depend on the seriousness with which we approach it.

WHY POLITICAL THOUGHT?

Thus, we begin with the question, "Why political thought?" and particularly from the standpoint of what it can do for the social sciences.[1] What help can the social scientists expect to get from mining the political ideas of the past? There appear to be useful materials of at least three kinds in this storehouse: it yields theory; it yields evidence for testing theory about theory; it constitutes a source of descriptive information about the political culture. Each of these points merits fuller explanation, for taken together they describe the purpose of this book.

That political thought yields theory will be demonstrated, if demonstration is required, by the substantive chapters that follow. At this point, we may confine our attention largely to the nature and role of theory in social science. What we are claiming here is not that to be theory, ideas had to be developed sometime in the past, nor that any set of ideas developed in the past is, ipso facto, theory, nor that any theory developed in the past is necessarily worthy of attention. We are, rather, making a claim so modest as to appear obvious to some— namely, our accumulation of political ideas can help us fulfill one of the major requirements of social science—that we have theory.

As the succeeding section of this chapter will suggest, the term theory is subject to a variety of interpretations. We are interested here in the kind of theory that generalizes about our interrelated expectations of the existential world—the kind of theory now commonly called empirical. The entire scientific enterprise is devoted to the development and testing of this kind of theory, which may, of course, be more or less elaborate according to its "level"—the sphere of experience with which it deals. It is through theory that our observations become more than the mere gathering of facts; it tells us where to go for evidence and what to expect when we get there. As it provides a framework for linking one set of observations to another, it provides the means through which our experience with the past becomes a basis for expectations of the future.[2]

---

[1] Discussions of the place of political thought in political science have been numerous in the literature. For a suggestive essay on the particular matter of American ideas, see Robert G. McCloskey, "American Political Thought and the Study of Politics," *Approaches to the Study of Politics*, ed. Roland Young (Evanston: Northwestern University Press, 1958), pp. 155–71. More generally, see Thomas I. Jenkin, *The Study of Political Theory* (Garden City: Doubleday & Co., 1955); Charles S. Hyneman, *The Study of Politics: the Present State of American Political Science* (Urbana: University of Illinois Press, 1959); Harry Eckstein, "Political Theory and the Study of Politics: a Report of a Conference," *American Political Science Review*, Vol. L (June, 1956), pp. 475–87.

[2] On the place of theory in science, see Ernest Nagel, *The Structure of Science: Problems in the Logic of Scientific Explanation* (New York and Burlingame: Harcourt, Brace & World, Inc., 1961), esp. chaps. 1 and 5; on the behavioral sciences, see Abraham Kaplan, *The Conduct of Inquiry* (San Francisco: Chandler Publishing Co., 1964); also Vernon Van Dyke, *Political Science: a Philosophical Analysis* (Stanford: Stanford University Press, 1960), esp. chap. 9.

Thus, it is through theory that predictions are developed, and prediction, in turn, is the testing mechanism of theory and the central part of the scientific process. At the practical level, it is theory that helps us to organize our contact with the environment in such a way as to make life workable. For example, through a generally unarticulated theory of physics, we predict (i.e., "know" and relate to specific events) that when we apply heat to paper, the paper ignites. This prediction does a number of things for us, telling us, among other things, how to build bonfires and warning us about smoking in bed while reading the *New York Times.* Much of our lives we run by signals inferred from low-level physical, chemical, and biological theory.

The same is true, both on the day-to-day level and at a more sophisticated plane, of the theory of social science. It is a prediction about human behavior deriving from a behavioral theory (actually an interdisciplinary theory borrowing from psychology, sociology, political science, and law) that permits us to cross the street with a green light when a truck is bearing down on us. Our generalized experience permits us to predict that the truck driver will stop (or, in certain cultures and subcultures, will not). In politics, a crude theory of voting behavior tells a candidate that kissing babies will do him good, and a somewhat more elegant one tells experts how unskilled urbanites or suburban professionals will cast their ballots. If political science is to be more than storytelling or the random collection of discrete facts, it must be on the basis of consciously developed and tested theory.

Theory is nothing mysterious; it is symbolic representation of what we think the world is like. What is said above does not solve many of the problems that social science theory involves. It does not tell us, for example, about the requirements of testability or settle the question whether theory or observation comes first in the logic or practice of the sciences. Some of these questions we will touch on below, some will wait for treatment in the context of the substantive part of our discussion, and some we will ignore altogether. At this point, our main interest lies in the centrality of theory to social science, and our case must rest on assertion and what demonstration the preceding paragraphs provide.

The other side of our claim is that theory is to be found in the storehouse of political thought. Here, too, we must rely on assertion and on deference to the evidence that follows. However, in support of our claim, we may suggest that ideas are where you find them, that the development of significant political theory is no easy task. The political thought of the past is the product of some of history's finest minds—minds whose eminence has withstood the test of time and the criticism of successive generations. It would seem foolish and arrogant not to use it for whatever it is worth, and we cannot know what it is worth unless we know what it is.

Our plea is simply that those who wish to develop explanatory theory about political life could do worse than turn to the accumulation of political ideas for inspiration. Certainly, to do so confronts us with dangers, for it can hold us in bondage to the past, stifle creativity, and promote the silly notion that because an idea was stated in a given period or by a big-name star of political theory, it merits uncritical adulation. These are, indeed, pitfalls against which political science has only recently begun to learn to protect itself. However, while acknowledging that such pitfalls exist, we might also remind ourselves with confidence that they are not so onerous as to forbid us the use of the wisdom of the past in developing a testable and systematic political science for the present and future. Hence, as we will try to show, the work of a Madison, a Tocqueville, or a Calhoun may still be (and in these cases has been) a source of forward thrust for the study of politics.[3]

We also suggested that political thought may be important as a testing ground for a specific kind of theory—namely, theory about the role of ideas in politics.[4] Whatever other tasks one may fancy for the discipline of political science, it will generally be agreed that one of its appropriate goals is to explain the relationship between political "things" (e.g., events) and other kinds of phenomena. Many hold that this is the only meaningful political science activity. But the question of scope aside, among the elements in these networks of political science explanation are ideas themselves. Ideas, that is to say, are variables in the explanation of political behavior. Whether they "cause" behavior we may not be able to know for certain, but they are unmistakably links in the chain of political phenomena at the level of the individual, the level of the group, and the level of the society. As ideas appear, as modes of thought disappear, as intellectual and communicative styles change, we expect related changes in other aspects of the political system.

---

[3] One of the most striking recent examples drawn from the American field is Robert A. Dahl, *A Preface to Democratic Theory* (Chicago: University of Chicago Press, 1956). See also references in the chapters following, particularly those on Jefferson, Tocqueville, and Calhoun.

[4] See McCloskey, *op. cit.;* Frederick M. Watkins, "Political Theory as a Datum of Politics," *Approaches to the Study of Politics*, ed. Roland Young (Evanston: Northwestern University Press, 1958), pp. 148–54; Karl J. Friedrich, *Man and His Government* (New York: McGraw-Hill Book Co. Inc., 1963), esp. chap. 4, pp. 83–93; Jenkin, *op. cit.*

More will be said about the characteristics and mechanisms of this relationship of ideas to political action, institutions, and policy. This is obviously a question that can be treated at many levels. Survey research on attitudinal correlates of voting behavior is research on this problem at the level of the individual. We shall be concerned with it in a much more macro sense, with the flow of a "tradition" and its effect on a political process and policy. If the generality of our concern and the fact that we are working with a single case prevent our bringing concrete hypotheses to test, this should not obscure the fact that we are still concerned in a systematic way with the question of ideas in the political system.

Further, political ideas tell us things about the culture, and this is a matter of importance both for social science and for responsible living. In a literate society, the social records of values, habits, customs, patterned interactions, etc., are kept in part by those whose business it is to think and write. Poets and storytellers and historians and philosophers all set down pieces of their culture in durable form. Their pictures of it are piecemeal, but they provide a kind of conglomerate understanding of ways of life among those whose ways we can no longer observe and among their survivors of today who still bear on their shoulders the cultural commitments of the past.

For clues about the political culture, we may turn to novels, to dramas, poems, public records, and to writings about politics. These last include much of what we call political thought. They may, of course, be used selectively, since they are clearly not of equal value for all purposes. However, they constitute a supply of data from which much may be drawn.

For political science, this supply is useful if culture is an important part of the political system. If, to put it in other terms, we see the political culture as an element in a macrotheory of politics, then the test of our theory may draw on political ideas for evidence. Such a model of politics will be sketched out in a subsequent section of this chapter. For political action—indeed, perhaps for citizenship itself—the supply of information about one's own culture is useful as a set of indications about the valuable and/or the possible, depending on one's ideological point of view. It yields clues to such things as the trajectory of development of institutions and the root sources of value commitments. Although the rationalist and the metaphysician, the liberal and the conservative might go about the study and use of political ideas in different ways, they would doubtless agree that one's cultural context is worth knowing. While we do not propose that these sets of ideas are complete or adequate guides to the culture, we shall go far enough to claim that they will provide as useful a source of political socialization as anything available.

THOUGHT, THEORY, AND IDEOLOGY

Certain terms that frequently recur in our discussion should probably be clarified at this point. Particularly central are the concepts of thought, theory, and ideology which, though closely interrelated, are not to be treated as identical.[5] While it does not seem necessary to offer formal definitions, some indication of tendencies and patterns of usage may help keep our discussion in order.

Of the three, thought is the most general category; in both technical and common use, its meaning is perhaps as big as the entire product of the human mind. In our discussions here, we have accordingly used it as a broad, residual label, though, clearly, a book on American political thought must take a subject somewhat narrower in scope than the entire political product of American thinking. In practice, therefore, our treatment of thought is selective.

Conventionally, political thought refers to the ideas of writers who have addressed themselves consciously and explicitly to such central problems of politics as liberty, authority, and order, at a fairly high level of abstraction. Usage has invested some with the status of major figures in political thought, others it has not. Generally speaking, our selection will follow convention. Other considerations, however, also enter the picture, some of them peculiar to this book, some inherent in the subject matter of American political thought.

One of these is that the principle of selectivity itself be recognized, that it be explicitly understood that "coverage" is out of the question. Another is that the thought with which we deal will be chosen with an eye to its representativeness of period, subject matter, and tone. Yet a third consideration is that our definition of thought will be sufficiently flexible to accommodate some materials not always classified under this heading—the miscellaneous ideas and comments of public figures, court cases, public documents, some institutional and social history into which ideas can be read, and others. The sample of "thought" on which we will draw and from which we will attempt our larger analysis of the American political process will include, in other words, more than statements of formal political philosophy. There have been, indeed, few such statements of much importance.

---

[5] A helpful discussion of these terms may be found in Jenkin, *op. cit.*, pp. 6–11. See also Friedrich, *op. cit.*

Implicitly, we are suggesting that the line between ideas and behavior is thin, and the two may be nearly indistinguishable when we are doing our analysis at the level of society and nation-state.

This, then, will be our raw material. What we shall expect to find among our collection of evidence are ideas—ideas that contain theory, that influence action, that describe the political culture. On occasion, these ideas may be described as ideology—a term with somewhat more specific reference than thought.

The term ideology is an old one, used for a variety of polemical and scientific purposes. There is little agreement about the specific terms in which it *should* be defined and about its merits and limitations as a concept in social research. An examination of the literature indicates that thought labeled ideology has been distinguished by such diverse criteria as prescriptive content, internal structure, personal and social functions, organizational locus, purpose, and group or class locus.[6] Among them, there is no single standard use, but the most common tendency is probably toward a composite. When we use the term here, it will be to refer to a preconceived set or structure of beliefs, including both values and propositions about the way the world is thought to be. Thus, an ideology is a "world view" with judgment and action implications.

Theory is likewise a term with a variety of common uses. Something of the sense in which we use it here has been suggested in the preceding section. Some confine it to a particular type of generalizations, usually empirical, i.e., generalizations that tie together propositions about the existential world.[7] This is a matter of choice which has to do not with reality but with clarity of purpose and communication. As we do not propose to limit our use of the term in this way, it becomes even more important to distinguish between kinds of theory and to clarify their various meanings.

Basically, our analysis rests on the view that propositions about fact and propositions about value are different kinds of statements that require different kinds of handling. Hence, we begin with a distinction between theory about the one and theory about the other, between empirical or explanatory theory and normative theory. The empirical is the theory we accept or reject according to its ability

---

[6] For discussion of the literature and perceptual problems of ideology, see David W. Minar, "Ideology and Political Behavior," *Midwest Journal of Political Science*, Vol. V (November, 1961), pp. 317–31.

[7] See the discussion in Carl G. Hempel, *Fundamentals of Concept Formation in Empirical Science*, Vol. II, No. 7, *International Encyclopedia of Unified Science* (Chicago: University of Chicago Press, 1952), pp. 29–39.

to predict. It is subject to disverification by the systematic use of procedures of sense experience, i.e., by systematic observation, experiment, and comparison. While it cannot be "proven true," it can be established to such a level of confidence that we use it as a basis for dealing with the world.

Normative theory, on the other hand, deals with questions of what should or ought to be rather than what is—with matters of moral quality. Whether questions of this kind are subject to verification (or disverification) is a matter of controversy in contemporary political science and philosophy. The problem is one of basic metaphysical and epistemological perspective which we cannot attempt to solve here. It should be clear, however, that the assumptions behind our work are those which indicate negative answers. That is to say, our assumptions suggest that normative propositions are not to be proven by reference to sense experience, at least in the fashion that the ordering of such experience undertakes to test propositions of fact. If value questions can be solved, they cannot be in the same way we "solve" questions of fact.[8]

A further type of theory, commonly called "prescriptive," seems to combine the other two, though not in the sense that it puts values in the role of facts or contends that value statements are subject to empirical validation. Prescription refers to theory about the factual prospects of bringing about desired conditions.[9] Thus, it tells you that if you wish to reach certain goals (either ultimate or instrumental), you should undertake such and such a prescribed course of action. To put the case in a slightly different way, prescriptive theory predicts the relative costs of alternative means to valued ends. It says empirical things about reaching a certain condition, if that condition happens to be valued; it does not tell whether the things should or should not be valued.

Most abstract political writing, i.e., political thought, is an amalgam of these kinds of theory, with historical description and a variety of other elements thrown in. For most kinds of analysis, it is important to distinguish one from the other. Our purposes are empirical; we aim to explain some aspects of the political system. In doing so, how-

---

[8] The classic formulation of this position was David Hume's. Commentaries are numerous. See, e.g., A. J. Ayer, *Language, Truth, and Logic* (New York: Dover Publications, 1953); John G. Kemeny, *A Philosopher Looks at Science* (Princeton: D. Van Nostrand Co., Inc., 1959), chap. 14; with particular reference to social sciences, see Arnold Brecht, *Political Theory* (Princeton: Princeton University Press, 1959); Kaplan, *op. cit.*, pp. 370–405; Van Dyke, *op. cit.*, chap. 1.

[9] Short discussions of prescription are to be found in Van Dyke, *op. cit.*, pp. 10–13; Kaplan, *op. cit.*, pp. 393–96.

ever, we must and will deal with values, norms, and statements of philosophy as variables. These have made up large portions of the body of American political ideas, and as such they have had demonstrable effects on the course of political development.

POLITICAL THOUGHT, POLITICAL STRUCTURE, POLITICAL PROCESS

What role does this thought about politics, be it theory, ideology, or whatever else, play in the operation of the political system? The question was raised above in terms of the influence of ideas as variables in the explanation of political behavior; in this case, we are interested in the impact of broad tendencies of ideas on the institutions of a society, on the regularized patterns of behavior that characterize a society's political life. An answer would demand more than we are able to give here, for some methodological reasons outlined below. We can, however, add clarity to some of the terms in which it might be stated, and cast the problem itself into finer relief. One way of getting at this objective and setting the stage for our later discussion of the substance of the thought–action relationship in American politics is to outline the main features of the political system as we see it. What follows is a sort of macromodel of politics presented as a framework for viewing the political role of political thought.

Our fundamental premise is that politics is dependent on the interplay of the social structure and the culture in which it is set. By politics, we mean the multilayer complex in which authoritative decisions are made; by culture, the repository of habitual ways of looking at things and responding to stimuli; by social structure, patterns of interaction. The order that makes society possible is basically a property of the culture, an understanding embodied in established usage. Over and above this basic level of order the ongoing business of politics proceeds, dealing with conflicts and discordances cast up by the social structure. As the political mechanisms attempt to handle these problems that get on the public agenda, new experiences, in turn, modify the cultural setting, e.g., specify new limits to action, redistribute decision-making authority, and develop new modes of problem identification. In practice, then, the motivating power of politics as a form of activity is change in the social structure. Culture, itself liable to change, carries the institutions (the persistent formal behavior patterns) of politics and indicates the limits of political activity.

In somewhat greater detail, this picture of politics has four major elements. Of these, social structure and culture are basic; though at risk of some oversimplification they may be considered as independent variables. Their interaction gives shape to politics. The way we are using the term here, social structure has reference to a bag of elements descriptive of the characteristic patterns of interaction of the society. Data about such things as population (age, distribution, etc.), urbanization, and technology indicate aspects of the shape of the social structure, as do such things as statuses, roles, and mobility. Out of the social structure and its concomitant demands and expectations grow frictions and disadjustments that come to be defined as problems. These problems are the raw materials of politics.

Culture, on the other hand, is intended to describe the accumulation of ways of doing and looking at things developed in a given social group. Hence, culture is the baggage of perspectives and values, rules, routines, and habits through which a society becomes accustomed to handling its variety of human relationships. What we commonly call institutions are such—i.e., regularized patterns of behavior. Culture provides political life with established means and limits; it shows the way for recognizing political problems, putting them on the agenda, stating them properly; it indicates the routines and procedures to be followed. A constitution may be a codification of the major features of the political culture.

The forces of culture and social structure merge in the political process—the making of authoritative decisions about the problems that afflict the society. Here is the "visible" part of the political system, the scene of recognizedly "political" activity. From the political process emerges "policy"—laws, administrative rules, judicial decisions, the variety of pronouncements *and* refusals or failures to make pronouncements that determine in authoritative fashion things about the life of the society. Policy, in turn, feeds back on social structure by changing relationships among its elements, and on culture by inducing changes in habituated ways.

Political thought fits into the model on the cultural side; it both indicates and shapes the culture. In political writing, values are articulated, meanings are explored, and the body of usage is preserved and explained by one generation for the next. It is also an intervening force for change as it interprets new forces for the system. In this fashion, the implications of the growth of capitalism, for example, were "brought to the attention" of the political system by the writings of the philosophical radicals, the Marxists, and a few other groups. In the ideas of a Jefferson, to bring the case closer to home, one finds both a description of the culture of his age—in, among other things, the liberal democratic symbols—and a stimulus to redefinition of those symbols. In Jefferson's case, some of the redefinitions were so persuasive or so congenial as to stay with us to the present day. Similar illustrations could be drawn from any of the periods dealt with below.

Hence, we are suggesting that political ideas do have an influence on the action of politics, though to say this leaves unsaid much about the nature, direction, intensity, and conditions of such influence. The subject is one on which the interests of students of the history of political thought converge with those of students of structure and behavior. It involves the use of the data storehouse provided by political history in the exploration of a persistent and central social relationship. It is a subject that provides one of several bridges between segments of the political science discipline sometimes thought to have dissimilar and even antithetical purposes. This bridge, however, is one that can be used only with some difficulty. The operations required to uncover the linkages between idea and action are, in any case, troublesome. They are perhaps particularly so at the level of the gross units of analysis with which political science characteristically deals. Because of the centrality of the problem, these difficulties are worth a few pages of our attention.

SOME PROBLEMS OF METHOD IN LINKING IDEAS AND POLITICS

Without pretending that they can be solved, we may address ourselves to five items on which the process of demonstrating influence often fails. One of these, the question of identifying concepts and units of analysis, has already been a subject of some of our attention. Thus, the character of research on theory and action depends on the way these concepts are defined and made operational. If theory is defined, for example, as something like "national tradition," it is almost impossible to identify in any but the most impressionistic terms. If theory, alternatively, is identified as ideology, the problem is nearly as difficult.[10] In both cases, the analyst runs the risk of identifying theory, the independent variable, by the behavior of action, the dependent variable, and demonstrating nothing but a neat circularity of design. If by theory we are to mean the ideas of theorists, the problems are somewhat different, involving the method of selection of theorists and the difficulty of assessing influence. As to the use of the nation

---

[10] For a more extended discussion of this point, see Minar, *op cit.*

as a unit of analysis, without quibbling about the problem of defining a nation (which, after all, does not seem so acute where nineteenth- and twentieth-century United States is concerned), it may fairly be suggested that the job of sorting out the strands of theory that have influenced the institutions, processes, policies, and behaviors of a nation is, at least, an extremely complex one. To say that the New Deal was influenced by pragmatism seems to slight the influence of Jeffersonian democracy, Hamiltonian mercantilism, Keynesian economics, social pluralism, syndicalism, and others on that complicated web of innovational and conservative phenomena. To say that it was influenced by all is to say nothing very definitive. Another alternative —the piecing together of imputed influences on specific policies and political figures—is a more acceptable method and also a more painful one.

A second item of difficulty has to do with handling variables other than theory or, to put it in another way, with the pitfalls of attempting explanation by reference to one variable only.[11] It is clear that the simple explanation of national political development entirely in terms of political theory is not satisfactory. To account for the variances in national development caused by political theory (either longitudinally or by comparison across units) requires holding other factors constant—geography, demography, external pressure, technology. Here again, complexity is a source of trouble, and we must usually be content with something less than is desirable by ordinary standards of verification.

A third problem has to do with the nature of influence and the direction of causation. The theory–practice relationship often raises a chicken-and-egg question of which causes which. It is not necessary to assume a hard sociology of knowledge position to suggest that thought can never be entirely disservered from its historico-environmental context. Perhaps the point is most apparent in American theory, where ideas are so often obviously stimulated by events and so often embedded in social movements.[12] Consider, for example, the theory and institution of separation of powers. Its greatest American commentary is doubtless found in three of Madison's *Federalist* papers. These, of course, followed in time and were directly stimulated

---

[11] Cf. Hartz, *The Liberal Tradition in America* (New York: Harcourt, Brace Co., 1955), pp. 20–23.

[12] A consideration which has prompted some commentators to conclude that there is no American political theory, or very little, or very little that is significant and original. On this matter, see Daniel Boorstin, *The Genius of American Politics* (Chicago: University of Chicago Press, 1953).

by the incorporation of separation into the federal Constitution. But we know that Madison and other framers were acquainted with Montesquieu's commentary (evidence of the influence of foreign theory), and that was, in turn, an examination of English constitutional practices. Meanwhile, the entire developing structure of American government was heavily conditioned by colonial and post-Revolutionary state political experience. Given such a sequence of theory and event, the disentangling of influences is probably impossible.

Suppose one seeks, however, to short-cut this problem by undertaking what seems to be a simpler task—assessing the influence of a particular theorist or group of theorists on a particular political actor. Here, evidence may be available in documents and public and personal papers, and it may be possible to size up background influences by the examination of school curricula, reading habits, associations, and others. The sorting of effective from ineffective elements of the environment, and of post hoc rationalization from introspective understanding in autobiographic evidence, however, requires a most careful type of imputation. The linking of outside ideas to behavior is an extremely intricate operation, probably impossible to perform with precision in most situations. Thus, when the influence of theory on political practice is sought at either the level of the nation or the level of the individual, the problem of identification of linkages is acute, and one must be satisfied with inferring relationships rather than proving causes.

A fourth problem, probably the most important of the list, is closely related to the one just mentioned. The discussion of political theory and national development is likely to be focused almost entirely on propositions about the effects of the one on the other. But not so much is usually said about the mechanisms of influence, about how theory operates on practice as distinct from what it has done. The consideration of mechanisms would add another dimension to the analysis, and this would seem to be a vital dimension if one aim of studies of this kind is to develop a generalized framework for understanding the impact of political theory on practice. The problem here is again one of identifying linkages, of discerning the processes by which ideas at the level of theory are translated into institutions and policies. This facet of the subject highlights the importance of studying political theory and national policy in close harmony, for knowledge of the mechanisms of influence would seem to depend on understanding of the processes of policy-making. It also suggests the importance of studying ideology, because the folk theory of ideology is probably one of the fundamental and most interesting of the pertinent channels of influence.

This discussion also has not taken account of the limitations on generalization and testing of hypotheses imposed by the scarcity of pertinent units of study, particularly where inquiry is aimed at the nation-state level. If one seeks to develop truly general theory about the relationship of political thought to macro political institutions he has a relatively small sample with which to work. The seriousness of this problem probably depends on the view one has of the nature of political science, the importance he attaches to comparison as part of the process of verification, and the intensity of his insistence that the nation-state is a unit that cannot be compared with other units of social organization. At least to some extent, it would seem to be a problem with which political science on the gross level will have to live.[13]

In view of these problems of method, it may well be asked what future there is in studies of the relationship of political theory and political action and similar subjects. One alternative is to abandon the quest for rigor and the ambition to adhere to standards of verification. Some think such standards are irrelevant to the study of politics, anyway. If this position is accepted, the study of political thought, insofar as its ends are descriptive rather than normative, would seem to resolve to intellectual history and literary criticism. It will yield appreciation, perhaps, but not explanation, and its relevance to the systematic understanding of current politics and to prediction would seem to lie only in the models and propositions it might incidentally suggest.[14] This comment is not intended to question the defensibility and importance of intellectual history or literary criticism or political prescription, but only to wonder about their contributions to systematic knowledge about politics. Anyway, since political scientists will without doubt continue to discuss such empirical problems as the influence of political theory on political practice, it seems very hard to defend the claim that questions about evidence and verification cannot and should not be asked.[15]

Granting the propriety of such questions, however, it can still be

---

[13] See Roy C. Macridis, *The Study of Comparative Government* (Garden City: Doubleday & Co., 1955), esp. pp. 26–27.

[14] See the discussion of the relevance of classical theory to the study of local politics in Norton E. Long, "Aristotle and the Study of Local Government," *Social Research*, Vol. XXIV (Autumn, 1957), pp. 287–310.

[15] A stimulating discussion of the thought–practice relationship in politics from a vastly different perspective than that of this book may be found in Hannah Arendt, *Between Past and Future* (New York: The Viking Press, 1961).

argued that studies of the influence of political theory on action should be carried on in traditional fashion, both at the level of national tradition and at the level of individual influence, lacking rigor but reaching for the best evidence available. This contention seems defensible on the ground that studies of this kind are in themselves interesting, that the discipline must continue to do what it can with the questions it is asked, and that one way of improving method is through trial and error with substance. Semi-impressionistic studies as well as the accumulation of additive analyses of specific political events and individuals have created a significant store of theory and evidence on the relationship of thought and political practice.[16]

At the same time, it seems important that improvement in method be sought consciously. Many of the specific points at which attention is in order have been identified above. In a more general vein, it might be added that studies at the macro level, at which political science has excelled, might gain in precision if explicit attention were paid to the techniques and results of studies at micro levels, and if studies of the data of the past were done in the light of what we discover we can find out about the present.[17] While problems of translation and conversion from level to level are themselves difficult, the more empirically manageable studies of the impact of ideas on policy in small groups and in local communities, for instance, might suggest a great deal about the study of their impact on the grand scale of the nation-state. And lessons learned in examining the construction or growth of contemporary policies and structures might yield clues for understanding the forces involved in the development of national politics in the past. Particularly, our vital understanding of the operation of mechanisms of influence seems likely to be enhanced in this way.[18]

---

[16] The number and variety of works that have made this kind of contribution are so great that it seems unnecessary to specify examples.

[17] Here again, the number of potential examples is so large that it is difficult to single out any particular one or few for citation. See, however, the following note for a few items dealing with the concept of influence.

[18] By attention, i.e., to current studies of "influence" in political affairs on various levels and to conceptual analyses of influence. See, for example, Edward C. Banfield, *Political Influence* (New York: The Free Press of Glencoe, 1961); James G. March, "An Introduction to the Theory and Measurement of Influence," *American Political Science Review*, Vol. XLIX (June, 1955), pp. 431–51; James G. March, "Measurement Concepts in the Theory of Influence," *Journal of Politics*, Vol. XIX (May, 1957), pp. 202–26; James G. March, "Influence Measurement in Experimental and Semi-Experimental Groups," *Sociometry*, Vol. XIX (December, 1956), pp. 260–71; Robert A. Dahl, "The Concept of Power," *Behavioral Science*, Vol. II (July, 1957), pp. 210–15. Also Floyd Hunter's "power elite" studies, and commentaries on them, e.g., Floyd Hunter, *Community Power Structure* (Chapel Hill: University of North Carolina Press, 1953); Herbert Kaufman and Victor Jones, "The Mystery of Power," *Public Administration Review*, Vol. XIV (Summer, 1954), pp. 205–12; Nelson W. Polsby, "Community Power: Three Problems," *Amer-*

Thus, our subject suggests attention both to the materials of political thought and to a variety of other focuses and developments in the social science disciplines.

THE STUDY OF A TRADITION

The preceding pages have suggested some of the potentials and problems of the study of political thought. In a sense, they describe the aims and limits of the present volume, though these matters call for further elucidation, particularly as they concern the relationship of the materials of political thought to the problems of political science. The scope, depth, and form of the substantive discussion in the chapters that follow necessitate considerable qualifications as to what they can and cannot show.

It was indicated above that there would seem to be three places where the study of political thought can contribute to the tasks of political science: the development of theory (and its conceptual and propositional components); the testing of theory about ideas; the description of the political culture. The first and last of these as they are manifest in the chapters that follow are substantially self-explanatory. The other, however, raises more questions, and as it is in some ways the main task of the book, it merits further explanation. The problem is what the examination of American political thought in the context of American political and social institutions and processes can tell us about the relationship of ideas and action.

A fully developed social science of the subject would consist of a set of interrelated theoretical propositions stated at a high level of generality and tested by reference to the experience of a large sample of societies. The content of the propositions would depend on the orientation of the theory, but they would be applicable to a variety of social–cultural situations, and at the highest level to all.

It will be widely agreed, however, that our social science in its present state falls far short of such a goal. In theory development and in the equipment of testing, it is in a primitive stage. Hence, much discussion of political thought is not even stated in terms of systematic questions. Some portions of political science are pushed further than others; the study of this particular relationship is, for a number of rather obvious reasons, among the less elaborate, especially when it comes to the statement of the question in fairly gross terms—i.e., in

---

ican Sociological Review, Vol. XXIV (December, 1959), pp. 796–803; Robert A. Dahl, "A Critique of the Ruling Elite Model," *American Political Science Review*, Vol. LI (June, 1958), pp. 463–69; Nelson Polsby, *Community Power and Political Theory* (New Haven: Yale University Press, 1963).

terms of large societies and traditions of thought. Yet, it is on this
macro level that we wish to proceed.

In this situation, it might perhaps be most bold and most defensible
to move immediately to the statement and testing of theory at the
highest possible level. However, at least in some situations, it would
appear that another step is more feasible and fruitful. The point can
perhaps best be approached by suggesting that various kinds of theories play their roles in explanatory science. They are described in different ways and given different labels, but this is beside the point.
When we discuss the "theory" of science, especially from the posture
of those who are defensive about the situation of social science, we are
inclined to think of the high-level theory that explains cause and effect in a completely generalized and mechanistic way. Such, however,
may be the product of the addition and exploration of theories of a different kind, theories that are particular, that are detailed descriptions
of unique events or systems. The particular theories are sometimes
called "ideographic," as distinguished from the generalized, "nomo-
thetic" explanations.[19] Whether the more general must be built on
a systematic treatment of the more specific is debatable, but it is
clear that much of modern science has taken shape that way.

Our substantive discussion of American political thought and its
action implications is largely concerned with this ideographic kind of
statement. It is hoped, however, that exploration of this kind is contributory to the development of more general explanation both by its
heuristic power and by virtue of the restatement and ordering of the
evidence it provides. What follows is largely concerned, then, with
posing questions, seeking hypothetical explanations, and putting the
materials of American political thought in such form as to make them
useful for the tasks of a developing social science. As preceding pages
suggested, we are interested particularly in political thought as an intervening variable between culture and social structure on the one
hand and the political process and its policy products on the other.
Such matters as relationships of social scale, consensus, and institutional forms will constitute the network of theoretical concern against
which we shall examine the materials of American politics, both from
the standpoint of static analysis and from the standpoint of the analysis
of change. While we may not be prepared to give the grand questions
final answers, consideration of the American experience can tell us
much about the forms, potentials, and probabilities of the relationship
of ideas and politics.

---

[19] See Nagel, *op. cit.*, chap. 15, esp. pp. 547-51.

II

BACKGROUNDS TO AMERICAN POLITICAL CONSENSUS

Seldom can the political tradition of a nation or a society be understood apart from the ideas of the world that predated and surrounded it. American political thought is part of a Western political culture from which it has drawn heavily and to which it has contributed significantly. Its total philosophical and ideological context clearly cannot be treated here in comprehensive fashion, for such treatment would have to reach to the time of the pre-Platonics. However, in the pages that follow, an effort will be made to select from the history of Western thought some of the major strands of ideas that have come to constitute the core of the American tradition of political thought and practice. Three of these will be subjects of major emphasis: the individualist and contract elements in Puritanism; the mechanistic theme in English revolutionary thought; and the pre-Enlightenment and Enlightenment conceptions of science and progress. The major aim of the analysis will be to clarify the central terms of the American political consensus. Given the consensus in which these three themes converged, most typically American political theory has either dealt with the means appropriate to the realization of basic values or reargued in different forms the nature of the consensual goals.

In a fairly immediate sense, the American political tradition took shape in the early "modern" period, i.e., the period reaching from the thirteenth to the seventeenth century. During this era, the Western world underwent a revolution, cultural and theoretical, which shook its very intellectual roots. This revolution had economic, technological, ideological, institutional, and theological causes and manifestations, all central to the breakdown of a synthesis through which the men of the Middle Ages in Europe understood their world and responded to it. New commitments and new demands arose to give shape to the ways of politics. In good measure, American political life was preconditioned by the thrust of the modern reaction to medieval thought and society. A few words about the most basic characteristics of the premodern world will help to make the content of this reaction clear.

The life of man in the Middle Ages, insofar as one can speak about the life of "man" in an age, was lived in a static and closed society, a society turned in on itself and largely confined by the geographic horizon. The individual seldom experienced either the pleasures or the pains of detachment from the community of his birth. Only a war or an occasional and short trip to a fair or market drew men outside the circumscribed area in which their daily lives were passed, and these were not common occurrences from the standpoint of individual involvement. And as men were bound geographically, they were also bound socially, to a society and to a station in that society to which they were born. Thus, life in this era was defined for the individual from outside—his situation, his status, his calling, nearly all his social relationships determined as if naturally. Society was to a great extent both localistic and organic, that is, organic in the sense that people lived as articulated parts of a greater whole rather than as integral and self-fulfilling individuals. These would seem to be the social facts that lay behind the institutions of manorial feudalism and of the guild structures of medieval towns.

Several of the implications of this social situation are suggested in the phrases localistic, organic, and status; others that are closely related also deserve mention. The idea of the organic society implies interdependence and hierarchy. Though indeed society itself probably entails interdependence, societies may be differentiated according to the degree of interdependence characteristic of them (e.g., measured by a man's ability to fulfill his needs and perform his social roles without interaction) and according to the extent to which the consequences of interdependence are acceptable to common values. The society of the present day is, as we shall observe later, highly interdependent in a technological sense—more so than the Middle Ages. But it is distinguished on the value or ideological dimension. Interdependence in the Middle Ages appears to have been something man accepted and understood. Closely related is accepted hierarchy—the expectation that some men are and will be "above" others in a variety of ways. In temporal society and in church, relations and positions were fixed in terms of an understood hierarchical organization. Everything in society was thus part of a system, part of an established and fundamentally inalterable set of social relationships. These relationships, sealed in habit, also came to be fixed by law, to be supported by customary, positive, and divine sanctions, each of these types of norms being seen in itself as part of an interrelated set of systems.

In most respects, medieval political thought follows what might be expected from this gross description of medieval life.[1] It was, in other words, an ideational expression of the culture. Best known through its representation in the works of St. Thomas Aquinas, its emphasis lay on synthesis, on the interdependence of social parts, and on the control of the whole by a purposive hierarchy of systems of law capped by the Eternal Law of God.[2] Like the thought of Aristotle, on whose work Thomism is supposed to be heavily dependent, St. Thomas emphasized the innate sociability of man, the differences in capacities and natural stations among people, and the integration of all parts of life down to the most mundane. Everything is in system, everything fits into place, and the higher rule over the lower. The whole is permeated by social purpose. Acts of subjects and rulers are understood by and justified according to their relationship to a common good of the whole. Thus, politics is part of a universal synthesis into which all elements of life are articulated. The rule of kings is validated by its reference to or role in the entire complex structure of human society.

Our interest in the thought of the Middle Age lies chiefly in its negation, for American ideas are the ideas of modern liberalism, and modern liberalism was substantially a direct reaction against the ideas and social arrangements of the Middle Ages. However, it is not to be supposed that the Middle Ages disappeared. Both its ways of thought and its modes of social organization and action remained very much a part of the Western world. The tradition of St. Thomas has been carried forward in modified form in the social and political doctrine of the modern Catholic Church, and his political ideas may be traced forward from his time in the main current of modern liberalism, particularly

---

[1] For sources and commentary on medieval political thought, see R. W. Carlyle and A. J. Carlyle, *A History of Medieval Political Theory in the West* (6 vols.; London: W. Blackwood & Sons, 1903–36); A. P. d'Entreves, *The Medieval Contribution to Political Thought* (New York: Humanities Press, 1959); Otto von Gierke, *Political Theories of the Middle Age*, trans. F. W. Maitland (Boston: Beacon Press, 1958); Ewart Lewis, *Medieval Political Ideas* (2 vols.; London: Routledge and Kegan Paul, 1954); an interesting article from the standpoint of our main theme is Ewart Lewis, "The Contribution of Medieval Thought to the American Political Tradition," *American Political Science Review*, Vol. L (June, 1956), pp. 462–74.

[2] Political selections from Aquinas may be found in *Aquinas: Selected Political Writings*, ed. with introduction A. P. d'Entreves, trans. J. G. Dawson (Oxford: Basil Blackwell, 1948); *The Political Ideas of Saint Thomas Aquinas; Representative Selections*, ed. with introduction Dino Bigongiari (New York: Hafner Publishing Co., 1953).

reflected in the ideas of such conservative thinkers as Edmund Burke, the English "father of modern conservative thought." [3] Further, there are today societies and portions of societies, ever fewer, to be sure, that are characterized by the predominance of status and by social and, to some extent, geographical immobility. There are also societies in which public acts are referred to the public interest, societies in which political activity is explicitly judged in terms of a common good finally referable to ultimate divine purpose. The theory of the Middle Ages is still descriptive, then, of some minor elements of modern Western social life. Probably to an even greater extent, this medieval thought indirectly provides for some men the value standards by which they judge the political and social arrangements in which they live. The application of these standards is apparent both in contemporary demands for a politics conducted in terms of community interest, and in a euphoria expressed by diverse people, probably for diverse reasons, for what is taken to be the security of the small, closed, face-to-face society. [4]

Nonetheless, under the pressure of social change, new modes of thought have largely replaced the "medieval synthesis" at the core of Western culture. Probably the most obvious and dramatic reactions to the Middle Ages were those that took the form of theological disputation as well as debate over the nature of Christian church structure. Discontent with the church both as temporal authority and as intermediary between man and God became increasingly a part of the social, political, and intellectual setting of the late Middle Ages. Certain practices of the church and of church personnel were bitterly attacked both from within the institution itself and from outside. From the beginning of the Christian period, too, the church had from time to time engaged in disputation with civil authority as to the proper division of the functions of rule between spiritual and temporal hierarchies. As the secular movement to confine the church to spiritual matters grew, within the church the Conciliar movement in the fourteenth and fifteenth centuries struck to decentralize the structure of church power. Thus, on several fronts, the ways of the Middle Ages institutionalized in Christianity began to be called into question.

At the same time, it must be recalled, the Western world was begin-

---

[3] On the former point, see especially the writings of Jacques Maritain, e.g., *St. Thomas Aquinas*, trans. J. F. Scanlan (London: Sheed and Ward, 1938); *Man and the State* (Chicago: University of Chicago Press, 1951).

[4] For example, for comment on one such school of thought, see Reinhard Bendix and Lloyd H. Fisher, "The Perspectives of Elton Mayo," *Review of Economics and Statistics*, Vol. XXXI (November, 1949), pp. 312–19.

ning to change in several other ways. Technological, intellectual, and artistic stirrings began to make themselves felt, and the development of the nation state imposed new demands on political thought and institutions. New and nonpurposive modes of thinking about social relationships, best typified by the ideas of Niccolo Machiavelli, attacked head-on the intellectual foundations of the structure of medieval political ideas. During this period, political thought was obliged to confront in new form the two fundamental questions faced by political theory in general: How is authority to be justified, and how may it be limited? The problem of the justification of authority became a substantially new problem with the increasing importance of the development of politics on the level of the nation state. And as political authority took on new and broader and, in some senses, more pervasive form, the need to think through the grounds and institutions of the limitation of authority likewise became more pressing. While the thought of leading figures of the Reformation is, properly speaking, chiefly theological in nature, the Reformation made major contributions both to the political theory of the justification of authority and to the political theory of the limitation of that authority. This thought was both the product and the producer of new social arrangements characteristic of the Western world when the American nation began to take form.

SOME CONTRIBUTIONS OF THE PROTESTANT REFORMATION

Our analysis of the political theory of the Reformation will be confined to the ideas of the two major thinkers in the movement, Martin Luther and John Calvin. Luther, a German theologian, instituted his major attack on the Catholic Church in Wittenberg in 1517. His principal contributions to the intellectual developments in which we are interested were theological, but out of these theological views grow Luther's main implications for political thought.[5]

The cornerstone of Luther's contribution to theology rests on simplification of the relationship between man and God, epitomized in the idea of salvation. In the medieval period, good works and sacraments were seen as the vital elements of salvation; Luther substituted salvation by grace through faith. Thus, simple faith replaced ritual

---

[5] For commentary on Luther's political thought, see Sheldon S. Wolin, *Politics and Vision* (Boston: Little, Brown Co., 1960), chap. 5. Also R. H. Murray, *The Political Consequences of the Reformation* (London: E. Benn, 1926); Ernst Troeltsch, *The Social Teaching of the Christian Churches*, trans. Olive Wyon (New York: Macmillan Co., 1931), Vol. II, pp. 515–76.

and philosophy as the key to man's relationship with God. The accumulated wisdom of the ages was no longer so directly relevant to man's fate, and the elaborate hierarchy of theology, philosophy, and social and political structure in the Middle Ages came to seem rather irrelevant to this central human concern. According to the Lutheran view, man did not require mediation in his relationship with God, for all believers were in an intimate personal relationship with their Creator. This is not to say that Luther rejected the notion of a visible church. But while the visible church was a fitting place for the tutelage of those in a less perfect state of faith, there was relatively much less emphasis on hierarchy and on the intervention of church authority between man and God. What sort of implications for political theory and practice may be drawn from this theological reorientation? Most importantly, the Protestant abandonment of the medieval conception of an elaborate and articulated cosmic order, of which politics was a part, drew politics out of its cosmic setting. Politics was no longer to be regarded, that is to say, as one aspect of a divine plan. While political theory still bore the marks of the close relationship between theology and social ideas, the theory of politics could take on a much more rudimentary form. While Thomism postulated a human life and a nature regulated in terms of a series of layers of law whose application was dependent on rational understanding, the Lutheran theory postulated a more mystical God and a human existence regulated through simple faith. Politics came to seem not part of a complex but rational world regulated through higher purpose, but a simple relationship imposed by the shortcomings of individual man.

The Lutheran conception of politics, then, was much more related to the needs of man than to the complex structure of nature. Politics seems in this formulation to be something almost utilitarian. The doctrine of original sin and its reflection in the psychology of individuals runs very heavily through Lutheran theology. Order is a condition needed in the face of the human materials with which society is put together, a fragile worldly value, imposed through politics on sinful man. Secular government is useful for the repression of unrighteous, unregenerate, and un-Christian instincts. It is guided not by rational purpose, but by worldly function. Government exists, said Luther, "in order that the good may have outward peace and protection; and that the wicked may not be free to do evil, without fear, in peace and quietness." [6] Human government may, and indeed probably must, be repressive in response to the nature of the material with which it deals.

---

[6] Quoted in Wolin, *op. cit.*, p. 161.

Further, in its assumption about the direct relationship of man to God, Lutheranism began to lay the theological basis for a politics that emphasizes fundamental equality among men and the control of authority by individual conscience. Luther was saying in effect that the unmediated individual conscience counts. While he was not himself a liberal democrat, in the notion of the sanctity of will and of the personal relationship between man and God, his theology helped sow the seeds for the individualistic liberal democracy of a later period.

Of more direct importance than Lutheranism in the development of American political thought were the ideas of John Calvin, the Genevan Frenchman who in the sixteenth century developed the doctrines on which Puritanism came to be largely based. Through the Puritanism of early New England and through the diffusion of elements of Calvinism in England and Western Europe, Calvin's theology and politics had a very substantial impact on the development of an American political tradition.[7]

Calvin's doctrine, like Luther's, was strict, authoritarian, and pessimistic, was based largely on the Old Testament, and emphasized original sin and the low state of man. Like Luther, too, he assumed the essentially personal and individual relationship of man to God. Perhaps his principal revision of both existing Christian theology and of Lutheranism lay in his approach to the problem of salvation, a problem that seems to have been of much greater moment to men in the age of the Reformation (and before) than it commonly is to men today. Where traditional Catholicism found salvation in works and sacraments and Luther found it in faith, Calvin raised the logical question how deeply sinful man could ever be expected to make his way to salvation through any kind of effort of his own. To gain grace through sufficient works is unthinkable, to achieve it through sufficient faith is improbable. How can a mere human being undertake either ritual or faith that will qualify him for the favor of eternal life? Calvin's answer was, in short, that he cannot, that man cannot himself overcome sin. This is something only God, acting through grace, can do. Thus, there follows in logical train the well-known Calvinist doctrine of predestination: Only the elect of God are saved, and man can do nothing about it.

This curious doctrine seems to have had a variety of effects on those

---

[7] On Calvin's political ideas, see John Calvin, *Institutes of the Christian Religion*, trans. F. L. Battles, ed. J. T. McNeill (2 vols.; Philadelphia: Westminster Press, 1960); selections may be found in *John Calvin on God and Political Duty*, ed. John T. McNeill (New York: Liberal Arts Press, 1950). Among commentaries, see particularly Wolin, *op. cit.*, chap. 6; Murray, *op. cit.*, Troeltsch, *op. cit.*, Vol. II, pp. 576–688.

who embraced it. It differentiated the elect from the rest of mankind, and placed on the shoulders of the elect the righteousness of the world. Whether men themselves felt able to gauge their destiny seems doubtful. Practically, however, within the structure of the Calvinistic religious institutions, it seems to have been up to the elect, that is the congregation itself, to determine the acceptability of individuals within the fold. Man might believe in his destination and seek to join that earthly society symbolic of one's standing in grace, but a measure of doubt and anxiety would seem to be nearly inevitable. Calvinism embodied an interesting doctrinal combination of a simplistic and direct relationship between man and God, and a temporal society which, while it did not mediate between man and God, played an integral role in the psychological adjustment of the person to his own religious comfort. Both these aspects of Calvinism seem to have had some political importance.

The political aspects of Calvinism can be examined both in theory and in practice, since Calvin not only wrote politics, but also played for a period a predominant political and theological role in his native Geneva. Geneva under Calvin was an authoritarian theocracy, a political society in which rule was in effect consigned to those earthly saints whose predestination was understood. Formally, the role of the church was that of overseeing matters of doctrine and public morals, a process in which, Calvin insisted, religious authority must be freed from secular restraints. The distinction between public morals and the proper sphere of state activity, however, was a shadowy one. Perhaps inevitably, the religious leaders became the "dominants" in all aspects of community life, and civil authority became virtually indistinguishable from the authority of the church. Within the church itself, power lay, in theory, in the hands of the congregation and the elders, the prescribed internal structure being democratic. But as observation of the oligarchic tendencies of organization might lead one to expect, power in Calvinist Geneva and in Calvinist New England tended to flow into the hands of the clergy, heightening the theocratic cast of the social power structure.

Thus, in the context of a society where Calvinist ideas were predominant, Calvinism became a harsh and repressive political force. In situations where the distribution of social power was different, Calvinism might and indeed sometimes did inspire another type of political result. In Scotland where John Knox and others developed Presbyterian Calvinism in an unfriendly context, resistance became almost a matter of Calvinist faith. This offshoot, however, can hardly be called representative of the main doctrine. In its more pure form, Calvinism taught that private man has no calling to judge the ruler, that a bad or heretical ruler may be a visitation of God on the people for their sins, and the best that Calvinists can hope for in a setting of this kind is the passive resistance of prayer and communion with the congregation. In such a setting, man without the political equipment to give force to his special role in the society of God must patiently wait for his destiny to be realized. The operational force of this doctrine of quietism seems to have been contingent on the power position of its adherents in a given society. Where that power position was very high or very low, the doctrine seems to have been effective. Where it was middling, i.e., where resistance might bear political fruit, the doctrine seems to have been of little effect.

The political influence of Calvinism is manifold and ambiguous. Its doctrines emphasized the personal relationship of man and God and the integrity of the individual human being. It helped cut away the medieval tradition of mediation between man and God by earthly authority, and formally embodied some of the practices of democracy in its approach to church government. On the other hand, as has been pointed out above, Calvinism differentiated among people and gave to some the equipment by which they might feel justified to impose their wills on others. Thus, this theory seems to come down on both sides of the questions: Is government the creature of man and ought it to be limited by his consent on behalf of his rights? Likewise, Calvinism made an ambiguous contribution to the development of the American political heritage. Its practice in New England was harsh. At the same time, it developed in New England the basis for a measure of that individualism and social conscience typical of American political practice. In England, Puritanism went to war with absolute authority. In America, Puritanism became absolute authority, though only in a limited context for a limited period of time. In both settings, the domination of a society by Calvinistic ideas immediately preceded the formal bloom of liberal individualism, and probably influenced that bloom both by challenge and by the implications of its own attitude toward life. In America, Calvinism still lives in respect for the individual on the one hand and in overbearing social moralism on the other.

One of Calvinism's most substantial, though indirect, contributions to political thought and political practice is the idea of the social contract. The concept of contract bears close theoretical and historical relationship to a late-Reformation Calvinistic doctrine of the Covenant of Grace.[8] This doctrine, not a part of the theology of Calvin himself, was developed in England in the early seventeenth century to answer certain basic problems that came to trouble Puritan belief and church practice. A basic deficiency in Calvinist theology seems to lie in the question of the grounds for moral obedience, that is, for obedience to the laws of God. Assuming, as Calvinism does, that man is fundamentally sinful, what will account for his adherence to those rules of morality to which Puritanism was firmly committed? Why should men live morally if their fate is predetermined?

The obvious answers to these questions are two, neither satisfactory to Calvinism in its main tenets as a religious doctrine. On the one hand, those who questioned why predestined men should live morally might simply be told that there is no answer to this question. If men are delivered, no matter where they are delivered, there is no persuasive reason why they should devote themselves to studying scripture, living morally, praying, and obeying the rigid puritanical rules of conduct. They may as well, indeed, "surrender to the intoxication of certainty" and give no thought to the propriety of behavior. The difficulties moralistic Calvinists would have in accepting this type of answer are obvious. On the other hand, these queries were sometimes answered in terms that represent a significant modification of Calvinistic doctrine. Thus, it might be said that it is within the power of the individual to receive grace or reject it, and that by his mode of living he might vindicate the choice of God or might render it useless by in effect refusing it through immoral conduct. This approach to the problem reintroduces the element of works, which Calvinism itself, and Lutheranism too, had earlier rejected.

In an age when spiritual support seemed required for the norms of social living, the idea of the covenant was developed as an answer to this problem as well as counter to the answers, specious in terms of Calvinist doctrine, which we have just reviewed. The notion of the covenant is venerable in origin. It is based on the Old Testament story of the covenant of Abraham found in Genesis and Deuteronomy. While we need not be interested in these finer points of theological doctrine, the idea of the covenant has very significant political implications in itself, contributing generously to the heritage deeded to American politics by Calvinism.

---

[8] See Perry Miller, *The New England Mind: the Seventeenth Century* (New York: Macmillan Co., 1939), chaps. 13 and 14, respectively, on the Covenant of Grace and the Social Covenant.

Genesis 17 describes the compact between Abraham and God in these terms:

And when Abram was ninety years old and nine, the Lord appeared to Abram, and said unto him, I *am* the Almighty God; walk before me, and be thou perfect. And I will make my covenant between me and thee, and will multiply thee exceedingly. . . . As for me, my covenant *is* with thee, and thou shalt be a father of many nations. . . . And I will establish my covenant between me and thee and thy seed after thee in their generations, for an everlasting covenant, to be a God unto thee and to thy seed after thee. And I will give unto thee, and to thy seed after thee, the land wherein thou art a stranger, all the land of Canaan, for an everlasting possession: and I will be their God. And God said unto Abraham, Thou shalt keep my covenant therefore, thou, and thy seed after thee in their generations.

The covenant was thus a gift of God at His pleasure in which He voluntarily contracted with mankind to grant life in exchange for belief and obedience. God is absolute, but He has granted His subjects an inviolable bill of freedoms or happiness.

The importance of the covenant lies in the restrictions it levies on individuals. The covenant implies an obligation on all men associated in society to honor God's law. It creates both an inward obligation to external behavior and a social obligation shared with one's fellow men. Thus, all men are bound to righteousness and subject to the punishment of their fellows if they do not honor the covenant on their side. In this fashion, the covenant provides a theological explanation for the obligation of moral law.

But even more important from the standpoint of politics, the covenant provided a model of social relations, a model of use in explaining the relations both among men in society and between society and ruler. The terms of the covenant doctrine became the common standard terms of political theory. If God binds His rule by contract, are not human rulers surely obliged to do the same? Puritan doctrine helped revive the ancient idea of the covenant and raise the contract relationship to the level of common consciousness. By transmutation from theological to social terms, the doctrine of the contract became a cornerstone of both English and American political thought. Forthright use of the compact device and implicit evidence of its ideological importance is to be found in various early New England sources: in the Mayflower Compact, in Governor Winthrop's famous "Speech to the General Court," in John Wise's "Vindication of the Government of New England Churches," in the Fundamental Orders of Connecticut.[9] The organization of political power in both civil society and church in New England of the seventeenth and early eighteenth centuries generally followed contract form. It is important to note, however, that contract doctrine also had other sources and took other forms, and that its implications are not completely explored in the paragraphs above. A further discussion of the social–political version of the contract idea will be found in the section to follow.

In part, the impact of Puritanism on American politics was mediated through the Puritan settlements of early New England.[10] A review of the ideas and practices of the society of seventeenth century New England suggests two particularly significant political aspects: typically, this society was on the one hand authoritarian, on the other hand localistic. Church government was congregational in structure. The church founded upon the covenant thus introduced some measure of democratic principle into religious life. But the covenant that established the New England church was a covenant among the elect, a covenant among the saints. Only those whose predestination was sure were allowed membership in the church, and only those who belonged to the church were full members of the civil society. In theory, church and state were separate and mutually helpful, and the duties of each were distinct. In practice, society was dominated by the church. Taxes were levied for church support, and the customary functions of civil government in the policing of norms for social conduct were shared with the church congregations. Puritan Massachusetts of this period has been called a "Bible state," a "New Zion," a "Calvinist theocracy." Even within the church, the power of ministers, deacons, and elders appears to have exceeded doctrinal prescriptions. Outside the church, ministers took an active part in politics and church officers an active part in the regulation of society. Opposition to the established order and to the state was condemned, and religious toleration was deemed impossible.

If the seeds of democracy and liberty were growing in this time, as

[9] See, e.g., excerpts from Winthrop and Wise in Perry Miller (ed.), *The American Puritans: Their Prose and Poetry* (Garden City: Doubleday Anchor Books, 1956), pp. 89–93, 121–37.

[10] The literature cited on the political ideas of the period and place is large. See the selections in Perry Miller (ed.), *The American Puritans: Their Prose and Poetry, op. cit.*, esp. chap. 1. For commentary, see Perry Miller, *The New England Mind: the Seventeenth Century, op. cit.*, and *The New England Mind: From Colony to Province* (Cambridge: Harvard University Press, 1953); see also Herbert W. Schneider, *The Puritan Mind* (New York: H. Holt & Co., 1930), and, more generally, Ralph Barton Perry, *Puritanism and Democracy* (New York: Vanguard Press, 1944). For a provocative historical discussion, see Thomas J. Wertenbaker, *The Puritan Oligarchy* (New York: Charles Scribner's Sons, 1947).

indeed we may suspect they were, they lay buried beneath the soil of authoritarianism. For example, Winthrop and others, speaking of the meaning of liberty, made much of the equation of liberty to order. The liberty of this time was the liberty of a society in which man was made not to want to dissent from the norms that the society imposed on him. As for democracy, Cotton, in a statement that seems typical of the times, said God never did "ordeyne [it] as a fitt government eyther for church or commonwealth." [11] However, even this closed society seems driven toward democracy by some of its major tenets: separatism and the congregational organization of the church, the doctrine of priesthood of believers, and the commitment to the compact or covenant as a basis both of church and of society.

The localistic tendencies of church and society during this period were partly a reflection of doctrine, partly a matter of the adaptation of doctrine to social and economic situation. The New England community was small in scope and population and the church itself was a small and primary unit. A large degree of autonomy, both political and religious, was left to individual towns. The church became the center of the society, a largely face-to-face society, and thus religious organization was a decentralizing influence. The basic locus of authority at the civil level was the town meeting which reviewed local political policy and chose selectmen to carry on between its sessions. Localism itself is probably to some extent democratic in its influence. It has also been a very important part of the development of a distinctly American attitude toward politics, revived in strong terms in the thought of Thomas Jefferson. Repeatedly in American political practice, the notion of local self-rule has been invoked as an ideal, and, indeed, the image of the New England town meeting has to some extent persisted as a distinctly American model for government. Even in our own time, Americans seem to long to recreate the primitive conditions of localistic isolation and government by "primary assembly."

At length, but not great length, the wilderness Zion of Puritanism broke down of its own weight, when economic and ideological, intellectual and educational influences, and probably the force of human nature itself brought the authoritarian structure under attack and forced its modification. Many of the ideas of Puritanism and some of its practices indeed lived on. Here is the point where the impact of Puritanism on American political ideas and practice filtered from its specific representations in Puritan New England society. While it may be somewhat misleading to list these implications in simple form, it

[11] Quoted in Miller, *The New England Mind: the Seventeenth Century, op. cit.,* p. 423.

would seem they can be enumerated under four basic tenets, all central to American development. One of these is the doctrine of equality implicit in the idea of the priesthood of believers and the personal relationship of man to his God. The second is the idea of democracy, the idea that government is founded on consent among men to whom the restrictions of government are applicable. The third, previously unmentioned in our account of Puritanism, is what has been called the Protestant ethic, the idea that work and economic accumulation are reliefs from the uncertainty of the society in which men's destinies are thought to be predetermined. This theme has been elaborated in a number of commentaries on Puritanism itself and on Puritanism in American society.[12] The fourth is respect for public education and scholarship, which many think was one of the sources of the breakdown of Puritanism itself. The interweaving of these tendencies into a basic set of American value commitments will be discussed further at the end of the present chapter.

SECULAR LIBERALISM: THE MECHANISTIC THEORY OF GOVERNMENT

While the Christian theology of medieval Europe was undergoing the challenge of the Protestant Reformation, other forces were taking shape in secular thought, including secular theories of politics. To an extent, the development of liberalism on the secular level bears some of the same characteristics and carries some of the same implications for political ideas as the Protestantism of Luther and Calvin. This liberalism, however, casts into different terms the breakaway from the medieval synthesis described above. Here again, our analysis of a complex philosophical movement will be greatly simplified to highlight its main tendencies, since our goal in this section is to explore the principal forces behind the development of the American value consensus and to provide some "models" by which later developments in American political thought may be tested and understood. This brief analysis of the development of liberalism will be focused on the systems of the three major architects of the political theory of the period: Machiavelli, Hobbes, and Locke.

---

[12] Especially well known are Max Weber, *The Protestant Ethic and the Spirit of Capitalism,* trans. Talcott Parsons (New York: Charles Scribner's Sons, 1948), and R. H. Tawney, *Religion and the Rise of Capitalism* (New York: Harcourt, Brace, 1926). More recently, the theme has been explored with reference to its relevance to present American society by David Reisman, *The Lonely Crowd* (New Haven: Yale University Press, 1950), and William H. Whyte, Jr., *The Organization Man* (New York: Simon and Schuster, 1956).

One of the most significant aspects of the political theory of the time with which we are now dealing lies in its methods of approach to the problems of political analysis. Secular liberalism embodied a sharp break with the methods, predominantly Aristotelian, of medieval philosophy. But not only does this analysis differ from the analysis of the medieval period, there are also methodological differences among the people to whom we will refer. These differences will be treated more exhaustively in the paragraphs to follow. But they are most dramatically illustrated in the difference between the fundamentally inductive method of Machiavelli and the fundamentally deductive method of Thomas Hobbes. Both approaches contributed to the shaping of social and political analysis and to the philosophical method which accompanied the growth of modern science. Both the process of induction from the observation of experience and the process of deduction from a set of assumptions about the nature of the world figure heavily in the scientific method, and the development of science as a characteristic mode of approach to nature is one of the most important aspects of this period of transition from the medieval to the modern world. It should also be noted that we are treating a time not only of changes in ways of abstract thought, but also of changes in ways of living. Technological developments, the exploration of new worlds, the development of the nation state, and the freer social and geographic circulation of peoples all conditioned outlooks on the problems of politics. This was a period of deep running social and philosophical change.

Niccolo Machiavelli

Although a commentary on Machiavelli may seem strangely out of place in the discussion of American political thought, Machiavelli was one of the most dramatic figures in the historical process of developing the modern orientation to politics. Few people regard Machiavelli as a liberal, but our thesis here is that both the philosophical method and the perspectives on politics that are fundamental to modern liberalism are embodied in his ideas. The common central elements are a rudimentary empiricism and a mechanistic interpretation of the nature of social life.

Machiavelli was not a systematic political thinker, his major works being tracts on the politics of the time, written for specific purposes. They may be interpreted as mere personal appeals for the favor of rulers with whom Machiavelli wished to ingratiate himself, or as pleas for a political program; or as parts of the "mirror of princes" literature of the period. The attempt to develop a systematic political theory from *The Prince* and *The Discourses,* however, would seem to be one of the most instructive available exercises in theoretical analysis.[13]

The fundamentals of Machiavelli's approach may be understood by an analysis of his conception of the nature of society and man. Typically, medieval thought saw society as a natural organism with a purpose; Machiavelli, on the other hand, saw society as a collection of men and not as a thing in itself. Society to Machiavelli was an aggregate rather than an organism. Concepts of status, of hierarchy, of natural differentiation and the division of labor play rather little part in the development of his system. While in medieval thought the principle of life was inherent in the social whole, to Machiavelli the principle of life was inherent in each individual. Thus, the unit of analysis becomes the integral man rather than the integral society. The overall approach is one of atomism, social phenomena being explained in terms of the interaction of the atoms that are individual parts of the agglomerate of human society.

As Machiavelli's thought was not organic, likewise it was not historical. It postulated no grand plan or pattern of social development, but rather the individual interplay of men acting as forces on one another and on their environment. The materials of human society remain fundamentally the same, only the forms and combinations differ. As social materials form and reform, the experience of one era is likely to be repeated in another, but the basics do not go through a predictable evolution. This is not to say that there are no regularities in human behavior. It is to say, rather, that the regularities are fundamentally the regularities exhibited in the interactions of individual men, and not regularities dictated by an ulterior force or purpose. Regularities are to be detected by the observation of social phenomena and not inferred by the operation of human reason.

In consonance with his philosophical method, Machiavelli's theory of politics proceeds by generalization from observation, not by refinement of received hypotheses. Basic to his theory was a set of empirically based propositions about human nature, a form of political psychology at a very crude level. Machiavelli viewed men as being basically seek-

---

[13] Citations of Machiavelli's works that follow are to *The Prince* and *The Discourses* (New York: The Modern Library, 1940), trans. Luigi Ricci and Christian E. Detmold, respectively. For commentary on Machiavelli, see Leonardo Olschki, *Machiavelli the Scientist* (Berkeley:The Gillick Press, 1945); Herbert Butterfield, *The Statecraft of Machiavelli* (London: G. Bell & Sons, 1940); Wolin, *op. cit.,* chap. 7. For a quite different perspective from that discussed here, see Leo Strauss, *Thoughts on Machiavelli* (Glencoe, Ill.: The Free Press, 1958).

ers of security and comfort, ultimately motivated by a fear of death. Men want to survive, and, secondarily, they want power and goods as instruments of survival. These ends they seek with any means at their command. In considering human society, Machiavelli suggests one "must start with assuming that all men are bad and ever ready to display their vicious nature";[14] they "act right only from compulsion": and respond better to fear than to love.[15] ". . . Men have less scruple in offending one who makes himself loved than one who makes himself feared; for love is held by a chain of obligation which, men being selfish, is broken whenever it serves their purpose; but fear is maintained by a dread of punishment which never fails." [16] They cannot be relied on because "they are bad and would not keep their faith with you." [17] "For it may be said of men in general that they are ungrateful, voluble, dissemblers, anxious to avoid danger and covetous of gain." [18] ". . . Men forget more easily the death of their father than the loss of their patrimony." [19] This pessimistic view of human nature is fundamentally not unlike that of the classical Christian doctrine. The difference, however, is that with Machiavelli it is the material by which the entirety of society is to be explained, while in Christian doctrine or in medieval Aristotelianism it is a counterpoint against which divine purpose or the motivations grounded in divine salvation are played. Machiavelli's social and political theories are constructed on this crude hedonistic conception of the nature of the human material of society.

With this egoistic concept of human nature as his building block, Machiavelli built a hypothetico-historical picture of the origin of the political community. If the free play of egos were allowed, life in society would be an unbearable jungle for everyone. Dissatisfaction with this human condition therefore, drives men into the creation of political units which afford them a measure of security they would not otherwise enjoy. Passages in *The Discourses* suggest how this development of political authority came about.[20] This is not, it should be noted, a contract theory, since no element of explicit consent seems to be introduced into the picture. Rather, man is driven by his natural propensi-

---

[14] *Discourses*, p. 117.
[15] *Ibid.*, p. 118.
[16] *Prince*, p. 61.
[17] *Ibid.*, p. 64.
[18] *Ibid.*, p. 61.
[19] *Ibid.*, p. 62.
[20] *Discourses*, pp. 105–13.

ties to seek refuge in the security of the state. Here in the thought of Machiavelli, the artificial, mechanical conception later to characterize liberal thought compromises with the naturalistic, and individualism meets Aristotelianism.

The fundamental political act, then, is the making of a situation of security out of a situation in which no security can exist. The basis of politics is this process, the process of making and maintaining the community. Man's basic need is protection, and protection is to be found only within the community political structure, "For when men are well governed, they neither seek nor desire any other liberty. . . ." [21] The remainder of Machiavellian political theory is concerned with the implications and alternative forms of this basic proposition.

Closely related is a set of implicit generalizations about the requisites for the establishment of political order or the ingredients from which political order is erected on the foundation of man's desire for security and stability. The first of these is power. While the nature of man brings power naturally into the political association, power being implicit in the energy of human life, the organized power of the state is the vital tool in the creation of community. Organized power is thus an ever-present basic datum of politics, really in a sense what politics is built of. Machiavelli's emphasis on power is well known and is often thought to be his major contribution to a new perspective on politics. The importance he attached to the role of physical coercion, a specialized but obvious kind of power, is apparent in his emphasis on armed might, his demand for boldness, and his sanctioning of cruelty. "Thus it comes about that all armed prophets have conquered and unarmed ones failed." [22] In *The Discourses,* he suggested that good military order is the very foundation of the state.[23] The point, however, is not that Machiavelli held that naked force is the only instrument through which politics may function. As we shall see later, he held it often better if force is only exerted through or concealed behind a shield of institutions. Nonetheless, the sanction of force is always there, implicit in political relationships, but only one of the instruments of power through which the organizational effect of community is maintained.

The second Machiavellian requisite for political community is leadership. Leadership is, like power, a sine qua non of political community. Without it, the social body is formless and ineffective. Leader-

---

[21] *Ibid.,* p. 409.
[22] *Prince,* p. 22.
[23] *Discourses,* pp. 500–504.

ship is, in a sense, the active principle which makes force applicable to social situations.

The third requisite of political community is social pliability, i.e., the pliability of the social materials from which the community is made. Society itself, according to the Machiavellian formulation, is the product of the impact of politics, that is to say, an artificial set of relationships manipulated out of nature by men acting in concert. This formulation suggests that Machiavelli viewed the social situation as one that can be to a large degree shaped according to the needs and desires of those with power. Except a few inherent in human nature, there are hardly any limits to what can be done to give shape to society. This proposition about the pliability of human society is fundamental to the idea that stability can be engineered into the human social situation.

The fourth of these requisites of stability in the political community is centralization. Reflecting, probably, the disorder created in Italy on the collapse of the feudal structure as well as the impossibility of creating an effective Italian state in the face of political fragmentation, Machiavelli seems to have believed in the need for one government with power undifferentiated either on a geographic or a functional basis. The diffusion of power among the parts of a state would create that fractionalization of power and disputation over power which inhibits the assertion of effective political control. The implicit proposition is that the diffusion of political power on any basis yields instability in government and, hence, instability in the structure of the political community. On this proposition, the American political institutions of separation of powers and federalism have often been attacked. That is to say, those who are concerned about the development of governmental power sufficient to meet social needs have often cast doubt on the safety of society given such devices for the dispersion of power. The converse of the case is the defense usually offered for the separation of powers and the federal system in American government. This argument runs to the safety from overbearing political authority assured to minorities and to individuals by the dispersion of power. The difference between the two positions lies in the difference in assumed ends, on the one hand community stability, on the other hand individual or subcommunity freedom.

A particular expression of Machiavelli's argument for the concentration of political power and a point of emphasis in itself, i.e., a major element in Machiavelli's description of the specifics of political organization, was his concern with the development of political authority effective over a relatively large area. Machiavelli argued that political authority could be effective in his time only if organized in the scale of the nation state. He held, in other words, that the maintenance of freedom and security in the political community could be maintained only if the community organized itelf as a large political unit extensive in population and resources and the other components of political and military power. The successful formation of one nation state dictates the formation of others, and thus, in the face of the growing national power of France and Spain, the position of Italy could be maintained only by union of the discrete principalities which then made up the nation. Machiavelli ended *The Prince* with an exhortation to create national power in Italy.[24] "And certainly," he wrote in *The Discourses,* "a country can never be united and happy, except when it obeys wholly one government, whether a republic or monarchy, as is the case in France and in Spain. . . ."[25] In *The Prince* and *The Discourses,* he made repeated references to France and Spain, whose political and military successes as nation states were then profoundly influencing the course of affairs in Europe.

The four "requisites" of community just discussed comprise the necessities of adequate politics according to the Machiavellian theory. These are the basic ingredients, the components out of which a political society is made. Machiavelli devoted a major part of his attention, however, to further refinement of these basics, to the development of prescriptions for optimal political organization. Many of these prescriptions have to do with rulership or statesmanship, i.e., the effective application of political power through leaders for the achievement of social stability and security. Machiavelli assumed that the ambition for political power is part of the natural equipment of some men, and that part of the fundamental process of politics is the harnessing of this ambition for power to social ends.

What particular characteristics set apart the effective exercise of political power? What distinguishes statesmanship from the mere wielding of the authority of government? The final test of rulership, of course, is its result, and this result is judged in terms of the stability and security that rulership creates in society. Machiavelli does, however, devote considerable attention to the specific means suitable for the attainment of this end. The basic ingredient in the exercise of statesmanship seems to be insight and boldness. It is not merely an ambition for power that characterizes the statesman, but that plus a

---

[24] *Prince,* chap. 26, pp. 94–98.
[25] *Discourses,* pp. 151–152.

combination of willingness to apply power where power is needed and appreciation of the needs of the particular social situation. Thus, statesmanship requires not the following of a predetermined recipe, but rather a flexibility in adaptation of means to ends and an almost intuitive ability to grasp and master circumstances. This quality is treated by Machiavelli through the concept *virtu,* the quality of the virtuoso. *Virtu* is not synonomous with virtue in the ordinary sense. The ruler with *virtu,* like the artist who can be described as a virtuoso, is one who knows his instrument or medium and is able to get the best out of it. The statesman grasps the situation of his social material, acts with confidence, and through the combination of judgment and skill exercises power effectively in the modes most appropriate to circumstances. *Virtu* is the quality of creative genius in the exercise of political power. In a famous passage, Machiavelli describes the combination of qualities necessary for effective political leadership as follows: "A prince being thus obliged to know well how to act as a beast must imitate the fox and the lion, for the lion cannot protect himself from traps, and the fox cannot defend himself from wolves. One must therefore be a fox to recognize traps, and a lion to frighten wolves. Those who wish to be only lions do not understand this." [26]

Complementary to Machiavelli's concept of *virtu* is his concept of *fortuna,* the circumstances of the time, the "ins and outs" of history. As we noted before, Machiavelli did not hold that history moves in predetermined patterns. *Fortuna,* therefore, is not completely predictable nor even completely manageable, but it is rather the challenge of fortuitous circumstances to the political leader. It is the test of his virtuosity, part of which is the sense of the situation. *Fortuna* thus imposes on the ruler an obligation to sense the situation and judge social needs and the modes of exercise of political power in complete appreciation of what is happening and what is likely to happen. But the quality of the statesmanship is not simply the quality of prudence, not only appreciation of the situation, it is also boldness and readiness to act. ". . . Fortune," said Machiavelli, "is a woman, and it is necessary, if you wish to master her, to conquer her by force; and it can be seen that she lets herself be overcome by the bold rather than by those who proceed coldly." [27] This is not a prescription of violence but a prescription of courage and determination.

Machiavelli's concept of statesmanship is not dissimilar from the modern concept which we now frequently hear contrasted to the qual-

---

[26] *Prince,* p. 64.
[27] *Ibid.,* p. 94.

ities of the politician. The modern statesman is the political leader who knows his country, who knows his world, who knows his history, and who acts boldly in the face of the circumstances with which he finds himself dealing. He may bend with the wind when necessary, but bending with the wind is not the prime quality of his political leadership. He is the leader who does not hesitate to lead. He is the Lincoln, the Bismarck, the Churchill, the de Gaulle of the modern world.

Within this framework of general requisites of stability in the political community, Machiavelli also develops some more specific rules for exercising political power in particular kinds of situations. Basically, the problem is twofold: (1) the establishment of power in an instable society, (2) the maintenance of political power in a stable society. The first of these situations is the main focus of *The Prince*. In the instable society, boldness and surehandedness in the exercise of political power are needed to maximum degree. The creation of a true and stable community must largely be accomplished through authoritarian means. It is in this connection that Machiavelli advocated those tactics of ruthlessness and cruelty which have popularly become associated with his name. He felt, however, that the issue of events and not the means used by the ruler is the final criterion by which his rule is evaluated. "Let a prince therefore aim at conquering and maintaining the state, and the means will always be judged honorable and praised by every one, for the vulgar is always taken by appearances and the issue of the event; and the world consists only of the vulgar, and the few who are not vulgar are isolated when the many have a rallying point in the Prince." [28] Confronted by instability, the prince must concern himself not with the acceptability of the means which he uses, but with the acceptability of the situation he creates.

The exercise of political power in already stable societies, however, must be more subtle and must involve institutions and forms not generally associated with Machiavelli. This is the subject of *The Discourses*. The difference between the stable and the instable situation is fundamentally the difference between maintaining and creating. Both situations require the application of *virtu,* and in both situations, power is the prime ingredient of politics even though the problems in its application differ.

In treating the maintenance of political power in a stable society, Machiavelli's work focuses on two preferred aspects of political ar-

---

[28] *Ibid.,* p. 66.

rangements. One of these is predictability, a most helpful situation in
a society relatively settled in its relationships. Predictability in political practice means such things as an established code of laws, established and recognized political procedures, and equal rewards and
equal punishments. ". . .[A]ll novelties," wrote Machiavelli, "excite
the minds of men. . . ." [29] Novelties, as they generate excitement,
threaten to upset the stability of a well-situated society. Machiavelli's
formulations about predictability resemble in content and, to some
extent, in function, later liberal ideas about the need for and effect of
the "rule of law."

A second political device effective for the maintenance of stability
in an established society is balance. In his admiration of political balance, Machiavelli seems sometimes to be almost an advocate of systems
in which powers are separated by functions and recombined by checks.
If one were to take this prescription seriously, Machiavelli would take
his place in the long line of political theorists advocating balance as
the answer to man's needs for political community. Included in this
group, though with vast differences among them, are Aristotle,
Polybius, Montesquieu, and the Founding Fathers of the American
Constitution.

It is difficult, however, to make this interpretation of the notion of
balance consonant with other aspects in Machiavelli's political
thought. We have noted his central emphasis on the concentration of
political power. The type of balance with which Machiavelli seemed
concerned is balance among social and economic interests in society.
This balance is not one institutionalized in government but one made
use of by government as it deals with society. Conflicting social and
economic forces in society tend to cancel out the power of one another,
that is, to limit the effectiveness of any one interest in its demands on
the political order. The political leader, appreciating the mutually
checking role of these countervailing forces in society will capitalize
on them, will permit them to flourish, but will maintain a situation
such that no one is able to overcome the influence of all others. This
theory is not unlike that expounded by James Madison in *Federalist*
No. 10, nor is it unlike the arguments of the later pluralists who maintained, in part, that political stability is the product of the interplay
of the various and competing elements in modern society.

In concluding our analysis of Machiavelli's theory of politics, we
might confront his work with the question: "What of the role of the
people?" This is particularly apropos, since our interest in Machiavelli

[29] *Discourses*, p. 182.

is chiefly an interest in his contribution to the liberal tradition, and the liberal tradition is defined in part by its emphasis on the role of the people and the institutionalization of that role in political arrangements. There is a sense and, we have argued here, a basically liberal sense in which Machiavelli's theory postulates that government is based in the people. Individual needs, it suggests, provide the justification for the establishment and maintenance of political power, and the social world is a world made up of integral individual human units. Society is but a collection of these individuals.

But the question may be pushed much further, as liberalism did, to ask, "Do the people have a moral claim to some particular role in the working out of political policy and political arrangement?" In Machiavelli's terms the answer to this question must be no. The question with which Machiavelli confronts any society or any set of political arrangements is: "Who can rule best?" There are situations in which the people in some institutionalized form might be the best— that is, the most effective—locus for political power. Despite his low estimate of human nature, Machiavelli seems to concede that a people acting together have some measure of the appropriate political virtues as well as what Leonardo Olschki calls "an elementary common-sense and a determined, stubborn courage of despair."[30] In any society, it is the practical obligation of government to attend to the needs of the people of that society. This is one of the conditions for the maintenance of political stability. It must be emphasized, however, that the obligation is not a moral one. It is an obligation to understand the people's needs and to maintain stability in the face of threats to stability which the needs of the people may create. The way of *virtu* is to accommodate and manipulate the people as the situation and disposition of force in society dictate.

Machiavelli's theory of politics may be summarized as an interrelated set of propositions about the nature, characteristics, and functions of political power. The whole is founded on the assumption that the social world is to be understood in terms of the interactions of individual men. The propositions are as follows:

1. Human beings are fundamentally egotistical, weak, and unpredictable creatures.

2. Man seeks the security of stable social relationships. Security in social relationships is established only with the creation of the political community. The political community is defined as the conjunc-

---

[30] Olschki, *op. cit.,* p. 41.

tion of four attributes—power, leadership, social pliability, and an adequate combination of territorial, population, and natural resources.

3. In terms of active political arrangements, power must be exercised by leaders in certain ways to achieve social stability. These ways may be defined in terms of *virtu*.

4. The adequate modes of exercise of political power differ in stable and instable societies.

As here stated, these propositions are on a very general level, and as such they would be very difficult to operationalize and test except against the gross phenomena of world history. In form, however, they are testable propositions that deal with the political world as we ordinarily understand it, and they do constitute a comprehensive system of theory about political relationships. Some of the propositions as stated above may, of course, be refined along lines previously noted or in different fashion.

The work of Machiavelli is important to us in two ways. As a system of theory, it has much in common with ways of political thought characteristic of the present age. As such, it provides a basis for the development and modification of systematic political theory. Secondly, it is important because both in a historical and conceptual sense it embodies many of the ideas crucial to the development of the liberal heritage of which American political thought is a part. Particularly in its emphasis on the individual and in its formulation of the social function of political authority, it points toward but, of course, does not comprehend the theoretical basis of American politics.

Thomas Hobbes

Even more closely related to the development of American political thought and the Western liberal tradition than the ideas of Machiavelli are those of Thomas Hobbes. Like Machiavelli, Hobbes is often condemned as an absolutist when seen from the perspective of more recent liberal theory. However, in many respects the contribution of Hobbes is similar to that of Machiavelli, both having formulated approaches substantially different from those of the Middle Ages and related in a basic way to the shaping of the modern liberal—individualistic interpretation of politics. As we will attempt to demonstrate later, Hobbes' absolutism is not the central element in his political thought. His major contributions lie in the application of new methods and new assumptions in the analysis of political relationships.

Hobbes lived in a century of turmoil in England, a century during which political, social, and religious bases of English life underwent much of the trauma of adjustment to the modern world. His life spanned most of the seventeenth century, when England was experiencing two civil wars, the execution of the King, the Cromwellian protectorate, and the Restoration of the Stuarts. Schisms in the British society of this period ran deep, social tensions were punctuated by violence, and there was frequent conflict over political authority. Hobbes' political thought doubtless reflects not only the conditions of the time and place in which he lived but also the needs and experiences of an era in which the larger world was undergoing dramatic change. His relation to the development of American politics was temporal and direct as well as intellectual, for he was contemporary with the first substantial English efforts at colonization in the New World. The colonization movement, of course, was itself closely related to the disorders and oppressions of the home country. Leo Strauss says that Machiavelli discovered the continent on which Hobbes' theoretical edifice was erected.[31] In a similar sense, Hobbes may be said to have constructed the individualist basis on which the architects of the British and American political systems built structures designed by John Locke and other English and American liberal political theorists. Both in time and in temper, he wrote at a critical juncture in the development of the American tradition.[32]

A note on Hobbes' method is in order before we describe his political ideas. It is to be distinguished in important ways both from the characteristic method of the Middle Ages and from the method of Machiavelli discussed in preceding pages. Where the medieval approach was theological or purposive, seeking "reasons" deduced from ultimate purpose, Hobbes' was mechanistic, nonpurposive, and directed to explanation in terms of cause. The first was metaphysical in ultimate reference, the second physical; cause is the fundamental concern of the modern scientist, reason, in this sense, of the metaphysician. Thus, Hobbes was dealing not with reality of some ultimate sort but with necessary relationships between nominally identified forces. His contribution was a part of the shaping of the distinctly

---

[31] Leo Strauss, *Natural Right and History* (Chicago: University of Chicago Press, 1953), p. 177.

[32] Citations that follow are to Thomas Hobbes, *Leviathan,* ed. with introduction by Michael Oakeshott (Oxford: Basil Blackwell, n.d.). For commentary on Hobbes, see Oakeshott's introduction in *ibid.;* Leo Strauss, *The Political Philosophy of Hobbes,* trans. Elsa M. Sinclair (Chicago: University of Chicago Press, 1936); John Bowle, *Hobbes and His Critics* (London: Jonathan Cape, 1951).

modern approach to knowledge in which such contemporaries as Descartes, Newton, and Leibnitz also notably participated.

His methodological difference from Machiavelli was noted above.
Where Machiavelli proceeded by induction from experience, Hobbes
began with first assumptions about human nature from which a social
theory was deduced as by the processes of mathematical logic. Where
Machiavelli's theory, systematically analyzed, works from observation
toward generalization, Hobbes' works from generalization and ideal
conception of relationships against which observation might then be
checked. Both are in a sense empirical and complementary. Both
methods are integral to the procedures of modern science, and both
differ radically from the typical ways of thought of the Middle Ages
which we have analyzed above.

The keystone of Hobbes' social thought is an assumption about
human nature which, in turn, had its natural social ramification in
the political state. Human activity, he suggested, is rooted in desire
and aversion, particularly in a passion for survival. Like many other
thinkers of his period, Hobbes explained his notion of human nature
through a conceptual device, a fictitious state of nature. His framework was fundamentally utilitarian, though with a greater emphasis
on vitality than on pleasure and pain. Basically, he held that men's
actions stemmed from a pervading fear of death from which may be
inferred a train of less compelling but still influential pleasures and
pains. In their fear of death, men seek the power to prevent it, and
in doing so they come into conflict with others trying to maximize
their own powers. A fundamental equality in the state of nature makes
it impossible for anyone to impose his will on the rest. Therefore,
man naturally faces a predicament—a predicament in which he and
his fellows are compelled to seek power, but at the expense of one
another, a situation in which everyone must suffer. The life of man
in the state of nature is, in Hobbes' familiar words, "solitary, poor,
nasty, brutish, and short." [33] There is, however, in the natural man
the ability to transcend passion and to solve his predicament. This
ability arises from the fact that man is not only passionate but also
gifted with a measure of reason, and the road to security through political association is discovered by man through reason mediated in
the act by passion and prudence. Passion impels men to follow whatever path seems to promise the most hope for survival, and prudence
—the lessons men learn in their day-to-day experience—brings to them

[33] Hobbes, *op. cit.*, p. 82.

the realization that only through association can each and all be saved. The answer to the human predicament, then, lies in the formation of civil society. The state is, therefore, a work of human will, an arti- fact, a mechanical contrivance created out of the minds of men to satisfy their desires.[34] The state has no teleological purpose, no growth, no decay, no existence independent of the men who make it. Like- wise, on the other side of the coin, the state gives to man nothing he did not have before. It only assures him that he is safer in the pos- session and use of his natural attributes, that is, of what the liberal tradition has come to call "natural rights." The obligation of men to the state stems from the acts of will of those men themselves. Obliga- tion is the rational commitment of the free will prompted by passion.

The interpretation of the civil society as the product of acts of human will leads quite logically to the explanation of political obliga- tion in terms of social contract, again a conceptual device, not a his- torical description. In Hobbes' version, the contract is a single one running among the members of the society and embodying their agreement to establish common authority. Being what they are, men require sanctions to assure the performance of their promises. The state, therefore, is recognized to be a coercive agency. The execution of the contract means the mutual surrender by men of the right to act freely as well as their acknowledgement of the legitimacy of a govern- ment to judge and punish violations of the promise to surrender that right. In Hobbes' words, the promise men make might be phrased this way, "I authorize and give up my right of governing myself, to this man, or to this assembly of men, on this condition, that thou give up thy right to him, and authorize all his actions in like manner." [35] Men will government to assure social peace, and government is expected to take whatever actions are necessary to maintain that peace by assuring observance of the contract.

The form of government is logically a matter of indifference to the mainstream of Hobbesian thought. Any political organization that could assure the performance of the contract or, in other words, fulfill the duties of the sovereign established by the contract, would pre- sumably be acceptable government. Hobbes, however, expressed a decided preference for government that takes on what we would call an authoritarian form. This is a preference of judgment and not a preference logically implied in the context of the theory.[36] The prime

---

[34] Cf. Oakeshott, *op cit.,* p. lii.
[35] Hobbes, *op. cit.,* p. 112.
[36] Cf. Oakeshott, *op. cit.,* p. xl.

consideration is authority based on adequate power to assure obedience, and hence the question of form of government resolves into
the problem what form is most likely to command sufficient power.
Hobbes, himself, was disposed to favor monarchy as the most satisfactory form for obvious reasons. Its councils are not divided, the
locus of authority is clear, it is not subject to internal intrigues. In
circumstances other than those in which Hobbes lived, the Hobbesian
theory might well be called into defense of a variety of forms of
government. Indeed, Hobbes himself said, "The legislator in all com-
monwealths is only the sovereign, be he one man, as in a monarchy,
or one assembly of men, as in a democracy or aristocracy." [37] Hobbes'
renowned preference for authoritarianism can thus be seen as a testable proposition about the political form most likely to succeed in
fulfilling the functions of the state.

The emphasis placed above on the nature of the state as the creature
of man's individual will may have obscured to some degree Hobbes'
formulation about the active relationship of man to the sovereign.
Man's surrender to the sovereign is a willful surrender, yet it is an
absolute surrender of his freedom to act contrary to law. Law is the
command of the sovereign and not subject to appeal. The individual
binds himself and is bound by the force of the government to observe
those rules of human conduct which the sovereign deems fit. Further,
claims cannot be made against the sovereign on the grounds that the
sovereign has breached the contract, because the sovereign is not a
party to the contract and therefore has made no agreement which he
can breach. His command, by dint of the delegation provided in the
contract between men, is absolute. As long as government fulfills the
functions of sovereignty, i.e., the keeping of social peace, there is no
ground for moral appeal against it. Thus, it is often said Hobbes implied no right of revolution. This is true if taken literally. There is
a sense, however, in which the locus of sovereignty can be shifted—
that is, a sense in which the government may cease to satisfactorily
fulfill the functions of sovereignty and thus be deprived of the position of sovereign. In such a case, it could not be said that a revolution
was made against a sovereign, since a government no longer effective
would no longer be fulfilling the functions of sovereignty. However,
it is possible to justify revolution as the response to a situation in
which the sovereign no longer is able to maintain civil order, i.e.,
within the Hobbesian framework, to countenance revolution as the
overturning of what had been authority when that authority ceases

---
[37] Hobbes, *op. cit.*, p. 173.

to be adequate. From this point of view, the success of revolution might even seem to be its own justification.

Hobbes' thought, on analysis, seems to be a curious combination of individualism and authoritarianism; his later influence has probably run in both directions. We are primarily interested, however, in those elements in Hobbes' theory which point in the direction of modern liberalism. Among the implications that should be emphasized here are particularly those that find the roots of political behavior in the psychological makeup of man, those that imply that power is characteristic of all political relationships, those that hold that the state is the artificial product of human will, and those that hold men to be basically equal in nature and before government. These are largely points that found elaboration and further liberal refinement in the theory of John Locke.

John Locke

Locke published his major contribution to political thought immediately after the Glorious Revolution, which, in a sense, has proved to be the final English political revolution to the present day. With the Glorious Revolution, the House of Stuart was deposed from the English throne and the crown settled on William and Mary of the House of Orange, and conditions were established for the development of English politics along their characteristic contemporary lines. Perhaps more clearly than any other, the time of the Glorious Revolution was the time of systematization of the English political system, the time of its settlement into a "steady state." Locke has been called the philosopher and sometimes the apologist of the Glorious Revolution, and in a sense he was also the advance ideologist of the American Revolution. He developed a set of political ideas which has very largely served as the basis for American political values and for the institutional structure which American and British government has since assumed. His importance for American political thought can hardly be overestimated; indeed, there is probably no better short summary of the ideas of Locke than the American Declaration of Independence.[38]

---

[38] Locke's major political work was the second of his *Two Treatises of Government*, entitled *An Essay Concerning the True Original, Extent and End of Civil Government*. Citations that follow, labeled *Civil Government*, are from the version found in E. A. Burtt (ed.), *The English Philosophers from Bacon to Mill* (New York: Modern Library, 1939). A definitive edition of *Two Treatises*, edited with introduction by Peter Laslett, was published by Cambridge University Press, 1960. Students of Locke should also be referred to *A Letter Concerning Toleration* and *An Essay Concerning Human Understanding*. For commentary on Locke, see, *inter alia*, John W. Gough, *John Locke's Po-*

Locke was not so rigorous in method or in execution as Thomas Hobbes, and some commentaries find more importance in the divergences between the two than in their similarities. However, it is also possible to see their theories as complementary, to see Locke beginning where Hobbes left off. At basis, the two formulations seem very much the same, although Locke's perspective was somewhat modified by the conditions of his time. Like Hobbes, Locke built a utilitarian description of the origin and nature of political power. Although Locke's version did not make human nature seem so antisocial, he interpreted life in the state of nature as being sufficiently difficult to prompt man to find a way out of it. Although he sometimes seems to describe the state of nature as a state of high sociability, it is a condition, after all, that men leave by consent. Despite the fact that men in nature are endowed with natural liberty, its enjoyment, he said, is very uncertain and "constantly exposed to the invasions of others." The state of nature "however free is full of fears and continual dangers" and is, in fact, "an ill condition." [39]

The basic difficulty in the state of nature arises from tension over the control and use of property. The product of man's labor is by right his; however, other men in the state of nature may refuse to observe such right. Thus, man is driven, according to Locke as according to Hobbes, to seek some artificial means for amelioration of a situation which is otherwise untenable. In other words, Locke elaborated Hobbes' definition of interest—a definition restricted pretty much to preservation of life—to include a wider range of things that make up man's essential humanity. These he subsumed under the general name of property—a broad term including life, liberty, and estate; they form the nexus of Locke's moral system, and they are the things which men should and do try above all else to preserve. They are the moral rights which prompt men to enter civil society and which, as we shall see, limit the sphere of the justifiable operation of social control on the individual man. They lie behind both authority and the drive to restrain authority.

Locke, like Hobbes, used the metaphor of the social contract to explain the development of political authority in a fundamentally atomistic, individualistic human world. Their contract formulations

---

litical Philosophy: Eight Studies (Oxford: Clarendon Press, 1950); George H. Sabine, "The Two Democratic Traditions," *Philosophical Review*, Vol. LXI (October, 1952), pp. 451-74; Willmoore Kendall, *John Locke and the Doctrine of Majority Rule* (Illinois Studies in the Social Sciences, Vol. XXVI, No. 2) (Urbana: University of Illinois Press, 1941).

[39] Locke, *Civil Government*, pp. 453–54.

were not basically dissimilar, and both implied that government is based on at least a rudimentary kind of consent. While it is sometimes claimed that Locke's was a dual-contract theory, postulating one "social" contract that runs between individuals and creates civil society plus a second "governmental" contract that runs from society to government, only the first seems to have been a true contract relationship. In other words, we are saying that Locke, like Hobbes, made use of the contract metaphor only to explain the relationship of man to society (actually of man to man), not of man to political structure. The importance of this distinction may be seen by considering the character of the governmental relationship as Locke's theory developed it.

That relationship he saw as having the form of a trust, not the form of a contract.[40] A contract, on the one hand, implies mutual obligations on both parties to the agreement, a quid pro quo. If you and I execute a commercial contract for services, for example, I exchange my services for your money; without some obligation on each side, the contract is not a binding relationship. A trust, on the other hand, is a tripartite relationship among trustor, trustee, and beneficiary, and it establishes quite a different set of obligations. The central relationship in a trust arrangement, that between trustee and beneficiary, is not a relationship of mutual obligation. Obligation rests entirely with the trustee. If a man (trustor) sets up a trust fund to be administered by a third party (trustee) for the benefit of his minor children (beneficiaries), for example, the trustee, not the children, is under obligation by the terms of the relationship. The children will have other obligations arising out of other relationships, of course, but that is another matter.

Applying this formulation to political arrangements, Locke suggests that the society as trustor assigns to the government as trustee a fund of power to be exercised on behalf of the safety (or pleasure) of the individuals of the community. This power is limited in application by the terms of the agreement, and the agreement does not fix the political obligation of the citizen directly to government. This is not to say, of course, that the people of the society are under no obligation, that they have no political duty. The idea of political obligation here, as elsewhere in political philosophy, is a crucial one. However, the obligation of the citizen in this scheme is an obligation

---

[40] Cf. John Gough, *The Social Contract: a Critical Study of Its Development* (2d ed.; Oxford: Clarendon Press, 1957), pp. 142–44.

that derives from his relationship to society (i.e., to his fellow men collectively) and not to government.

The distinction between society and government is thus an important one. The contract is one that runs among the individuals in society, a contract that seals their obligation to one another. The power of the government, however, is derivative power, and it in no way entails moral claims or rights held by the government in and of itself. The importance of the use of the trust concept in Lockean political thought is not in its elegance as a fancy legal device, but rather in the nature of government and the nature of the political relationship that it implies. For reasons to be explained shortly, Locke's system prescribed limited government, and the trust concept helps to emphasize the limited and fiduciary role that government as the active arm of society is supposed to play in human arrangements.

Thus far in our examination of Locke's theory, we have a model of the political system with three central components: first, the individual, a free creature with psychological and moral rights; secondly, the society or community, a construct of individual wills; and third, the government, entrusted with the exercise of the limited and delegated authority of the society to maintain social peace. One of the elements in this model that is not sufficiently treated in the foregoing paragraphs is the relationship between the individual and society. We have described this as a contract relationship—that is, a relationship in which the individual freely surrenders something to society in exchange for the protection society offers him in amelioration of the ill condition of the state of nature. It is not accurate, however, to describe this contract merely in terms of free surrender. The question of what is surrendered remains, and this is a matter on which Locke's theory has had particular bearing on latter political development, especially in America. It is at this point that the familiar idea of natural rights enters.

It was mentioned earlier that man's life can be described in terms of a cluster of what might be called interests, namely, life, liberty, and estate—attributes of life to which, Locke held, man had a natural right. Here, the psychological hedonism of Locke (and of Hobbes) is transmuted into a moral theory through a proposition that runs something like this: Here is what man is, and furthermore, he should be treated in recognition of what he is. Natural rights comprise the core of man's humanity, a humanity which ought to be respected. They are eternal, indefeasible, unalienable components of the human personality. The doctrines of individualism imply the deepest respect for those elements of individual life which define that individual life in terms of its distinction from and freedom from all others.

The execution of the social contract does not and, indeed, cannot involve the giving away of natural rights. The relationship between man and society is a relationship in which rights are not surrendered, but the defense of rights is delegated. The rights remain with the individual. What the individual gives up is what Locke calls "the executive power of the law of nature." This point is an important one. Civil society and its governmental arm are developed by man to protect him in the exercise of his basic human rights, and in executing this protective power, the government is in no way justified in abridging these rights. There is, in other words, a natural sphere of privacy for the individual which government is obliged to protect and not to violate.

From its statement in the *Declaration of Independence,* this doctrine was carried into its most effective operational form in the American Bill of Rights. Since that time, it has been continually reasserted and frequently modified, but Locke's theory has remained as the cornerstone of the doctrine of freedom which, as doctrine, still plays a fundamental part in the limitation of political power in the United States, as well as in attacks on and rationalizations of various extensions of governmental power into zones of activity formerly thought to be private to individuals. Problems inherent in making the notion of natural rights operational and meaningful for a society will be discussed in greater detail at a later point in our analysis.

On the basis of this conception of the nature and limits of political authority, Locke built his justification of the political forms of liberal democracy. One might read his theory of government as though it were answering the question: Given the values of individualism and the need for political authority as described above, what political means are most appropriate for their realization? In effect, the criterion of forms of government under this theory is the two-sided criterion applied by liberal democratic thought in general—authority commensurate with the maintenance of social stability, and limits on authority commensurate with the protection of individual freedoms. These criteria are met on the one hand by a set of institutions that transform the principle of consent into a principle for the dynamic control of authority through the institutions of political democracy, and, on the other hand, by the development of a set of strictures on political power through the institutions of what is commonly called "constitutionalism."

In the matter of democracy, Locke took the steps that Hobbes did not by suggesting that policy for the settlement of social disputes can best be developed by those who represent the will of the majority through legislative institutions. With Locke, the notion of dynamic consent as the validation of political authority became a principle. His theory seems to suggest not only that active consent is the most effective policy-making mechanism for maintaining stability in society, but also that since government is a creature of men, men *ought* to have a right to participate in the development of general and specific policies under which they are to be asked to live. Thus, figuratively speaking, he makes consent both the foundation of political authority and the means of its continuing legitimation. Drawing the implications of the theory of consent even further, Locke comes close to stating a theory of legislative supremacy. Ultimate authority in the state is to rest in the hands of a representative legislature with the power to promulgate laws but without power to delegate its own power which, in turn, has been delegated to it by the body politic. One might say that in this theory the active principle of political authority is the principle of legislative democracy. This is not to say, of course, that Locke advocated the radical democracy which would have made the legislature a perfect mirror of the society or would have accorded an active part in the selection of government authority to all the people in society through some plebiscitary device. The extension of the principle of consent into the principle of political equality was a later development in England and America—a development for which, as the experience of the Levellers suggests, Anglo-Saxon society in the eighteenth century was not yet ready.

In the interest of Locke's other basic principle, the principle of limitation of political authority, his democratic prescription becomes somewhat attenuated. The principle of individual rights dictates the limitation of social authority, and Locke would have institutionalized this limitation through the imposition of certain checks on the exercise of government power. He sets out, for example, a version of the age-old doctrine of separation of powers which later was to become so integral a part of the American political ideology and procedure. Suggesting that safety in the face of authority is to be found partially in that arrangement which separates authority and requires that it be shared and exercised jointly, he divides the functions of government into three, each to be exercised by a different structure. Of these structures, the legislature is in some sense central, but the executive is empowered to exercise a healthy prerogative. The third organ, which he called the federative power, was substantially to exercise the function of handling external affairs. In consonance, too, with the developing British practice of the time, Locke argued for an independent judiciary and paid his respects to the doctrine of the rule of law, the doctrine which says that the acts of government as they operate on citizens must be public and predictable.

In its approach to political form and structure, Locke's theory dealt with the relationship of means to ends, the ends being those of the limitation of political power in behalf of individual rights; the means being those of separation of powers and structuralization and delimitation of political functions. Essentially, Locke's theory of government, emphasizing as it did both consent and limits, reflected his fairly optimistic view of human reason and sociability and his less optimistic view of political power. In these respects, it seems safe to say that he stands conceptually much closer to the center of the Western liberal democratic tradition than does his predecessor liberal, Hobbes.

A note should be added about some problems inherent in the interpretation of Locke's political ideas. Because of his importance to the Western political tradition and because of some inconsistencies in his political thought which have made him a rather easy target for criticism, Locke has been one of the most widely interpreted of all the major figures in the history of Western political ideas. The more common interpretations of Locke seem to fall into four categories: One of these emphasizes Locke's moralistic bent, his emphasis on self-evident moral injunctions. In this interpretation, Locke becomes substantially a metaphysician dealing in the propositions of natural law which are not testable except perhaps in the light of a specially gifted human reason. A second type of interpretation of Locke emphasizes his empiricist side. This approach, finding no great difference between him and Hobbes, treats Locke's theory as an inductive system derived from observations about human nature. Locke did, it should be noted, elaborate a systematic and influential theory of human psychology.[41]

Third and fourth interpretations of Locke direct attention to the political implications of his system of theory. One of these emphasizes the majoritarian aspects, suggesting that the main burden of his theory is that which points toward the implementation of the will of the majority through the devices of democratic consent. The other is constitutionalist, emphasizing, as we have above, the interplay be-

---

[41] See the *Essay Concerning Human Understanding*.

tween Locke's insistence on the need for political authority and his insistence on the need for restrictions on political authority on behalf
of the individual human personality. While the interpretation we
have offered here is not represented as necessarily accurate or best, it
does seem faithful to Locke, closest to the center of the Western
liberal tradition, and most influential in the development of American
political ideas and practices. It highlights the difficulties of living with
seeming tensions and contradictions—the tension between liberty and
authority, the tension between psychology and morality. Yet, these
are the tensions with which the Western liberal tradition has had to
deal, and these are perhaps tensions inherent in the human being and
the human social situation. In this major sense, and in a number of
more specific ways, Locke's work helped to shape the American political tradition as a distinctive version of Anglo-Saxon liberalism.[42]

THE AMERICAN POLITICAL TRADITION AND THE
DEVELOPMENT OF MODERN SCIENCE

The third major element in the intellectual-cultural setting out
of which American political thought developed is typified in the
growth of modern science. The influence of the spirit of modern
science on the development of political ideas is neither so direct nor
so easy to illustrate as the influence of theological and explicitly
political ideas. Perhaps nothing is so characteristic of the modern
Western world, however, as its scientific outlook, and certainly the
development of this outlook has made itself felt in the conception of
theories, ideologies, and institutions of politics. There are, of course,
a variety of relationships between the development of the spirit of
science and the development both of Protestant theology and of the
liberal political ideas which we have reviewed in preceding pages. It
is clearly impossible to discuss here in any comprehensive fashion the
development of science in its historical, philosophical, or inventive
aspects. The reader is cautioned, therefore, that what is said comes
far from plumbing the full depths and implications of the scientific
revolution. For our purposes, however, the important problem lies in
understanding not the details of modern science but its broad characteristics as a way of thought, and its implications for ideas and developments in the political and social sphere.

Like modern social and political thought, modern science can be
understood as a reaction to the typical intellectual postures of the

---

[42] On the contribution of Locke to the American political tradition, see especially
Louis Hartz, *The Liberal Tradition in America* (New York: Harcourt Brace & Co., 1955).

Middle Ages. While it is an oversimplification to treat in black-and-white terms the contrast between the ideas of the middle period and those of the modern age, in science as in other reaches of intellectual life, the changes were great. Perhaps even more than its social philosophy, the science of the Middle Ages was dominated by the classics. In its effort to understand the natural world, the medieval period borrowed not only the epistemology, logic, and characteristic modes of stating questions from the golden age of Greece, but also in large part the Greek and Roman answers. Thus, the great events of medieval science were the rediscoveries of ancient Greek texts or the translation, often by Arabic scholars, of texts not previously available. Insofar as this is true, medieval science was not science at all in the sense that science is new discovery; it was rather a kind of literary philosophy, largely without new problems, new theoretical formulations, new methodology, or new systematic observation. Its tendency was to receive and, in some cases, to attempt to reinterpret the authority of the classics.[43]

It is not easy to characterize or summarize the methodology of classical science. It is important, however, to do so in a fashion sufficient to illustrate its differences from the approaches of modern science to natural phenomenon. Aristotelian science dealt with things, not with relations among things, and its efforts were directed toward the delineation of their unique characteristics. Each category of things was somehow understood in terms of its uniqueness, that is to say, of its distinctive purpose or natural course of development. The function of science was to achieve an orderly picture of the world out of rationally constructed categories into which existential phenomena were to be sorted. Such science is interested in the "oakness" of the oak and in the incipient "oakness" of the acorn. It is interested in the qualities that make a dog a dog and not something else and in the qualities that cause a puppy to grow into a dog and not into a horse or a sheep or a cat. This is not to say that classical science dealt with each phenomenon individually. There was in classical science as in classical social thought a good deal of integration, the development of things being leveled off by final purposes at succeedingly more general levels of existence. The laws of motion, for example, depended on the final conception of a prime mover whose purpose provided a reason for the motion apparent in physical phenomena.

---

[43] Particularly helpful in interpreting the shift from medieval to modern science are Herbert Butterfield, *The Origins of Modern Science* (New York: Macmillan Co., 1960), and *A Short History of Science* (Garden City: Doubleday Anchor Books, 1959), esp. chap. 2.

The science of the Middle Ages was based on perspectives such as these, and the revision of science in the modern period reached to the most basic of scientific questions. The development of the outlook and techniques of modern science was not, of course, a sudden result of the overnight collapse of medieval ways of thinking. It was part of the general awakening of the period reflected in a wide variety of social, technical, and intellectual manifestations. Only a history of science could capture the full flavor and impact of this revolution in man's way of looking at his world. The re-stimulus of interest in classical culture during the Renaissance probably in itself is typical of the heightened interest in scholarship and in the conditions of man's own existence. Interest in the classics did not simply disappear; indeed, quickened interest in the classics probably stimulated interest in striking for new modes of understanding of the natural world. The adventurous inventiveness of the Da Vincis, the Christopher Columbuses, the Vasco da Gamas, suggests impatience with existing bodies of knowledge and styles of scholarship.

We have already suggested the ways in which the social ideas of Machiavelli foreshadowed a reorientation of typical ways of looking at the social world. The great age of modern science, like the great age of modern social thought, did not, however, follow immediately on some event that marked the "close" of the Middle Ages. Their gradual development is suggested by the fact that for both the most significant early period of discovery and reorientation fell in the seventeenth century. It is interesting, in fact, to note the extent to which the development of the two fields ran concurrently. There is, doubtless, no period in intellectual history when the development of natural science and the development of social thought can be separated. The ambition to create a new and scientific social science in our own day, for example, illustrates the close relationship between the two as it is also illustrated in the codevelopment of scientific and social thought in the early reaches of the modern period.

While we are not able to deal in detail with the variety of significant instances of scientific reorientation of the sixteenth and seventeenth centuries, a few examples may illustrate the ways modes of thought underwent the shock of radical change. The study of celestial mechanics has always been one of the more advanced sciences, and some of the early significant breakthroughs of modern science occurred in this field. The classical view of the motion of heavenly bodies accepted in the Middle Ages had been developed most comprehensively and influentially by Ptolemy in the second century A.D.

His theory, a careful statement of the centuries-old folk theory, depicted as the center of the universe the earth around which revolved
numbers of crystalline spheres to which the heavenly bodies were
attached. The motions of the sun, planets, and stars were explained in
terms of the revolutions of these spheres. The common sense and
scientific merits of Ptolemy's theory are great, and it resisted any but
piecemeal revision. Probably the main step in the early modern revision of the Ptolemic view was that taken by Copernicus when he
proposed that the sun, not the earth, lay at the center of the universal
system, a possibility Ptolemy had considered but rejected. Copernicus
did, however, continue to depict the world of the heavens as a world
of spheres, though reducing somewhat their number and the complexity of their interrelationships. Thus, he did not reject completely
a preexisting conceptual system, but gave its modification an added
and important impetus.

Copernicus' major contribution was published only at the time of
his death, and it did not immediately excite scientific interest. A century later, however, it became the center of a major philosophical and
scientific controversy. The suggestion that not the earth but the sun
lies at the center of the universe and the demonstration of celestial
motion in terms of this concept opened the way for total rejection
of the spherical conception. It remained for others following Copernicus to take steps in this direction. Bruno, for example, proposed a
theory of the universe infinite in scope and without center. Keppler
contended that the planets move in ellipses rather than in circles.
Galileo, with the significant benefit of improved optical instruments,
probed both the Milky Way and the solar system to make discoveries
that confronted the scientific world with empirical evidence of the
inadequacy of the Ptolemic interpretation of the universe. Thus,
through the contributions of numerous scholars whose works built
upon one another's, the classical understanding of the nature of the
celestial universe underwent complete revision, and along with this
revision, the entire structure of medieval thought was threatened in
a number of ways.[44]

Concurrently and subsequently, discovery proceeded in other
branches of the natural sciences. Harvey, for example, using the
method of dissection and observation, discovered and described the
circulation of the blood and the operation of the heart. Like the
advances in celestial mechanics, this achievement in anatomy rested
upon the overturning of a classical description which had come to

---

[44] See Herbert Dingle, "Copernicus and the Planets," in *ibid.*, pp. 18–26.

have virtually the status of dogma. Boyle, in his experiments with the air pump, made observations about the properties of air which led to the expansion of knowledge in a number of scientific fields.

As developments of these kinds continued in the scientific world, a good deal of rethinking about the philosophical or methodological aspects of natural science was also under way. Indeed, change in theoretical and experimental science forced change in the philosophy of science. The significant science and the significant philosophy of an age are never separable, and many of the most prominent thinkers of sixteenth and seventeenth centuries were centrally concerned with the philosophical problems implicit in man's attempts to know his natural environment better by the application of new approaches. Francis Bacon, Spinoza, Liebnitz, and Descartes, are among those who contributed most prominently to the development of the philosophical and mathematical bases on which the evolution to modern science rests. Bacon's work, for example, emphasized inductive procedures, the development of scientific theory from careful observation, and the belief that it lies within the power of man to control nature. Descartes, operating from the principle of doubt, fashioned deductively a rational mathematical model of knowledge.

But perhaps the most significant milestone in the history of modern science was the statement by Isaac Newton of new laws of motion. Newton's genius pulled together a variety of speculations, observations, and discoveries in this most important field into a system so comprehensive and persuasive that it came to serve in some sense as the model for further development in both natural and social sciences. Newton suggested that the same laws could account not only for the earthly phenomena of gravity and motion but also for the observed and supposed behavior of the heavenly bodies. And, perhaps most important, he developed the mathematical statements through which the operation of common laws in seemingly diverse phenomena could be demonstrated. Put simply, his contribution could be said to be the framing of a few simple principles through which it is possible to explain the properties and behavior of the material things of the universe.

Newton's work in combination with that of Descartes and others suggested that the world can be treated most adequately in terms of quantitative relationships rather than in terms of qualitative differences. His version of the universe was a mechanical one, a picture of a universe of systematic cause and effect, whose regularities were universal and subject to mathematical description and interrelationship.

The mathematical laws of mechanics have applicability to all variety of phenomena. They are not confined in their operation to particular classes of the kind with which classical science was inclined to deal. Thus, the crucial properties of modern science as a way of thought were given shape, and the ground was prepared philosophically for two and a half centuries of spectacular scientific progress.

In summary, the principal features of the attitude and method of modern science are these:

1. The attitude of doubt. The indisposition to accept authority because it is authority, and the inclination to subject explanation to rigorous examination and reexamination. The principle of doubt requires the exploration of the theories of science both on the rational level of theory and on the experiential level of empirical observation.

2. The use of mechanistic, mathematical models in scientific theory. The development particularly of new concepts in mechanical physics and in celestial mechanics gave impetus to the tendency to see all relationships in terms of mechanical cause and effect. Questions about "the purpose of" and "the reason for" gave way to questions about "the cause of." The world came to be understood something in the fashion of a machine which operates through a series of sequential physical phenomena.

3. Measurement. With the development of mechanistic models, interrelationships among phenomena were described in terms of their mathematical regularities. Quantitative measurement became the way of operationalizing these concepts and their interrelationships. Thus, as suggested earlier, emphasis shifted from description by quality to description by quantity.

4. Observation and experimentation. As important as the development of the mathematical model is to modern science, of equal importance is the connection of abstract theory to sense experience through experimentation and observation. It is probably this insistence on testing theory against the reality of the sensual world that distinguishes modern science most clearly from the science of the classics. Modern science is finally empirical in the sense that it demands that its theory explain relationships among phenomena in the real world. Experimentation is fundamentally the planning and systematization of observation. In good part, the scientific advances discussed above were made possible by the development of empirical interest and technique, as illustrated in the works of Galileo, Boyle, and Harvey.

5. Technological development. The advancement of modern

science was both stimulated by and dependent on the development of new technological devices and techniques. In some instances, science grew out of man's ambition to discover machines and processes that would make his life more secure and comfortable. Boyle, it is said, was motivated by the desire to understand human respiration and thereby prolong the span of human life. Sometimes, scientific instruments were the product of tinkering with what amounted to toys or intriguing gadgets. But whatever the motivation behind it, the perfection of machines and devices of various sorts made possible the verification of theories in ways that were previously out of the question. Galileo's telescope, Boyle's air pump, Leeuwenhoek's microscope, all examples of the adaptation of craftsmanship to the problems of science, made substantial contributions to the advancement of empirical science and to the cumulative improvement of human understanding.

The impact of this scientific revolution on political thought and institutions has been touched on in our discussion of Machiavelli and Hobbes. Machiavelli's thought, it was suggested, represents a turning away from the hierarchical rationalism of the Middle Ages toward the orientation of theory to empirical phenomena. Hobbes' theory of government represents in itself a mechanistic and almost mathematical deductive system which, in a limited sense, did for political thought what Newton's ideas had done for physical mechanics. The factors which had led to Newton's success in developing mechanical laws stimulated others both concurrently and subsequently to attempt to develop similar systems and apply similar methods to the understanding of the human mind and to the understanding of the social world. The psychologies and political theories of the British empiricists—Locke, Berkeley, and Hume—represent perhaps the best known of such early attempts. Convergence of the ideas of Locke and Newton, who were contemporaries, probably had the predominant influence in eighteenth-century attempts, particularly notable in France, to reach a satisfactory and adequate scientific theory of political relationships.

A NOTE ON THE "SCIENTIFIC" FRENCH SOCIAL THOUGHT OF THE EIGHTEENTH CENTURY

The stimulus and excitement of the development of science elsewhere, along with the death of Louis XIV in 1715, created in the eighteenth century the conditions for the first significant French contributions to political and social thought. While there were important differences in the ideas of the French political philosophers of this period, i.e., the period up to but not including Rousseau, it is possible and adequate for our purposes to explain their ideas in a generalized way.[45] The group of French philosophers generally identified as the *philosophes,* including Voltaire, Helvetius, Holbach, Condorcet, Turgot, and others, was engaged in a struggle to free political thought and practice from the dominance of existing rigid authority. In a sense, they adopted not only the method but also the substance of Newton's approach to science. In method, they stressed not only the development of theory but also the need for empirical verification. In substance, they tended to see men as objects in nature whose interactions are to be understood like the interactions of atoms or physical forces. Above all, perhaps, they emphasized the role of reason in the ordering of sense experience.

To some of the advanced thinkers of this time, the prospect of breaking through in the understanding of the human mind and its operation was even more exciting than had been Newton's achievements in understanding the physical world. Among some grew the conviction that there are regularities in human behavior about whose operations laws could be found. An empirical sociology could then investigate man's real wishes, bring them to light, and demonstrate the means by which these wishes could be satisfied most efficiently. Thus, through reason and investigation, it would be possible to create a wholly just and satisfied society which would vindicate the *philosophes'* faith in reason and their faith in human perfectability. Under the impact of this man-centered rather than God-centered world view, the authority of traditional philosophy, of traditional theology, and finally in France the authority of traditional political institutions were rejected as inadequate.

There is in much of this philosophy of the Enlightenment an element of utilitarianism, demonstrated, for example, in the ideas of Holbach and Helvetius. They, like Bentham a few years later, seized on the notion that it is possible to develop a scientific ethic, and through government apply the principles that this scientific ethic uncovers. They suggested that man's quest for happiness is the fundamental axiom of such a science, and that the chief utility of government lies in its ability to alter the relations between pleasure and

---

[45] Commentary on the period and ideas generally includes Carl L. Becker, *The Heavenly City of the Eighteenth Century Philosophers* (New Haven: Yale University Press, 1932); Ernst Cassirer, *The Philosophy of the Enlightenment,* trans. F. C. A. Koelln and J. P. Pettegrove (Princeton: Princeton University Press, 1955); Kingsley Martin, *French Liberal Thought in the Eighteenth Century* (London: Ernest Benn, Ltd., 1929).

pain. The approach of science, therefore, is integral to the development of a better world of human relationships.

Another wing of French social thought in the eighteenth century is represented by a group commonly called the physiocrats. The physiocrats, like others of their contemporaries, believed it was possible to develop a science of enlightened justice in all social relations through the application of enlightened human reason. The principal departure of the physiocrats, however, was to hold that social relationships are basically economic, and that reform in society is accomplished, therefore, largely through the manipulation of economic affairs.

Yet another prominent figure of this period, Montesquieu, attempted to translate the scientific attitude into a theory of civil law.[46] Montesquieu likewise saw human behavior as governed by observable regularities which man might attempt to translate into positive law and therefore put to use in artificial regulation of human affairs. He believed the positive action of the state, that is to say, might be made to conform with the natural dictates of the regularities of nature. He was particularly interested, however, in the fact that the positive law does differ from time to time and from place to place. This fact in itself, he suggests, may be explained by the operation of predictable regularities, for environment itself has different and observable effects on civil arrangements, and, therefore, the differences in positive law can be explained in the sociological schema. Thus, such factors as geography, climate, soil, and the extent of a country have integral effects on the shape human institutions take. Montesquieu's was an early and very influential statement of this sociological interpretation of human institutions.

Three political aspects of this French Enlightenment thought deserve particular emphasis. All were influential, at least indirectly, on the American tradition.

First, the Enlightenment embodied, again, the attitude of doubt, the attitude which led to the questioning of established institutions, of traditions, of sentiments, and of established ways of thought. The attitude of doubt characteristic of scientific thought generally has obvious implications both for the thinking and practice of politics, as the agonizing French political experience in the last decade of the eighteenth century was to demonstrate.

Second, the ideas of the French Enlightenment led to the statement

---

[46] See especially *The Spirit of the Laws,* ed., with introduction, Franz Neumann (New York: Hafner Publishing Co., 1949).

of a strong case for liberty, particularly intellectual and scholarly liberty. If it was possible and desirable to develop a science of human relationships in terms of which men might be governed, it was necessary that those who were to create the science be freed from the artificial restrictions of established authority in their search for scientific principle. Thus, freedom for the development of science became a prime consideration in the arrangement of the affairs of men, and the expansion of the principle of freedom for scientists into the principle of freedom for all men was only a step away. The last step not all the *philosophes* were prepared to take. The arguments for freedom in scientific pursuit, however, are to be found in the writings of such people as Voltaire, whose statement of the principle is classic.[47]

Third, the central political thrust of this strain of thought was more manipulative than democratic. Democracy might elicit the sentiments of the mass, but the problem of politics from this perspective is to discover through the measures of science the proper principles of human behavior. If this outlook is rigorously developed, the laws and institutions by which the lives of human beings are given shape are no more properly subject to popular vote than would be Newton's law. Thus, politics would become the preserve of the rationally informed, enlightened despot, and the institutions to be favored would be those of strong central authority brought to the service of mankind by applying the insights of the new science.

The effects of the revolution in science on the American political tradition, on the ends and means that America has favored in the development of her political system, are both great and somewhat obscure. No vital social experience like that of Puritan New England, nor any dramatically borrowed manifesto like the obviously Lockean *Declaration of Independence* documents the influence of science on American politics. But the fact that America as a nation, as a society, and as a polity, was taking shape during the period of the most dramatic changes in science has doubtless had a great deal to do with the shape she has taken. Many of the influences of the scientific revolution on American ideas and practices are subtle, hidden in the complexities of social relationships and commitments. It is possible, however, to detect certain characteristics of the American political style to which the spirit of modern science seems basic:

1. An atomistic and mechanistic view of the universe, man, and

---

[47] For commentary, see Peter Gay, *Voltaire's Politics: the Poet as Realist* (Princeton: Princeton University Press, 1959).

social relationships. In general terms, the American political tradition has been inclined to view men as individuals and their interrelationships as the confrontation of individual physical and psychic energies. In this, it has taken its cues from Newtonian physics as well as from the social ideas of such figures as Hobbes and Locke. The American tendency to emphasize the individuality and equality of men and to regard political arrangements as the mechanistic contrivances of men reflect this kind of commitment. To put the case this way is perhaps a gross oversimplification, but if it is viewed as a generalization requiring qualification, the proposition seems both accurate and fair. This does not mean, of course, that the American heritage has been devoid of classical influences, of a sense of community and common destiny, or of religion and a theistic concept of God.

2. A disposition to regard progress as inevitable. This disposition, while not universal, seems to have been a very important element in the characteristic American perspective. As the social thought of the *philosophes* may be seen to suggest, science regards relationships as explainable and, therefore, problems as solvable. The conflicts with which politics as a form of human activity must deal are problems which lie within the realm of rational understanding. As science moves ahead, it can be called, therefore, into the service of more orderly human relationships. Thus, the development of science would seem to promise not only advance in the control of the material environment, but also advance in terms of the betterment of the human environment. Overtones of this point of view are apparent in the development of American political thought down to the present time, when the movement to create a scientific social science has often taken its impetus from the belief that it could contribute significantly to the betterment of the human life.

3. The penchant for experimentation. Politics in America has generally been an activity which allowed for the possibility of experimentation and development. While Americans have not always been receptive to change, they have on the whole been an adventurous people willing to innovate in politics as in other types of social, economic, and technical fields and, particularly, to experiment with political structure. Pragmatism, a very important philosophical and practical posture of the twentieth century, perhaps typifies this orientation at its most extreme. While formal pragmatism is an outgrowth of the later history of the nation, its spirit among the American people was not new with the philosophy of William James and John Dewey. It would not seem unreasonable to say that a willingness to experiment

is particularly apparent, for example, among the framers of the Constitution, and in the ideas and actions of Thomas Jefferson.

4. The importance of education. America is also a nation that has attached much value to education and enlightenment, and has supposed that with the advancement of knowledge, men would be better able to master their social affairs. America developed early and well a system for universal public education. The assumptions behind this passion for education would seem to be twofold: it assumes, first, that man is perfectable at least to the extent that he can profit in his ability to deal with his environment by or through the learning process; second, it assumes that the environment is subject to understanding and control. Education, then, is a channel of communication from scientific discovery to the improvement of social and individual lives. This faith in enlightenment has been a favorite theme of American political philosophers from Jefferson to Dewey, and is very much a part of the American popular ideology, as is suggested perhaps by the support Americans have given their educational enterprise, by the growing emphasis on the necessity for nearly universal higher education, and even perhaps by the passion for learning represented in the phenomenal growth of the paperback book industry.

III

THE NATURE AND JUSTIFICATION
OF POLITICAL CHANGE:
THE AMERICAN REVOLUTION

The problems raised in the political analysis of revolutions are problems of general interest to students of politics. Revolution in a sense lays bare the crucial innards of the political process and always somehow involves a crisis in the eternal political relationship between authority and liberty. Even if the American political society had taken on its major form and value commitments by the time the American Revolution developed, still that Revolution and its aftermath provided the conditions under which the society's commitments were articulated and put to test, and under which the tradition assumed political form. From this point forward, our attention will be directed in large extent to the processes by which fundamental ideas were institutionalized, i.e., translated into regular practice.

THE CONCEPT OF REVOLUTION

Treatment of the American Revolution from the standpoint of its implications for the understanding of political events requires attention to some conceptual and definitional problems. A social science approach to a phenomenon of this kind is interested not in the uniqueness of events but in the generalities or regularities they may suggest which have application to other social situations. Concepts which permit comparison, therefore, must be part of the intellectual equipment one takes to such a task of social analysis.

The analysis of revolution is dependent, at least in small part, on definition of the concept revolution. Any definition may, of course, be purely a matter of stipulation on the part of the person using the concept, but considerations of communicability, utility, and economy generally condition effective usage. Like most terms commonly used in social discourse, the word revolution is charged with emotion and

66

its meaning obscured by vagueness. If revolution is a genus, however, of which the American Revolution is a species, there must be some common characteristics that differentiate this genus of social phenomena from others.

For our purposes, revolution will refer to a specific form of political change. It is clear, however, that revolution is not a term commonly applied to all forms of political change, indeed not even to all forms of political change achieved in a violent manner. Some claim that revolution is a distinctly modern phenomenon, a type of social event that could occur only in conditions that have existed in the modern world.[1] This distinction would seem to be a useful one, though this is not to say that any political change in modern social circumstances is to be considered a revolution. Revolution as the concept is used here refers to a social movement having two distinguishing characteristics: [2] (1) Its sources lie in pressures of discontent fairly general to the society; that is to say, the term does not include some kinds of political change—for example, a palace revolt—occurring at the instance only of those who would seize the reins of government. This is not quite to be taken to imply, however, that the revolution is necessarily a mass movement in the distinctive modern sense, a point to which we shall return later in the present chapter. (2) A revolution is a social movement which effects or attempts to effect a change in the form of political authority. Given the first definitional element above, this change in authority is almost certain to be one that can in some fashion be described as democratic. This point too, however, is one which we will leave for more extended discussion at a later point.[3] It also follows, but as an empirical proposition and not as a matter of definition, that a revolution defined according to these criteria is almost necessarily a movement which requires physical armed force in the pursuit of its objectives.

The problem of revolution for the political theorist is not, of course, entirely a problem of definition. It is a problem in the explanation of political change. The questions of theory that revolution raises may be stated in a variety of ways, but they would seem to deal at heart with the conditions, style, and justification of revolution and

---

[1] Among commentaries on revolution, see especially Crane Brinton, *The Anatomy of Revolution* (New York: W. W. Norton, 1938), a systematic comparison of the American, English, French, and Russian Revolutions; Hannah Arendt, *On Revolution* (New York: The Viking Press, 1963); R. R. Palmer, *The Age of the Democratic Revolution* (Princeton: Princeton University Press, 1959). On the essential modernity of revolutions, see Arendt, *op. cit.*, pp. 13–23, and Palmer, *op. cit.*, pp. 5–13.

[2] Cf. Brinton, *op. cit.*, pp. 35–36.

[3] Cf. Palmer, *op. cit.*, esp. pp. 13–20.

with the effects of its ideology on political institutions. The discussion that follows will attempt to describe the American Revolution along these lines and to deal with theoretical questions raised by comparison of the American Revolution with other modern and contemporary instances of revolutionary political change. It should be noted at this point that there is no agreed interpretation of the American Revolution. Scholars, particularly historians, have for years been in disagreement about its major characteristics and their significance. It should also be noted that what follows is not an attempt to describe the American Revolution as a historical event. Our concern is with the nature and source of revolutionary ideology and its impact on American institutions.

THE ECONOMIC AND SOCIAL BASIS OF THE AMERICAN REVOLUTION

The "historical situation" of the American Revolution was so complex and its memory is still so emotion-laden that the job of sorting the crucial from the incidental is extremely difficult. This difficulty does not, however, relieve the student of the burden of assaying the strengths and effects of the various background factors of the Revolutionary period. In general terms, the thesis of this chapter is as follows: (1) Because a revolution is a movement based on discontent fairly general to the society, a prime requisite of revolution is a social basis for common action. (2) There were in the colonies at the time of the Revolution many sources of disunity—forces for disunity that prima facie outweighed the forces for unity. (3) The key to common action in the American Revolution lay in an ideology that was the product of the socioeconomic–political situation and the instrument for achieving political unity sufficient to the circumstance. The empirical evidence offered in support of this thesis is gross and sketchy and insufficient to demonstrate its verity; what follows is concerned chiefly with the content of the ideology. However, it is proposed as a framework for analysis of the relationship between ideas and action in a revolutionary situation.

Perhaps the most striking aspect of American society in the Revolutionary period is the curious mixture of heterogeneity and homogeneity—of disunion and union that did then and continues to provide a major social influence on practice and a major theme in political ideas.[4] Subsequent American political history seems to demonstrate

---

[4] For background and historical summary, see Clinton Rossiter, *Seedtime of the Republic: the Origin of the American Tradition of Political Liberty* (New York: Harcourt,

clearly even down to the present day that America has been both nation and antination. The heterogeneity and divisiveness of colonial
life is probably somewhat more impressive than its basic social unity.
The individual colonies, it should be recalled, were formally separate
units of the British Empire; their union was created largely out of the
necessities of the situation. They differed among themselves in time
of settlement, economic interest, social pattern, and, to some extent,
in predominance of national origin. While the majority of the colonists were of British stock, there were also at the time of the Revolution significant numbers of Scotch-Irish, Germans, Dutch, some
Swedes and Frenchmen, and a scattering of other nationalities along
the length of the Atlantic seacoast. While, in the style of the times, the
legitimacy of British rule was generally accepted, there lay in ethnic
diversity the basis for rejection of the British tie and also the basis for
factional internal struggle among the colonies. The colonies had also
witnessed, even during the seventeenth century, occasional outcroppings of attenuated class struggle. While it would probably be exag-
gerated to describe the structure of American society during the period as even a pseudoaristocracy, the internal division of classes along
economic and social lines was clear by the time of the Revolution.
Sometimes, as in the Regulator movement of the Carolinas, the tension between yeoman and gentry even gave rise to violence.[5]

The more interesting facet of the American Revolutionary movement, however, is the extent to which it succeeded in bringing together
a people whose grounds for internal conflict were so many and patent.
Like later American political history, the American Revolution raises
the question how such common commitment and action is possible
among a people with so many bases for difference. For all the differences the colonials had, they did, after all, achieve a basis for common action sufficient to pursue to successful conclusion a war against
one of the world's great powers. This is not to minimize the internal
divisiveness of the colonies during the period, nor the halfhearted
military and political support that General Washington received in
his role as Continental commander in chief, but to emphasize that the
Revolutionary venture provided the basis for an enduring political
arrangement and drew support from a wide range of elements in
American society.

The Revolution cannot be satisfactorily interpreted as entirely the

---

Brace & Co., 1953). A brief sketch of the condition of colonial society is found at pp. 3–11
and much information in the succeeding chapters. On population, see pp. 150–56.

[5] Rossiter, *op. cit.*, p. 115: Palmer, *op. cit.*, pp. 194–96.

product of the economic greed of a special-interest group, for its sources of support, such as they were, ranged geographically up and down the coast and socially up and down the status scale. Probably the two most active centers of Revolutionary sentiment and deed were Massachusetts and Virginia—colonies unlike in social structure and economic interest. Revolutionary support from the merchants of Boston was forthcoming at a very early period, just as the so-called planter aristocracy of Virginia early rallied its forces to the cause of colonial independence. And the war was fought, it should be recalled, not only by farmers and backwoodsmen, but also by urban dwellers and planters and merchants.

Probably no single factor can be called on to explain this measure of unity apparent in the American Revolution. But in the search for an explanatory key, we should pay particular attention to two factors that seem of central importance—a political–social ideology and the pressures of a socioeconomic situation. The importance of these factors perhaps becomes more clear on consideration of the economic and political situations of the colonies at the time of the Revolution.

It is indeed not at all difficult to detect the importance of economic relationships in the developments of this period. Until about the time of the Seven Years' War, 1756–63, there had been relatively little British interference with the developing polity and economy of the colonies. In its beginning the American economy was, of course, dependent on British trade and promoted by British capital. But overt restrictions were light-handed and did not seem particularly repressive in view of the state of economic development. By the end of the Seven Years' War, however, Britain began to tighten her mercantilist grip on the American colonial economy and to yield to the temptation to attempt to collect a colonial revenue. It was probably more the thrust for an American revenue than the design for American trade that hurt British relationships with the colonials in an economic way. In any case, a series of political–economic measures adopted by Parliament between 1763 and 1770, including the Stamp Act and the Tea Act, provided the basis for some of the specific colonial actions and complaints against British treatment of the colonies. The new British policies, it should be noted, alienated New England merchants who played key roles in stimulating the movement for an adjustment in political relationships. Economic restrictions and the principles behind them led, in turn, to occasional outcroppings of popular unrest, the most famous of which were the Boston Tea Party and the Boston Massacre. These incidents, in turn, led to the stationing of British troops in Boston, which in itself was a source of colonial resentment and discontent.[6]

The economic problem, however, is important to us only as it is reflected in political arrangements and political doctrine. And these, in turn, are most clearly illustrated in arguments that run to the heart of the relationship between consent and the economic support of political activity. Mottoes about taxation without representation may seem revolutionary calls to battle. They are also, however, statements of a venerable and basic normative proposition in political theory. The device of central taxation, i.e., taxation by central national political authorities, had come into prominence in Western Europe only at the point when kings began to demand support for large national armies. The problems with which we are dealing thus are problems caused by the development of political organization on the scale of the nation-state. As kings sought revenue to sustain central nationalistic military ventures, people, particularly nobles, demanded a say in making the policies in pursuit of which tax funds were expended. Thus, there developed in England, for example, a House of Commons whose early powers were largely fiscal in character.

By colonial times, it was expected by Englishmen that consent, at least in a general sense, was prerequisite for the levying of taxes for revenue purposes. Taxes for purposes of trade regulation, incidentally, raised different questions. The extent to which taxation by consent was an issue to the colonials is reflected in the commentary of Franklin on the "Plan of Union" adopted at the Albany Convention in 1754: ". . . it is essential to English liberty, that the subject should not be taxed but by his own consent, or the consent of his elected representatives."[7] As Parliament therefore moved closer and closer to demanding revenue of the colonies, it moved closer and closer to exciting not only temporary and specific economic interests but also to exciting some of the basic components in the constitutional ideology of the British people. The problem of taxation is illustrative of and central to, though it does not exhaust, the problems which gave rise to colonial demands for adjustment in political relationships. Fundamentally, what found expression in the situation was a democratic ideology: the assertion that taxation without representation is tyranny

---

[6] Rossiter, *op. cit.*, pp. 60–84, discusses the colonial economy, and summarizes the events of the period 1765–76 at pp. 317–25. See also J. Franklin Jameson, *The American Revolution Considered as a Social Movement* (Princeton: Princeton University Press, 1940), pp. 47–73.

[7] *The Writings of Benjamin Franklin,* ed. A. H. Smyth (New York: Macmillan Co., 1905), Vol. III, p. 209.

is a special and powerful form of the assertion that government must legitimize its exercise of power by reference to popular consent.

EARLY STATEMENTS OF THE REVOLUTIONARY IDEOLOGY

The extent to which the Revolution was a broadly based demand for government by consent is suggested in the statements of political theory that came out of the pre-Revolutionary and Revolutionary period. These statements were directed first to the point that British policy was in violation of the rights of the colonials as Englishmen, later that British policy was in violation of their rights as men. Some students have laid great emphasis on this change in the style of the colonial argument. Though these arguments are different in object, they are not different in kind. Their underlying theme is the demand for common consent to the operation of political authority, a theme which, as we shall see in greater detail, runs back to the classic statements of Hobbes, Locke, and Harrington, particularly the last two.

During the earlier period and down perhaps to as late as 1775, the theoretical statements of colonial discontent were directed toward supposed parliamentary abuses of power and stated in terms of violations of the supposed rights of Englishmen. It was early proposed that the conflict might be resolved by the development of colonial representation in Parliament, but as early as the Stamp Act Congress, practical considerations suggested that this solution would not be an adequate one. That meeting, for example, resolved "That the people of these colonies are not, and from their local circumstances, cannot be, represented in the House of Commons in Great Britain." [8] This position was either the source or the result of an interesting theoretical divergence between Britain and the colonies on the nature of political representation. British practice and British theorists suggested that to be satisfactory, representation might be "virtual," i.e., based on classes and interests but not necessarily direct. Colonial practice (and typical subsequent American practice) has tended to insist on direct representation as the only legitimate kind. The distinction, of course, is not one of black and white, but it is suggestive of the ways tenets of political theory may grow out of the demands of circumstance. The tradition in America that representatives should reside in the legislative districts they represent is in contrast to the British tradition which imposes no such limitations and thus opens the way for virtual representation in the Commons taken as a whole. It should also be noted

---

[8] Quoted in Rossiter, *op. cit.*, p. 319.

that this early Revolutionary argument was directed in form toward the authority of Parliament and not toward the authority of the Crown. It was the legitimacy of specific constitutional arrangements for consent and not the legitimacy of the authority of the sovereign that the colonials first called into question. Even here, however, we may suggest that the differences between earlier and later arguments is more a difference in form than in content, that the fundamental problem is the problem of consent to the exercise of authority, and that this problem is not answered by abstract arguments about the location of sovereignty.

The heart of the colonial position can be found in such tracts as James Otis' *The Rights of the British Colonies Asserted and Proved*, published in 1764, and John Dickenson's *Letters from a Farmer in Pennsylvania*, published in 1767–68. Otis, for example, stated a moderate position based heavily on Lockean contract theory. Government, he said, in terms like Locke's, is the answer to man's quest for "the security, the quiet and happy enjoyment of life, liberty and property." [9] Man's need for authority and his obligation to obey is not questioned, but as the source of government lies with the people, reason indicates certain limitations that may be placed on its exercise. These are the limitations secured to Englishmen by the British Constitution. The rights of colonists are no different from, nor less than, the rights of Englishmen in the mother country. It is instructive to note the contents of these rights as they are set forth by Otis:

1st. That the supreme and subordinate powers of the legislation should be free and sacred in the hands where the community have once rightfully placed them.

2dly. The supreme national legislative cannot be altered justly 'till the commonwealth is dissolved, nor a subordinate legislative taken away without forfeiture or other good cause. . . . .

3rdly. No legislative, supreme or subordinate, has a right to make itself arbitrary. . . . .

4thly. The supreme legislative cannot justly assume a power of ruling by extempore arbitrary decrees, but is bound to dispense justice by known settled rules, and by duly authorized independent judges.

5thly. The supreme power cannot take from any man any part of his property, without his consent in person, or by representation.

6thly. The legislature cannot transfer the power of making laws to any other hands. [10]

---

[9] James Otis, *The Rights of the British Colonies Asserted and Proved* (Boston: Eades and Gill, 1764), p. 10.

[10] *Ibid.*, pp. 35–37. Italics in original eliminated.

Locke's principle of consent runs consistently through Otis' argument. It is, of course, explicit in point five. The immediate effect of Otis' tract was to raise questions about the legitimacy of Parliamentary authority over colonial affairs. In the longer run, it points toward the testing of all political authority in terms of the rightness of the doctrine of consent and the consonance of the exercise of authority with natural law. It is, incidentally, also interesting to note that Otis in certain paragraphs of *Rights Asserted and Proved* seems to defend the doctrine of judicial review later to become so important a part of American constitutional arrangements, although the suggestion is not entirely clear. He wrote:

The supreme *legislative* and the supreme *executive* are a perpetual check and balance to each other. If the supreme executive errs, it is informed by the supreme legislative in parliament: If the supreme legislative errs, it is informed by the supreme executive in the King's courts of law.— Here, the King appears, as represented by his judges, in the highest lustre and majesty, as supreme executor of the commonwealth; and he never shines brighter, but on his Throne, at the head of the supreme legislative. This is government! This, is a constitution! to preserve which, either from foreign or domestic foes, has cost oceans of blood and treasure in every age; and the blood and treasure have upon the whole been well spent.[11]

Dickinson's argument in *Letters from a Farmer* assumes the same general tone but is directed somewhat more specifically toward Parliament's right to tax in the colonies. Dickinson contested the authority of Parliament on the taxation-without-representation ground and held that taxation is a type of power which must be controlled if liberty is to mean anything. In interesting fashion, he drew the distinction mentioned above between taxes levied for the restriction of trade or the regulation of economic enterprise and taxes laid for revenue purposes alone. The British constitution, he asserted, forbids that revenue taxes be laid without representation. The attempt of the Parliament to raise a revenue in the colonies he called "an innovation; and a most dangerous innovation." [12] Quoting the resolutions of the Albany Convention, he maintained that any tax "if laid any other way, than 'with their consent, given personally, or by their representatives,' was not only 'unreasonable, and inconsistent with the principles of the *British* constitution' but destructive 'to the freedom of a people'." [13] Dickinson's argument thus ran both to the rights of a man and to the rights

---

[11] *Ibid.,* p. 47.

[12] "Letters of a Farmer in Pennsylvania," *The Writings of John Dickinson,* ed. Paul L. Ford (Philadelphia: The Historical Society of Pennsylvania, 1895), Vol. I, p. 316.

[13] *Ibid.,* Vol. I, p. 332.

of Englishmen to consent to the political policies under which they are to live. He also argued, quoting Machiavelli as his authority, for a reexamination and return to first principles.[14]

While the arguments of Otis and Dickinson went to the basic principle of consent, their more immediate effect was to contest the right of Parliament to levy certain kinds of acts without the direct consent of the colonies. Later tracts written by colonists began to push the fundamental principle of consent toward different institutional conclusions. James Wilson's *Considerations on the Nature and Extent of the Legislative Authority of the British Parliament*, written in 1774, for example, denied all Parliamentary authority over the colonies. Wilson, like Otis and Dickinson, invoked the principles of Locke and Harrington in explanation of the legitimacy of political authority. He did not deny the legitimacy of the colonists' relationship with the Crown. "The colonists," he said, "ought to be dependent on the King, because they have hitherto enjoyed, and still continue to enjoy, his protection." [15] He did deny, however, that there was any principle in the British Constitution or in the fundamentals of legitimate government which justified hegemony of the laws of Parliament over the American colonies.

The youthful Alexander Hamilton in *A Full Vindication*, 1774, likewise denied the jurisdiction of Parliament while supporting the sovereignty of the King. "Besides the clear voice of natural justice in this respect, the fundamental principles of the English constitution are in our favor." [16] Both Wilson and Hamilton directed their arguments more to the absence of a general consent to the legislative powers of Parliament than to the absence of consent on specific measures or specific types of measures. They held that a contract relationship did not exist between colonies and Parliament rather than that acts of Parliament were invalid because the colonists had no representation in the constitutional body which was the author of those acts.

A similar position was stated by John Adams during the same pre-Revolutionary period.[17] Adams granted that Parliament had legitimate power to regulate Colonial trade but claimed that the legitimate

---

[14] *Ibid.*, Vol. I, p. 386.

[15] "Considerations on the Nature and Extent of the Legislative Authority of the British Parliament," *Selected Political Essays of James Wilson*, ed. R. G. Adams (New York: A. A. Knopf, 1930), p. 78.

[16] Alexander Hamilton, *Works*, ed. John C. Hamilton (New York: Charles S. Francis & Co., 1851), Vol. II, p. 3. See esp. "A Full Vindication," *ibid.*, Vol. II, pp. 1–36, and "The Farmer Refuted," *ibid.*, Vol. II, pp. 37–126.

[17] John Adams, "Novangelus," *Works*, ed. C. F. Adams (Boston: Little, Brown & Co., 1851), Vol. IV, pp. 3–77.

powers of Parliament ended at the American shore. Thus, the main line of the colonial political case, while keeping its basis in the doctrine of consent, tended to move toward broader and broader ground. By 1776, of course, the principal statements of the American position had gone the full way to the claim for independence.

The foregoing discussion of the social, economic, and political facets of American society in colonial times only points up the main aspects of the period in such fashion as to illustrate our basic theme of interpretation of the Revolution. The economic and political considerations are closely intertwined. The predominant theme is the political one—the demand for government by consent, a demand deeply rooted in the Anglo-Saxon American political tradition. The statement of this position as an ideology was both the verbal representation of the position and a phenomenon of importance in itself. This ideology, like ideologies generally, was neither cause nor effect but both—the effect of accumulated grievances and an instrument for mobilization of a heterogeneous society behind a political movement. Thus, the social condition, the economic and political circumstances, and a set of ideas were welded into an important historical event.

THE *DECLARATION OF INDEPENDENCE* AS REVOLUTIONARY THOUGHT

Two famous tracts of the Revolutionary period stated the ideology of the movement in a more mature and full form, and deserve extended analysis. These are the *Declaration of Independence* and Thomas Paine's *Common Sense.* They differ sufficiently to merit separate treatment, though the *Declaration,* because it is based clearly on ideas reviewed above, permits a rather summary review.[18]

The *Declaration* is so tersely stated that a careful reading of its first two paragraphs unearths a set of fundamentals that outline the nature of man and government and provide an ideological justification of the American Revolution. The *Declaration* may, of course, be analyzed in terms of its purpose, as a kind of advertising tract for revolution. Such analysis, however, seems likely to fall far short of comprehending the full implications of the document either as theory or

---

[18] Commentaries on the *Declaration* include Carl Becker, *The Declaration of Independence: a Study in the History of Political Ideas* (New York: A. A. Knopf, 1956); Edward Dumbauld, *The Declaration of Independence and What It Means Today* (Norman: University of Oklahoma Press, 1950). For textual analysis, see Julian P. Boyd, *The Declaration of Independence; the Evolution of the Text as Shown in Facsimiles of Various Drafts by Its Author, Thomas Jefferson* (Princeton: Princeton University Press, 1945).

as ideology. It is not enough to dismiss it as a tract, because it provides a valuable key to the world view and political norms of its time and place.

At bottom, the *Declaration* states a deductive theory derived from first assumptions about man, God, and power. It is clearly a product of the age of reason, the "golden age" of the rise of liberalism, though much closer theoretically to the English liberalism of Locke than to the French liberalism of the period in which it was written.[19] Its key lies in a basic axiom. "We hold these truths to be self-evident, that all men are created equal, that they are endowed by their Creator with certain unalienable Rights . . ." Man, according to this view, is an integral creature with innate moral qualities, a creature in personal relationship with God. The moral quality of individual human life is a matter established in natural law which the reasonable man understands. This is a first assumption from which flows a train of prescriptive consequences for political life.[20]

While man is the child of God, he is also to some extent the child of the Devil, not only a creature with innate moral qualities but also a creature of passion. Man's moral qualities, that is to say, are not necessarily qualities of consciousness; to describe man as a creature innately moral is not to say that man is a creature who necessarily acts in moral ways. He is, indeed, the child of the Garden of Eden, a creature in whom lust is constantly at war with love. It is this fact, of course, that explains the development among men of civil government. "That to secure these rights, Governments are instituted among Men": to secure these rights from the threats of other men and from the quirks of nature which would deprive men of their benefits. Furthermore, since human lives are the fundamental fact of the social system, and since men develop governments to serve their ends, the legitimate powers of government are based only on consent and are limited by the unalienable rights of men. Thus, civil society is a joint venture through which men turn reason and prudence to the work of controlling the passions. The principal problem of concern to the framers was the problem of control of authority, but this is only one problem of control faced by man in social relationships. In broad terms, the problem to which political theory was then and in nearly all other times has been addressed is the problem of the relationship of liberty and authority. The *Declaration* emphasizes this relationship by juxtaposing

---

[19] See above, pp. 47–54, 60–63.
[20] Cf. Becker, *op. cit.,* pp. 24–79.

a liberty it assumes to be natural and unalienable with an authority it assumes to be necessary but overbearing.

The *Declaration* assumes an absolute metaphysics from which are derived the ideas of self-evident rights and the equality of men. The propositions that men are equal and have unalienable rights are moral axioms understood through reason but not subject to proof in the empirical sense. They are expressive of the fundamental moral reaches of a natural law that governs the universe. Whether they are understood or honored does not affect their verity. They outline ways in which men ought to act. They cannot be verified or disverified by reference to ordinary experience. Neither are they, if one is to take the theory literally, to be modified or qualified in the interests of community security. They are unalienable and absolute.

In the face of modern positivism and ethical relativism, propositions of this kind are less likely to be taken seriously than they were in the different philosophical atmosphere of the eighteenth century. Whether they are acceptable as truth or not is dependent on the ethics and epistemology which the commentator brings to their judgment. Whatever the answer to that problem, self-evident rights and equality have been important operative ideals. The controversy over the interpretation of the Bill of Rights provisions that later wrote these limitations into the American Constitution seems to demonstrate convincingly the extent to which the basic moral demands of the *Declaration of Independence* have been translated into political expectations of the American people.[21] The century-long movement to assure equality of treatment to the Negro, for example, is hinged to the assumption of the rightfulness of the doctrine of equality. The judicial interpretation of some provisions of the Bill of Rights likewise continues on occasion to invoke the symbols of absolute freedom. More will be said later about mechanisms by which these ideals have been applied in general and specific ways.

Also derived from basic assumptions but in a somewhat different way is the principle of consent, which we have called the basic operative ideal of the Revolutionary movement. "Governments," the *Declaration* reads, "are instituted among Men, deriving their just powers from the consent of the governed." The principle of consent implies that government is not a natural creature but an artificial construct, something developed by men to serve their ends. It assumes that since government is the creature of the men of society, it is rightly subject to their control. This, according to the revolutionary theory, is the

---

[21] Cf. chap. 4, below, on limits on political power.

basic principle of political legitimacy. It is also the basic principle of American democracy. The principle of consent, as we have already noted, has two implications into which it may be extended. It implies at its most fundamental level that men must in some general sense commit by consent their obedience to a political authority and to a set of rules under which that authority is conducted. It is in this sense that the theory of Hobbes, for example, is a consent theory. Hobbes' thought suggests that the foundation of political authority is its creation by the men of society.[22] Consent may also be an active or dynamic principle, a principle which requires that men must be accorded some kind of regular and institutionalized voice in, and check on, the specific rules by which political authority governs the society. This is the principle of Locke's extension of the liberal theory of consent as he modified Hobbes' basic doctrine. The theory of the American Revolution established a claim for consent in both its senses. Where earlier it rejected the notion that the rule of Parliament was legitimate, in the *Declaration* it rejected the notion that either Parliament or the King ruled by the agreement of the American colonists. At the same time, as has been pointed out above, the theory of the Revolution suggests that in its specific reaches the authority of the British government had extended too far, and that these exercises of authority were illegitimate because not based on a satisfactory foundation of consent.[23] The *Declaration* thus claimed for the people the right "to alter or to abolish" government and to institute new political forms. This is basic. It also argued the illegitimacy of a "long train of abuses and usurpations," fundamentally abuses of the right to consent and usurpations of the power of the people to develop the regulations under which they would live.

Thus, from an examination of the *Declaration of Independence*, one can discern some of the values and institutional claims which have continued to lie at the center of the American political system. The values that are implied in the assumption of individual integrity and equality, the values of the individual rights of life, liberty, and property (the last for rhetorical reasons couched in the more general term of pursuit of happiness), are of evident importance in the theory of the *Declaration*.[24] The importance of the instrumental principle of consent is also clear. A careful examination of the *Declaration*, particu-

---

[22] Cf. above, pp. 42–47.

[23] Becker, *op. cit.*, pp. 89–124, discusses the "theory of the British empire" vis-a-vis consent.

[24] See Dumbauld, *op. cit.*, pp. 60–63, on the phraseology.

larly in the later and more specific parts, also suggests an inkling of some of the institutions later to become characteristic of the American system. For example, some of the claims made against the King seem to be basically claims that stem from a belief in the separation of powers as a protection for rights and an extension of the principle of consent. We will subject the doctrine of separation of powers to more extended analysis later.[25]

Two themes in the *Declaration* that depart in some degree from its individualistic and rationalistic tone deserve special mention. These are important both as they raise theoretical problems for the liberal individualism of the age and as they have come to constitute in themselves important elements of the fundamental set of American operating values. One of these is the theme of prudence, which strikes a cautionary note in an otherwise rationalistic and revolutionary tract. The principle of prudence can perhaps be invoked to explain the very framing of the *Declaration,* which the founders attributed to "a decent respect to the opinions of mankind," though this phrase can also be explained in rationalist terms. Prudence is explicitly invoked in the clause which states, "Prudence, indeed, will dictate that Governments long established should not be changed for light and transient causes." The invocation of prudence is the invocation of experience rather than of the abstract dictates of natural law. A moral theory of prudence suggests that men ought to act as their experience with the world dictates in order to maintain a continuity between past and present that is valuable in itself. Its principles of behavior are experiential rather than a priori. The immediate thrust of the phrase quoted from the *Declaration* above is to soften the demand of the *Declaration* for adherence to abstract standards. It lends a conservative tone to a document that was otherwise epistemologically liberal but that rationalized a movement seeking to conserve established usages.

The notion of prudence was not entirely strange to liberal thought. Hobbes acknowledged the psychological role of prudence as well as of reason in informing man of the mode of solution of his social problems. Locke likewise honored prudence not only as a psychological concept descriptive of the mental makeup of man, but also as an instrumental guide in the preservation of the society on which the preservation of natural rights in turn must depend. Prudence is, thus, a concept employed both in prescription and description, as in "men ought to act prudently," i.e., by reference to past experience, either on principle or to be effective, or as in "men do act prudently," either

---

[25] Below, chap. 4.

consistently or on certain occasions, because of their psychological makeups. Both as prescription and as description prudence is important in the American political tradition, despite the fact that it is theoretically somewhat ambiguous in terms of the main tenets of that tradition.

A second concept in the *Declaration* that hovers between prescription and description and is somewhat inconsistent with the general framework of liberal theory is that of community. The point can only be stated with diffidence, for both the importance and meaning of the concept in the *Declaration* and its theoretical implications are subject to controversy. By community we mean not just space but space to which loyalty and meaningful political interaction are attached. Community in this broad sense has posed problems for political thought throughout history. The concept took on particular importance in the eighteenth century because of its rebirth in the theory of Rousseau and because of its relationship to the claims of the burgeoning nation-state.

English liberalism and in good part the liberalism of the French enlightenment tended to be anticommunity in bias. That is to say, they viewed the individual as the integral element in social life and the more inclusive units as his artificial creations. Thus, community was not a thing in itself but an aggregate without independent existence and will, at best an instrument to individual welfare. Rousseau, borrowing in this sense the classical position, saw community as something organic, morally prior to the individual, and having its own will. Perhaps in the labeling of political theories, Rousseau's may best be called "communitarian" as contrasted with "individualist." Its standards for judging political acts (or policy or regime) are framed in terms of the needs or goods of "the community," not those of individuals.

The *Declaration* seems to imply shadings of the organic interpretation of community, though they are only shadings and faint ones at that. The first sentence speaks of the necessity of "one people" to dissolve political bonds and to "assume among the powers of the earth" a "separate and equal station." These glimmerings are easily lost in the rationalist–individualist tone of most of the document, and, to be sure, the *Declaration* declares the independence of sovereign *states*. Significance does not lie, however, with quibbles about the "real" meaning of its words, but with what they suggest about a sense of community incipient in revolutionary society. This may, taking some liberty, be described as a seed of American nationalism, a nationalism destined to grow by fits and starts into a major political force three-quarters of a century later. It did not, of course, take that long to assume recognizable embryonic form.[26]

Nationalism is thought by many analysts of the current scene to be one of the principal characteristics and motive forces of present-day political activities and arrangements. The nation-state had well taken form by the time of the American Revolution, though its more extreme symbols developed later. But the point is that while the American Revolution can scarcely be interpreted as a nationalistic revolution, it did have nationalistic overtones that bind it, however tenuously in ideology, to the modern revolutions, from the French one forward, in which nationalism has been a central appeal. The American Revolution is a part of this slowly developing modern political outlook; it is not an antiquarian relic or a thing in itself, entirely detached from the nationalistic, community-centered demands of later periods.

In summary, as justification for change the American *Declaration of Independence* is based largely on the invocation of the principles of rights and consent. It judges the arrangements against which it was directed in terms of these abstract standards. When set in the context of the political history of the period, its emphasis particularly falls on the failure of the institutions of consent. In its appeal to prudence, it is almost antirevolutionary in tone, the expression of a people whose main object was to preserve or reinstate the fundamentals of English constitutional arrangements. It is on this ground that the great English conservative Edmund Burke could consistently defend the American Revolution as rightful but later attack the French Revolution as a blow at the very basis of society and human right. The *Declaration* is also a document which reflects, though dimly, the growing nationalism of the period, and which provided some of the symbols of community in a nation which had as yet rather little to hold it together. Some of these themes become even more explicit in the writings of Thomas Paine, whose justification of the Revolution we shall examine briefly in the section to follow.

THE POLITICAL THOUGHT OF THOMAS PAINE'S *COMMON SENSE*

Beyond the *Declaration of Independence*, probably the major theoretical statement of the American Revolution is to be found in the pamphlet *Common Sense*, published in January, 1776, by Thomas

---

[26] See the discussion of nationalism in chap. 9, below, and references cited there in note 23.

Paine. In some senses, Paine probably cannot be fairly considered representative of American political thought. Of course, he was himself, like many of the other colonists, of English origin, and after the Revolution he left America for France where he associated himself with the French Revolution. Paine was personally close to some of the American revolutionaries, for example, Franklin, but was disliked by others, for example, Adams. His major contributions to the rhetoric of the American Revolution were *Common Sense* and a later pamphlet, *The Crisis.* After his emigration to France, he published *The Rights of Man* and *The Age of Reason,* which embody substantial theoretical departures from the main themes of his American writings. As a result of his French activities, Paine largely fell out of favor with the American patriots, and even in later commentaries, he has been attacked and distrusted by some and much honored by others, generally depending on the commentator's position on the political spectrum. The analysis of Paine that follows is based almost entirely on the theory set out in *Common Sense.*[27]

Common Sense fell close to the liberal democratic argumentation already discussed, but with some interesting and significant deviations. Perhaps surprisingly in terms of Paine's later reputation, it was not overly optimistic about the natural sociability of men. It stressed both the mission of the young America as a nation and the brotherhood of all men in freedom. It often gave the argument for independence an economic cast not typical of the time. Politically, *Common Sense* clearly and unequivocally stated the case for complete independence from Britain. In this respect, Paine's tract caught the tone of the growing colonial demand for independence capped in the *Declaration* signed in the same year. It has been said that *Common Sense* probably more than anything else popularized the ideas of revolution and complete break with Crown and Parliament. Soon after its publication, *Common Sense* had been circulated in half a million copies. While it is probably impossible to document the effect of *Common Sense* on the Revolutionary movement at this late date, there can be no doubt that it had a tremendous popular impact.[28] The case of *Common Sense* is a striking example of the interplay between idea and action. Paine reflected both a basic ideology and the rising tide of popular senti-

---

[27] Citations to Paine in the pages following are to Thomas Paine, *Common Sense and the Crisis* (Garden City: Dolphin Books, n.d.).

[28] Philip S. Foner (ed.), *The Life and Major Writings of Thomas Paine* (New York: Citadel Press, 1945), p. xiv. For a less enthusiastic account of Paine's influence, see Philip Davidson, *Propaganda and the American Revolution, 1763–1783* (Chapel Hill: University of North Carolina Press, 1941), pp. 13–14, 131–33.

ment, and at the same time pushed the cause further than it had gone before.

Common Sense began with a brief discussion of the nature of man, society, and government as Paine saw them. His version of the basics puts one in mind of the ideas of Hobbes and Locke and of the Christian doctrine of original sin. The political problem, it suggested, arises from the tension between man's needs and his propensities. Man's strength is individually unequal to his wants, and his mind is unfitted for perpetual solitude. The intermediation of society helps man in the face of these natural deficiences. Deficiencies in sociability, however, prompt the development of government with its greater and greater complexity of authority. "Society is produced by our wants, and government by our wickedness; the former promotes our happiness *positively* by uniting our affections, the latter *negatively* by restraining our vices." [29]

The need for government in the face of man's weakness, however, he seemed to find undoubtable. In describing the development of social institutions in the state of nature, he stated the case as follows:

Thus necessity, like a gravitating power, would soon form our newly arrived emigrants into society, the reciprocal blessings of which, would supercede, and render the obligations of law and government unnecessary while they remain perfectly just to each other; but as nothing but heaven is impregnable to vice, it will unavoidedly happen, that in proportion as they surmount the first difficulties of emigration, which bound them together in a common cause, they will begin to relax in their duty and attachment to each other; and this remissness will point out the necessity of establishing some form of government to supply the defect of moral virtue.[30] [Thus] Government, like dress, is the badge of lost innocence; the palaces of kings are built upon the ruins of the bowers of paradise.[31]

Society is necessary to compensate for the deficiency of man's ability, government to compensate for the defect of his moral virtue.

Paine's theory proceeded, on a foundation of these basics, to discuss the nature and form of government—political institutions being built on the needs and characteristics of human beings: "*Wherefore,* security being the true design and end of government, it unanswerably follows, that whatever *form* thereof appears more likely to insure it to us, with least expense and greatest benefit, is preferable to all others." [32] His prescription for political forms had two main elements:

[29] *Ibid.,* p. 13.
[30] *Ibid.,* p. 14.
[31] *Ibid.,* p. 13.
[32] *Loc. cit.*

government must be simple and responsible, the first characteristic being instrumental to the second. Consideration of the needs of man in the light of reason demonstrates the virtues of simplicity in political arrangements. "I draw my idea of the form of government," he wrote, "from a principle in nature, which no art can overturn, viz. that the more simple any thing is, the less liable it is to be disordered, and the easier repaired when disordered; . . ."[33] He even admitted that absolute governments, though they have other distasteful characteristics, do have the virtue of simplicity.

In terms of these general prescriptions, Paine placed a low value on English political institutions and the institutions under which the colonists had been governed. His charges against British government were twofold, directed toward its complexity and toward the principle of monarchy itself. In summary, he described it as "two ancient tyrannies, compounded with some new republican materials."[34] The mixed British constitution, which was the object of considerable admiration in the time and, to some degree, the model for characteristic later American institutions, he attacked for obscuring responsibility. His principle has been popular with later critics and admirers of democratic institutions—namely, the concentration of authority makes possible the assertion of popular control. It may indeed remind one of some of the "principles" of recent public administration doctrine, e.g., "unity of command" and "authority commensurate with responsibility." It was, then, an attack on the principle of the separation of powers. Paine, like later radical democrats, assumed that democratic institutions would be sufficient to check the arbitrary exercise of political power.

He went on to suggest that the system of separation of powers is a logical absurdity and a practical failure. It supposes first that the king, being not wise enough to govern responsibly, must be checked by the Commons; then it supposes that the Commons, being no wiser than the king, must, in turn, be checked by him. ". . . [I]t first excludes a man from the means of information, yet empowers him to act in cases where the highest judgment is required. The state of a king shuts him from the world, yet the business of a king requires him to know it thoroughly; . . ."[35] The practical upshot of the arrangement of political institutions according to this impossible theory is the gravitation of political power to the king himself. Over the long run, the

[33] *Ibid.*, p. 15.
[34] *Ibid.*, p. 16.
[35] *Ibid.*, p. 17.

separation of powers breaks down, and that structure which starts strongest will finally come into complete control. Thus, he feared that the system of separation of powers will ordinarily if not inevitably yield to executive dominance, a fear not unreasonable in view of the historical context, and a proposition perhaps not unreasonable, if modified, in view of the later development of American political institutions. His assumptions and conclusions about separation of powers, however, should be read in the light of our later and more complete discussion of this principle as it was incorporated into the American Constitution and analyzed by others in the period immediately following the Revolution. It may be noted here that Paine's orientation is based more on his fear of irresponsibility and arbitrariness in government than it is on fear of the ineffectiveness of government in the maintenance of security. This point will be picked up again below when we discuss Paine's suggestions for the development of American institutions.

Paine's attack on the principle of monarchy itself as distinct from his attack on its effects on the exercise of political power stems from his commitment to the assumption of human equality. There are distinctions among men, he said, that are congenial to reason, distinctions between men and women, between good and bad, even between rich and poor. But the distinction between kings and subjects is one "for which no truly natural or religious reason can be assigned. . . ." [36] The case is a simple one but not one commonly encountered in the revolutionary rhetoric.

Paine supplemented his attack on the principle of monarchy with an equally strong attack on the practice of hereditary succession, which he considered "evil and foolish." If the elevation of a man to kingship violates the canons of reason, even more must the elevation of his progeny. This Paine considered an imposition on posterity for which there can be no defense. Even if the establishment of a monarchy were defensible in terms of the needs of the time, the perpetuation of a dynasty is clearly not: "A French bastard landing with an armed banditti, and establishing himself king of England against the consent of the natives, is in plain terms a very paltry, rascally original.—It certainly hath no divinity in it." [37] Paine further documented his case against hereditary monarchy with several more or less miscellaneous arguments. One of these runs to the frequent incompetence of people who occupy hereditary thrones, which he said is proof that nature dis-

---

[36] *Ibid.*, p. 19.
[37] *Ibid.*, p. 24.

approves of the institution when she gives mankind "an ass for a lion." [38] He further pointed out the disruptive effects of the hereditary principle when it advances a minor to the throne or leaves political power in the hand of the senile. In either case, he said, the public is left at the mercy of political schemers. The institution of hereditary monarchy does not even, as some of its defenders claim, provide for an orderly succession in political power; history refutes the claim that hereditary succession saves a nation from civil war.

Thus, on several basic political principles, Paine found Colonial political arrangements and the British constitution itself to be faltering instruments of government. Even aside from the fact that the constitution was a foreign imposition on an American people, it was a charter with many imperfections. He also extended the argument for immediate independence in a number of other specific directions in some sense tactical in nature. He argued the commercial and economic advantage of separation from Britain, claiming that the economy of America would flourish when separated from the ties and restrictions of the mercantilist system. [39] Citing the probability of help from abroad and the adaptability of America's people and resources to such a conflict, he argued skillfully and in detail the ability of America to sustain a fight for independence. [40] And he stressed the long-run political importance of a fight for independence in binding the American people together as one nation. The common cause of revolution would yield the initial cohesive to make the American people a community. [41] His case for independence pulled out all stops—economic, military, political, and psychological—as it translated the basics of a political theory into a set of prescriptions for political action.

Similar themes were also carried into what Paine had to say about the development of a set of political institutions appropriate for the American nation once independent. What was said above about his commitment to simplicity and responsibility indicates the general tone of his preferences for institutions which would translate consent into policy as directly as possible while taking account of the size and complexity of the nation. Paine would apparently have preserved the federalistic structure for America, with each colony legislating for its internal affairs but subject to the authority of a Continental Congress. But he would have developed national institutions of the utmost sim-

---

[38] *Ibid.*, p. 22.
[39] *Ibid.*, p. 28.
[40] *Ibid.*, pp. 42–48.
[41] *Ibid.*, p. 49.

plicity: a single legislature consisting of at least thirty members from each colony, doing its business by three-fifths majorities; an executive chosen by the congress annually, each year from a different colony in an order chosen by lot until the entire group of colonies had been represented.[42] He proposed that a continental charter establishing institutions such as these should be drawn by a continental conference of two legislators and five representatives of the people at large from each colony. The constitution should be drawn "Always remembering, that our strength is continental, not provincial" and "Securing freedom and property to all men, and above all things, the free exercise of religion, according to the dictates of conscience. . . ."[43]

The principles of such a form of government, beside adherence to a federalistic system of division of powers, would be legislative supremacy, a corollary of which is weakness in the executive power, and a bill of rights embodying limitations in consonance with the major value commitments of the period. The principle of consent would seem to be the overriding consideration, reflecting the radical democrat's faith that a government in the control of the people would be a government least likely to abuse its power.

Paine's political theory was fundamentally a simple one based on the more important assumptions common to the main stem of the Anglo-American tradition. Like most thought of the Revolutionary time, it emphasized the principle of consent, which, in turn, grew out of assumptions about the artificial character of political institutions and about the integrity and equality of the men who framed them. In at least three respects, Paine's theory is, however, unique and deserving of particular attention. First, the institutional prescriptions Paine based on his liberal assumptions called for a simpler and somewhat more direct operation of the principle of consent in the development of political policy than did those of Locke, Harrington, and most of his contemporary colonial commentators on politics. His preference for a pervasive kind of democracy would seem to be in contradiction to his almost Hobbesian picture of man, for it is the kind of prescription one usually expects to be based on an optimistic view of the human potential. Perhaps the difference is one of degree. At any rate, his rejection of principles of check and balance suggests the extent of his faith in the reasonableness of man acting in the mass. American political ideas and practice may reflect reliance on checking principles and institutions more than on Paine's pervasive principles of consent.

---

[42] *Ibid.*, pp. 39–40.
[43] *Ibid.*, p. 40.

Paine's position, however, has contributed heavily to the American tradition through ideas which may be lumped under the generic term "populist." While the main burden of the populist theory will be analyzed at a later point, it may be noted here that the position of simple democracy has been constantly present in the give-and-take of American ideas about politics.

A second element which deserves reemphasis is the element of incipient nationalism. We have frequently noted above and will note again the importance of this theme in the justification of modern political change. Here we may simply cite the importance of some of the primitive symbols of nationalism in Paine's appeals for American independence. In the context of his later activities and writings, they are perhaps surprising. Though he often wrote like a world revolutionary, a citizen of the universe, he also stressed the importance of political organization in the parochial community, even in a world ideally characterized by the brotherhood in equality of all men. Here again, perhaps, we see reflections of the ambiguity between his realistic assessment of the human condition and his commitment to rationalistic first principles. The nationalism expressed in Paine may, of course, also be seen as a tactical part of the web of ideas set out as incitement to revolutionary action. The difficulties of distinguishing between theory as explanation, theory as prescription, and ideology as a weapon of persuasion are here manifest.

Our third and concluding comment about Paine's theory is no more than a reminder of Paine's importance as a stimulant to action, as a case in the relationship between thought and practice. His thought was important not only as one alternative verbal model of the political system but also as a part of the causal chain between social structure, culture, and policy that political science seeks to clarify.

LOYALISM IN THE AMERICAN COLONIES

While it is not our intention to provide a comprehensive intellectual history of the development of American politics, it would be misleading to fail to mention that the political rhetoric of the time did include arguments on behalf of maintenance of the attachment to Britain as it already existed. There was, of course, in the American colonies a body of loyalists very considerable in number.[44] Before the *Declaration* and the commencement of the war, these loyalists' spokesmen wrote in answer to the tracts that advocated the alteration or de-

---

[44] See Palmer, *op. cit.*, pp. 185–90, on the extent and character of loyalism in the colonies.

struction of the British tie. While we will not attempt a sustained analysis of these ideas, their main tendencies may be quickly analyzed in summary form. Perhaps the most noted of the loyalist publicists were Samuel Seabury and Jonathan Boucher, both clergymen, and Daniel Leonard, a Boston lawyer.

A brief summary cannot do full justice to the intricacies and individual variations of the loyalist position. The loyalist arguments, however, seem to emphasize variously four major themes. First, they leaned heavily on a view of the ultimate necessity for the maintenance of political power. Major changes in the relationship with Britain or its dissolution would, they held, threaten the strength and continuity of political authority on which social stability must rest. This assertion is akin to Hobbes' position that nothing is so important as the maintenance of the sovereignty. A second argument used by the loyalists, also Hobbesian in its tone, emphasized the inviolability of obligation once established. On both natural law and scriptural grounds, the loyalists were inclined to argue that only the most extreme circumstances could justify the severance of obligations like those which bound the American colonists to the British constitution. There is in much of the loyalist rhetoric an almost puritanical equation of liberty with order, restraint, and obedience. Third, the loyalists argued against separation in terms of the advantages afforded in the past by the operation of British institutions in America, by the extent to which these institutions provided the framework for the settlement and development of the country as well as the sustenance of an orderly and pious way of life. They failed to see as abuses those regulations and restraints which their adversaries attacked so wholeheartedly. Fourth, the loyalists sometimes employed constitutional arguments against some of the claims of Adams, Hamilton, Otis, Dickinson, and others. They claimed, for example, not without logic, that it was impossible to separate the authority of Parliament and Crown and to lay the abuse of the colonies strictly at the door of the Parliament, as was commonly done by those who were attacking the British relationship in the early period.

On grounds such as these, some of the political pamphleteers of the time attempted to leaven the colonial view and to push the case for accommodation with Britain. The loyalists' view deemphasized the importance of consent in favor of the importance of maintenance of authority. In doing so, it restated one of the principal viewpoints on the major problem of the reconciliation of liberty and order. The Hobbesian argument about the primacy of authority is one that frequently finds restatement in the later reaches of American political thought. Thus, even the loyalists who historically fell outside the central American political tradition were themselves substantially engaged in the level and kind of controversy that has constituted the subject for the bulk of American political thought: the problem of the ordering of ends and selection of means to those ends.

THE NATURE AND IMPACT OF THE AMERICAN REVOLUTION

How is the American Revolution to be understood in terms of its impact on ideas and political practice, and how does it compare with other recent manifestations of revolution as a political phenomenon? These are the questions to which we may now turn.

At the beginning of the chapter, it was suggested that modern revolution may be understood in terms of two criteria: the generality of its source among a people and the effects of its action on the form of political authority. It was also suggested that confined by these definitional elements a revolution is by implication democratic in the broadest sense of the term. Both in ideology and in action, the American Revolution falls within these criteria. The basic theme of the ideas we have been analyzing is the theme of consent, the theme that political authority gains legitimacy by the agreement of the people who are to live under it. To the Revolutionary spokesmen of the colonials, this was a principle which governed not only the proper establishment of government but also the proper development of political institutions. Consent thus was seen not only as the basis of obedience but also as the basis of proper public policy. In the pre-Revolutionary tracts, the *Declaration,* and the writings of Paine, this consideration seemed to be paramount.

Corollary to the basic theme of consent and much more subtle was a weak but growing nationalism which, as the Revolution progressed, came to distinguish the aims of an American people from the aims of the people of British America. This nationalism, tenuous in social basis, was to await for years its full development, but it is not surprising that it should have taken shape at a time when the colonies began to modify their demands from accommodation within the British structure to independence and the development of structures *de novo.* With its democratic rationale and its latently nationalistic base, the American Revolution can begin to be seen from the perspective of its position among revolutions of the modern age. These, from the French Revolution that followed the American Revolution by only a few years to the most recent movements for separation from colonial powers, have been characterized at base by their demands for political equality and national independence.

There are, to be sure, some variables on which the American Revolution differs from other modern revolutionary movements with which it can be compared. One of these is the extent to which a revolution reaches to what might be called the social basics. It is on this question that the American Revolution and the French Revolution are commonly contrasted. The French Revolution, it is said, was much more total than the American Revolution. Change reached not only the political institutions but a good deal of the inner fabric of society. Social distinctions and relationships underwent basic and sometimes enforced alteration. The American Revolution seems to have had substantially less impact at this level. It affected fewer of the common run of relationships which give society its informal and formal structure. It is probably easy, however, to overemphasize this difference between the American and French Revolutions. The American Revolution, it should be recalled, did entail substantial unsettlement in many of the reaches of society: large amounts of property changed hands, many social ties were broken, and the customary patterns of action disrupted. What we are suggesting, however, is that revolutions may be considered along a continuum according to the extent to which they reach into the sphere of social relationships. Along this continuum, if the French Revolution of 1789 were somewhere near the middle, the American Revolution would be close to one end and the Russian and Chinese Revolutions would be close to the other. The latter revolutions have effected radical and compressed changes in the patterns of social life.

Two factors perhaps help explain differences between or among revolutions on this variable. One of these is the political object of the revolution in question. Fundamentally, the object of the American Revolution was to destroy political ties relatively external to the society. The French Revolution, on the other hand, had in the nature of the situation to be directed toward the destruction of an internal and indigenous power structure whose roots ran deep into and not outside the society. Revolutions of the internal type entail something more than the destruction of a ruling class. By this criterion, some recent moves by peoples in "underdeveloped" areas to end colonial ties are perhaps closer to the American than to the Russian or French Revolutionary experience. What we are suggesting is the rather simple proposition that the nature of the political object of a revolution conditions the impact of the revolution on social basics.

A second factor runs to the scale of the society undergoing revolutionary change. Our proposition here is that as social scale increases, the social impact of revolution increases. This is simply to suggest that an increase in social scale quickens the pace of change and renders the entire social system sensitive to alterations in one part, for example, the political. While this proposition is harder, perhaps, to defend with the historical evidence, it would seem to be very important in the understanding of modern relationships between politics and society.

A second major variable along which the American Revolution may be distinguished is ideological, having to do particularly with the degree of crude democracy and the stridency of nationalism embodied in revolutionary appeals. Despite the extent to which the American Revolutionary ideology was directed to demands for government by consent, its appeals were mild compared with those of a good many modern revolutions, including the French and Russian. The American demand for democracy was of an attenuated and very much mediated sort. French and Russian demands, particularly the French, were more specifically directed toward freedom for the people than freedom for the system. Likewise, other modern revolutions, including many contemporary revolutionary movements, have strongly emphasized the mission of the people as a nation, national destiny, and other such organismic aims and goals. A cursory consideration of this factor in the history of revolutions suggests that perhaps the higher the intensity of democracy and nationalism in revolutionary ideology, the more likely is the revolution to fall prey to Bonapartistic control —that is, to total control based on the manipulation of democratic forms to gain consent for authority through the seeming mass approval of the national will. Perhaps differences on this variable too can be explained by differences in the political precondition, the objectives, and the social scale of the society undergoing a revolutionary movement.

The point of these distinctions between the American Revolution and other revolutions of modern times is that the American Revolution differs chiefly in degree, not in kind. On the spectrum of such movements, the American Revolution is relatively conservative. Its aims could be realized through relatively moderate changes in political relationships and through moderate impact on the texture of society. Its ideology could be relatively specialized, relatively specifically focused on certain political–constitutional forms and problems. It did not in the nature of the situation require far-reaching altera- tions in the social structure. It did not really entail the destruction of a ruling class but rather the displacement of a political authority. For these reasons, the American Revolution may be, and usually is, seen as an orderly step in the development of the political tradition of a nation, not as a break in national or social continuity. Nonetheless, it did give rise to a change, an important change in the locus of au- thority, and paved the way for political alterations which were to be- come characteristic of the American form of government.

This raises a final point in our analysis of the American Revolu- tion—namely, its impact, immediate and long run, on the political institutions of the American nation. At various points in the proceed- ing discussion, it has been suggested that the American Revolution was a revolution in the sense that it left a substantial imprint on the political practices of the country, and the specific characteristics of this impact will be treated comprehensively in the following chapter. It may be useful here, however, to indicate a few of the general as- pects of this impact. In these terms, the political results of the Revolu- tion seem to have been twofold: first, its effect was to conserve the in- fluence of existing constitutional relationships and attitudes; but second, it had the countereffect of setting the stage for the modification of these relationships and attitudes in the direction of broader and more specific incorporation of the consent principle in constitutional usage. The institutions conserved were largely those of British con- stitutionalism, most evident, perhaps, in the carrying over of the com- mon law tradition by the colonists along with the retention of certain guarantees to the individual established in the traditional British documents and practices. Thus, as we have suggested before, the core of the American political tradition is a liberal constitutionalist core shared with the British nation, embodied in specifics as well as in a general attitude toward the nature and responsibilities of political authority.

At the same time, the American Revolution was also realized in some specific revisions of British institutional relationships, generally undertaken to modify the constitutional tradition in the direction of more immediate and broader based popular control on the exercise of political power. Thus, we might suggest that from the American Revolution stems the American disposition toward such institutions as equal representation, broadening of the franchise, and limitation of the power of the executive. The position of the executive, for obvious reasons suspect by the colonials because of their experience with the King and the colonial governor, can be seen as a manifestation of the attitude which regards the basic evil of government as uncontrolled and arbitrary power set beyond the reach of the people. The general reading of the political history of the time suggests that the executive was seen as a greater threat to popular control of political power and responsibility in the exercise of political power than was the legislature. The democratization of American politics is, of course, something that was to follow only gradually and after a period of years in all its specifics. What we are proposing, however, is that to a substantial degree the experience of the revolution conditioned the American people to demand and expect the extension of the democratic principle.

In summary, we might interpret the political impact of the American Revolution as follows: It found and left the American people in basic satisfaction with British constitutional relationships. At the same time, it fostered an ideology which would dictate changes in those relationships in the direction of greater democratic control. The interplay of this satisfaction and dissatisfaction prompted a search for the political institutions of accommodation, institutions that would satisfy both demands for limitation and demands for democratic control, institutions that would make bearable if not resolve the tensions between liberty and authority.

IV

THE FRAMEWORK OF INSTITUTIONS: THE AMERICAN CONSTITUTION

We may now turn to what is perhaps the most theoretically revealing and interesting juncture in American political thought—the framing of the American Constitution. The history of the framing of the 1787 Constitution is familiar and need not claim our attention. We need to be concerned, however, with the American Constitution for what it demonstrates about the relationship between ideas, institutions, and political practice. From this point of view, the American Constitution should have much to tell us, for the Constitution *is* idea, or, perhaps better, the embodiment of the ideas of the culture as they bear on political relationships.

The American Constitution has served to represent and bind together the various parts of the political system in its broadest sense. This system has its base in the culture, the complex of values, needs, habits, and ways of life of people living together in a society. In the culture, ideas take shape about the role and proper organization of political authority, and these ideas come to be equipped through the development of a set of political institutions, i.e., of an understood and regularized set of ways to get things done. The institutions are media for action toward the solution of social problems, action predicated on policy. Action, along with the policy that gives it form, is the end product of the political system. This action, in turn, feeds back to the culture, modifying ways of doing things, modifying demands on the political system, and, through experience, modifying the culture's conception of proper social ends and means.

The working of the American Constitution is an illustration of the operation of such a political system. It is important to the study of political ideas and political theory because (1) it is the manifestation of one of those rare points in history where the dominant ideas of a culture are codified; (2) its development and history illustrate through gross phenomena the relationship between ideas and political action; (3) it has exerted a major influence on subsequent political ideas and action. This is emphatically not to say that the American Constitution set down a set of novel ideas which thenceforth served as a sole and static guide to political activity. Such a claim would grossly misrepresent the idea of a constitution. On the contrary, the ideas embodied in the American Constitution were clearly those the society had developed out of its traditions and experiences with the past. The Constitution is important because it is the codification and summarization of those ideas, and because it is a concrete representation of the political culture with which the society has subsequently worked. It became what A. D. Lindsay has called a set of "operating ideals," setting out basic relationships between acceptable ends and means in a prescriptive fashion, a framework for political action.[1]

Thus, we are viewing the Constitution as part of the political system, not as something over, above, apart from, or prior to it. By politics we mean a process for the seeking of authoritative solutions to social problems, by constitution, a generalized guide to this process. There are, of course, a variety of interpretations of the concept of constitution in use, of which two seem to merit further attention. First, constitution can be considered to mean those functioning mechanisms of political problem-solving that are created out of the needs of a community and given shape by community characteristics. According to this conception, it is assumed that if these mechanisms do actually function and persist over some period of time, they are at least in a general sense responsive to community needs. The constitution is, thus, as we have suggested above of the American Constitution, a political representation of the culture. This conception of constitution is related to both classical and contemporary usages. In classical use, the constitution referred to the entire culture of the *polis:* not only the mechanics of decision-making but its entire context of social relationships, values, esthetic and economic activities, and so on. This concept of constitution, though not necessarily normative, is generally normative in use. Thus, Aristotelian political thought, emphasizing the dependence of the good life on its relationship to all elements of community being, makes of the constitution a kind of nexus of existence and growth out of which springs all value. Edmund Burke, taking the Aristotelian view, similarly saw the constitution as the

[1] A. D. Lindsay, *The Modern Democratic State* (New York: Oxford University Press, 1947), Vol. 1, pp. 37–38 and *passim*.

distinctive and organic spirit of the nation which preserves the fabric of the past and points the way to the future. In these usages, constitutions are things that ought to be preserved and served.

In more contemporary usage—the usage of some current social science—this conception of constitution does not, at least explicitly, have a normative cast. From this viewpoint, politics is seen as basically a problem-solving activity, but emphasis is put on its sociological roots. Thus, a constitution becomes a descriptive representation of the political process as the process grows out of the rationalities and irrationalities, the needs and desires, the social, economic, geographic, and demographic configuration of community life. Politics is what the culture dictates, though whether it ought or ought not to be is beside the point. Constitution is distinguished from other aspects of the political process only by its more general and enduring content. It is chiefly from this perspective that we will pursue our analysis of the American Constitution.

There is a second sense in which the term constitution is often used —a sense very important in the history of Western political ideas, more specialized, and related in a central way to the Western liberal political tradition. In this sense, constitution is interpreted as a set of effective, regularized restraints on the exercise of political power. The term constitutionalism as it is commonly used is a derivation of this meaning of the term constitution. "Constitutionalism" has, hence, come to describe a political system in which political power is limited in certain understood ways, as contrasted, for example, with a totalitarian system, the scope of whose political power is total.[2]

Although this conception of constitution can be used in descriptive fashion, its roots too are deeply normative. It takes its modern impetus chiefly from the ideas of those like John Locke, who saw man as having rights that lie beyond the scope of proper political power, and is ordinarily based on some such conception of the priority of individual rights to social authority. But this conception of constitution is distinguished from the first stated conception mainly by its specification of the kind of political processes and relationships that may be labeled as constitutional, and by its lesser attention to the social and cultural context of the political system. It defines as constitutional only those systems of problem-solving that cut off substantive spheres of action as lying beyond the range of legitimate social power.

---

[2] Carl J. Friedrich, *Constitutional Government and Democracy* (rev. ed; Boston, Ginn & Co., 1950), pp. 25 ff.; C. H. McIlwain. *Constitutionalism Ancient and Modern* (Ithaca: Cornell University Press, 1940).

The American Constitution is a constitution in both these senses. The second is somewhat the more narrow, referring more specifically to the document drafted in Philadelphia in 1787 along with its amendments, as it is this document which provides explicit direction for the checking of political power. In the first sense, the American Constitution is something broader, reaching, as we have suggested above, into the culture beyond political relationships, reaching in time from before 1787 to the present day, and, incidentally though not at all unimportantly, embodying pervasive checks on political power of a substantive and procedural sort. This interpretation views the document, and the specific American institutions which it established, as outgrowths of the search for accommodation between social values which demanded authority and social values which expressed fear of it. And these values and the means the society selected for their implementation lay deep in the core of the American social condition.

One aspect of this interpretation of the idea of constitution that deserves special emphasis is its dynamic character. It is tempting to think of the American Constitution as a document as Gladstone put it, "struck off at a given time by the mind of man." But given a broader perspective, this view is not adequate, for the description of a constitution is the description of a process that necessarily reaches over time. While the terms of the document and the conditions of its conception are not unimportant, the more pertinent questions for the study of politics are questions about the guidelines that enduring constitutional commitments have provided for the settlement of specific social disputes and the distribution of specific community resources. A static view of the constitution would, therefore, be a view which failed to penetrate to the place of the constitution in the political system. Furthermore, it would fail to take account of the fact that the constitution itself is a flexible and constantly changing framework, for a constitution responds to changes in culture or it fails to survive. As new demands are made on it, as the culture throws up new types of problems and new values, the constitution accommodates to provide the means for their settlement. Too, political action itself produces changes in the culture which, as was suggested above, feed back to find reflections in the basics of the political system.

Perhaps the most striking feature of the American Constitution has been its adaptability to the demands of changing times. It is the generality and, hence, flexibility of the document of 1787 that has enabled the nation to preserve it as the basic framework for political action. This point is perhaps most strikingly illustrated in the contrast between the American people's experience with the national constitution and their experience with state constitutions. State constitutions, drawn in specific and detailed terms to meet all contingencies, have of necessity undergone frequent and sometimes complete revision. Over a period of a century and three-quarters, the federal Constitution has undergone formal revision only 24 times, 10 of these amendments the product of the first Congress. But while the words of the document have remained largely the same, its meaning as a set of guides to action has radically evolved. The institutions it described are now capable of handling political problems unthought of at the time of the framing. This is not to claim the virtues or disvirtues of change, but only to suggest that if the Constitution is to be understood as a part of a political system, it must be seen with a long view. That view we will initiate with attention to the basic commitments embodied in the document of 1787.[3]

THE BASIC COMMITMENTS

The framing of the American Constitution was, thus, the explication of a basic set of values and a prescription of institutions by which these values were to be implemented. Our model of the political system suggests that these values and institutional commitments grow out of the social culture in which they are established. This suggests, in turn, that the constitution is the product of some kind of consensus of the society, and the examination of the American experience with constitution-making in 1787 seems to lend some credence to this scheme of interpretation. It is difficult, if not impossible, to measure or document the extent to which a set of political instruments is the expression of a social consensus, particularly long after the fact, but the indicators that can be found in the political thought and practice of the time seem to lend weight to the claim that the American Constitution was rather firmly founded on agreement. The theoretical consonance of the *Declaration of Independence,* of the state constitutions drafted between 1776 and 1787, of the Articles of Confederation, and

---

[3] Historical and other commentary on the Constitution of the United States is nearly endless, and it is difficult to choose among the many suggestive sources. On the framing itself, see the documents collected in *The Records of the Federal Convention of 1787,* ed. Max Farrand, (4 vols.; New Haven: Yale University Press, 1937); also Max Farrand, *The Framing of the Constitution of the United States* (New Haven: Yale University Press, 1913); Carl Van Doren, *The Great Rehearsal: the Story of the Making and Ratifying of the Constitution of the United States* (New York: Viking Press, 1948); Broadus Mitchell and Louise P. Mitchell, *A Biography of the Constitution of the United States* (New York: Oxford University Press, 1964).

the instrument of 1787 itself affords a gross index of the common tendencies in American constitutional thought. This is not by any means to claim that the basic principles of the American Constitution were the subject of 100 percent concurrence in the society. That there were differences in viewpoint among sections, classes, and interests is perfectly apparent: these differences have been rather thoroughly documented by the historical scholarship of the last hundred years.[4] Such events as Shays's Rebellion as well as differences of opinion expressed in the Constitutional Convention and over ratification of the Constitutional instrument reveal political disagreement. Our claim is simply that the Constitution institutionalized a set of preferences firmly rooted in the American society of the time. Buttressed by the traditions and experience of the American people, this agreement, like most political charters, was crystallized on a very general level, not on the level of specifics. The interpretation of generalities into specifics has provided most of the stuff of American political conflict, both theoretical and practical, in subsequent periods.

To list the features of this basic commitment is to list the principles of the Constitution of the United States, a task that may be done in any number of ways. The fundamentals we will deal with in the pages to follow include these:

1. The establishment of authority. This is, of course, a feature of any political organization. That it was in good measure the major aim of the Constitutional Convention is suggested by the circumstances in which the Convention was convened. The commitment to authority means simply the commitment to the establishment of some institutions to maintain order and affirm policy for the settlement of conflicts and distribution of resources in the community. It is the step that creates a political community out of a social agglomeration, represented in traditional liberal political thought by the metaphor of execution of a social or political contract.

2. The establishment of an authority national in scope, but preservative of a measure of local autonomy. This principle, and elaboration of the first along more specific lines, was realized in the American society by the development of the federal system.

3. The legitimation of policy by consent. The principle of consent, institutionalized through the procedures of democracy providing for policy-making by institutions responsive to popular will, was incorpo-

---

[4] See esp. Charles A. Beard, *An Economic Interpretation of the Constitution of the United States, with a new introduction* (New York: Macmillan Co., 1954); and J. Allen Smith, *The Spirit of American Government* (New York: Macmillan Co., 1912).

rated in attenuated form into the charter of political practices established by the Constitution of 1787.

4. The organization of the institutions of authority according to the principle of separation of powers. The system of separation of powers, though not unique to America, has been brought to its most complex development in American political practice. Its importance is attested in the documents with which we are dealing and in their contemporary commentaries. Under this heading, we are subsuming a number of important and typical structures and practices—"presidential government," checks and balances, judicial review, and others.

5. The explicit enumeration of substantive restraints on the exercise of political authority. These restraints, embodied chiefly though not exclusively in the Bill of Rights, are the constitutional representation of the doctrine of natural rights, of the doctrine that some aspects of human existence and activity lie beyond the appropriate exercise of the power of government. They express in specific terms the more general liberal orientation that would restrict the scope of political power to certain agreed and understood functions, i.e., they are the explication of the principle of constitutionalism in the liberal sense discussed above.

These constitutional principles have two intermingled sides, the positive and the negative, one directed toward the establishment of social authority, the other directed toward limitation of that authority. They institutionalized that tension between authority and liberty to which we have already made frequent reference, a tension which stimulates most political thought and conditions most political action. Rather than examine the American Constitution in the fashion of the student of history, we will examine it through the analysis of these principles, asking what values they imply, how they came to be a part of the American consensus, how American constitutional arrangements would realize them, and, in brief, how their institutional manifestations have worked through American constitutional experience. Since some principle of selection is necessary to this analysis, our focus will fall largely on the ideas found in the major work of political thought of the time, *The Federalist* papers.[5]

THE ESTABLISHMENT OF AUTHORITY

The American commitment to the principle of authority probably does not require much embellishment beyond attention to its basic

---

[5] Citations below are to *The Federalist*, ed., with introduction and notes, Jacob E. Cooke (Middletown, Conn.: Wesleyan University Press, 1961).

importance. So closely intertwined is the idea of authority with political life in general that it is easy, particularly in reference to a
liberal society whose emphasis has been on limitation, to slight the
fact that government is based on a need for order that is important
and perhaps even universal. Whether man can live only in a society
characterized by the presence of political institutions is here beside
the point. What is pertinent is the realization in the American Constitution of the need for development of authority. The liberal tradition,
it should be noted, has not denied authority, as often seems to be
asserted. Its roots are too deep in the doctrine of original sin to entertain seriously or for long the notion that man can live satisfactorily
in a society without political constraints. The liberal tradition has
characteristically sought to limit authority, but the effort to limit is
not in itself a rejection of the principle. The social condition of the
times seems to determine whether or not the tradition's explicit
spokesmen and characteristic ideas emphasize authority or its limitation. On this matter of emphasis, the focus in American political
thought shifted between the Revolutionary period and the period of
adoption of the federal Constitution.

The shift was stimulated by commonly noted politico-social developments. In general terms, perhaps the most significant characteristic of the Articles of Confederation was their failure to establish
firm institutions for the exercise of authority. The national government under the Articles was given neither the terms of reference nor
the fiscal and coercive power requisite to the maintenance of order
in matters of national concern. The Articles, as might be expected
in terms of the time of their development, were written in the spirit
of suspicion of authority. Likewise, the political institutions of the
states during this period were typically inadequate to the task of performing fundamental political functions. Terms of office were customarily short, legislative and executive powers severely hampered
by mutual checks, and popular expectations of the performance of
government were low. In these circumstances, the operation of political authority was apparently near the point of breakdown. Civil
disorders, of which Shays' Rebellion was only the most famous,
provided stimulus for reexamination of the basis of authority in
existing political institutions. This reexamination, though not so
systematic as we are making it sound, resulted in evolution toward the
framing of the Constitution.

The movement that led eventually to the framing of the federal
Constitution was focused explicitly on the development of a more

adequate national authority over some kinds of economic affairs. The Annapolis meeting of 1786, which formally set the stage for the Philadelphia Convention, was called to discuss relationships among the states in respect to trade and commerce, and resulted only in a resolution calling for a further meeting to consider these relationships. "The power of regulating trade," the resolution read, "is of such comprehensive extent, and will enter so far into the general system of the Federal Government, that to give it efficacy, and to obviate questions and doubts concerning its precise nature and limits, may require a correspondent adjustment of the Federal system." Even this Annapolis resolution, however, did not deal exclusively with commercial regulations but included in its terms general statements about the situation of authority in the United States. The resolution proposed a meeting ". . . to devise such further provisions as shall appear to them necessary to render the Constitution of the Federal Government adequate to the exigencies of the union." [6]

The interest in commercial authority, of course, while it may have been basic to the initiation of the Philadelphia meeting was broadened into a more general concern with effective political authority. The Philadelphia Convention quickly transcended questions of economics to deal generally with the powers and institutions of the national government. The concentration of this pre-Convention interest on economic relationships, however, throws emphasis on an important point. This is the vital place the ownership and protection of property occupied in the political ideas and developments of the liberal period. The right to property, it may be recalled, was central to Locke's formulation of the political relationship, and this right and its institutionalization in American and British constitutional usage played a key role in preparing a social context for the development of the institutions of capitalism on which contemporary Anglo-American civilization has been built.

The relationship between power and property has been shaped, particularly by critics of the Constitution, into an interpretation of its framing and development as a class phenomenon, sometimes even as a class conspiracy.[7] Some recent sociological perspectives suggest

---

[6] *Documents Illustrative of the Formation of the Union of the American States* (Washington: U.S. Government Printing Office, 1927), pp. 953–56.

[7] See Beard, *op. cit.*, and Smith, *op. cit.* But also see the following commentaries: Forrest McDonald, *We the People: the Economic Origins of the Constitution* (Chicago: University of Chicago, 1958); Robert E. Brown, *Charles Beard and the Constitution: a Critical Analysis of "An Economic Interpretation of the Constitution"* (Princeton: Prince-

the viability of such a "ruling class' interpretation of political events, and this point of view is not necessarily Marxist or even anticonstitutional.[8] It is a framework of analysis, however, which seems to overstress certain aspects of American political development at the expense of certain others, and particularly to slight the breadth and importance of an American consensus.

The commitment to authority is given operational meaning in the Constitution of the United States in those provisions which vest power in the national government and which equip institutions for the exertion of that power. The establishment of a satisfactory social authority in the national community is recognized in the Preamble itself as the basic aim of the Constitution where it reads, for example, "in order to establish justice, insure domestic tranquillity, provide for the common defense, promote the general welfare." Most specifically, the authority of the national government is established in Article I, Section 8, which enumerates the powers of Congress, these in effect being the bulk of the substantive powers of the national government. It may be noted for future reference that this section established authority to "provide for the common defense and general welfare of the United States" and "to make all laws which shall be necessary and proper for carrying into execution the foregoing powers, and all other powers vested by this Constitution in the government of the United States, or in any department thereof." These grants of authority, vague in tone, were to be used later, as we shall see, in the embellishment and broadening of specific terms of power—power, for example, to regulate commerce, to coin money and regulate its value, and others enumerated in the rest of Section 8. Elsewhere in the Constitution, the authority of the national government was also made explicit, for example and in the long run of Constitutional history very importantly, in the establishment of the office of President and in the vesting in him of "executive" powers—powers over foreign affairs, military affairs, and so on.

In some sense, the principle of authority is the foundation of American Constitutional commitments. Its operational manifestation in individuals is obedience, the standard on which a structure of political order rests; its institutional manifestations are rules or policy and the threat of sanctions for failure to obey. Authority in the Amer-

---

ton University Press, 1956), Lee Benson, *Turner and Beard: American Historical Writing Reconsidered* (Glencoe: Free Press, 1960).

[8] Gaetano Mosca, *The Ruling Class,* trans. Hannah D. Kahn (New York: McGraw-Hill Book Co., Inc., 1939).

ican tradition is not, of course, a naked principle. It blends into questions of how, on what basis, and by whom authority should be used—in other words, questions about the geography of politics, the element of consent, the institutions of authoritative office, and the scope of proper political power. These questions, and the answers of the American constitutional tradition, will be considered in the sections that follow.

THE GEOGRAPHIC BASIS OF AUTHORITY: THE PROBLEM OF FEDERALISM

While the process of establishing authority is basic to any political organization, more specifically in dispute at the framing of the American Constitution and the fundamental source of the deepest of subsequent political divisions in the American nation was the problem of the geographic basis of authority. In other terms, the problem is the relationship between nation and states and of the relative powers of each. Prior to the drafting of the Constitution, the American people had experienced in a practical way the difficulties that can grow out of such a relationship. Under British rule, the colonies had been separate political entities with only their ties to the Crown and geographic and cultural propinquity to bind them together. By the middle of the eighteenth century, they began to sense the need for some common political action. Formally, they acted in unison in declaring independence from Great Britain, and they developed in the Continental Congresses a tenuous basis for united action during the war. The Articles of Confederation, establishing a more permanent and structured relationship among the states, were not adopted until the war was nearly over. The Articles themselves proved, too, to be a shadowy basis for common action. They were ill equipped in institutions for exertion of authority, but even more acutely, they were founded on a concept of national power extremely limited in scope. The national government, such as it was, operated only on and through the various states. It was dependent on state governments for revenues, and these were not forthcoming in the amounts requested. It could and did print money, but its power in this vital sphere was not exclusive. Even in military and naval matters, its predominance was not clear, for the Articles only provided that the states might not keep armies or vessels of war *except* as they were "necessary for defense," a flexible and equivocal arrangement. Perhaps the spirit of the Articles is best summarized in the clause of Article II which stated that "each state retains its sovereignty, freedom, and independence."

While the national government under the Articles did achieve some notable accomplishments, particularly the negotiation of peace with Great Britain and the adoption of the Northwest Ordinance, its authority over matters of national concern—especially commercial problems, monetary arrangements, and the general maintenance of order—was so limited as to stimulate certain elements of the community to seek a more firm, pervasive, and effective general power.

The arguments in the Convention over this matter are usually described in small state–large state terms. While it should be noted that the dispute over the extent of national power did not confine itself to this division alone, it is most clearly seen in the best-known conflict of the Convention, that which juxtaposed the "Virginia plan" for a more extensive national power to the "New Jersey plan" for national arrangements more modest in character.[9] The Virginia plan proposed what amounted to complete revision of the Articles. It would have established a legislative branch of two coordinate houses, representation in both of which would have been by population or by contribution. The lower house would have been elected directly by the people, the upper house by the lower from the nominees of state legislatures. It would have established a national executive and a judiciary with rather vaguely defined powers, and a Council of Revision to exercise a judicial review extending even to acts of state legislatures in conflict with national law. As to substantive powers, it would have given Congress all the authority of the national institutions under the Articles of Confederation, plus competence in matters in which the separate states were incompetent. The breadth and vagueness of the terms of the Virginia plan suggest that if it had been adopted, like the final Constitution of 1787 it would have come to serve as a vehicle for the extension of national authority at the expense of the authority of the states.

The New Jersey plan embodied a revision of substantial proportions in the arrangements of government under the Articles of Confederation. It proposed no changes in the structure of Congress, a plural executive, and a judiciary with jurisdiction over matters of purely national concern. It did not, like the Virginia plan, extend the jurisdiction of the judicial branch to "questions which may involve the national peace and harmony." As to the powers of the national government, it would not have extended them much beyond those specified in the Articles of Confederation, though it would have given the national government power to raise revenues by imposing

[9] For the texts of the two plans, see Farrand, *op. cit.*, pp. 20–28, 242–45.

an import duty, as well as the significant power over interstate commerce. Fundamentally though, it would have established a basis of government operating on the states rather than directly on the people. Beyond import duties, revenues would have had to come through requisitions on the states, with the national government to be given power to make these requisitions effective by collecting revenues directly in states failing to comply with requisition orders.

The so-called Connecticut compromise found a middle course on the question of relationship between state and nation. The compromise itself hinged around the structure of a legislative body in which one house incorporated the principle of state representation, the other the principle of proportionate direct representation. This compromise pointed the way toward solution of some of the other outstanding Convention problems and, in some respects, reached even beyond the Virginia plan in its implications for national power.

If the final constitutional pattern is to be regarded as a compromise, it is a compromise in which more was conceded on one side than on the other, for the Constitution was extensive in its grants both of specific and of general powers to the national government, and it established instrumentalities for the exercise of authority which made it possible for national power to be mobilized on an effective basis. Broad national powers would probably be fruitless without the structures and institutions capable of carrying them into effect in a vigorous and sustained way. Thus, the executive power was concentrated in the hands of one man and the terms of executive power were vague enough to promise the office an expansive future. Likewise, the Constitution established a national judiciary with expansible jurisdiction. Again, the question of the geographic basis of authority blends into the question of political structure.

The formalities of the distribution of authority under the federal Constitution are well known, and history has proved them to be nondefinitive. The Constitution established a national government of enumerated powers, but these powers provided an adequate fiscal base and an adequate reference to substance to permit the national government to assert its authority without disregarding the terms of the document. The "general welfare" and "necessary and proper" clauses clearly opened the doors to the expansion of national power, though this expansion was not, of course, unaccompanied by dispute.

The fate of the formal Constitutional distribution is perhaps best illustrated in the history of the Tenth Amendment, which explicitly reserved "to the States respectively, or to the people" those powers not delegated to the national government nor prohibited to the states in the Constitution. The Tenth Amendment would seem to be a concrete affirmation of limitation to specific terms of the power of the United States government. Its later career, however, suggests the extent to which Constitutional formalities are bent by the situation of their application. During the period when the nationalism of John Marshall dominated the Court—1801 to 1836—the Tenth Amendment cautionary would appear to have little practical effect on the development of national power. During the subsequent period from 1836 to perhaps as late as 1936, the Tenth Amendment seems generally to have been regarded as a meaningful though wavering limitation on the national government. Its spirit was often apparent as the courts struck down attempts to extend the power of the national government, particularly into social and economic fields.[10] On occasion, as in cases involving the establishment of federal regulation over transportation and some cases involving interpretation of such statutes as the Sherman Act, its seeming restriction on national power was less effective. During and since the 1930's, feeling the full impact of technological development and under the pressure of social, economic, and political change, the Tenth Amendment seems nearly to have been written out of the Constitution as a real limitation on national authority. Mr. Justice Stone, speaking for the Court in the Darby case in 1941, called the Tenth Amendment "a truism" as he held valid the Fair Labor Standards Act extending the power of the national government into the previously largely reserved fields of regulation of wages and hours, working conditions, and child labor.[11] This alteration over time of the pattern of relationships between nation and states is a more important feature of the American Constitution from the standpoint of understanding politics than the formal arrangement of power set out in the original document.

To this point, we have described the structure of the geographic distribution of authority in the United States and the conditions of its adoption.[12] More might be said, however, about the general way in which the federal system is rooted in the condition of the American nation. The federal system, both in its original form and in its historical development, may be described as the product of the forces of

---

[10] See, e.g., *Hammer* v. *Dagenhart,* 247 U.S. 251 (1918); *Bailey* v. *Drexel Furniture Co.,* 259 U.S. 20 (1922); *Carter* v. *Coal Co.,* 298 U.S. 238 (1936); *United States* v. *Butler,* 297 U.S. 1 (1936).

[11] *United States* v. *Darby Lumber Co.,* 312 U.S. 100 (1941), 124.

[12] See the comparative commentary in K. C. Wheare, *Federal Government,* (4th ed.; New York: Oxford University Press, 1964).

union and disunion which provide one of the most persistent themes in American political thought and practice. These forces are various in nature, and a number of them have already been discussed in our treatment of the Revolutionary and Constitutional periods. Four major types of factors seem to have worked to make the American nation a testing ground for the federal form of political organization.[13]

1. Geography. The basic geographic fact is the territorial dispersion of the American people. This factor was at work in the earliest days of Colonial settlement, when pockets of immigrants were widely separated in space. The development of localistic traditions began early in the history of the nation, and though the space–time ratio decreased with the invention of new modes of travel and communication, spatial dispersion continued with the opening of the west. Thus, social localism and spatial movement sustained geography as a salient factor in the development of the political system. The push of this factor has been decentralistic, its gross effect tending to disunite the total structure.

2. Culture. The cultural characteristics of America, in themselves to some degree dependent on geography, have, likewise, tended to be a decentralizing force in American politics. Not only did culture patterns tend to be distinguished by area—New England, South, Middle Coast, Piedmont—but the introduction and development of various ethnic and religious factors resulted in the cultural heterogeneity is undoubtedly a source of resistance to political centralization. A counteractive cultural force should also be noted, however, for the spread of the scale of interaction, external pressure, and common political experience have certainly over the long run led to the development of something like a national American culture. The forces of this evolution were at work before the Revolution, and they continue with mounting force down to the present. From the initiation of national political action before the Revolution to the revision of racial attitudes in the contemporary South, the working of the forces of cultural nationalization have been apparent.

3. Economy and technology. Economic forces have, likewise, been both centralistic and decentralistic in effect. Economic sectionalism based on product differences and differences in predominant form of economic activity has long been a force in American politics. It was manifest in an early period, for example, in different types of regional concerns with British regulations on trade, and for a long time

---

[13] Cf. *ibid.*, pp. 35-52; Leslie Lipson, *The Great Issues of Politics*, (2d ed.; Englewood Cliffs, N.J.: Prentice-Hall, Inc., 1960), pp. 316–40.

it persisted in attitudes toward the tariff, one of the most divisive specific problems with which the national political structure had to deal. This economic differentiation is still clearly a fact in the American nation, dividing region from region on both a macro and a micro scale. It is inevitably a source of conflict between city and farm, and it remains to separate the interests of large sections of the nation from one another. However, like the culture, the economy has also provided impetus toward national union. We have previously noted the impact of economic relationships in bringing the states together in Philadelphia for the drafting of the Constitution. This movement is emblematic of the growth of interdependence, and continuing technological development has increasingly made of the American nation one economic unit for many purposes. The extent to which evolution of the federal system has proceeded through extension of national economic power, especially through commerce and tax clauses, suggests the importance of economic considerations as a unifying force. The development of national markets and a national labor force through increased product and human mobility explains the extent to which industrial organization, labor, distribution, and others have become matters of true national concern. In sum, economic factors have probably been powerful forces toward centralization in the American political structure.

4. Political experience. Finally, political factors themselves have been important in determining the shape of the distribution of power. While we have implicitly to this point been treating political arrangements as a dependent variable, over time this dependent variable feeds back on the other elements of the system to create further political effects itself. We have repeatedly pointed out that by the time of the drawing of the Constitution, the American people had had experience both with political separation and with political interaction. The predominant political experience of the colonies had been separatistic, and the sustenance of state loyalties in America probably reflects indirectly these earlier political conditions. We have also noted, however, the growth of instruments and sentiments for common action, as well as both the successes and failures of these conveyed lessons in the importance of working together. Threat and pressure from other nations, too, have been political reasons for union as young America faced English, French, Spanish, and Indian difficulties, and as the more mature America faces involvement in global conflict. The development of an ideological nationalism, of a sense of an American people and an

American destiny, has made possible the acceptance and extension of national power.

Thus, the geographic, cultural, economic, and political condition of the United States has thrown up a complex of forces influential on the distribution of power under the Constitution, both toward centralization and toward decentralization. In typical fashion, the American attempt to resolve counterpressures has resulted in a compromise, a federal system designed to accommodate the need for national power *and* the various forces for local autonomy. This compromise has been a dynamic one, able to accommodate changes in the underlying causal factors by revision of institutions and gradual, sometimes subtle redistribution of the powers to which those institutions give effect. A comparative perspective on this political phenomenon is instructive. Those nations which have developed and maintained federal systems— for example, Canada, Australia, and Switzerland—are nations built on geographic, cultural, economic, and political bases in major respects similar to those of the United States.[14] In the contemporary world, federal institutions have appealed to those peoples who for similar reasons have sought political means to reconcile both national and particular interests.

A final and very important aspect of American federalism has been mentioned only by implication in what has been said above. This is the relationship of federalism to constitutionalism, i.e., to the basic demand for institutions that limit the exercise of political authority. In a general discussion of federalism, this factor is both cause and effect; the desire of the American people to insure themselves limited government doubtless was one of the major factors propelling them toward adoption of federal institutions, and, at the same time, these institutions have helped in practice to maintain a politics limited in scope. The theory behind the relationship between federalism and limited government is simple and obvious. It is the geographic extension of the fundamental idea that division of power renders it less subject to abuse and more subject to control. Thus, federalism anticipates that the nation and the states will be mutual counteractives, often competitors for authority, and that the people will thereby gain the advantage in liberty of this mediation of political power. It is often argued that it is the pluralistic social basis of the American nation which has made the preservation of liberty both desirable and possible. Federalism is, in some sense, a geographic recognition of social

---

[14] See Wheare, *op. cit.*

pluralism and one of the forms in which this basic social characteristic is translated into specific political institutions.

This argument for federalism is probably most elegantly and memorably stated in one of the greatest and best known essays of *The Federalist:* Madison's No. 10. *Federalist* No. 10 is a far-ranging and closely reasoned piece of political theory. Its applicability and importance are so wide that it might be treated at any one of a number of points in our discussion of the American political tradition. Since it is important to look at this paper as a whole, however, and since one of its major themes is the subject with which we are now dealing, we may at this point turn to its consideration at some length.

Madison's explicit concern in *Federalist* No. 10 was with faction. "Among the numerous advantages promised by a well constructed Union," it begins, "none deserves to be more accurately developed than its tendency to break and control the violence of faction." [15] By faction, Madison meant simply a portion of the community set off from the rest by special interests: "By a faction I understand a number of citizens, whether amounting to a majority or minority of the whole, who are united and actuated by some common impulse of passion, or of interest, adverse to the rights of other citizens, or to the permanent and aggregate interests of the community." [16] He apparently saw faction as based on a substantial sort of interest sufficiently vital to impel men to intrude on the interests of others. By analogy with the contemporary political scene, Madison's faction would seem to be what we now call interest groups, either organized or unorganized. The spirit of faction, Madison suggested, stands in the way of common agreement over social policy.

Why did Madison see faction as a phenomenon that must be "broken or controlled" in the interests of good government? The basic answer to this question is not explicit in *Federalist* No. 10, though Madison does write there of the ill effects of faction on justice and the "public good." Underneath these phrases seems to lie Madison's axiomatic belief in the personal and individual rights of eighteenth-century liberalism. It is apparent that his chief practical concern was with the threat of majority factionalism, for the spirit of faction would impel men in the majority to move against the rights of defenseless minorities or individuals. The heart of the liberal tradition is its commitment to the protection of innate, individual personal rights with emphasis on the right to property. It is the first object of government

---

[15] *The Federalist,* No. 10, *op. cit.,* p. 56.
[16] *Ibid.,* p. 57.

according to this tradition to protect these rights, "to secure these rights governments are instituted among men." Unchecked, the spirit of faction would render rights subject to the dangers of instability, injustice and confusion. "To secure the public good, and private rights, against the dangers of such a faction, and at the same time to preserve the spirit and form of popular government, is then the great object to which our inquiries are directed." [17]

The essay then proceeds to a systematic examination of the relationship between faction and popular government. It first notes two methods of curing the mischiefs of faction—removing its causes and controlling its effects. As to removing causes, there are again two methods—to destroy liberty or to give every citizen the same opinion. The first remedy Madison dismissed as "worse than the disease." Here, his argument recurs, in effect, to his axiomatic first principle. The second remedy he dismissed as impracticable, and in doing so he discussed in most fascinating fashion his theory about the causes of faction, a utilitarian "interest" theory. Opinions, he said, are based on desires, and as long as human desires differ and the means for satisfying them are unequally distributed, there will be differences in attitudes among men, differential abilities and needs inevitably given to conflicting demands and points of view. "The latent causes of faction are thus sown in the nature of man; and we see them every where brought into different degrees of activity, according to the different circumstances of civil society." [18] Thus, factions grow out of what Madison calls "a zeal for different opinions" concerning the variety of things toward which human interest is directed, "the most common and durable" of these being "the various and unequal distribution of property." [19]

In arguing the impracticability of giving every citizen the same opinions, Madison seems to have assumed rigid linkages between interest, attitude, and political behavior. He suggested that since interests cannot be changed because rooted in objective differences in condition, attitudes and political associations based upon them must necessarily be as different as the interests. Such a conclusion in not surprising, perhaps, in the circumstances of Madison's time. However, experience with modern techniques of persuasion may lead us to wonder about this impracticability. It is worth noting that even Rousseau, a contemporary of Madison's, seems to have regarded it as possible if not

---

[17] *Ibid.*, p. 61.
[18] *Ibid.*, p. 58.
[19] *Ibid.*, p. 59.

easy to destroy, at the source of opinion, the causes of faction in civil society. Modern men, especially those in mass societies, seem to be fairly common prey to techniques that manipulate opinion to the point where men will believe there are no differences between them and their needs and desires are common. From advertising through brainwashing to the manipulation of the masses in nation states, this kind of persuasion has been tried and often found to work.

Madison, however, turned his major attention to the second method of curing the ills of faction—controlling its effects. Here, he dealt with the mediating effects of political arrangements on human social activity. If a faction is a numerical minority, he said, its effects may be controlled through the devices of what he called the "republican principle." But in the context of popular government, the control of majority faction is obviously a more onerous problem. His solution is to prevent the impulse to oppression and opportunity to exercise such impulse from coinciding. Madison's analysis led him to conclude that two forms of political arrangement would be valuable in this respect —one the institution of representation, the other the geographic extension and federalization of political power. The first of these not only filters and mediates popular demands and attitudes, but it is also instrumental to the effectuation of the second. That is to say, it is the representative type of institution which makes it possible to extend political power over a large area. The inclusion of a large area within a common political authority implies the inclusion of many and varied interests. The extent of this heterogeneity or pluralism in a big country is the best insurance that on matters of important public policy predatory factious interests will not add up to numerical majorities. Furthermore, the federal Constitution, in dividing power between nation and states, provided a vehicle for the satisfaction both of local needs and of aggregate interests at two different levels.

The smaller the society, the fewer probably will be the distinct parties and interests composing it; the fewer the distinct parties and interests, the more frequent will a majority be found of the same party; and the smaller the number of individuals comprising a majority, and the smaller the compass within which they are placed, the more easily will they concert and execute their plans of oppression. Extend the sphere, and you take in a greater variety of parties and interests; you make it less probable that a majority of the whole will have a common motive to invade the rights of other citizens, or if such a common motive exists, it will be more difficult for all who feel it to discover their own strength, and act in unison with each other.[20] [A factious interest] . . . will be less apt to pervade the whole body of the Union, than a particular member of it. . . .[21]

Thus, Madison concludes, "In the extent and proper structure of the Union, therefore, we behold a Republican remedy for the diseases most incident to Republican Government." [22]

A few of the main tendencies and implications of Madison's argument in *Federalist* No. 10 are worth brief review. While the essay explicitly strikes a strongly normative tone, it can also be seen as descriptive theory of the if–then variety, i.e., as theory which explores the empirical consequences of certain modes of action. Basically, as we noted above, it is an interest theory of politics, assuming that the basis of social action lies in individual desire. This interest-based interpretation of political phenomena is central to the Western liberal tradition, as is its combination with a moral commitment to the notion of individual human rights. Madison's interest theory has sometimes been treated as an economic theory of politics. Indeed, Madison has sometimes been made almost a pre-Marx Marxist as far as his understanding of the basis of social life and action is concerned. Such treatment, however, seems to extend unduly Madison's interest interpretation in the direction of economic motivation.[23]

Federalist No. 10 also suggests what is in later scholarship called a group theory of politics, that is, a theory based on the assumption that men tend to combine for political action as shared interests and attitudes intersect and bring them together in the satisfaction of wants.[24] This has been a major note in American political thought nearly throughout its history, reflective probably of the social condition of heterogeneity in the American culture. This thought may be either normative, i.e., saying grouping is good by casting group in an instrumental role in protection of human rights, or it may be descriptive, saying merely that the group is the basic datum and group theory the basic framework through which politics may be understood. But the tone of *Federalist* No. 10 seems to point in both directions. Despite the adverse effects of faction on human justice, Madison suggests, we

---

[20] *Ibid.*, pp. 63–64.

[21] *Ibid.*, p. 65.

[22] *Ibid.*, p. 65.

[23] Beard, *op. cit.*, pp. 156–61; Douglas Adair, "The Tenth Federalist Revisited," *William and Mary Quarterly*, Vol. VIII (January, 1951), pp. 48–61. One of the most interesting commentaries on Madison's theories is Robert A. Dahl, *A Preface to Democratic Theory* (Chicago: University of Chicago Press, 1956), pp. 4–33.

[24] See esp. David B. Truman, *The Governmental Process* (New York: A. A. Knopf, 1951), esp. pp. 4–13.

must accept the fact of social grouping and durability of factional human action. Normatively, the group is in some sense an extension of
highly valued liberty, and with the multiplication of groups within
the civil society, it is instrumental to prevention of the tyranny of
the majority.

Finally, *Federalist* No. 10 states and emphasizes the importance of
institutions in the achievement of the goals of a liberal society. It ex-
amines in some detail the proposition that the structuring of the political system has a strong influence on the policy product of that system
and, more specifically, the proposition that certain kinds of structures
are least likely to yield the kind of political policy abusive of private
human rights. The discussion of *Federalist* No. 10 is confined largely
to the policy effects of representative and federalistic institutions, and
it is particularly the federalistic of which we wish to take note here.
Madison's phrase about "the extent and proper structure of the
Union" is a succinct summarization of the case. Both the size of the
union and the division of political power between nation and states,
he suggested, are in themselves important, if not necessary or sufficient,
features of the constitutional instrument for seeking political realization of the values of the American society.

LEGITIMATION OF POLICY BY CONSENT OF THE PEOPLE

The American commitment to the idea that public policy must be
given legitimacy in a dynamic sense by the consent of the people requires somewhat different and perhaps briefer treatment than the two
items discussed in the preceding sections. The idea of consent is one
with which we have dealt at some length above, and the manner of its
incorporation into American political institutions is such that more
can be said specifically about it at later points in the development of
our analysis than can be said here.[25] Nonetheless, if the Constitution
is viewed as the dynamic development of the American political tradition, probably no element is more notable or further advanced in
the course of constitutional growth than this one.

The idea of consent we introduced above as an outgrowth of the
liberal view that political structure is the creation of individual men
working in concert and, therefore, somehow morally under the control of those whose creature it was in the first instance. It has already
been noted that the liberal concept of consent has two sides, one of
which refers to consensus as the basis for the creation of political au-

---

[25] See esp. the section on extension of the franchise during the Jacksonian period,
chap. 7, pp. 215–20, below.

thority, the other to consensus in the sense of immediate requisite to legitimate political activity. Here we are dealing with the second side. Locke, though hardly a basic democrat, seems to have felt that the principle of democracy, i.e., the legitimation of policy through the instruments of consent, was a logical corollary of liberal individualism. This idea in attenuated form was promoted through the development of the British House of Commons, and we have interpreted it above as the basic if often implicit demand of the American revolutionaries. The drive for controllable, responsible institutions seems to have been the main political goal of the revolutionary movement. Paine, whose democratic proclivities outran those of a good many of his contemporaries, was clear in his demand that governmental struc-tures be so arranged as to be under immediate and effective popular control.

The idea of democracy, of course, dates back at least to Periclean Athens; the eighteenth century witnessed a rebirth of this old politi-cal principle based on a largely new philosophical foundation. Whether this idea is *the* foundation idea of the American Constitu-tion, a question sometimes debated now of whether America is funda-mentally a republic or a democracy, seems rather beside the point. Whether the principle of consent was perfectly incorporated in Ameri-can institutions at the beginning or even today likewise is somewhat beside the point. The point here seems to be that the American politi-cal tradition has been centrally informed by the basic idea of consent —the idea that the machines of government must constantly be re-fueled by consent of the people.

This basic commitment, like all the basic commitments with which we are dealing, is the instrumentation of a part of a central value cluster. American tradition is such that one element alone of that cluster could not be given effect at the expense of all others. But the continuity and strength of the idea of government by consent would seem to be demonstrated by a look at the development of democratic institutions through American political history.

The institutionalization of the principle of consent in American po-litical practice has been achieved through the device of representation. Representation, it is true, entails a modification of the consent idea. The introduction of a mediating structure between popular will and public policy was commonly recognized even by the Founding Fathers, to attenuate responsibility to the people. By most public figures of that period—for example, Madison in *Federalist* No. 10—this attenua-tion was regarded as salutary in itself. On the other hand, it can be

seen as a kind of necessary evil acceptable only because of the inopera-
bility of direct democracy in the context of the large nation. In any
case, in the framing of the Constitution, representation was regarded
as the feasible and desirable form of the operation of the principle of
consent, and thus it was put into practice in the political institutions of
the period. While it is doubtless true that some elements in American
society, particularly many of the economically powerful, were skeptical of the idea of democracy, the strength of democracy was sufficient
to force its measured acceptance in the framework of the new Constitution. Hamilton, scarcely to be regarded as a radical, concluded
Federalist No. 22 with these words: "The fabric of American empire
ought to rest on the solid basis of *the consent of the people.* The
streams of national power ought to flow immediately from that pure
original fountain of all legitimate authority." [26]

Institutions, however, may differ according to the extent and style
in which they endeavor to incorporate popular will into the ongoing
processes of politics. These differences appear to be functions of (a)
feasibility and (b) a desire in the culture to achieve certain ends other
than consensus through the use of representative institutions, such
ends as mediation of popular will to keep the people's power under
reasonable control. Simple or direct democracy—the democracy of the
town meeting or the Greek forum—built in few checks to the translation of popular will into political policy. The British House of Commons, however, as it existed at the time of the framing of the American
Constitution, imposed a number of barriers between popular will and
policy. The "rotten borough," for example, was defended (most notably by Edmund Burke) as a way of modifying immediate popular will
in the interests of longer-run traditions and spirit of the nation. The
American tradition, even from its earlier periods, has typically leaned
toward a fairly direct and simple relationship between the voice of the
people and their organ in the political system. While liberal values
dictated the limitation of political authority through a variety of
checks on the development and assertion of policy, insofar as the democratic ingredient itself is concerned, the application of consent was
fairly unencumbered. Thus, the lower house of the typical American
legislature, the forum of popular will, was constituted of members
elected directly by the people, on a fairly broad franchise, to short
terms of office, from districts of relatively equal size. These lower bodies were devised to provide responsive organs of political power dependent rather immediately on public opinion for direction of their

---

[26] *The Federalist,* No. 22, p. 146.

deliberations. State constitutions generally embodied this attitude, as did the United States House of Representatives established in the Constitution of 1787. Hamilton summarized it in *Federalist* No. 52:

> . . . [A]s it is essential to liberty that the government in general, should have a common interest with the people; so it is particularly essential that the branch of it under consideration, the House of Representatives should have an immediate dependence on, and an intimate sympathy with the people. Frequent elections are unquestionably the only policy by which this dependence and sympathy can be effectually secured.[27]

Thus, the House of Representatives was designed as the sounding board of popular will in a government of mixed institutions. Here, the principle of consent was given effect in the body which, it is interesting to note, was given sole formal power over the initiation of fiscal legislation. Given the situation of the time, the democratic basis of the House of Representatives was reasonably broad. Whatever the motivation of the framers, whether they went as far as they did toward democracy as an act of appeasement is rather beside the case. For it is clear from this democratization itself that the demand for consent was a common one at the time and was deemed important by the political elite. It is also clear that the principle of consent became operative to an important extent with the development of the House of Representatives into an active and fundamental political institution. But more important is the extent to which the framing of the Constitution of 1787 opened doors to further and radical development of a democratic political structure.

For democracy in America on both state and national levels has undergone a radical growth both in the extension of its popular base and in the penetration of its spirit into the institutions of government. If the actual institutionalization of democracy in the Constitution of 1787 was modest, it was a step in the development of a government basically informed by popular will. As E. E. Schattschneider puts it:

> It is a change not brought about by an act of Congress, a decision of the Supreme Court, a constitutional convention or a constitutional amendment, but by a kind of general consent. Somewhere along the line the owners of the government decided to read the Constitution as if it were a democratic document. This is unquestionably the most important interpretation of the Constitution in our history.[28]

---

[27] *Ibid.*, No. 52, p. 355.

[28] E. E. Schattschneider, *The Semi-Sovereign People* (New York: Holt, Rinehart, and Winston, Inc., 1960), p. 116.

The dramatic growth of the franchise in the extension of popular government in America will be a subject of discussion at a later point, as will the democratization of the Presidency, the Senate, and the spirit of American politics generally.[29] It must be noted here, however, that on the basis of the institutional arrangements given formality in 1787, nearly every aspect of political authority in America has been in some sense democratized. The Presidency, for example, was rather rapidly converted from an office of vague powers whose occupants were selected in a peculiarly mediated manner to an office of great powers whose occupancy became the subject of the greatest contest for popular approval in the world and whose occupant came to be regarded as the spokesman of the American nation. Given the basis of the Constitution of 1787, the American President quickly became, as Henry Jones Ford put it, "the elect of the people and the presidential office became the organ of the will of the nation." [30] At a later time, the Senate, a bastion of privilege and continuity, likewise became the subject of approval of the popular will.

The spread of mechanisms of consent through the institutions of the American government certainly was not a development unique to American politics. Though it took root and found institutional expression early in the framework of the American government, the idea that the legitimate exercise of political power must be based on common will is, perhaps, the most characteristic political doctrine of the modern age. It still provides, though now generally on a more organismic and nationalistic basis, a central ideological theme for revolution. The mixture of the principle of consent with a variety of mediating forces in the American Constitution reflects the fact that American political institutions were given their general form in a period before the development of mass society, a period when the demand for consent was leavened with concern for individual and minority rights, particularly the right of property. Indeed, American political experience would seem to indicate that even down to the present, American political ideology as contrasted with that of most if not all other areas of the world continues to hold the idea of limitation in as high regard as the basic democratic principle. Debate surrounding the extension of the franchise in the third and fourth decades of the nineteenth century, and the theoretical and political posture of the American New Deal of the 1930's, were probably influenced as much by a respect

---

[29] Chap. 7, pp. 215–27, below.

[30] Henry Jones Ford, *The Rise and Growth of American Politics* (New York: Macmillan Co., 1900), p. 196.

for property as by the demand for extensive popular control of the political mechanism.

Both theoretically and historically the principle of consent is closely related to the phenomenon of the political party, though at this point we will refer only briefly to this relationship. Historically, of course, it is often noted that the Founding Fathers, or at least the articulate among them, feared the development of political parties as Madison feared faction. At the time of the framing of the Constitution, party was regarded as a divisive force which could flourish only at the expense of a sacrifice of common good. It is also notable that the growth of political parties followed hard on the heels of the institution of government under the federal Constitution.[31] This development could scarcely have been accident. The parties probably not only reflected natural divisions in the society that long predated the Revolution, but they also are probably a sort of natural institutional accompaniment or corollary to the structure of government by consent. In the light both of logic and of historical experience, it may indeed be proposed that the principle of consent is not operable in the large-scale society without some form of political party system, that the two-party system is the outgrowth of American political society, and that it provides the most stable if not the only basis for the sustained operation of the democratic mechanisms. If consent implies meaningful choice, it is difficult to see how man in the large-scale mass society can be expected to make real choices, isolated as he is from control over and understanding of his environment, without the party as an institution to structure the political situation. This process of structuring as the parties carry it out includes both the promotion of candidates and policies for public approval and also the simplification of the alternatives among which voters may choose. Without the party device to perform these tasks, mass democracy seems likely if not certain to become an exercise in the choiceless and often irrational Bonapartistic expression of mass adulation for leadership. The operation of the principle of consent at some points in the French Revolution and often in subsequent political history has taken this course.

Consent in the framework of American institutions has persistently come to mean consent rendered only in the context of a system in which there is real choice between parties, usually two in number. Given the long constitutional view, it is impossible to consider the

---

[31] For party history, see Wilfred Binkley, *American Political Parties: Their Natural History*, (2d ed.; New York: A. A. Knopf, 1947); William N. Chambers, *Political Parties in a New Nation* (New York: Oxford University Press, 1963).

American Constitution as an operating guide for government without considering the political party as a basic constitutional instrumentality. While questions may, of course, be raised about whether choice in the context of a party system is free, whether choice between two alternatives is adequate, and whether choice between nonprogrammatic American parties is meaningful, the American political party system in practice has seemed to yield a satisfactory approximation of the political standards of the American ideology.

ORGANIZATION OF AUTHORITY BY SEPARATION OF POWERS

A fourth commitment embodied in the Constitution was to the organization of national authority by the principle of functional separation. In specific terms, this principle called simply for the vesting of formal power in three coordinate agencies designated, according to the classic model, executive, legislative, and judicial. More generally, the idea of separation of powers reflected a fundamental and long-lasting American taste for the dispersion of authority, a taste that has many manifestations in the development of the nation's political institutions. No theme has been more influential in shaping American modes of policy-making and execution.

Like other tenets of the political culture, this one is rooted in historical experience, in philosophical precedent, and in the logic of constitutionalism. Both the idea and the practice of separation of powers long predate the American Constitution. In political thought, it can be traced back as far as Heroditus and Aristotle. For example, Aristotle divided the functions of government into three analytically separate parts, corresponding to the legislative, executive, and judicial, and noted that these three powers could be located in separate agencies.[32] He also mentioned and, indeed, favored the institutionalization of balance among elements of society as an instrument of political moderation and stability. While neither of these formulations completely comprehends the system of separation of powers in its later sense, both point in similar directions. Polybius, describing the political institutions of Rome, stated a theory of stability even more directly based on the concept of political balance among agencies. Locke and Harrington, in a much later period, also advocated the use of functional division for containing political power.

---

[32] Aristotle, *The Politics*, trans. Ernest Barker (Oxford: Clarendon Press, 1946), pp. 188–89. For contemporary comment on the doctrine of separation of powers, see Dahl, *op. cit.*, pp. 4–33.

The best-known intellectual oracle of separation of powers, however, was the Frenchman Montesquieu who, in *The Spirit of the Laws,* published in 1748, found in separation and balance the secret of liberty under the British constitution.[33] The theory of separation of powers was not Montesquieu's sole contribution to political thought, and the accuracy of his interpretation of the English system is questionable. Nonetheless, his ideas about the effects of separation and balance on the condition of liberty may be suggested to have, when tested against American experience, a surprising predictive quality. His work was also known to the Founding Fathers, and he is cited with favor in *Federalist* No. 47, the leading tract on the subject to come out of the Constitutional period.

Experience as well as ideas headed the American nation toward the practice of separation of powers. Though the evolution of British practice had by the late eighteenth century largely cast the Commons into the predominant role, the existence of King, Lords, and Commons as separate but complementary institutions afforded the Americans a familiar model. Their own political evolution, too, suggested a similar lesson. Formally, the separation of powers was not built into most of the colonial governments, the authority of the royal governor being supreme. By the time of the Revolution, however, colonial legislatures had come to exercise real checking power, especially through their control of the fisc. Both the problems of executive predominance and the therapeutic effects of balance had thus suggested themselves to the Americans before they achieved their independence, as some aspects of Revolutionary theory have made clear. The *Declaration of Independence,* in its later reaches, has overtones of separation of powers theory, e.g., "The history of the present King of Great Britain is a history of repeated injuries and usurpations, . . ." and "He has made Judges dependent on his Will alone. . . ."

The early state constitutions, devised during and after the War of Independence, ordinarily stated the principle of separation in explicit terms like the following from the North Carolina constitution: "The legislative, executive, and judicial powers of government ought to be forever separate and distinct of one another." Such statements were buttressed by the establishment of some independence in different spheres of activity. It should be noted, however, that these governments leaned decidedly toward legislative supremacy, again a product of experience with royal governors and crown. Short terms of execu-

---

[33] *The Spirit of the Laws,* ed., with introduction, Franz Neumann (New York: Hafner, 1949).

tive power, selection of the governor by the legislative body, denial of the veto power (in all states but one during the early period) limited the weapons of initiative and defense available to the executive branch. The development of "energy in the executive," later characteristic of American politics at some levels, came only after trial and disillusionment with the predominance of the legislature. In general, however, the institutional frameworks established in the states were faithful to the separation model, the model built into the national structure with the writing of the Constitution.

The logic of the separation of powers is simple and evident. By requiring that the public business be transacted in parts by counterpoised authorities, it assumes that the tendencies of government to arbitrary, unlimited, or illegitimate action can be checked. The root value is that of liberty, in the American version the liberty of the individual, and separation has been thought a major device for its maintenance. In our constitutional usage, it seems often to have been regarded as a necessary, though not a sufficient, safeguard. The tripartite division prescribed in the federal and most state constitutions is thus one form of institutional limitation on the arbitrary exercise of authority, an end sought through use of this and other instruments.

The general principle of separation of powers seems to have been taken on faith and virtually without examination by the articulate political elite of the Constitutional period. Certainly in part, the system assumed shape out of the practical demands of constitution-making, out of the juxtaposition of office to office, out of the confrontation of political requirement to political requirement. Some of the theoretical symmetry of the system, some of the rationalization it has inspired, is doubtless post hoc reflection on fortuitous structures. It should be pointed out, however, that the premises of separation had been examined in abstract terms by the time of the framing, and the idea itself seems to have had some direct impact on the practice.

In the Constitutional Convention, the general issue whether or not to separate powers does not seem to have been a central problem. The Convention's debates about structure of government revolved about specific aspects of the organization of the specific branches. One of its best-known conflicts, of course, centered on the legislative organization, but theoretically this had more to do with the matter of federalism than with the matter of separation of powers. Some features of the system of separation, e.g., the veto power, were the subject of fairly thorough discussion, and others, like the political role of the courts, were, perhaps purposely, left vague.

The resultant overall pattern was faithful to the model of separation suggested by the scattered prescriptions of political thought on the subject, by aspects of the British constitution, by American experience and state usage. The pattern has been enduring and influential—certainly one of this nation's most important contributions to political usage. The relative contributions of accident and idea to its development must remain obscure, but it cannot be doubted that this is one of the places where the influence of political thought extrudes into action.

The evidence of *The Federalist* papers suggests that the idea of separation of powers was widely and thoroughly established in the Constitutional period. Madison's attention in No. 47 was devoted not to the defense of separation but to defense of the proposed Constitution from the charge that it did not separate powers enough. The preferability of separation he took to be axiomatic:

One of the principal objections inculcated by the more respectable adversaries of the constitution, is its supposed violation of the political maxim, that the legislative, executive, and judiciary departments ought to be separate and distinct. . . .

No political truth is certainly of greater intrinsic value or is stamped with the authority of more enlightened patrons of liberty than that on which the objection is founded. The accumulation of all powers legislative, executive, and judiciary in the same hands, whether of one, a few or many, and whether hereditary, self appointed, or elective, may justly be pronounced the very definition of tyranny.[34]

Paying due respects to the separation of powers idea, Madison proceeded to examine the problem of how much separation is necessary (and tolerable) for the preservation of liberty. In doing so, he further cited the authority of "the celebrated Montesquieu" and examined the evidence provided by state and British constitutions. Though the point of separation is to separate, Madison noted that complete separation is an impossibility, and that even if it were possible, it would destroy the potential of authority for which government exists. Separation, in other words, must be a matter of degree; for government to operate, power must also be reblended. The functional agencies must be provided the mutual stimuli to move at least partially in a common activity. Otherwise, the political system would achieve an equilibrium of repose; all energies would be forestalled, and the system would die in paralysis and frustration.

Thus, the logic of politics requires not only separation but inter-

---

[34] *The Federalist*, No. 47, *op. cit.*, pp. 323–24.

action among agencies, a set of channels and prods to mutual activity. The experience of the states and England, said Madison, demonstrates how this may be achieved. He proceeded to cite the abstract statements of the principle in the state constitutions and also the institutional devices in use in the states, these contributing to the "blending" of authority. What Madison demonstrated here is that separation of powers must be complemented by what we often call "checks and balances" to form a complete and operating system of government. The principle of separation of powers provides that political energies that might be turned to arbitrary exercise of authority is displaced on the adjustment of relationships among departments whose concert is required for the solution of political problems. And in these adjustments through formal (veto, advice and consent, judicial review, presidential messages) and informal (political parties, patronage, personal persuasion) devices, the departments acquire some mutuality of perspective and interest.

American experience with the separation of powers is thus a dual experience of problem-solving and adjusting the mechanisms of problem-solving. Like other elements in the American system, the framework of national institutions has felt the impact of change, and some of this impact has pushed toward the redistribution of functions among the branches of government. Especially interesting has been the evolution of relationships between executive and legislative.

It seems fair to say that both the overall ideological tradition and the colonial historical background dictated some tendency to lean toward legislative supremacy. Still, as *Federalist* No. 48 suggests, there has also been awareness of the threat of "legislative tyranny" and some concomitant appreciation of the crucial character of the executive leadership.[35] Hamilton, for example, though his views may be more typical of a later time than of his own, wrote in *Federalist* No. 70 that "Energy in the executive is a leading character in the definition of good government."[36] While this hardly threatened presidential predominance, it indicates another of the many tests against which the framework of institutions must be set.

Over the long run, the thrust of events has pushed the balance toward the executive power. The causes of this development are manifold, and any attempt to summarize must do them less than justice. Complexity has created the need for expertise; the expanded scale of life and government has created the need for dispatch. The nation's

[35] *Ibid.,* No. 48, pp. 333 ff.
[36] *Ibid.,* No. 70, p. 471.

involvement in foreign affairs has heightened the importance of that aspect of governmental functions. These factors taken together, along with the force of personality of some who have held the office, have added to the relative advantage of the Presidency, an advantage probably summarized in the capacity for sustained leadership.[37]

These tendencies are nearly everywhere visible in the contemporary world. What may be most notable about the American experience is the extent to which executive predominance has been forestalled by the nation's commitments to the limitation and sharing of power. By comparative standards, it is not so much presidential aggrandizement as congressional self-defense that looks impressive. Nonetheless, in terms of internal distribution in the American system, the loose framework of the Constitution has been pulled more strongly toward executive than legislative control.

Note should also be taken of the other branch, the judicial, as we consider the development of national institutions. At various points in the chapters to follow, the institution of judicial review will be examined in fairly exhaustive fashion. For the present, we will confine ourselves to two simple observations. First, the principle of an independent judiciary is deeply embedded in English and colonial usage. It is, to be sure, a considerable jump from judicial independence to a judiciary coordinate with the other branches of government, but the two concepts are not unrelated, and the coordination was not an innovation of 1787.

Secondly, the analysis of the judiciary from the standpoint of separation of powers emphasizes the courts' role as a part of the political system, not as an institution of a different kind set apart from the mainstream of political processes. From the early days of the nation's political experience, the high Court has had a place in the political scheme of things, both as adjuster of relationships between the other two branches and as a contestant for political power itself. The courts are not to be considered, in other words, special things in a legalistic world of their own. They play a fundamental part in the dynamic adjustment of policy and institutions to new social situations. The nature and justification of that role is, of course, a subject of theoretical interpretation and ideological controversy, as the development of Constitutional law from *Marbury* v. *Madison* to *Baker* v. *Carr* suggests. The important thing to note, however, is the extent to which

---

[37] See Ford, *op. cit.;* Clinton Rossiter, *The American Presidency* (New York: Harcourt, Brace & Co., 1960); Richard Neustadt, *Presidential Power: the Politics of Leadership* (New York: John Wiley & Sons, 1960).

the judicial power is involved in virtually every broad area of political problems that has confronted the American system.

Two implications of the foregoing deserve notice. First, the idea of separation of powers, though basically an instrumental device, has been so prominent in American political life as to make it an object of commitment in its own right. Second, the acceptance of the separation concept as the guiding principle of governmental structure has fostered an extremely complex and intricate approach to the organization of political authority.

This is apparent in the conception and growth of national political institutions. When all is taken into account, the American system can only be described in terms that portray it as an almost incredibly complicated and finely balanced piece of machinery. In part, this can surely be explained as the product of the heterogeneity and complexity of the underlying social structure. But it may also be partly attributable to the counterdemands for separation and integration of power.

It may also be suggested that the commitment to separation has had manifestations beyond those written into the Constitution of the United States. On the national level, for example, it helps explain the ambiguous device of the "independent regulatory commission" and the diffuse character of political party organization and policy. On state and local levels, it has probably contributed much to the popularity of such structures as the plural executive (i.e., multiplication of independent, elective executive officers), administration by boards and commissions, and elective judiciaries. While these are not necessary components of a system of separation, they reflect its fundamental assumptions and some of its political logic. Thus, in a variety of ways, the American experience with separation of powers may be called on to demonstrate the translation of idea into practice.

EXPLICIT LIMITS ON POLITICAL AUTHORITY

Most of what we have said to this point has dealt in some way with the basic tension in political theory between the commitment to authority and the commitment to liberty. The problem of the establishment of constitutional political devices has been the development of a set of structures and guides to political authority that would realize both the control over human will that social living requires and the measure of freedom of will that Americans have customarily thought desirable. The problem is met in its purest and most direct form in the matter of explicit constitutional limits on the exercise of legitimate political power.

The ideological–political background of these limits as they were woven into the fabric of the American Constitution in 1787 and after should be clear from what has been discussed in this and preceding chapters. As we have several times maintained, the idea of an individuality or privacy with certain substantive accoutrements lies at the heart of the liberal tradition. According to this tradition, political authority can only be legitimate when it observes (or is held within) commonly understood bounds. *In its broad form,* this principle seems to have been so pervasive in American ideology as to be very nearly beyond argument. The principle was worked into the constitutional framework in two fashions. In the first place, as we have seen before, many of the institutional arrangements of the federal Constitution were so devised as to provide in themselves restrictions on the exercise of authority. In the second place, the federal Constitution includes in its body and in several amendments a statement of specific limits. It is with this statement that we are here concerned.

A comprehensive treatment of the lineage of the idea of express limits on political authority would take us deeper into history and philosophy than we are able to go here. However, a cursory examination of its background will make possible a better appreciation of the place of these rights in the operation of the constitutional system. These background questions can be divided into two sorts—ideological and philosophical—the first dealing with the social and historical sources of specific limitations on political authority, the second dealing with the principles on which they are established and defended.

With respect to the ideological dimension, we may note first the weight of tradition and previous experience both in England and in America. The battle over constitutional rights in England, of course, had been going on for centuries by the time of adoption of the American Constitution; it had, indeed, not been won by 1787, if it can ever be said that such a battle is won. But along the way, considerable concessions had been wrung from British monarchs guaranteeing rights of special kinds or in limited degree, and these concessions had on occasion been incorporated in the formal documents which have historically come to form the heart of the "unwritten" British constitution. The most important of these are the Magna Charta, the habeas corpus acts, and the Bill of Rights. In each case, these acts did not so much establish limitations as formalize and regularize those which English people already asserted by practice or common law. This practice of formalizing claims to rights in constitutional documents was carried over into American experience, where it was even more actively used and developed to an even higher degree.

The drawing of compacts and fundamental agreements is, as we have seen before, an American practice dating back to the time of earliest colonial settlement. The *Declaration of Independence* itself represents a formal statement of constitutional principle. Seven of the state constitutions adopted in the period between independence and the framing of the federal document included bills of rights embodying formal limitation of governmental authority. The Virginia Bill of Rights of 1776, perhaps the most famous of these, began as follows:

> That all men are by nature equal free and independent, and have certain inherent rights, of which, when they enter into a state of society, they cannot by any compact deprive or divest their posterity; namely, the enjoyment of liberty, with the means of acquiring and possessing property, and pursuing and obtaining happiness and safety.

These bills of rights customarily enumerated at some length restraints on the substance and procedure of governmental action.

Not only did the development of a constitutional bill of rights in America reflect Anglo-Saxon experience, it also reflected the rationalism characteristic of the liberal eighteenth century. Indeed, the very drawing of a constitutional document is an exercise in reason and in a sense a declaration of faith in the reasonability of men. The fact that people would bother seriously to state what kinds of things political authority might not legitimately do suggests their belief that such statements will have at least some effect on political action. That is to say, it assumes that political action is thoughtful action taken in the light of reason and the wishes and needs of fellow men. There is, of course, an element of persuasion as well as an element of commitment in constitution-making. This is clear in the "political" role of the bill of rights idea during the period of adoption of the federal document. But this motive is probably not in itself adequate to explain American constitution-writing in an age when respect for reason ran high.

Thus, the American Constitution guarantees those traditional rights for which Englishmen had fought political authority over a long period and for which the colonists themselves had struggled with British authority. These include free speech, historically an offshoot of the British controversy over free debate in the parliament; free press, previously a subject of controversy in Britain and America; and a variety of procedural protections developed out of British ex-

perience with the arbitrary exercise of political power and the faltering step of British justice in such institutions as the star chamber. To
these, a few distinctly American items were added, one notable extension being freedom of religion, which was still to be realized in
Britain at the time but whose importance in America can probably
be explained on the basis of the religious pluralism of American society. Here again, we might suggest that the condition of the society
is directly reflected in its formal approaches to political power.

The matter of the philosophical roots of liberty is different from
the matter of its ideological roots. Ideology raises questions about how
liberty became a value and what forms that value takes; philosophy
raises questions about the grounds on which liberty is defended as an
attitude, institution, or social commitment.

The philosophical aspect of human freedom has engaged man's attention probably for as long as he has been able to approximate philosophical thinking. Its record is as old as ancient Greece. In major
respects, however, the case for freedom has taken on a distinctive cast
in the modern age, a cast that has as its central element the liberal
theme of individualism. In the formative years of the American political tradition—i.e., in the years when modern liberalism was taking
shape—the theme was influentially stated in such places as the
Vindiciae Contra Tyrannos and the writings of Milton, Hobbes, and
Locke. It is important to realize, however, that the modern case for
liberty is not monolithic. The limitation of political power can be and
has been defended from a variety of philosophical perspectives. At
least four different positions with different implications for politics
have been fundamental in modern political thought.

One of these, the individual–liberal point of view stated by Locke
and embodied in the Declaration of Independence, represents what
we have called the central tradition in American political thought.
This is the tradition that derives absolute individual human rights
from natural law, claiming that there is a sphere of private human
activity indefeasible in all circumstances. It defines rights in terms of
its understanding of the moral stature of the individual human being
and often in terms of his relationship with God. It holds individuals
and their rights to be prior to the civil society and the state, not dependent on social arrangements for their existence but only for their
protection, and, therefore, interprets rights as morally inviolable limits on the permissible operation of political authority. This position is
reflected in the statement of the American Bill of Rights in terms of
absolutes: "Congress shall make *no* law respecting an establishment

of religion," * and so on. The doctrine has commonly been given abstract statement in American constitutional documents like that of the Virginia Bill of Rights quoted above.

A second position, often thought identical with the liberal point of view, is that set out by John Stuart Mill in his famous essay, *On Liberty*.[38] This we will call the utilitarian argument. Basically, the utilitarian point of view defends liberty as useful to some ulterior end, usually the advancement of knowledge. It makes of liberty not so much a good in itself or something to be defended through the abstract invocation of rights, but something whose defense is argued for the sake of something else deemed to be a good. Thus, Mill stated that a society cannot reach truth if it is not permitted the free interplay of ideas through which falsehood can be tested and detected. A modern Platonist might restate this fundamental view of liberty in terms of its utility to the search for an ideal pattern of good or virtue. The central point is that a utilitarian view of liberty embraces it as useful, i.e., instrumental, and not as an ultimate value in itself.

Third, liberty may be defended from the viewpoint of what may be called classic conservatism. This position, as it is found in the ideas of Edmund Burke and the so-called new conservatives in the contemporary United States, is also sometimes mingled with and confused with the doctrines of liberalism. Basically, however, the conservative outlook is a commitment to the defense of social arrangements that embody what Burke called "the spirit of the nation." It is a perspective on politics that sees in the nation a kind of living organism whose identity is bound up to its continuity with past, present, and future. Man takes his nature from his participation in society, and the society's constitution embodies the arrangements discovered through social experience which conduce in the place and circumstance to the sustenance of individual life in the context of the community. If a bill of rights is a part of the settled arrangements through which the society is governed, that bill of rights bears an organic relationship to the society and, therefore, deserves defense. It cannot be severed without harm to the balance of the body and the danger of slow death. Thus, in a society like the English or American where principles of liberty were deeply rooted in the "native political arrangements," a bill of rights is not only a permissible but a vital part of the good society. In France, by contrast, as Burke was at pains to show in his *Reflections*

---

* Author's italics.

[38] Available in many editions. See, e.g., the Everyman ed., *Utilitarianism, Liberty, and Representative Government* (New York: E. P. Dutton & Co., Inc., 1948).

on the Revolution in France, the revolutionaries were attempting to impose a kind of liberty that would have represented a radical departure from the characteristic way of the French nation. This to Burke was a prime example of political illegitimacy.

Fourth, liberty may be defended from a point of view which seems to incorporate elements of both the liberal and the conservative outlooks, but which in its basics represents a departure from each. We have reference to what might be called an organic or societal defense of freedom like that found in the works of Rousseau or Thomas Hill Green.[39] Theirs were philosophical positions that held society to be prior to man and, like conservatism, regarded human development as possible only within the social setting. In contrast to individual-liberalism, they believed human morality to be derived from social relationships rather than from the peculiar individual qualities of human beings. Mill's utilitarian defense of liberty in some sense developed a theoretical bridge between classical individualistic liberalism and the later organic liberalism of Green. For, on the one hand, utility can have a social meaning, and, on the other hand, the organicist can see the institutions of liberty as useful in the quest for individual self-development which they may, like Green, regard as an important consequence of social organization. But the organic interpretation of liberty tends to define it, in effect, in terms of the adjustment of the individual to the needs of society, which, in turn, represented the *real* needs of the individual, as in what Rousseau, for example, called the General Will.

Each of these positions embodies philosophical difficulties. The major problem of the liberal individualist point of view probably lies in its metaphysical basis, a source of difficulty which seems particularly acute in a pragmatically oriented age. In a period accustomed to the demand for verification, the bald assertion of self-evident rights may seem an inadequate basis for a political philosophy, even if the propositions asserted are clearly value propositions. Such assertions may seem to be only mystical appeals to absolute authority. Thus, both the defensibility and the classical content given to natural rights is often brought into question. Furthermore, the individualist doctrine of natural rights is accompanied by a corollary assumption about the reasonability of men. That is to say, rights according to the classical liberal position are rights that reasonable men will understand. Mod-

---

[39] J. J. Rousseau, *The Social Contract,* e.g., in the Everyman edition, trans. G. D. H. Cole (New York: E. P. Dutton & Co., 1950); T. H. Green, *Lectures on the Principles of Political Obligation* (London: Longmans, Green & Co., 1895).

ern psychological and sociological theory has laid new emphasis on irrationality and brought the assumption of rationality under severe question. In the face of the failure of modern man to recognize and respect the rights of others, it may be questioned whether assumptions about the ability and willingness of men to exercise their reason regularly in social relations is a very useful one. Philosophically, the problem would seem to be whether the supposed value assumptions of the liberal position are truly value propositions and, therefore, shielded from the requirements of empirical verification. At the ideological level, the question is whether this liberal defense of individual liberties can be a very effective one in a world in which human rights are often and obviously ignored.

The utilitarian position is likewise open to question. It may in the first place be driven back to ultimate assumptions which are themselves metaphysical in nature. Who is to prove, for example, that truth is the proper ultimate goal of human activity unless the proof is offered in the definition of value itself. Thus, the proposition that man ought to be free because only in freedom he can seek the truth would seem to rest on an ultimate commitment to truth in a sense as metaphysical and perhaps as mystical as the proposition that freedom itself is an absolute good. Further, the utilitarian position would seem inadequate on practical grounds if the end of the person who uses it is to find a convincing basis for the defense of liberty. For it is surely conceivable that at least in the short run the disutility of freedom of expression and action may be as convincingly demonstrable as its utility. If the argument runs to what is useful for securing some ultimate social goal, may it not sometimes be the case that freedom can be shown to be destructive of that goal?

This would seem to be the sense of the clear and present danger doctrine enunciated by Mr. Justice Holmes in the Schenck case and often used by the Supreme Court in testing subsequent civil liberties problems.[40] The clear and present danger doctrine seems to say that liberty is to be honored except in certain situations where it can be shown to be destructive of common social goals like the preservation of peace or stability in society. While this doctrine may be a tool for striking down the arbitrary exercise of authority, it may also be a rationalization for the exercise of that authority at the expense of individual liberty when liberty seems to have bad effects on accepted social goals and values. In short, the argument that defends liberty

---

[40] *Schenck v. United States*, 249 U.S. 47 (1919).

from the point of view that it is useful risks the counterdemonstration that freedom is not useful at all. An assertion, on the other hand, that freedom will *always* be found to be useful because it is somehow ultimate is merely a disguised return to the absolutism of the doctrine of natural rights.

The difficulties of the conservative and societal–organic positions as defenses of individual human rights would seem to lie in their inherent relativism and community bias. The conservative doctrine lays individual rights beyond the reach of those whose societies have not honored them. It suggests that whatever has been must be right because it has been, and that changes in the social condition, even if they are changes in the direction of greater individual freedom, can be achieved only by the grinding process of the evolution of justice in human relationships. This position would make fact and value identical—a position of small comfort to those who seek amelioration of their conditions in the short run of an individual life. Both these theories, furthermore, tend to read individual life into terms of the life of the society and redefine freedom as a social rather than an individual good. From this perspective, the individual may be asked to sacrifice for the welfare of the larger whole, may indeed in Rousseau's terms be "forced to be free." For those who must live their lives as individuals as well as for those who see in the individual the basic point of reference for human value, such a definition of freedom may seem a cruel joke.

The interesting thing is the mode in which these diverse basic political philosophies are brought to the defense of a common set of restrictions on political authority. That they are would seem to be a token of the hegemony of the fundamental liberal point of view in modern political thought. Individual liberty has been called the theme of the modern age. It has provided a standard of expectation to which ideologies and systems of political philosophy have been forced to pay heed. Thus, one finds across a broad spectrum of recent political ideas concern for limitations on the power of the state. One of the major aspects of importance in the diversity of views about the nature of liberty is that each point of view has somewhat different consequences when it is used in the judgment of specific political acts. Some of these consequences will be reviewed briefly in the paragraphs to follow.

The substance of American constitutional liberty has been suggested above. A reading of the American Constitution and of state constitutions generally indicates those types of activity which constitutional restriction has attempted to place in some special position vis-a-vis the exercise of authority. There is among these charters of liberty a striking degree of consonance; the American constitutions have drawn on a common stock of symbols to indicate those types of individual and social activity which are to be regarded in the exercise of authority as falling into specially protected categories. We will not attempt here to catalog these rights or discuss them in terms of such familiar categories as "substantive" and "procedural." Such an effort would take us deeper into particular information than we need to go. More important for our purposes than identification of the specific symbols written into American constitutionalism is consideration of the operative political role of these symbols in the dynamics of government. Whatever their source, American constitutional commitments to the limitation of power are important as they have conditioned the operation of political authority in the process of social problem-solving. This is a sphere where the relationship of ideas and practice has clearly been of great importance.

The key considerations are twofold, involving the ways constitutional limits get worked into the genuinely operational principles of a nation and the ways they influence social behavior once there. The first matter takes us back to our concept of constitution as a codification of the culture which acts as a generalized set of cues to acceptable public activity. We have spoken of the Constitution as a set of commitments, as a set of rules established to guide national political life. Our tradition is such that the very establishment of these rules, i.e., placing them in constitutional status, assures them a place in the process of making social decisions. The quality and quantity of their role, however, is dependent on at least three further things: the way and extent in which they "live" in the social consensus, in the context of opinion and ideology within which social decisions are made; the operation of the institutions of decision-making; and the character of the social problems with which the social dynamic is confronted. To put it in more concrete terms, the effect of constitutional liberty depends on the interaction of social problems (cold war threats, threats of internal subversion, threats to common moral standards), the strength of the community's commitment to established, traditional norms (free speech, free worship, due process of law), and the propensities of the active agencies of social authority (legislatures, executives, courts, police). All these forces are variable, their effects problematic. Thus, when individual liberty is claimed as a defense for seemingly deviant or threatening activity and ideas, a weighing process (not necessarily a conscious one) is triggered in the political system. The question becomes whether the society through its authoritative institutions is prepared in the name of freedom to risk some measure of security, stability, and freedom. It is worth noting that these "situations" become more notable with the increase of social scale—with, that is, the sensitization of society that comes about as the scope and intensity of interactions expands.

The fundamental political problems involved in the protection of individual rights can be illustrated briefly through consideration of the interpretations given free religion and speech over the past few years. The first important case involving the meaning of religious freedom, for example, raised the question whether the practice of polygamous marriage among the Mormons in the Utah territory was protected from Congressional interference by the First Amendment. Mormons claimed that this practice was dictated by their religious doctrine and was, therefore, beyond the legitimate power of Congress to control. In the case *Reynolds* v. *United States,* the Supreme Court disagreed, holding that the First Amendment protected belief, not practice, and that practice contrary to the commonly established moral principles of the community, therefore, lay within the police powers of government and fell outside the scope of First Amendment protection.[41] A series of interesting tests of the meaning of religious freedom followed in the 1930's, growing out of the religious style of the Jehovah's Witnesses sect. This sect, every member of which is regarded as a minister of the Gospel, requires extraordinary militance of its adherents in the proselytization of new members and the propagation of its doctrines. Because of their militance and hostility to organized religions and some of the other accepted institutions of the American community, the activities of the Witnesses have repeatedly raised questions about the protection afforded religious activity through the First Amendment. The Supreme Court, for example, has considered questions about the extent to which the Jehovah's Witnesses are subject on solicitation and sale of religious pamphlets to taxes ordinarily levied on peddlers,[42] whether so-called "green river ordinances" are applicable to religious groups,[43] whether Witnesses must pay to hold parades,[44] are subject to the operation of child labor laws in using youngsters to distribute pamphlet literature,[45] and whether in a vari-

---

[41] *Reynolds* v. *United States,* 98 U.S. 145 (1879).
[42] *Cantwell* v. *Connecticut,* 310 U.S. 296 (1940); *Jones* v. *Opelika,* 319 U.S. 1903 (1943).
[43] *Lovell* v. *Griffin,* 309 U.S. 444 (1938).
[44] *Cox* v. *New Hampshire,* 312 U.S. 569 (1941).
[45] *Prince* v. *Massachusetts,* 321 U.S. 158 (1944).

ety of ways their religious activities lay beyond ordinary policy powers designed to prevent the disturbing of the peace.[46]

In seeking an answer to these questions, the Supreme Court has endeavored with its characteristic mixture of pragmatism and rationalism to find some defensible line between those types of activities that could safely be protected as freedom of religion under the First Amendment and those activities which so violate established policy and community standards as to make it infeasible to accord them First Amendment protection. From the political point of view, it is apparently impossible to maintain the position that *any* kind of behavior justified as religious in nature deserves the protection of constitutional limitations. An extreme case is found in the ritualistic handling of snakes, which has been held by courts to be beyond the sphere of First Amendment protection. In the Jehovah's Witnesses situations mentioned above, the Court has generally leaned toward the side of permissiveness. It has held, for example, that Witnesses ministers may not be prohibited from their door-to-door activities by peddlers' laws nor required to purchase a peddlers' license, even when they are dependent on the sale of Bibles and tracts for their livelihoods.[47] It has held that the playing on public streets of phonograph records even of a somewhat inflammatory nature could not be prohibited as a breach of the peace.[48] On the other hand, the Court has upheld municipal authorities in attempts to apply child labor laws to the distribution of Witnesses pamphlets and in levying fees for Witnesses religious processions on public streets.[49]

The nature of the problem is again illustrated by a famous pair of cases heard by the Supreme Court on the question whether children in the public school could be required to salute the American flag as a part of the day's regular school exercises. A number of districts have had such requirements, in some cases given force by the expulsion from school of a refusing child and subsequent prosecution of the parent on truancy charges. The practice of saluting the flag runs contrary to the Witnesses doctrine prohibiting idolatry. In the first case to come before the Supreme Court on this issue, the Court held that the requirement was not an unreasonable abridgement of religion.[50] This freedom, it said, is not absolute, and the flag salute requirement,

---

[46] E.g., *Kovacs* v. *Cooper,* 336 U.S. 77 (1949).

[47] *Murdock* v. *Pennsylvania,* 319 U.S. 105 (1943).

[48] *Cantwell* v. *Connecticut,* 310 U.S. 296 (1940); but cf. *Kovacs* v. *Cooper,* 336 U.S. 77 (1949).

[49] *Prince* v. *Massachusetts,* 321 U.S. 158 (1944).

[50] *Minersville School District* v. *Gobitis,* 310 U.S. 586 (1940).

indeed, may contribute to national unity, a justifiable community end. The Court held, therefore, that the matter was one of educational and public policy better left to legislative bodies for decision. Three years after this opinion was announced, however, the Court reversed itself in the case, *West Virginia Board of Education* v. *Barnette.*[51] In the later case, the Court suggested that the compulsory flag salute abridges freedom of conscience for those whose religious commitments preclude such an exercise. Mr. Justice Jackson's opinion nearly but not quite runs to the extent of insisting on freedom of religion as an absolute kind of protection. "Whether the First Amendment to the Constitution will permit officials to order observance of ritual of this nature does not depend upon whether as a voluntary exercise we would think it to be good, bad or merely innocuous." [52] The opinion does not, however, go so far as to suggest that any religious exercise would be protected nor any denial of public obligation countenanced because of First Amendment claims. It argues the fundamentally utilitarian point of view that freedom of conscience is conducive to strength and not destructive of it. It denies that strength can or must be gained by compelling participation in patriotic rituals, and it sets forth a broad basis for the interpretation of the First Amendment as a protective commitment: "If there is any fixed star in our constitutional constellation, it is that no official, high or petty, can prescribe what shall be orthodox in politics, nationalism, religion, or other matters of opinion or force citizens to confess by word or act their faith therein. If there are any circumstances which permit an exception, they do not now occur to us." [53]

Thus, in handling these problems, the Supreme Court has felt its way case by case toward a socially acceptable definition of free religion suitable to a variety of times and circumstances. It cannot be doubted that as times and circumstances change, that definition too will change. Society will continue to feel impelled, perhaps increasingly, to protect itself from the odd, the deviant, the seemingly dangerous. And social policy will doubtless be developed accordingly. This is not to say, of course, that such commitments as the abstract constitutional doctrines of freedom are meaningless. They play the role of an integral variable that figures into the solution of public problems in this field. The point would seem to be, however, that public policy is settled

---

[51] 319 U.S. 624 (1943).

[52] *Idem,* at 634

[53] *Idem,* at 642.

(though not permanently fixed) in the interaction of abstract symbols, perceived community needs, and situational constraints.

Similar problems arise out of the social–political interpretation of other restrictions on governmental activity. Probably the most dramatic and revealing problems of liberty faced by the American community have been those growing out of the question whether and to what extent the speech clause of the First Amendment protects political activities contrary to the general disposition of the American people. Questions of this kind first began to confront the institutions of public authority in a persistent and major way during the First World War, when community concern with dangers from the radical left were heightened by international tension. The case that set much of the tone for later consideration of this problem grew out of an alleged violation of the Espionage Act of 1917, *Schenck* v. *United States*.[54] The immediate problem in the Schenck case was whether First Amendment restrictions protected in a wartime situation those utterances—in this case leaflets advocating refusal to cooperate in conscription for military service—that might endanger the security and stability of the community. The Court's answer was no. Speaking through Mr. Justice Holmes, the Court held these rights to be not absolute but subject to modification in terms of the situational needs of the community. In this case, Holmes enunciated the influential clear and present danger doctrine, which as nearly as anything has provided the nation in subsequent years with the rule by which it has attempted to distinguish protected from nonprotected kinds of activities. The clear and present danger doctrine suggested, in effect, that if a relationship could be shown between words and an imminent danger to the community, those words were drawn out from under the protection of the First Amendment. The test required the courts to judge whether the dangers created by the words were of sufficient "proximity and degree" to merit punishment of their author.

The difficulties of drawing a line between permissible and nonpermissible freedom may be illustrated by brief reference to selected later decisions of the Court in the speech area. A major countertest to that offered by Holmes in the Schenck case was developed in the case, *Gitlow* v. *New York*, in a holding to which Holmes dissented.[55] The Gitlow case again involved the circulation of radical literature, this time allegedly in violation of the New York Criminal Anarchy Act of 1902. In this case, the Court abandoned the clear and present

---

[54] *Schenck* v. *United States*, 249 U.S. 47 (1919).
[55] *Gitlow* v. *New York*, 268 U.S. 652 (1925).

danger test in favor of what has since been labeled a "bad tendency test." As the Court saw it, a showing of imminent danger was not required to draw speech out from under the First Amendment protection. The question rather was the looser one whether the speech in question had a *tendency* to create harm which legislative bodies had the power to prevent. The Court said:

A single revolutionary spark may kindle a fire that, smouldering for a time, may burst into a sweeping and destructive conflagration. It cannot be said that the state is acting arbitrarily or unreasonably when in the exercise of its judgment as to the measures necessary to protect the public peace and safety, it seeks to extinguish the spark without waiting until it has enkindled the flame or blazed into the conflagration. It cannot reasonably be required to defer the adoption of measures for its own peace and safety until the revolutionary utterances lead to actual disturbances of the public peace or imminent and immediate danger of its own destruction; but it may, in the exercise of its judgment, suppress the threatened danger in its incipiency.[56]

In subsequent litigation, the Court has tended to move between the somewhat more stringent clear and present danger doctrine and the somewhat looser bad tendency test. Neither of these has seemed to be fully satisfactory in the resolution of the conflict between the social need for order and the social commitment to liberty, and in recent years, of course, the incidence of problems has been heightened by a renewal of international tensions and by domestic fears of subversion and espionage growing out of the situation of the cold war. Thus, in the Dennis case, involving prosecution under the Smith Act of top echelon Communist party leaders, the Court was badly split, but the controlling opinion leaned toward a bad tendency rule:

Obviously, the words [clear and present danger] cannot mean that before the Government may act, it must wait until the *putsch* is about to be executed, the plans have been laid and the signal is awaited. If Government is aware that a group aiming at its overthrow is attempting to indoctrinate its members and to commit them to a course whereby they will strike when the leaders feel the circumstances permit, action by the Government is required. The argument that there is no need for Government to concern itself, for Government is strong, it possesses ample powers to put down a rebellion, it may defeat the revolution with ease needs no answer. For that is not the question. Certainly an attempt to overthrow the Government by force, even though doomed from the outset because of inadequate numbers or power of the revolutionists, is a sufficient evil for Congress to prevent.

---
[56] *Idem,* at 669.

The damage which such attempts create both physically and politically to a nation makes it impossible to measure the validity in terms of the probability of success, or the immediacy of a successful attempt. In the instant case the trial judge charged the jury that they could not convict unless they found that petitioners intended to overthrow the Government "as speedily as circumstances would permit." This does not mean, and could not properly mean, that they would not strike until there was certainty of success. What was meant was that the revolutionists would strike when they thought the time was ripe. We must therefore reject the contention that success or probability of success is the criterion.

* * * *

Chief Judge Learned Hand, writing for the majority below, interpreted the phrase as follows: "In each case [courts] must ask whether the gravity of the 'evil,' discounted by its improbability, justifies such invasion of free speech as is necessary to avoid the danger. . . ." We adopt this statement of the rule.[57]

The test of imminence seems to have given way here to a test of probability. In the interim since Dennis, the line between permissible and impermissible has several times been tested, often with somewhat different results.

What, in sum, can be said about the role of the idea of liberty in the American political system? In this chapter, we have treated liberty —i.e., the limitation in principle of political authority—as one among a number of commitments to ideas that have guided American political practice. The sources of this commitment and the meanings it can assume in a philosophical sense have been discussed above. Three questions, however, merit further discussion: In what sense is this commitment a commitment? How is it "applied" in political life? With what results?

The first of these questions raises those acute problems of methodology with which the entire study of the role of ideas in politics is plagued. The quality and depth of penetration of an idea as well as its influence on action are difficult to assay, particularly when one deals with historically remote periods. At best, one must be content with generalizations of a low degree of confidence, and much must be left to feel and impression. Given these qualifications, we will venture two very general propositions that experience seems to support. One is that the American commitment to liberty through limitation of authority has been a deeply embedded ideological element in the American culture. Note that we deal with it as a cultural char-

---
[57] *Dennis v. United States*, 341 U.S. 494, 509–10 (1951).

acteristic, not as a consensual item of individual belief. That is to say, while liberty has doubtless been an object of very widespread individual belief, it has been sustained, in addition, through habitual usage, institutional "concretization," and societal inertia. As evidence of the supportability of this proposition, we will be content to cite the staying power of the symbols of liberty and their persistent use in the rhetoric of public policy. The second proposition is that the commitment to liberty is a commitment in general, not in particular. The American society, in other words, has been dedicated to liberty in broad and undefined senses rather than in specific terms applicable to specific situations. This notion is supported by recent empirical research on the meaning of American values.[58] Out of this situation grows the flexibility that has been permitted to authoritative and nonauthoritative applications of "liberty" in periods of high social tension.

In respect to the how question, we will content ourselves with one vital observation. The application of civil liberties standards to public policy should be seen as an aspect of the entire interplay of forces in the political process. The form this process takes and the character of the outcome often leads us to an inordinate and deceptive emphasis on the judicial role in the resolution of civil liberties disputes. Two things should be noted in this connection. One is that the courts' proceedings and decisions are not isolated acts taken on their own volition. They are, on the contrary, acts stimulated by the conflicting demands and activities of private individuals, groups, and political authorities, set against a background of policy decisions by legislative and executive institutions. Second, it is tempting to fall into the easy conclusion that courts (particularly the Supreme Court) have the last word on these problems and are, therefore, in the position of "sovereign" authorities. But few of the problems in this sphere are ever finally resolved—for most of them there is no last word. The courts, along with the other federal, state, local, and private participants in the political process, are constantly seeking a line between the permissible and the impermissible in the face of constantly shifting social situations. Hence, the entire field should be seen in terms of a broad range of interactions rather than as a specialized single institutional function. Nonetheless, it remains true that the word of

---

[58] Raymond W. Mack, "Do We Really Believe in the Bill of Rights?" *Social Problems,* Vol. III (April, 1956), pp. 264–69; James W. Prothro and Charles M. Griggs, "Fundamental Principles of Democracy: Bases of Agreement and Disagreement," *Journal of Politics,* Vol. XXII (May, 1960), pp. 276–94.

the court is probably the best evidence we have of the authoritative interpretation of liberty at any given time.

The third question—what have been the results of application of the liberty idea to policy—requires a more lengthy answer, but again we shall not attempt to give it comprehensive treatment. We shall return to the actions of the court to illustrate in a more systematic way the results of the social processes mentioned in the preceding paragraph.

The fundamental question, as we have suggested several times previously, is how the tension between liberty and authority can be resolved in a given social context. Theoretically, attempts to answer this question may be ranged along a continuum from resolution in favor of absolute liberty to resolution in favor of absolute authority. The answers of history, however, may conveniently be sorted into a few categories; in the paragraphs to follow we shall discuss two major types of answers and two subtypes of each, all familiar in commentaries on the law and practice of the First Amendment.

One broad category includes those answers that would accord the Constitutional protections of freedom, particularly the First Amendment protections, a preferred position, a status beyond that of other Constitutional provisions, a position that would insulate First Amendment-protected types of activity from the normal processes of social problem-solving. This preferred position, on the one hand, is sometimes the outgrowth of the view that First Amendment freedoms must be held absolute, that either on natural law or on utility grounds, speech, religion, and others must be accorded full free play regardless of the consequences for the society. The leading adherent of such a view in recent years has been Mr. Justice Black. In the case, *Carlson v. Landon,* for example, Black wrote, "I further believe that the First Amendment grants an absolute right to believe in any governmental system, discuss all governmental affairs, and argue for desired changes in the existing order." [59] In the Wilkinson and Braden cases, decided in 1961, Black again stated the absolute position:

This country was not built by men who were afraid and it cannot be preserved by such men. Our Constitution, in unequivocal terms, gives the right to each of us to say what we think without fear of the power of the government. That principle has served us so well for so long that I cannot believe it necessary to allow any governmental group to reject it in order to preserve its own existence. . . . For I believe that true Americanism is to be protected not by committees that persecute un-

---

[59] 342 U.S. 524, 555 (1952), in dissent.

orthodox minorities, but by strict adherence to basic principles of freedom that are responsible for this Nation's greatness. Those principles are embodied for all who care to see in our Bill of Rights. They were put there for the specific purpose of preventing just the sort of governmental suppression of criticism that the majority upholds here. Their ineffectiveness to that end stems, not from any lack of precision in the statement of the principles, but from the refusal of the majority to apply those principles as precisely stated. For the principles of the First Amendment are stated in precise and mandatory terms and unless they are applied in those terms, the freedoms of religion, speech, press, assembly and petition will have no effective protection. Where these freedoms are left to depend upon a balance to be struck by this Court in each particular case, liberty cannot survive. For under such a rule, there are no constitutional rights that cannot be "balanced" away.[60]

This category would also include, on the other hand, the position of those who would accord an unusual but not absolute place to First Amendment rights and whose rule of discrimination is such that it is likely to bring them down on the side of severe limitations on state authority. In the resolution of social conflict over dangers in the exercise of individual freedom, they would feel that a unique standing is to be accorded the particular prescriptions found in the First Amendment. This standing inhibits any exercise of social power that cuts across these particular areas of freedom except in the most extraordinary circumstances. In the case, *Thomas* v. *Collins,* for example, Mr. Justice Rutledge wrote as follows: "The case confronts us again with the duty our system places on this Court to say where the individual's freedom ends and the state's power begins. Choice on that border, now as always delicate, is perhaps more so where the usual presumption supporting legislation is balanced by the preferred place given in our scheme to the great, the indispensable democratic freedoms secured by the First Amendment." [61]

A second major set of answers grows out of what is often called the balance of interests doctrine. It has gained increasing favor and frequent restatement from some members of the Court in very recent years, but it would also seem to subsume the classic clear and present danger position. From this point of view, the conflict of individual liberty and social authority is to be resolved by a process of weighing individual needs on the one hand and social needs on the other. Enunciating the balance of interests doctrine in the Barenblatt case, Mr. Justice Harlan wrote: "Where First Amendment rights are

---

[60] *Wilkinson* v. *United States,* 365 U.S. 399, 422–23 (1961).
[61] 323 U.S. 516, 529–30 (1945).

asserted to bar governmental interrogation, resolution of the issue always involves a balancing by the courts of the competing private and public interests at stake in the particular circumstances shown." [62] Only by indirection do cases decided according to this doctrine indicate how or on what principles public and private interests are to be compared. An examination of the cases suggests that those who would use the doctrine are relatively permissive of the exercise of governmental authority. In the Barenblatt case previously quoted, for example, the majority of the Court, speaking through Mr. Justice Harlan, held Barenblatt legitimately required to answer questions about his political beliefs and affiliations, despite his claims of First Amendment protection. Similar conclusions were reached in the Wilkinson and Braden cases, also on questions involving the right of investigating committees to compel testimony.[63]

A question that arises from a balance of interests doctrine but is also pertinent to the general matter of institutional resolution of these conflicts over the scope of individual liberty is the problem of identification of the appropriate governmental vehicle to determine the way the balance must swing. The Harlan opinion quoted above emphasizes the role of the courts in this process. This position might be called "judicial activism," seeing courts as independent participants in the political decision-making process. From an alternative point of view, however, the role of the court is seen as more appropriately limited to the consideration of the procedures by which other political institutions have undertaken the process of balancing. This is the posture often adopted by Mr. Justice Frankfurter. It would accord to the legislative and executive bodies, particularly the legislative, the active decision-making power to determine whether public or private interests should prevail. Not the balancing doctrine but the process of its application differs if this procedure is followed.

It has been suggested in this section that there are several types of theoretical questions important to consideration of the limiting effect of constitutionalism on political power. Thus, the American Constitution provides a codification of basic values that are the subject of a consensus sufficiently broad to give them fundamental weight in the resolution of constitutional relationships. These limits raise normative problems about their extent and defensibility, and empirical problems about the process and content of their impact on

---

[62] *Barenblatt* v. *United States*, 360 U.S. 109, 126 (1959).

[63] On the balancing doctrine see Mr. Justice Black's caustic comments in Wilkinson at 420–21.

politics as a dynamic problem-solving system. We are thus suggesting that a complete political theory must include consideration not only of the abstract prescription of limitations but also of the operation of these prescriptions as ideological forces in the solution of human problems. From the first standpoint, the central questions have to do with the abstract logic and implications of prescriptions for the operation of political institutions. From the second point of view, the central problem is the societal interpretation of prescriptions into dynamic operating rules which deal with the difficult problem of conflicts between public and private interest. American political history suggests (1) that the ideology of liberty is both persistent and generalized, and (2) that the relationship between rights and authority will be particularly problematical in periods of national tension. This history has provided a protracted period of exploration for a satisfactory rule; the lesson of this exploration seems to be that solution lies in a pragmatic and sustained process rather than in an abstract, permanent "resolution." That is to say, political institutions have apparently dealt with rights as variable factors to be weighed in a framework of consideration of the entire range of political and social problems of an age. Thus, if one is to ask what liberty is from an existential rather than a normative view, the answer apparently must be that liberty is a process of seeking carried on in the light of some abstract commitments continually redefined in terms of given social circumstances.

This chapter has attempted to lay the basis for consideration of the Constitution of the United States from two points of view; first, from the standpoint of the sources and character of the prescriptions the Constitution has embodied; second, from the standpoint of the Constitution's operational relationship to political processes. These subjects, very much intertwined, illustrate the dual central concerns of political theory as a scholarly venture. The first mentioned set of concerns is normative in character, and the subjects are the kinds with which students of political theory have customarily been concerned—analysis of systems of ideas, intellectual history, and moral philosophy. The second kind of question has become increasingly of explicit interest to political theorists as efforts have mounted to provide a systematic, theoretical basis for the scientific examination of political processes. As it relates to the study of the Constitution, this kind of theory eschews both moral considerations and history for its own sake, and concerns itself with models of analysis and with ideas as variables. It seems important while treating the political theory of the Constitution to distinguish these two senses in which the term may be used and to call attention to the close interrelationship between the two. Whatever the possibilities, impossibilities, probabilities, improbabilities of a scientific political science, the human enterprise of living with a constitution certainly involves the dual activities of evaluation and prediction from experience.

V

THE SCOPE OF POWER:
THE FEDERALIST INTERPRETATION

In the preceding chapter, we examined in some detail a set of basic commitments codified in the American Constitution. These commitments formed an enduring framework for American government, but their application to specific situations and problems has required much elaboration of means. The subsequent development of the American political system has been largely a process of shaping institutions and policies within the shell provided by the original constitutional process.

What we have suggested to this point is that the American Constitution comprises a fundamental set of rules for the authoritative handling of social problems. These rules represent the convergence of social and political experience and the ideas of the culture in the vacuum of power left by the breakdown of established political relationships. While the constitutional process has been treated in general terms as a process of establishing ends, it will be readily recognized that these ends are not all of the same order. The Constitution, on the contrary, is an ordering of various levels of ends, a few of them ultimate but most instrumental and, therefore, in themselves means for the realization of ulterior goals. We have suggested, for example, that the ultimate goals of political organization in our culture are authority and liberty; the establishment of an executive and legislative, then, is a means to the assertion of authority, and their separation by function and the explicit statement of limitations on the scope of political authority are instrumental to the maintenance of liberty.

We have been working to this point with two models—a model of the process of building political arrangements and a model of the working of political arrangements. The first contributes to the second an ordered or hierarchical set of ends and a set of structures through which those ends, proximate and ultimate, are sought. These seem to assume the status of givens, but since we wish the working model as well as the building model to be a dynamic explanation, i.e., an explanation capable of accounting for change, we must make it capable of accommodating social change in the broadest sense. The American Constitution required amplification not simply because it was stated in general terms, but also because as a dynamic instrument it has reflected the change of the social context in which it works. The givens of end and structure themselves are givens only in a limited sense, for they are modified by the feedback of new ideas and attitudes. Thus, the movement of the social structure triggers the system, excites the explication of means, and requires the redefinition of the so-called givens.

Historically, this process of amplification of means and revision of ends in the American nation was first undertaken in terms of the theoretical–ideological positions of the Federalists and the Jeffersonians. We shall be concerned here not with recounting the political history of the process but with considering successively the two political ideologies in terms of the demands they made on the constitutional framework and the social forces those demands reflected. We refer to them as theoretical–ideological positions because, like so much of American political thought, each represents not simply the cohesive ideas of a political philosopher or even the cohesive ideas of a political practitioner. Each found expression both in the writings of articulate practitioner–theoreticians of various shadings and in the practice of politics during the early period of the Constitution. Each has, furthermore, contributed heavily to the American ideology and, therefore, to the enduring qualities of the American political culture.

Though the term Federalist has meant many things, we are using it here to characterize a position reflected in the Washington and Adams administrations and in the party called "Federalist," and made explicit in the writings and political activities of Alexander Hamilton and John Adams. This chapter will be concerned principally with the Hamiltonian version of politics and briefly with the contributions of Adams and of the Federalist jurisprudence of John Marshall.

THE CONTRIBUTIONS OF ALEXANDER HAMILTON

No man maintains perfect consistency over the span of a long life or even a short one. Alexander Hamilton has been particularly subject to charges of inconsistency, perhaps because his political involvement reflected the tension between theoretician and practitioner, and because his writings on politics spanned the diverse eras from pre-Revolution to post-Constitution. There was without doubt some shift in Hamilton's views between his Revolutionary tracts written at seventeen and the state papers of his maturity, prepared when he was Washington's prime lieutenant and Secretary of the Treasury. In the circumstances, however, these changes are probably easy to overestimate, and it may be suggested that the shifts were more in emphasis than in position. Our principal concern here is with the ideas of the Hamilton of the post-Constitutional period, which comprise an integral though not very philosophical statement on the means of political organization.

Hamilton has often been pictured by his detractors as a conservative without faith in human nature and without respect for the political claims of the great body of the people.[1] This view of the basics of Hamilton's political ideas seems oversimplified and inadequate. Certainly, his earlier Revolutionary papers professed a strong adherence to the principles of rights and consent. But even in the later reaches of his career, Hamilton did not disagree significantly with those basic conceptions of human nature and politics that we have described as fundamental to the American ideological commitment. We are suggesting that Hamilton was at bottom a liberal in the broad sense of the term, that in the last analysis he saw human society in terms of the interaction of relatively equal individuals, each with claims for participation in and protection by the state. There was, of course, a decided difference in emphasis between the Hamilton and Jefferson estimates of human nature. This difference however, was not so great as to carry Hamilton outside the liberal tradition.[2]

Though, in his controversy with Seabury, Hamilton explicitly rejected and attacked Hobbes, it does not seem unfair to suggest that the position he himself adopted is not far from that of Hobbes, if Hobbes is seen as a leading figure in the shaping of the liberal tradition. Like Hobbes, Hamilton emphasized the self-interested side of human nature, stressing those factors in the makeup of man that render social life more difficult rather than easier. Hobbes and Hamilton both seemed to adopt the posture of orthodox Christianity, with its emphasis on man's potential for sin rather than on his potential

---

[1] See, e.g., Claude G. Bowers, *Jefferson and Hamilton: the Struggle for Democracy in America* (Boston and New York: Houghton Mifflin Co., 1953).

[2] Cf. Broadus Mitchell, *Heritage from Hamilton* (New York: Columbia University Press, 1957); also Louis Hacker, *Alexander Hamilton in the American Tradition* (New York: McGraw-Hill Book Co., Inc., 1957). While Hacker labels Hamilton a "conservative," his interpretation is not dissimilar to the one offered here.

for sociability. Both, too, saw man as the integral building block in social relationships and derived the state from his consent. While liberalism more than alternative theories emphasizes the rationality in man's makeup, so long as liberalism is a political theory, i.e., treats social relationships in terms of the need for the application of authoritative power, it professes a limited belief in man's reasonability. Hamilton's and Hobbes' skepticism was greater than that of Jefferson and Locke, but in neither case so great as to deny man the fundamental role in arranging the sociopolitical conditions for his existence.

Their relative skepticism about human nature had its corollaries in political theory. It was felt in emphasis on power rather than on limitation of power. Hamilton's political ideas seem to revolve around questions of the sort "Is political power adequate to the circumstances with which it must deal?" and "How can adequate political power be effectively institutionalized?" It is partly because of this emphasis that Hamilton seems somewhat ahead of his time, for he asked questions that remain central for a world that has experienced increasing complexity and steadily growing demands on political authority.[3]

Thus, Hamilton's ideas may best be described as belief in the need for strong organs of authority balanced by a genuine liberal commitment to consent. His writings are such as to make the authority factor somewhat more prominent than the popular control factor. A man of action, Hamilton wrote not so much in abstractions as in terms of political, social, and economic problems to which answers had to be sought through the application of the authority of the state.

The balance he sought between liberty and authority is suggested by the following passage from one of his speeches in the New York Convention of 1788 on the adoption of the federal Constitution:

Sir, the general sense of the people will regulate the conduct of their representatives. I admit that there are exceptions to this rule. There are certain conjunctures where it may be necessary and proper to disregard the opinions which the majority of the people have formed; but, in the general course of things, the popular views, and even prejudices, will direct the actions of the rulers.

All governments, even the most despotic, depend, in a great degree, on opinion. In free republics, it is most peculiarly the case. In these, the will of the people makes the essential principle of the government, and the laws which control the community, receive their tone and spirit from the public wishes. It is the fortunate situation of our country, that the minds of the people are exceedingly enlightened and refined. Here, then,

---

[3] Cf. Mitchell, *op. cit.*

we may expect the laws to be proportionately agreeable to the standard of a perfect policy, and the wisdom of public measures to consist with the most intimate conformity between the views of the representative and his constituent.[4]

In the light of such commitments as this, it would be a mistake not to recognize Hamilton's basic sympathy with the authority of popular consensus. At the same time, it is apparent in his writings that he feared the power of demagogues in the classic sense, i.e., the power of those who are able to manipulate the mass of people and turn it against the people and to their own particular uses. This fear was probably heightened by Hamilton's observations of the success of totalitarian democracy in the French Revolution. The balance factor is again suggested in Washington's speech to Congress delivered in 1796 and said to have been drafted by Hamilton: "No plan of governing is well founded, which does not regard man as a compound of selfish and virtuous passions. To expect him to be wholly guided by the latter, would be as great an error as to suppose him wholly destitute of them."[5]

Hamilton's specific attitudes toward the nature and needs of political power, reflecting this general orientation, were directed toward the many policy problems and action situations in which he found himself in the pre- and post-Constitutional periods. Since his activities and interests ranged widely, they embodied a great variety of political stimuli. In terms of his own interests, of the clarity with which he expressed himself, of the problems on which his ideas were tested in action, and of his impact on American political ideas and institutions, three categories of political problems seem particularly worthy of attention. These are: first, the distribution of political power between the whole and the parts, the nation and the states; second, the problem of the nature and strength of the executive component in government; third, the appropriateness and character of governmental economic programs. On all these subjects, Hamilton stated an articulate point of view, theoretically coherent and of great importance for the American perspective.

National Power

Nothing is so clearly the outgrowth of fundamental Hamiltonian ideas on government as his attitude on the distribution of power

---

[4] Alexander Hamilton, *The Works of Alexander Hamilton,* ed. John C. Hamilton (New York: Charles S. Francis Co., 1851), Vol. II, p. 438.

[5] *Ibid.,* Vol. VII, p. 614. The comment occurs in the context of a discussion of rates of pay for public officials.

within the federal system. It has been suggested that Hamilton could be an ardent nationalist, because his origins were foreign and he therefore had no attachment of long standing to a specific part of the American nation. In abstract terms, perhaps one's ability to understand the claim to political power of a given area depends on whether or not he is able to see that area as a community. Hamilton was, like Paine, to some extent a citizen of the entire American nation. While others saw community in localistic terms, the entire nation was his community. Out of this broader point of view came Hamilton's ability to argue persistently and effectively for the nationalization of political power.[6]

But these genetic considerations are peripheral to the central point that over a long period of time Hamilton was an articulate and ardent advocate of a national point of view. His role in the series of events leading to the Philadelphia Convention is well known, as are the line of attack he took on political problems at the Convention and his contribution to the adoption of the new framework of government. As early as 1778, he was arguing for the provision of adequate powers to make the Continental Congress a real organ of national authority, and his role as Secretary of the Treasury and adviser to Washington focused very largely on efforts to extend the scope of the national government and provide it the equipment by which it could assert its claims to power.

Hamilton's preference for firm national power grew directly out of his general ideas about the need for adequate power in the political society. The fundamental question is whether government has the means to do what is expected of it—settle social conflicts and distribute resources within a given geographic sphere. A confederal system would fractionalize power and leave the national community without means for pursuing its common ends. Such a government is, indeed, by logic worse than none at all, for its very existence prompts the translation of political needs into national terms without providing instruments at that level through which those needs can be met. Thus, governments like those of the Continental Congresses and the Articles create more expectations than they can satisfy. While a unitary national power would be preferable to the federalistic arrangement of the Constitution of 1787, that Constitution did provide both an expansible framework for the development of effective national govern-

---

[6] Mitchell, *op. cit.*, pp. 7–8, suggests that his settlement in New York also made it possible for him to adopt a "continentalist" perspective.

ment and a set of working tools in the immediate situation. The constitutional arrangement was, furthermore, as much a modification in the direction of union as could reasonably be expected given the conditions of the period.

Hamilton's position was and can be stated in terms of the familiar concept of sovereignty which, though now out of vogue, retains certain explanatory merits. It was a pivotal idea in the theories of both Hamilton and Hobbes. The kernel of the notion of sovereignty is that there is some one locus to which highest authority may be ascribed. Sovereignty, then, comes to mean the ability to exercise power effectively, for only in the effective institution can highest or final authority rest. If a government keeps the peace, it passes the first test of sovereignty, which has to do not with the forms or distribution of power but with its adequacy to its functions. The problem of sovereignty is, "Is there a ruling body, i.e., a sovereign?" The problem of government is, "Does it have the equipment to enable it to rule, i.e., to be sovereign?" This is the question against which the government of the United States must be judged.

Within the general framework of our discussion, Hamilton's arguments about the need for national power can be seen as a set of prescriptions for the realization of the ends set forth by the liberal tradition, the ends of social peace and protection of the individual. He argued in effect that the nature of the political function and the character of human nature are such that prime attention must be given to the provision of adequate power, since the realization of all lesser political ends is contingent on maintenance of the more general end of stability in society. Set in these terms, the Hamiltonian version of politics does not represent even a substantial revision of the central liberal tenets, but simply stresses his conviction that community is to be found and, therefore, preserved on the larger national level. The questions of scope and definition of community are the central ones.[7]

This commitment to effective political power on a national basis was a persistent theme in Hamilton's commentaries on the Revolutionary question and on the Articles of Confederation in the events leading up to the Philadelphia Convention, in the Convention, to a lesser extent in *The Federalist* papers, and in the period when Hamilton was actively engaged in the exercise of national power. Its most

---

[7] Indeed, the concept of community is persistently central in political theory. See Carl J. Friedrich (ed.), *Community* (Nomos II; New York: Liberal Arts Press, 1959); Robert A. Nisbet, *Community and Power* (New York: Oxford University Press, 1962).

important and cogent statement is to be found in his reflections on the doctrine of implied powers under the Constitution. These were set forth in a report he rendered to President Washington on the constitutionality of the Bank of the United States. The controversy over the Bank's constitutionality was a vivid one. Both the theory and policy of the matter were points of dispute between Hamilton and Jefferson. The lengthy comments submitted to Washington by Hamilton as Secretary of the Treasury were in answer to a brief solicited from Jefferson by Washington in Jefferson's capacity as Secretary of State. Thus, the substance of the issue will be discussed further from the Jeffersonian point of view in the following chapter. It may be noted that when the issue again became prominent in connection with the constitutionality of the second bank, Hamilton's argument was followed very closely by John Marshall in *McCulloch* v. *Maryland*.[8] Hamilton's argument began with general reference to the theory of sovereignty discussed above:

> Now it appears to the Secretary of the Treasury that this *general principle* is *inherent* in the very *definition* of government, and *essential* to every step of the progress to be made by that of the United States, namely: That every power vested in a government is in its nature *sovereign,* and includes, by *force* of the *term,* a right to employ all the *means* requisite and fairly applicable to the attainment of the *ends* of such power, and which are not precluded by restrictions and exceptions specified in the Constitution, or not immoral, or not contrary to the *essential ends* of political society.[9]

This proposition Hamilton states is axiomatic and ". . . essential to the preservation of the social order. . . ." [10]

Hamilton was arguing that the Constitution is a specification of ends, the means to which lie within the permissible exercise of the United States government unless they are means specifically excluded by the terms of the Constitution. He did not, of course, hold that all legitimate functions of government in the United States fall within the permissible scope of national activity. He conceded that sovereignty was divided between national and state governments, a proposition that present-day Hamiltonians might not be so quick to admit. But the point for Hamilton was to establish that the government of the United States had in its own right a sovereignty which opened to it a broad scope of permissible and independent activity.

---

[8] 4 Wheaton 316 (1819).
[9] *Works, op. cit.,* Vol. IV, p. 105.
[10] *Loc. cit.*

He was interested in establishing the power of the United States to operate with effectiveness and relative freedom within a sphere of stated ends.

Hamilton then proceeded to attempt to demonstrate that it is within and, indeed, even incidental to the sovereign power to establish corporations. With specific reference to the constitutional position of the United States government, he noted that the power to establish corporations is incidental only in those areas in which exercise of the legislative authority of the national government is admissible. It remained, then, to demonstrate that creation of the bank was a proper object of the national power.

This, Hamilton did by the development of the crucial doctrine of implied powers. By an implied power, he meant an "instrument or mean" for carrying out one of the powers specified to the national government.[11] A corporation such as a bank, he stated, is not a "great independent substantive thing," but only a means to an end.[12] Much of the substance of Hamilton's paper on the constitutionality of the bank was devoted to a demonstration of the senses in which the bank could be considered a means to constitutional ends.

Intervening was a more expansive discussion of the doctrine of implied powers and the relationship of that doctrine to the necessary and proper clause of the Constitution. In paragraphs foreshadowing Marshall's treatment of the subject in the McCulloch case, Hamilton argued that there are degrees of meaning of the word necessary, that is to say, degrees of necessity, and that the term necessary in the necessary and proper clause is not to be read as though it were prefixed by the word absolutely or indispensably. "It is certain," he wrote, "that neither the grammatical nor popular sense of the term requires that construction. According to both, *necessary* often means no more than *needful, requisite, incidental, useful* or *conducive to.*"[13] Thus, Hamilton rejected Jefferson's argument that implied powers must be excluded because they do not carry necessity with them. Hamilton's position on the matter made the necessary and proper clause more a key to expansion of the substantive meaning of the Constitution than a key to its restriction. Claiming that a literal or stringent interpretation of "necessary" would "at once arrest the motions of government," he argued that "the exercise of constructive powers is indispensable," and that it is necessary to invoke the doctrine

---

[11] *Ibid.*, Vol. IV, p. 107.

[12] *Ibid.*, Vol. IV, p. 108.

[13] *Ibid.*, Vol. IV, p. 109.

of implied powers to justify the passage of nearly any legislation. This doctrine comprehends Hamilton's notion of the proper interpretation of what the national government must and must not be permitted to undertake, in his terms,

> . . . a criterion of what is constitutional, and of what is not so. This criterion is the *end,* to which the measure relates as a *means.* If the *end* be clearly comprehended within any of the specified powers, and if the measure have an obvious relation to that *end,* and is not forbidden by any particular provision of the Constitution, it may safely be deemed to come within the compass of the national authority.[14]

Hamilton did take account of the fact that a power may be unconstitutional if it abridges the preexisting right of a state or of an individual person. The establishment of a corporation, however, did not in his view abridge such a right; that is to say, the national government's exercise of the power to incorporate would in no way prevent the exercise of similar power on the part of the states. Although it might be true that the act to create a bank or nearly any other exercise of national legislative power would, in effect, alter the laws of the states, this alteration in itself is not sufficient basis to declare the unconstitutionality of the federal legislation. That constitutionality or unconstitutionality must be decided on other grounds—grounds running to the substance of the measure itself. If in substance the federal legislation is justifiable and if the alteration of state laws is incidental, it is within the power of Congress to proceed with the measure.

It remained, then, for Hamilton to demonstrate the senses in which the establishment of a national bank could be implied from specific powers granted the Congress in the Constitution. Without exploring the details of this argument, we may simply mention in passing the various objects of national power Hamilton cited in this respect— collection of taxes, borrowing of money, regulation of trade between states, provision of means for national defense. A national bank, Hamilton claimed, would be instrumental to carrying out all these explicit and undoubted ends of the national government.

Hamilton's case may be summarized briefly as follows: (1) Government of necessity implies the exercise of sovereignty. (2) Incidental to the exercise of sovereignty is the power to establish corporations. (3) In a government of limited powers like that of the United States, the establishment of corporations may proceed only within the powers

---

[14] *Ibid.,* Vol. IV, p. 113.

granted to the national government. (4) The powers granted to the national government include those specified plus the means implied in this specification. (5) The establishment of a national bank is clearly within the means in a broad sense necessary and proper to the realization of several of the enumerated powers of the United States government. Stated more generally, the burden of Hamilton's argument was that the power of the government of the United States must be adequate to its tasks and must, therefore, be flexible, expansible, and exercised so as to permit institutional innovation by the national authority. Hamilton judged national power not so much in terms of its relationship with state power as in terms of its relationship to the functions he thought the national government must carry out.

The Structure of Government: Energy in the Executive

Hamilton's views on the internal structure of government focused chiefly on the roles and needs of the executive power. His convictions about the importance of the executive were manifest in his writings as early as 1777, and they were frequently and emphatically reasserted in his reflections on the difficulty of government under the Articles of Confederation, in the arguments he advanced in the Convention of 1787, and in his actions and ideas as Secretary of Treasury and prime adviser in the Washington administration. Because of the role he played in the Washington Presidency, Hamilton has been seen as a major force in the shaping of the presidential institution.[15] The position and development of the Presidency in American political history suggests that this perhaps was Hamilton's most durable and impressive contribution to American political practice and ideas.

The articulation of the element of executive strength in Hamilton's political ideas does not require a feat of imagination. It would seem to be a commonsense implication of his Hobbesian emphasis on sovereignty. Hobbes' work prescribed concentration of power in an authoritarian sovereign who could speak clearly with a single voice of political command. Hamilton, of course, did not push his case that far in view of his commitment both to the theory of popular responsibility and to the doctrine of separation of powers, but his belief in the overriding importance of executive strength seems to permeate all his reflections on political structure, in a way doubtless conditioned by his acute observation of the nation's political ex-

---

[15] See Edward S. Corwin, *The President: Office and Powers: 1787–1948* (3d ed.; New York: New York University Press, 1948), pp. 18–20; Clinton Rossiter, *The American Presidency* (rev. ed.; New York: Harcourt, Brace Co., 1960), p. 91.

perience. While experience with the British Crown prompted some Americans to view executive power with suspicion, Hamilton's basic perspective pushed him toward greater emphasis on the dangers of lack of authority than on the dangers of its abuse.

In one of *The Federalist* papers, Hamilton wrote:

Energy in the Executive is a leading character in the definition of good government. It is essential to the protection of the community against foreign attacks: It is not less essential to the steady administration of the laws, to the protection of property against those irregular and high-handed combinations which sometimes interrupt the ordinary course of justice, to the security of liberty against the enterprises and assaults of ambition, of faction and of anarchy. . . .

. . . A feeble executive implies a feeble execution of the government. A feeble execution is but another phrase for a bad execution: and a government ill executed, whatever it may be in theory, must be in practice a bad government.[16]

In more generalized terms, Hamilton's argument for executive energy seemed to resolve to two characteristics, initiative and responsibility. Here, Hamilton's ideas share much with recent "orthodox" theories of administration. These hold that the executive must be accorded authority sufficient to make his leadership felt, and that only when authority is clearly focused is it possible for the validators of authority, i.e., the electorate, to rationally assess the executive's conduct of his office.[17] Hamilton thus stated, though this is not to say he invented, a theory of leadership in the most modern sense, a theory which emphasizes the need for a clear statement of policy from the top of the hierarchy. Such theory commonly goes on to propose that effective control of an organization is most likely to come to rest in the institution whose authority is singular and whose ability to move is not hampered by the need for an internal consensus. The movement of power to the executive in modern government, particularly in situations of crisis, would seem to validate this empirical version of Hamilton's prescriptive theory.

Hamilton's perspective on the executive power can be further illuminated by reference to his comments on the Constitution in and following the Philadelphia Convention. At the Convention itself,

---

[16] Alexander Hamilton, James Madison, and John Jay, *The Federalist*, ed. Jacob E. Cooke (Middletown, Conn.: Wesleyan University Press, 1961), No. 70, pp. 471–2).

[17] See, for example, Luther Gulick, "Notes on the Theory of Organization," *Papers on the Science of Administration*, ed. L. Gulick and L. Urwick (New York: Institute of Public Administration, 1937); President's Committee on Administrative Management, *Report with Special Studies* (Washington: U.S. Government Printing Office, 1937).

Hamilton argued for a single and strong president with an absolute veto over congressional acts. He commended the English constitution for the strength it accorded the executive power; in doing so, he was not so much advocating monarchy as emphasizing the need for an executive both republican *and* effective. Madison's notes summarize Hamilton's comments as follows:

As to the Executive, it seemed to be admitted that no good one could be established on republican principles. Was not this giving up the merits of the question; for can there be a good government without a good Executive? The English Model was the only good one on this subject. The Hereditary interest of the King was so interwoven with that of the Nation, and his personal emolument so great, that he was placed above the danger of being corrupted from abroad—and at the same time, was both sufficiently independent and sufficiently controuled, to answer the purpose of the institution at home. One of the weak sides of Republics was their being liable to foreign influence and corruption. Men of little character, acquiring great power, become easily the tools of intermeddling Neibours.[18]

Hamilton seems from the context of the notes to have been advocating an executive with long tenure, perhaps tenure for life, but founded on republican, i.e., indirectly popular, modes of selection.

The Presidency, as it developed out of the Constitution of 1787, was a long-run victory for Hamilton's prescriptions because of its provisions of power if not its provisions of tenure. Probably the crucial feature of the Presidency as it was written into the Constitution is its statement in broad and vague terms subject to development by those who, like Hamilton, were to participate in the shaping of American political institutions through practice. If one can judge from his attitudes expressed in *The Federalist*, Hamilton must have been reasonably well satisfied with the shape of the Presidency and its prospects under the Constitution. There, he vigorously defended and explained the nature of the Presidency on three grounds: (1) on the tactical ground of its differences from the British monarchy, an argument into which Hamilton was probably forced by the nature of his immediate task; (2) on the ground that the constitutional provision for the executive branch provided adequate basis for the development of an energetic executive component to government; (3) on the grounds that the Presidency as the Constitution established it was a republican office into which the safeguards of popular liberty

---

[18] James Madison, "The Journals of the Constitutional Convention," *The Writings of James Madison*, ed. Gaillard Hunt (New York: G. P. Putnam's Sons, 1902), Vol. III, p. 192.

were built on solid republican lines. We need not pause with the details of his discussion of the first point, but it is worthwhile to review quickly his statements on the other two.

"The ingredients, which constitute energy in the executive," he wrote, "are first, unity, secondly duration, thirdly an adequate provision for its support, fourthly competent powers." [19] Each of these theoretical elements of executive power Hamilton then proceeded to explain and test against the framework provided by the newly devised Constitution. As to unity, the argument was simple, following the lines suggested above:

> That unity is conducive to energy will not be disputed. Decision, activity, secrecy, and dispatch will generally characterize the proceedings of one man, in a much more eminent degree, than the proceedings of any great number; and in proportion as the number is increased, these qualities will be diminished.[20]

Several of the participants in the Convention had proposed a plural executive for the United States. Hamilton argued from logic and history that plurality of the executive weakens its operation and dissipates responsibility. On the matter of responsibility, he wrote:

> It is evident . . . that the plurality of the executive tends to deprive the people of the two greatest securities they can have for the faithful exercise of any delegated power; first, the restraints of public opinion, which lose their efficacy as well on account of the division of the censure attendant on bad measures among a number, as on account of the uncertainty on whom it ought to fall; and secondly, the opportunity of discovering with facility and clearness the misconduct of the persons they trust, in order either to their removal from office, or to their actual punishment, in cases which admit of it.[21]

He also invoked the common political experience of America with state government in support of his argument that the unity of executive power is not only an acceptable but an essential characteristic of an effective governmental framework. On this score, he found the provisions of the federal Constitution eminently satisfactory.

As to the second ingredient, duration, his case was similarly simple. "This," he wrote, "has relation to two objects: to the personal firmness of the executive magistrate in the employment of his constitutional powers; and to the stability of the system of administration which may

---

[19] *The Federalist, op. cit.,* No. 70, p. 471.
[20] *Loc. cit.*
[21] *Ibid.,* pp. 477–78.

have been adopted under his auspices." [22] The argument might be paraphrased in terms of commitment and continuity, again terms familiar to contemporary students of organization. Hamilton described as a general principle of human nature his belief that interest in a function or privilege is directly and positively related to the security with which a man holds it, and, therefore, interest in exercise of the functions of executive office by its incumbent would be enhanced if he knew his tenure was substantial in length. He rejected on basic principles the argument that an executive must be so pliant as to bend readily to the winds of public opinion. He also rejected an extension of the separation of powers principle—the notion that the executive must be servile to the legislative power—and insisted on the independence of the executive body, an end which would be served by long tenure in office.

The arguments above run largely to the policy-making functions of the executive and to the initiative he is able to take in suggesting, promoting, and pursuing the policy ends that fall within the scope of his duties. At the administrative level, Hamilton's arguments for duration were focused chiefly on continuity. He then connects these with the problem of responsibility—the problem of affording the people ample time to develop rational judgment about the behavior of executives in office, which they may then reflect in their exercise of the republican procedure of voting.

As to the adequacy of the federal Constitution on the test of duration, Hamilton was doubtless not completely satisfied. His preference for long tenure in office, perhaps even life tenure, was noted above. His statements in *The Federalist* reflect his disappointment while, at the same time, conveying the tone of approbation. "It cannot be affirmed," he wrote, "that a duration of four years or any other limited duration would completely answer the end proposed; but it would contribute towards it in a degree which would have a material influence upon the spirit and character of the government." [23]

Hamilton's third ingredient, "adequate provision for the support of the executive," requires little elaboration. It refers specifically to the emoluments of office and reflects the common concern of his and later times that those who hold political power will lay themselves open to corruption in seeking to profit financially through the holding of office. The principle seems to be a simple one, namely, pay an officeholder adequately from public funds in the first place, and you

---

[22] *Ibid.*, No. 71, p. 481.
[23] *Ibid.*, pp. 484–85.

have little to fear that he may go to private lengths to support himself in an adequate fashion. Incidentally, though the principle seems a simple one, its lesson appears to be hard to learn, as several generations of American political experience with ill-paid legislators and executives, particularly on the local level, would seem to demonstrate. On this count, Hamilton regarded the provisions of the Constitution of 1787 as admirable, and seemed to feel they provide sufficient safeguards for executive integrity as to lay this threat to good government to rest.

On the fourth ingredient, adequate powers, Hamilton's conduct as principle adviser to Washington speaks as loudly as the words of *The Federalist* papers in which he dealt specifically with the subject. In *The Federalist,* he discussed at some length the veto power—a matter which he regarded as of prime importance—as well as the President's power of appointment and a variety of other lesser presidential prerogatives.[24] During Washington's tenure, Hamilton encouraged the President to move independently and decisively in a number of policy fields. He defended vigorously, for example, the President's exercise of his foreign affairs power, describing the executive "As the organ of intercourse between the nation and foreign nations; as the *interpreter* of the national treaties, in those cases in which the judiciary is not competent—that is, in cases between government and government; as that power which is charged with the execution of the laws, of which treaties form a part; as that *power* which is charged with the command and application of the public force." [25] In defending Washington's neutrality proclamation of 1793, Hamilton advanced the argument that the Constitution meant to establish an executive with broad prerogatives, that is to say, with the power to exercise all executive powers except those explicitly denied him by the Constitution. "The general doctrine, then, is that the *executive power* of the nation is vested in the President; subject only to the *exceptions* and *qualifications* which are expressed in the instrument." [26] This broad interpretation of the executive power, sponsored and rationalized by Hamilton, was of great importance in laying the basis for expansion of the Presidency, particularly in respect to the exercise of foreign affairs, which has characterized the history of that office in later times.

Also worth noting in connection with the provision of adequate

---

[24] See especially Nos. 74 and 76.

[25] Quoted in Richard B. Morris, *Alexander Hamilton and the Founding of the Nation* (New York: The Dial Press, 1957), p. 196.

[26] *Loc. cit.*

powers to the executive is the role Hamilton played in the development of an administrative structure capable of rendering advice and carrying out executive policy. Again, Hamilton's role in organization of the first administration of the federal government provided him an opportunity to participate in the shaping of later practice.[27] His activities in the development of administration reveal what has been called a Hamiltonian theory in that field itself. In consonance with the other elements of his political thought, Hamilton's administrative theory emphasized unity of command and hierarchical responsibility. Here again, Hamiltonian theory seems to have run considerably ahead of its time and to coincide in many of its main features with later ideas. In view of the colonists' somewhat unhappy experience with bureaucracy and in view of the minimal nature of the national administrative establishment in Washington's time, it is significant that principles of administrative organization occupied Hamilton's attention as much as they did, and that he felt that in adequate administrative organization lay some of the principal elements of success in proper governance. Certainly more than the average commentator on politics during his time, Hamilton saw adequate administration as instrumental in an important and central way to the general success of the political enterprise.

Economic Policy

Hamilton also made substantial contributions to American political ideas and practice in the field of governmental economic policy. Many have thought his contributions here to be the most lasting in setting the American nation on a successful political course. Certainly, as events have proved, Hamilton's ideas in the sphere of political economy were far ahead of his time.[28] Their general tone, while to some extent foreign to the economic needs and circumstances of his agrarian America of four million people, sounds familiar to those accustomed to the overwhelmingly important economic role played by the American government in the twentieth century. To an unmeasurable but certain degree, Hamilton's policies prepared the American body politic and the structure of American government for the assumption of economic responsibilities thrown on it in the complex and sensitive world of today.

---

[27] Lynton K. Caldwell, *The Administrative Theories of Hamilton and Jefferson* (Chicago: University of Chicago Press, 1944); Leonard D. White, *The Federalists: a Study in Administrative History* (New York: Macmillan Co., 1956).

[28] This claim should probably be modified by reference to Hamilton's use of some elements of the theories of mercantilism, already well established in his time. See Hacker, *op. cit.*

Hamilton's originality did not lie in the field of economic theory. Here, he was under the influence of the nationalistic mercantilism predominant in his day, leavened by familiarity with the work of Adam Smith and other classical economists. In view of his general position on the ends and means of political organization, it is no surprise that his economics were directed chiefly toward heightening national strength and utilizing political power. His economic posture is of a piece with his general political theory, his economic ends instrumental to his ulterior political ends. More than its misuse, he feared the effects of disuse of political power in the economy, and he saw political authority as a positive participant in a national economic enterprise. Hamilton's inventiveness and initiative lay on the political side of the political economy problem. He moved with vigor and insight to seek, through political means, economic ends which were, in turn, to be contributory to the political ends of strength and stability.

Although Hamilton's ideas on economic policy ranged widely over nearly the whole scope of the subject, his best-known contributions lay in the fields of public credit and government policy toward manufacturing. During his tenure as Secretary of the Treasury, he developed thorough and thoughtful state papers on both of these subjects for presentation to Congress.[29] An examination of these documents reveals much about Hamilton's general attitudes toward politics, as well as about his specific attitudes toward the economic subjects with which they deal.

When Hamilton assumed the position of the first Secretary of the Treasury under the new federal Constitution, one of his primary objectives was to take measures to bolster the public credit, which had suffered much in the economic disorder and decentralization of the Revolutionary and Confederation periods. At the request of the first House of Representatives, Hamilton submitted to the Congress in 1790 a report on the public credit, and in 1795, shortly before he resigned from the Treasury to return to the practice of law, he submitted a second. These, along with his activities and pronouncements during the intervening period, indicate his broad views on the specific fiscal condition of the United States and on the more general problems of fiscal policy. It may be noted that in good part

---

[29] See especially Hamilton's two reports on the public credit (1790 and 1795) and his report on manufactures (1791), in *Works, op. cit.*, Vol. III. These are to be found in convenient form in *Alexander Hamilton's Papers on Public Credit, Commerce, and Finance*, ed. Samuel McKee, Jr. (New York: The Liberal Arts Press, 1957).

they embody theories and proposals Hamilton had developed in earlier periods of his life, his interest in economic policy dating from the early days of his participation in the Revolution. During the Revolutionary period and the period of government under the Articles of Confederation, Hamilton frequently proposed measures for improvement of the shaky financial situation of the American nation.

In respect to the public debt, Hamilton advocated a series of measures designed primarily to restore confidence in the fiscal stability of American government. A second important objective was to cast the federal government into an active economic role at its very inception so as to set precedent for a governmental role in the shaping of the American national economy. Hamilton did not fear debt per se—in fact, regarded the public debt as something of an advantage —but he did fear fiscal inactivity and loss of public faith in the financial integrity of public institutions. To achieve his ends, he proposed in the first report a four-step program providing for: (1) payment of the debt of the United States at par; (2) federal assumption of the debts of the various states; (3) establishment of a revenue system more than adequate to provide for the funding of the debt and the financing of national services; (4) establishment of a bank of the United States.

Politically, the second and fourth of these items were the most contentious. For some time prior to the drafting of the Constitution, Hamilton had advocated the national assumption of state debts. His reasons for doing so were fundamentally rooted in those broad principles of economic policy mentioned above. His difficulties in securing approval for this program were related in large part to the fact that some states, particularly those of the South, were less burdened by debts and had in many cases made provision for their retirement through state action, while in other states, particularly in New England, substantial debts were still outstanding. Congress at first refused to honor Hamilton's plan and finally did so only when he managed to exchange some votes with Jefferson on the location of the national capital.

The proposal to retire the public debt at par was also a subject of public bickering because of the advantages it would seem to give to those who had speculated in continental and state securities. Madison had proposed that securities no longer in the hands of their original owners be paid at one-half face value to the original owner and one-half face value to the person who held the security at the time of redemption. This plan Hamilton attacked as impracticable and lacking in good faith. But the question of favor to speculators became to some extent a class issue and, hence, a party issue, and is thought by many to have been the main factor in the development of parties dividing the Hamiltonians from the Jeffersonians. The question of the establishment of a bank, both as a matter of policy and as a matter of constitutionality, became one of the most celebrated and important issues of the time. It is on this issue that Hamilton and Jefferson stated their opposing views on the scope of national power, on the doctrine of implied powers, and on the meaning of the necessary and proper clause.

All these issues are of theoretical importance as they reflect Hamilton's ambition to lay a firm basis for national power. His tax policy is perhaps the best illustration of the tendency of his thought. In his reports to Congress, Hamilton advocated the establishment of a broad revenue system based mainly on excise and import taxes. The level of these taxes was somewhat more than ample to meet the fiscal needs of the federal government as he projected them, but Hamilton's aims were higher than those of meeting the federal obligations. Through a system of taxation, he hoped to create some of the energy in national government that was lacking under the Articles of Confederation and to provide the channel through which the national government could pursue an important part of its operation in direct contact with the people. Hamilton laid a good deal of emphasis on the levying of taxes on commodities, such as liquor, which were important to the social and economic life of the people, particularly those away from the seacoast whose style of life was such that they little felt the direct impact of national political power. The problems arising from collection of excise taxes on hard liquor and popular resistance to that tax led Hamilton to take direct federal action in the Whiskey Rebellion. Thus, the revenue system offered the occasion to make a direct show of national power in an area where consciousness of that power was both low and critical to establish.

Underlying these ideas and activities is an interesting proposition about the nature of political power and its relationship to the citizenry. Fundamentally, what Hamilton sought through the establishment of the revenue system was community—the sense that power exists and can be exerted effectively. He apparently believed the establishment of community was so important as to justify forms of political activity to which, by almost any standards, the citizenry was likely to feel resistant. That is to say, he apparently would rather the citizenry felt the impact of political power in an adverse way than that it not feel the impact of power at all. This attitude provides some gauge of the great extent to which he was committed to the notion that the prime requisite of government is its ability to make its power felt.

Hamilton's policies on manufacturing embodied a further representation of the same set of fundamental economic and political goals. They are interesting for this reason in itself, and because they provide an early justification for so much of later American economic policy and development. In his classic "Report on Manufactures," Hamilton stated a strong case for government action to encourage the development of a manufacturing economy. Except their implications about the general direction of public policy, Hamilton's arguments were not a direct confrontation of the Jeffersonian arguments in favor of agrarianism. Jefferson's, as we shall see in the chapter to follow, were chiefly moral and political, while Hamilton's were chiefly economic. It is perhaps fair to say that Jefferson favored the agrarian economy as an end, and Hamilton favored the manufacturing economy as a means.

Nonetheless, Hamilton did devote considerable attention in the report to the various arguments that could be made on behalf of agriculture as the base economic activity of the society. He made it clear that he did not seek the development of a manufacturing enterprise at the expense of agriculture, but that he saw the two types of economic activity as complementary and mutually supportive. At least explicitly, he sought the dual development of farming and industry. It is not surprising, however, that his tone is defensive; such a position was probably tactically essential in a period when the political and economic and social strengths of agriculture so far outweighed those of the industrial portion of the community.

We will not attempt to deal in detail with Hamilton's counterarguments to the position that manufacturing was less productive than agriculture. It is significant to note, perhaps, that in his report he scarcely touched on the common moral arguments on behalf of agriculture and the rural life. It is worthwhile, however, to note those aspects of the industrial society that he regarded as advantageous and put forward in support of his general position.[30]

1. The division of labor. The development of manufacturing enterprise, Hamilton argued, made division of labor possible through "the mere separation of the occupation of the cultivator from that of the artificer." This, in turn, had the effect of enhancing the productive capacity of each and, hence, "the total mass of the produce or revenue of the country."

---

[30] *Works, op. cit.,* Vol. III, pp. 205 ff.

2. Extension of the use of machinery.   Since manufacturing pursuits are adaptable in greater degree to machine operations, the development of an industrial enterprise makes possible the greater proportionate introduction of machinery into the total economic picture of the nation and thus again enhances the productivity of the community.

3. The additional employment of otherwise idle elements in the community.   The extension of manufacturing would make possible productive employment for those who must of necessity live in industrial and commercial centers. Particularly, Hamilton had in mind here the economic advantages of providing productive employment for women and children. He cites favorably in this regard the achievements of the factories of Great Britain. This point alone suggests the extent to which Hamilton's perspective was economic rather than moral or social, although it would be unfair to read him in the light of present-day standards for factory employment of women and children.

4. The promotion of immigration.   Manufacturing would promote immigration, adding again to productive capacity, consumption, and the general population of the nation.

5. Greater scope for the diversity of talent and dispositions natural to men.   Manufacturing, Hamilton argued, provided outlets for a variety of talents and interests which the agricultural enterprise alone would not accommodate.

6. A more ample and various field for enterprise.   This point is much like the one preceding. "The spirit of enterprise," Hamilton wrote, "useful and prolific as it is, must necessarily be contracted or expanded, in proportion to the simplicity or variety of the occupations and productions which are to be found in a society. It must be less in a nation of mere cultivators, than in a nation of cultivators and merchants; less in a nation of cultivators and merchants, than in nation of cultivators, artificers, and merchants." [31]

7. A more certain and steady market for the surplus produce of the soil.   This, Hamilton said, is the most important point of all—simply that a domestic market such as is created by the presence in the community of a manufacturing class will stabilize the farmers' economic position by creating a steady demand for their product. He rejected the notion of national self-sufficiency but, at the same time, urged that a domestic market is an important complement to unsteady foreign markets as an outlet for agricultural goods. He also pointed out

[31] *Ibid.,* Vol. III, p. 210.

that manufacturing stimulates the search for and production of new products and by-products whose utilities were not appreciated earlier.

Following his discussion of these general advantages of the development of manufactures in the community, Hamilton detailed a set of policies that could bring about such development through the application of national power. These he advocated applying in various degrees, depending on the particular situation of the country and the particular effect of the policies involved. In Hamilton's words, they are as follows: [32]

1 Protecting duties–or duties on those foreign articles which are the rivals of the domestic ones intended to be encouraged

2 Prohibitions of rival articles, or duties equivalent to prohibitions

3 Prohibitions of the exportation of the materials of manufacturers

4 Pecuniary bounties

5 Premiums

6 The exemption of the materials of manufacturers from duty

7 Drawbacks of the duties which are imposed on the materials of manufacture

8 The encouragement of new invention and discoveries at home, and of the introduction into the United States of such as may have been made in other countries; particularly those which relate to machinery

9 Judicious regulations for the inspection of manufactured commodities

10 The facilitating of pecuniary remittances from place to place

11 The facilitating of the transportation of commodities

Of these proposals, the last is particularly worth noting. Hamilton had in mind the development of roads and canals for the movement of persons and goods, and advocated national action in undertaking such internal improvements. In doing so, he once again gave expression to his disposition toward broad congressional power and energetic national policy. He also urged that in providing for the welfare of the manufacturing portion of the economy, the national government take care to avoid those policies, particularly tax policies, injurious to the prospering of manufacturing activities. It is also worth noting that Hamilton advocated liberal immigration policies to compensate for the scarcity of labor in the national economy, as well as a variety of other measures to encourage and safeguard invention, investment, and other activities which would enhance the industrial capacity of the nation.

The implications of proposals such as these need scarcely be noted.

---

[32] *Ibid.*, Vol. III, pp. 244–55.

They not only foresaw the course of American economic development but also portended that vast expansion of national power which has made the government a primary actor in the economic system. They bear little resemblance to the kind of policy one might expect from a literal reading of the American Constitution, but they indicated the potential direction of American policy and the possibilities in public power as a lever and guide for activity in the economic sphere. In an overall sense, Hamilton's economic policy has never achieved complete favor, but its general thrust has been much reflected in later policy. Contemplation particularly of the public programs of twentieth-century America suggests the extent of the Hamiltonian influence. Fundamentally, what Hamilton did was to provide some specific indications of the ways in which Hobbesian liberalism could be applied to a dynamic and expanding society.

THE FEDERALISM OF JOHN ADAMS

Though the mature political thought of John Adams fits better politically than theoretically into the present context of discussion, a brief analysis may be inserted conveniently at this point. Adams was an intelligent and learned man, widely read in political subjects. From well before the Revolution, he played an active part in Massachusetts government and in the movement for independence. His tracts in defense of the demands of the colonies have been noted above; they were surely among the more thoughtful and deliberate of the Revolutionary literature. Adams continued his writing on politics to the end of his life in 1826, particularly through an active correspondence with his friends in public life or retired from the public scene. Some of the most interesting letters of his later period were those addressed to his former political adversaries, Jefferson and Taylor, with both of whom John Adams developed an intellectual and personal friendship. Probably his major work on politics was a three-volume study published in 1786 and 1787, *A Defense of the Constitutions of Government of the United States*. This work was followed, in 1791, with a series of political essays called *Discourses on Davila*, which is likewise interesting from the standpoint of his political thought.[33]

---

[33] John Adams, *The Works of John Adams*, ed. Charles Francis Adams (10 vols; Boston: Little, Brown & Co., 1850–56). For commentary on Adams, see Correa M. Walsh, *The Political Science of John Adams* (New York: G. P. Putnam's Sons, 1915); Manning J. Dauer, *The Adams Federalists* (Baltimore: Johns Hopkins University Press, 1953), esp. chap. 3; Russell Kirk, *The Conservative Mind: from Burke to Santayana* (Chicago: Henry Regnery, 1953), chap. 3, pp. 62–98. Selections from Adams' works may be found in *The Political Writings of John Adams*, ed. George A. Peek, Jr. (New York: Liberal Arts Press, 1954).

Adams' writing was seldom brilliant and often ponderous. As theory, his ideas were not very original, much of his books, in fact, being occupied with lengthy quotations from a great variety of sources. Despite their lack of originality, however, and their sometimes turgid form, Adams' ideas merit notice for the somewhat different cast they put on Federalism as an outlook on the nature and scope of the state and its place in social relations. What follows is not a systematic analysis of any one or several of Adams' major political works, but an attempt to distill in abstract his major political ideas.

Like most writers on politics of his period, Adams gave prime attention to the characteristics of human nature. Indeed, like Hobbes, Adams' theory may be seen as a deductive system derived from an axiomatic belief about certain common human characteristics. As to the goodness and badness or sociability and unsociability of man, Adams' view was much like that common in the liberal tradition of the eighteenth century. Adams shared the common Christian perspective on man as the faltering child of God, perhaps in some sense well intentioned but basically unable to lift himself above the dictates of his fundamentally sinful nature.

His most significant angle on human nature, however, and the one that provided the starting point for his political theory, had to do not simply with the sociability and unsociability of man but with the differentiation of human talents, ambitions, and abilities. Humankind seemed to impress Adams most of all with its passion for pride and honor, its appetite for praise. The operation of this passion was to cause people to seek distinction, and Adams believed that this seeking for distinction comprised the most important and characteristic element in human society. The axiom is classical in nature, having found early expression in the writings of Aristotle.

Although he sometimes wrote in the common contract parlance of the time, Adams' view of human society also seems to have been Aristotelian in tone. That is to say, he regarded the social condition as the natural condition of mankind, man being by nature a social and political animal. It is in the context of society, a network of interpersonal relationships, that the life of man is human and moral, and takes on its characteristic and important shapes. The juxtaposition of these Aristotelian beliefs in a natural society and in human differentiation led Adams to his fundamental sociopolitical proposition, namely that what he called aristocracy is inevitable and comprises the main factor in determining social relationships. It is out of this proposition that Adams derived his system of theory.

As Adams himself discovered, the term aristocracy is deceptive unless it is taken in its purest classical sense. In his later years, Adams was at pains to explain that his concept of aristocracy had been misunderstood. By aristocracy, Adams did not mean a hereditary class recognized by the use of honorific titles. He meant, rather, the product of the social process of differentiation among men according to their various abilities, talents, and endowments. This differentiation proceeds, he thought, in any society, sometimes along different lines but always creating classes. "The controversy between the rich and the poor, the laborious and the idle, the learned and the ignorant, distinctions as old as the creation and as extensive as the globe, distinctions which no art or policy, no degree of virtue or philosophy can very wholly destroy, will continue, and rivalries will spring out of them." [34] In using the term aristocracy, Adams was referring to a social phenomenon which he regarded as natural, that is to say, inherent in the very nature of man and, hence, in the social structure in which he lived. A hereditary society of invidious distinction would be contributory but not equivalent to an aristocratic structure of this sort. Adams wrote to John Taylor:

> By *natural aristocrary*, in general, may be understood the superiorities of influence in society which grow out of the constitution of human nature. By *artificial aristocracy*, those inequalities of weight and superiorities of influence which are created and established by civil laws. Terms must be defined before we can reason. By aristocracy, I understand all those men who can command, influence, or procure more than an average of votes; by an aristocrat, every man who can and will influence one man to vote besides himself. Few men will deny that there is a natural aristocracy of virtues and talents in every nation and in every party, in every city and village. Inequalities are a part of the natural history of man.[35]

Thus, the sources of natural aristocracy are as numerous as the differences in natural endowments with which men are born, but the central criterion of aristocracy is influence, the quality that permits one man to induce another man to do his bidding. Politics is the process of structuring this influence, and the nature of the influence comprises the fundamental fact of politics. The interpretation of politics in terms of influence is very modern indeed. This concept is one which lies at the center of many of the most systematic contemporary efforts to explain political activity, though few modern students of politics would use a label like natural aristocracy. Indeed, Adams' use of

---

[34] "Discourses on Davila," *Works of John Adams, op. cit.,* Vol. VI, p. 280.
[35] *Works of John Adams, op. cit.,* Vol. VI, pp. 451–52.

the term natural aristocracy seems somewhat narrow to characterize his own concept, since he saw influence as growing not merely from the endowments of birth but also from the accoutrements picked up by man in his life in society, including such equipment as wealth, title, and position. Thus, insofar as his theory was concerned with depicting politics as the playing out of influence in society as well as the conflicts to which influence leads, Adams shared a good deal with those whose view of politics now centers on the disposition of power.

By implication, Adams was also modern in his depiction of some of the social processes that go on in human organizations. He seemed to be suggesting, for example, that human nature and the nature of the social body itself inevitably lead through the process of differentiation to the control of society by a few. This proposition may remind contemporary students of Michels' "iron law of oligarchy." At one point, again in a letter to Taylor, Adams explained how he believed a political society inevitably becomes a society subject to aristocratic control through the progressive narrowing of the number who command influence. "This," he wrote, "my dear sir is the history of mankind, past, present, and to come." This too sounds, indeed, like an iron law, the operation of which must have a good deal to do with the functions of politics and the way they are performed.[36]

Despite his axiomatic treatment of the distinctions among men, it would be a mistake to assume that Adams categorically and completely rejected the liberal commitment to equality. What lay behind Adams' theory and, for him, set the problem of government is a distinction between kinds of equality. In a moral sense—indeed, in the sense of the *Declaration of Independence*—Adams seems to have been committed to the notion that all men are created equal. The prescriptive standard of justice implicit in equality, the rule of law, is one of the basic universals of the liberal tradition, but it is also set in civil society against the many impediments to its realization; therein lies the problem.

That all men are born to equal rights is true. Every being has a right to be his own, as clear, as moral, as sacred, as any other being has. This is as indubitable as a moral government in the universe. But to teach that all men are born with equal powers and faculties, to equal influence in society, to equal property and advantages through life, is as gross a fraud, as glaring an imposition on the credulity of the people as ever was practiced. . . .[37]

Theoretically, the question with which Adams dealt is the question

---

[36] *Ibid.*, Vol. VI, p. 458.
[37] Letter to John Taylor, *ibid.*, Vol. VI, pp. 453–54.

raised by the gap between the moral right to equal treatment in the law and the ability of people to assert it in the face of natural distinctions of influence. This is still one of the fundamental problems with which liberalism in theory and practice has to deal. Projecting his analysis of human nature and human society into politics, Adams supposed that differences in influence would lead to the development of parties opposed in the quest for prizes of power. "These parties will be represented in the legislature, and must be balanced, for one will oppress the other." [38] Adams succinctly summarized the function and problem of politics in the following sentences: "The great art of law-giving consists in balancing the poor against the rich in the legislature and in constituting the legislative a perfect balance against the executive power at the same time that no individual or party can become its rival. The essence of a free government consists in an effectual control of rivalries." [39]

The solution of the problem for Adams as for most of his contemporaries lay in the proper structuring of political machinery. Given his basic view of mankind, he could not be optimistic about the prospects for moral uplift that Jefferson found so promising. Adams was inclined, rather, to seek institutions to contain those unsocial propensities which his "realistic" view of human nature found inevitable. The answer to his search he found in the complex and balanced institutions characteristic of British and American government during his period, and discussed and favored by philosophers of politics from Aristotle forward. Here again, the influence of the Aristotelian perspective on Adams seems to have been great.

Adams struck hard at simple institutions, holding that their simplicity only rendered easy their control by the parties contending for political power. The notion of a simple democracy was to Adams nearly a contradiction in terms, since a simple democracy did not maintain its democratic character. It too would be prey to the domination of those whose influence was greatest. "A simple and perfect democracy never yet existed among men." [40]

Thus, Adams favored the structuring of government through separation of powers and the system of checks and balances, and looked with favor on the characteristic forms that came to be taken on by the American states and the American federal union. The system of separation of powers he regarded as the extension of the natural division of inter-

---

[38] "Discourses on Davila," *ibid.,* Vol. VI, p. 280.

[39] *Loc. cit.*

[40] "Defense of the Constitutions of Government of the United States of America," *ibid.,* Vol. IV, p. 301.

ests in society. "By the authorities and examples already recited you will be convinced that three branches of power have an unalterable foundation in nature; that they exist in every society natural and artificial; and that, if all of them are not acknowledged in any constitution of government, it will be found to be imperfect, unstable, and soon enslaved. . . ." [41]

Adams' interpretation of the doctrine of separation of powers deserves explanation, for its elaboration is somewhat different than one familiar with American institutions might expect. As has been suggested above, the natural divisions along which social power is likely to fall are divisions between influential and uninfluential which are likely to be, in effect, the divisions between rich and poor. Each of these groups Adams would have represented in a branch of government—the one in a senate to which would be "ostracized" the more able men of the community, the other in a populous lower house of the legislative body. This arrangement leaves unanswered, however, the problem how to resolve the natural tensions between these two centers of power. Stability in society depended on the development of some institution to exert balance. This would be the function of the executive whose importance to stable government could in Adams' view hardly be overestimated. Adams saw in the executive power a kind of energetic mediator among interests on whom would necessarily devolve the ability of the government to seek the public interest. He advocated a strong executive with an absolute veto, an executive capable of defending himself against the demands of the legislative body. His three branches of government, then, were upper and lower houses and executive. The judiciary he does not seem to have seen as a political power. Though he was a strong advocate of independence in the judicial branch, he apparently regarded the function of the judiciary as somewhat specialized and as not including the political equilibration of social interests.

It is interesting to consider Adams' theory of checks and balances in the light of the subsequent history of American government and the development of the system of separation of powers. Superficially that development would seem to be such as to give Adams a high measure of satisfaction, for the balance among departments has been preserved, and more than anything else, it has been marked by the growth of a strong and independent presidency able to assert a substantial influence in the conduct of public business. However, it is not at all clear

[41] *Ibid.*, Vol. IV, p. 579.

that the departments have come to recognize Adams' natural divisions in society. Including the Presidency, they have to a substantial degree been captured for democracy, and the influence of "influentials," while not to be denied, does not seem to make itself felt systematically through one or the other branches. Politics has come to be played out in the United States in terms of a shifting and fluid structure of interests that relate more to sectional and functional considerations than to the clear responsibility of the various branches to specific elements in the community. The general result might be satisfying to Adams, but on the specifics, his theory does not seem to have predicted very clearly.

In terms of an overall evaluation of Adams, two points should be made. First, the thrust of his theory seems to have reached in generally the same direction as that of Hamilton's, and although the two men were not personally close, their theories, perhaps, are not unjustifiably grouped within a single category. For Adams, like Hamilton, developed a theory that lay considerable emphasis on the role of authority exerted through politics in settling the business of society. Though Adams' theory is not explicit on this point, and though he himself did not function as a notably strong executive, like Hamilton he was a devotee of executive power. There is little reason, on the other hand, to believe that Adams went nearly as far as Hamilton in his advocacy of positive and energetic political action. He saw political power ideally used more as a balancer of interests than as an active force of initiative participant in shaping social affairs. In these terms as well as in terms of his view of human nature in society, perhaps Adams is well classified on the conservative wing of the liberal tradition, which he shared with Edmund Burke.

Second, Adams, rather surprisingly, developed concepts and insights which are, as we have pointed out above, much like many of those in use in contemporary social science. Power, influence, organization—all these were concepts central to Adams' version of society, and from these, his view of the nature and ends of the state took form. By the standards of the "realist" who takes his cue from experience with modern social organization, it is inadequate and perhaps unfair to regard Adams only from the standpoint of his conservatism when he seems to have foreseen clearly many of the problems of liberalism which empirical social science has recently rediscovered. His implicit propositions about the nature of the social order, indeed, suggest that Adams' ideas may well be the subject of fruitful reflection on the part of students of society, even of those who may not share his basic value commitments.

FEDERALIST JURISPRUDENCE

A third example of the Federalist's approach to the question of the scope of political power may be lumped under the general heading, "Federalist Jurisprudence." Using jurisprudence here in a nontechnical sense, we are referring to the body of legal doctrines developed through the courts to set forth the Federalist position on certain basic questions of political and theoretical dispute. The major issues involve, first, the role of the courts themselves in the political system and, second, the conformation given the power of the national government through the actions of the courts in certain substantive disputes. The thrust of federal jurisprudence, as one might expect, was toward the extension of national power and toward the development of the court as a political instrument capable of counterbalancing the democratic power asserted through the national legislature. Federalist jurisprudence was shaped in overwhelming degree by the contributions of Hamilton and John Marshall. Marshall is often credited with having done more than any other person, certainly more than any other judicial figure, to give the American Constitution the characteristics it has taken on through the years of its development. The influence of Hamiltonian ideas on Marshall is apparent, and on many of the important questions through which Marshall asserted his views, his arguments closely paraphrase those developed at an earlier point by Hamilton himself. Nonetheless, the importance of John Marshall as a creative force in the development of Federalist theory as well as an influential and very vigorous channel for the communication and application of that theory should not be underestimated. Marshall served as Chief Justice of the United States for 35 years, during which period he dominated the Court by force of his intellect and personality. After Hamilton's death, he remained by far the leading politically active exponent and theoretician of the Federalist point of view.[42]

One of the interesting aspects of jurisprudence as a form of political thought, and, indeed, of all higher judicial proceedings within the context of the American constitutional system, is that it so clearly represents the application of theory to practice. That through Marshall, the federalist ideas had an impact on structure and policy is unmis-

---

[42] On Marshall and his impact on the Court and American politics see Albert J. Beveridge, *The Life of John Marshall* (4 vols.; Boston and New York: Houghton Mifflin Co., 1916–19); W. M. Jones (ed.), *Chief Justice John Marshall: a Reappraisal* (Ithaca: Cornell University Press, 1956); C. A. M. Ewing, *Judges of the Supreme Court: 1789–1938* (Minneapolis: University of Minnesota Press, 1938); Charles Grove Haines, *The Role of the Supreme Court in American Government and Politics* (Berkeley and Los Angeles: University of California Press, 1944).

takable, though this is not to say, of course, that the precise nature either of the theory or of the impact is so readily understood. But whether one regards the judicial opinion as rationalization or as sincere expression of theory, he cannot, it seems, help but be impressed by its demonstration of the relationship of ideas and action.

It would be needless and impossible here to attempt to explore all of those junctures where Federalist theory was incorporated into judicial practice. We will confine our attention, therefore, to a limited number of basic but familiar cases through which the main burden of the contribution can be understood. The necessity of treating the subject selectively means that inevitably most of the highlights of the 35-year dominance of the federal court system by Federalist ideas must be omitted. What followed will outline, in turn, the Federalist judicial position on three basic matters—judicial review, implied powers, and the federal commerce power.

Judicial review is certainly one of the more interesting and original American contributions to politics. It was not, as some seem to think, the invention of John Marshall as he decided the Marbury case in 1803. There was some precedent for judicial review in colonial practice and some rationalization for it in English jurisprudence. As a practicing attorney in a case before the New York courts, Hamilton had, in 1784, stated a position in favor of the power of the courts to review legislation.[43]

It is important that judicial review not be confused with the broader doctrine of judicial independence. The independence doctrine is firmly and historically embedded in the British constitutional tradition, and it seems to have been regarded as axiomatic by nearly all segments of political thought in the early United States. Judicial independence is substantially a doctrine safeguarding the courts from immediate political interference as they discharge their roles as referees in largely private disputes. In theory, judicial independence has almost never been at stake in American politics. But the question of judicial review is one that reaches much further than freedom of the judiciary from political interference on a case-by-case basis. It raises a question about the breadth of the role the judiciary is to play, more specifically about the breadth of its part in the political process generally—that is to say, in the process of framing the broader policy through which government contributes to the solution of social disputes and the distribution of social resources. The Federalists struck hard for an active judicial role in politics and, on the whole, made

---

[43] Morris, *op. cit.*, p. 216.

their demands effective, though, as we shall see, they did not strike in terms of a political judiciary but in terms of a judiciary discharging ordinary judicial functions under the Constitution. That is, while a political role for the judiciary was an effect and probably a goal of the Federalists' policy, their arguments were framed in other terms.

In the larger context of the Federalist position, judicial review was a lever for the extension of national authority. One needs only to observe the extent to which Hamilton's programs were given effect during the incumbency of John Marshall on the Court, i.e., to watch judicial review in operation, to understand how Hamilton might have hoped the federal judiciary would become an instrument through which national power would be made effective. Indeed, the results probably far outran even Hamilton's most optimistic expectations. Politically, the Federalists benefited greatly from the success of their doctrines of judicial independence and judicial review, for as a party their influence lasted longer in the federal courts than in any other department of the national government. In practice, judicial review came to embody not only the Hamiltonian prescription for national power, but also the "balance" of Adams' federalism. But theoretically, there would appear to be a great deal of John Adams too in the Federalist position on judicial review. For the courts have come to be an organ of balance and a seat of distinction, an institution through which a peculiar aristocracy, using the word in Adams' sense, was set apart to perform the function of referee among interests. Thus, it fulfills the role that Adams had mistakenly expected the executive to undertake. The courts became, as Adams might have wanted, a counterbalance to the thrust of democracy—both the ideology of democracy and the Jeffersonian party that came to bear that name. On either the short or the long view, it is too much to claim that the federal judiciary, operating under the doctrine of judicial review, has been a disinterested locus of power; it is indeed doubtful that an active political power in a dynamic society is capable of disinterest in any true sense of the word. But it does not seem to reach too far to suggest that the Federalists, fearful of the mass and representative of the established interests in society, may in the perspective of their time have been able to regard the courts as a disinterested institution capable of preserving balance in the social body.

The Federalist theory of judicial review is set forth succinctly in two places—by Hamilton in *Federalist* No. 78 and by John Marshall in his most famous opinion, *Marbury* v. *Madison.*[44] The arguments of

---

[44] 1 Cranch 137 (1803).

the two are highly similar. In *The Federalist,* Hamilton's position on judicial review is stated in the context of a paper on the tenure of federal judges under the new Constitution. The argument can be conveniently summarized using Hamilton's own words as follows:

[1.] No legislative act . . . contrary to the Constitution can be valid.[45]

[2.] If there should happen to be an irreconcilable variance between the two, that which has the superior obligation and validity ought of course to be preferred; or in other words, the Constitution ought to be preferred to the statute, the intention of the people to the intention of their agents.[46]

[3.] The interpretation of the laws is the proper and peculiar problem of the courts.[47]

[4.] A constitution is in fact, and must be, regarded as the fundamental law. It therefore belongs to them [the courts] to ascertain its meaning, as well as the meaning of any particular act proceeding from the legislative body.[48]

[5. Therefore,] . . . where the will of the legislature declared in its statutes, stands in opposition to that of the people declared in the constitution, the judges ought to be governed by the latter, rather than the former.[49]

Thus, Hamilton suggested that determing the constitutionality of legislation grows out of the ordinary function of the judiciary to interpret the laws and is, indeed, almost a routine extension of that function. He denied that this is a doctrine of judicial supremacy, maintaining that it is the Constitution which is supreme to all bodies or departments of the government. The basic element in his argument is the belief that the Constitution is an expression of fundamental law to which all else must be subordinated and from which all legitimate political authority must be derived.

Federalist No. 78 provides perhaps the purest statement of the Federalist theory of judicial review. But Marshall's opinion in Marbury not only rephrased the Hamiltonian argument but also demonstrated the principle of judicial review in operation. We will not review in detail the political background of the case nor emphasize the brilliant coup represented by Marshall's opinion. In brief, the case arose out of Marbury's plea, originated in the Supreme Court, for a writ of mandamus to compel James Madison, Jefferson's Secretary of State,

---

[45] *The Federalist, op. cit.,* No. 78, p. 524.
[46] *Ibid.,* p. 525.
[47] *Loc. cit.*
[48] *Loc. cit.*
[49] *Loc. cit.*

to deliver Marbury's sealed commission of appointment as Justice of
the Peace for the District of Columbia. Marbury was a last-minute
"midnight appointment" of the Adams' administration, though the
commission had not been delivered when Madison took over the Department of State from his predecessor. Madison and Jefferson, responding in political fashion, refused to deliver the paper to the
Federalist Marbury. The whole dispute developed out of political contention over judicial reorganization and court packing through which
the Federalists hoped to maintain their influence in government despite Adams' defeat by Jefferson in the presidential election, and the
atmosphere was one of bitter partisanship.

The case left Marshall in a peculiar dilemma. On the one hand, he
had no desire to satisfy the Jeffersonians by denying Marbury his
commission. On the other hand, it seemed certain that Jefferson would
refuse to deliver the commission even if ordered to do so by the Supreme Court; such an incident could only weaken the authority of the
judiciary, a result far from Marshall's desire. The solution on which
Marshall hit manifested his consummate skill as politician and legalist. The case had come to the Supreme Court under a provision of the
Judiciary Act of 1789 which gave that body original jurisdiction in
such matters, and this fact lay open to Marshall the tactic through
which he could pursue his seemingly contradictory ends: he held the
relevant portion of the Judiciary Act unconstitutional. In doing so,
he could lecture the Jeffersonians about their failure to fulfill their
duty under the law, thereby serving as much as possible the Federalist's
partisan advantage. At the same time he did not run the risk of demonstrating the political impotence of the judiciary by giving Jefferson
the opportunity to flout its order. But most importantly, the case gave
Marshall the opportunity to assert and, as events would have it, to
establish the doctrine of judicial review through which both the judicial institutions and the interests of the Federalist party were strength-
ened. Though the Court did not overturn another congressional statute until the Dred Scott case more than fifty years later, the precedent
established by Marshall in Marbury comprised one of the most important amplifications of the Constitution on record.

Marshall's justification of this act of judicial veto, though couched
in characteristic legal rhetoric, substantially restated the argument of
Hamilton in *Federalist* No. 78, as we noted above. The Constitution
establishes the fundamental principles of government approved by
the people. It is the supreme law, the fountain of legitimacy. In cases
where the Constitution conflicts with legislation, the Constitution

clearly must control. It is the duty of the judiciary to say what the law is. Therefore, the Constitution must govern what the courts say, and the courts in the exercise of their duty must strike down the lower in behalf of the higher law. Again, judicial review is depicted as a part of the routine legal function of a court fulfilling the role of court.

So strong was the Hamilton–Marshall precedent of judicial review and so much in consonance with the fundamental American commitment to limited government that the principle has seldom been effectively contested and rather seldom critically reexamined. In only one instance of any note has the principle of judicial review been attacked on broad grounds in a judicial opinion, that instance a dissenting opinion in a rather obscure 1825 case in the Pennsylvania Supreme Court.[50] Although specific instances of judicial review have been roundly condemned in a number of circumstances on a number of occasions, and although the New Deal experience with the courts in the early thirties created much popular and scholarly clamor about the subject, the institution itself has remained surprisingly intact. The doctrine of judicial self-restraint has made significant inroads in recent jurisprudence, but the power of the court over federal and state, particularly state, legislation continues to be an important element in the American political system. A present-day reexamination of the doctrine would seem unlikely to shake the foundations of the practice itself, although it may be supposed that given the temper of contemporary times such a reexamination might abandon the old grounds of defense and seek for new. The doctrine of the higher law, implicit in Hamilton's and Marshall's arguments and much in vogue in the late eighteenth and early nineteenth centuries, no longer carries its great appeal. Perhaps the role of the Court in reviewing legislation might now be persuasively stated in terms of its salutary political effect, in terms of the role the Court plays as a balancer in representation of certain otherwise relatively silent elements in the community picture. This, of course, is only speculation. One cannot even be sure what he means when he talks about a more satisfactory justification for the institution in current terms, since current terms themselves are not clear subjects of general agreement. But it may at least be noted that the court is much more likely now to be treated in forthright recognition of its political role and impact than fiduciary for the operation of a higher metaphysical law manifested through the Constitution in a

---

[50] By Mr. Justice Gibson in *Eakin* v. *Raub*, 12 Sergeant and Rawle 330 (1825).

kind of occult judicial understanding of what the meaning of that law might be.

Our other two examples of Federalist jurisprudence we will treat briefly and without detail. The doctrine of implied powers was expounded by Marshall in *McCulloch* v. *Maryland,* 1819.[51] Here again, the doctrine was not original with Marshall, for again his arguments had been anticipated by Hamilton, and the doctrine itself had been utilized by the Court in less notable cases. Through McCulloch, Marshall once again managed to give brilliant and effective expression to a doctrine which became intimately woven into the fabric of precedent through which the Constitution has since been interpreted.

The McCulloch case dealt with the power of the state of Maryland to tax the Bank of the United States—not Hamilton's bank but a second one chartered in 1816. It is interesting that both Hamilton's and Marshall's most famous elucidations of the doctrine of implied powers were developed in connection with the establishment of a federal banking institution. The McCulloch case dealt not only with the doctrine of implied powers but also with the somewhat more technical matter of intergovernmental tax immunity, an issue with which we will not deal.

Marshall, like Hamilton before him, boldly defended the establishment of the bank as an instrument through which Congress sought to carry out the enumerated powers granted to it in the Constitution. He noted the impossibility of a constitution that would spell out in accurate detail all the various instrumentalities through which its powers might be asserted. He dealt with the Constitution as a constitution, a set of political fundamentals whose meaning is to be determined through usage. Here, as in Hamilton's defense of the bank, the argument hinged on the power of the sovereign to exercise the authority required to carry out its functions, although Marshall did not explicitly use the concept of sovereignty so prominently as Hamilton had. Marshall argued that both the sense of the Constitution and the words of the Constitution itself were sufficient to justify this exercise of congressional power.

His opinion renewed the Hamiltonian argument about the meaning and importance of the necessary and proper clause, finding in it justification for the use of congressional imagination in establishing the instrumentalities of authority. Denying that necessary means necessary in the common sense of the term, he held, like Hamilton, that there are degrees of necessity short of the notion of absolutely necessary. The development of the doctrine of implied powers, of course,

---

[51] 4 Wheaton 316 (1819).

was of great importance in permitting Marshall's Court and the Courts to follow him as well as Presidents and Congresses to read the Constitution as a broad grant of authority rather than a narrowly restrictive code of conduct. Its importance in setting the stage for the broad development of American government in succeeding years can hardly be overestimated.

Finally, in illustration of Federalist jurisprudence, we might mention Marshall's treatment of the commerce clause. Here again, we may be brief in dealing with the specific arguments but emphatic in asserting the importance of the Marshall contribution in terms of the later shape of American institutions and practices. The leading case in the development of Marshall's commerce clause doctrine was *Gibbons* v. *Ogden*, decided by the Court in 1824.[52] In broad terms, the issue again was a matter of "strict" as against "loose" construction of the Constitution. Like the rest of the Constitution, the commerce clause is succinct in its relevant parts, granting Congress the power simply "to regulate commerce . . . among the several states." It fell to Marshall to interpret these words into specific meaning for public policy, and his initiative in jurisprudence in effect made it possible for him to exert maximum influence on the development of constitutional doctrine. He seized the opportunity of Gibbons, in other words, to give a Federalist cast to the commerce clause.

The Gibbons case involved a dispute over a monopoly on steamboat navigation granted by the state of New York, the question being whether such a monopoly imposed a burden on interstate commerce and whether this burden on commerce violated the terms of the Constitution giving Congress power over that commerce. More specifically, the problem boiled down to the meaning of commerce itself. Did commerce in the meaning of the Constitution comprehend only trading in goods, or did it comprehend other such activities as navigation? Marshall's answer, of course, was broad and permissive toward national power, since Gibbons, who opposed the New York monopoly, operated under the terms of a federal coasting license. Marshall found the monopoly to be unconstitutionally in restraint of a subject of national control. In discussing the definition of interstate commerce, he refused to confine it to the passage of a product over the border of a state, a move which in itself became important for later types of commercial regulation undertaken by the national government. Further, he refused to confine commerce to mere traffic. "Commerce," he wrote,

---

[52] 9 Wheaton, 1 (1824).

"undoubtedly, is traffic, but it is something more—it is intercourse. It describes the commercial intercourse between nations, and parts of nations, in all its branches, and is regulated by prescribing rules for carrying on that intercourse."[53]

The effect of Marshall's handling of the Gibbons case was twofold. In the first place, it launched a very expansive interpretation of the meaning of commerce itself and provided the Constitutional means by which Congress might later undertake a wide variety of types of economic regulation. The long-run impact of this wedge of broad interpretation in the facilitation of various Hamiltonian policies for the national economy was immense. Second, it established national supremacy over interstate commerce at points where the powers of national and state governments might conflict. As subsequent decisions of the Court provided, state governments were not shut out from *all* commercial regulation of an interstate character.[54] But the Gibbons holding did give Congress and the national government purchase on the exclusive exercise of the commerce power where it chose to seize the initiative. Since about the last two decades of the nineteenth century, the power of the national government to engage through the commerce clause in social, economic, and moral regulation has grown in measure that would doubtless have astonished even Hamilton himself. The regulatory and welfare programs taken up under commerce powers, from the establishment of the Interstate Commerce Commission and the passage of the Sherman Anti-Trust Act through the development of the Social Security system, minimum wage and hour regulation, child labor legislation, and laws promoting and regulating labor organization, have brought practical references time and again to the Federalist version of the breadth of meaning of interstate commerce. It is through the commerce clause more than any other single portion of the Constitution that the power of the national government has been "nationalized," that is to say, equipped to deal with the nation as one community. With the growth of technology, the nature of the federal system itself has changed, as we have pointed out above, and the commerce clause has provided a ready and flexible means for the accommodation of political power to new social needs and wants.

Thus, in a variety of ways in both theory and practice, the Federalist group put its stamp on the development of Constitutional instrumen-

---

[53] *Ibid.*, 189–90.

[54] See, for example, *Cooley* v. *Board of Wardens of the Port of Philadelphia,* 12 Howard 299 (1852).

talities for the effectuation of political authority. The emphasis of Federalist means lay on authority—authority adequate to achieve community stability. Against the Federalist ideology, of course, one must take account of the Jeffersonian counterpoint which, though of the same general tradition, exerted its force in quite a different direction. This Jeffersonian theory will be the subject of the chapter to follow.

VI

THE SCOPE OF POWER:
THE JEFFERSONIAN INTERPRETATION

A second broad set of political prescriptions offered to the American nation during its early development is commonly described as Jeffersonianism. It is tempting to label Jeffersonianism a set of alternatives to the ideas of the Federalists. The two categories are often treated both in intellectual and political history in that fashion and discussed in terms of their conflicts and contrasts.[1] While it is true that on both the political and theoretical levels there is very significant divergence between Jeffersonianism and the Federalist approach to politics, it is probably misleading to regard the two simply as opposed types, particularly insofar as political theory is concerned. They share much, including a common framework of aims and traditions. It is probably too easy to overemphasize the antithesis between Jeffersonian and Hamiltonian ideas, particularly if one wishes to take cognizance of the fact that they have been much intertwined in subsequent American perspectives on and practices in politics. This cautionary note, however, is intended to serve as the preliminary warning to a discussion which inevitably will point up contrasts and differences.

The power of the Jeffersonian influence on American ideas need hardly be noted.[2] It must be obvious to nearly anyone who has observed with some care American attitudes on man, society, and politics, and has taken the trouble to consider their probable intellectual sources. At the level of ideology, the level of rationalization of the

---

[1] See, for example, Claude G. Bowers, *Jefferson and Hamiliton: the Struggle for Democracy in America* (Boston and New York: Houghton Mifflin Co., 1953); Charles A. Beard, *Economic Origins of Jeffersonian Democracy* (New York: Macmillan Co., 1915).

[2] It is discussed in, among others, Merrill D. Peterson, *The Jeffersonian Image in the American Mind* (New York: Oxford University Press, 1960); and Charles M. Wiltse, *The Jeffersonian Tradition in American Democracy* (Chapel Hill: University of North Carolina Press, 1935), esp. chaps. 10, 11, 12.

practices and forms of political activity, Jeffersonianism is probably the greatest single identifiable influence in American political–intellectual history. Its force is illustrated by the extent to which Jefferson has been adopted by parties and groups, and lionized by both popular and scholarly writers of broad commentary on the American political tradition. Probably more than any other person through the years of American development, Jefferson has been regarded as the patron saint of the American way of life. One of the results of this grip of Jeffersonianism on American social perspectives is that the Jeffersonian outlook has been treated largely in terms of praise or blame, particularly in terms of praise. Jeffersonianism and Jefferson have come to be, more than anything else, symbols— symbols hard to analyze free from the instrusion of valuation and emotion. This fact in itself makes the interpretation of Jeffersonian political thought a problematic task.

Our approach to the Jeffersonian outlook on politics will take us through Thomas Jefferson's ideas and into a brief description of the ideas of his friend and follower, John Taylor of Caroline. Like those of Hamilton, the political ideas of Jefferson must be gathered from a variety of sources—occasional writings, pamphlets, state papers, and letters—he did not set down a systematic and comprehensive exposition on politics.[3] His writings were vast, and, following his interests, they ranged over a wide variety of subject matters. It would be stretching a point to call him a political philosopher; he was, rather, a thoughtful man of affairs who left a variety of remains from which can be constructed a fairly systematic picture of the ends and means of politics as he saw them. The nature of this constructive process, however, as well as the nature of the raw materials on which it is built make problems of identification and interpretation of ideas tricky, and make one's interpretation of the structure of the system liable to a variety of disputes and counterinterpretations.[4] The risk, however, is worth running, for the development of a system from the diffuse and sometimes contradictory Jeffersonian ideas is an instructive exercise in political theory as well as an exploration into the ideological ramifications of American political conflict.

---

[3] Jefferson's writings are collected in *The Papers of Thomas Jefferson*, ed. Julian P. Boyd (Princeton: Princeton University Press, 1950). This edition has not yet been completed. Also *The Writings of Thomas Jefferson*, ed. Paul L. Ford (10 vols.; New York: G. P. Putnam's Sons, 1892–99); *The Writings of Thomas Jefferson*, ed. Andrew A. Lipscomb (20 vols.; Washington: The Thomas Jefferson Memorial Association, 1905); and *The Political Writings of Thomas Jefferson: Representative Selections*, ed. Edward Dumbauld (New York: Liberal Arts Press, 1955), this offering a much-abbreviated choice.

[4] Cf. Beard, *op. cit.*, pp. 416–17.

JEFFERSON ON MAN, SOCIETY, AND POLITICS

Jefferson's outlook on human nature, an article of faith or first assumption, conditioned to an unusual degree his entire interpretation of social life and political authority. Sometimes it would seem at the expense of both realism and logic he clung to a gentle and humane view of his fellows. His outlook was quite typical of the eighteenth-century "age of reason," when many men, including philosophers, were sanguine about the potentialities of human nature. The marvelous discoveries of early modern science promised to set men free from bondage to the natural world, and it was widely anticipated that a similar understanding of the ways of men might show the way to freedom from oppressive social and political arrangements.[5] Furthermore, the very advance of science itself was thought to demonstrate the potential of men for rationality. In this setting of intellectual hope, it is not surprising that many might take an optimistic view of the human future.

Jefferson and those of like persuasion saw human beings as rational and perfectable creatures, and, therefore, as creatures at least potentially moral. Jefferson admitted for example, that some men are bad, but claimed that this "is no proof that it is a general characteristic of the species." [6] "I believe with you," he wrote to a friend, "that morality, compassion, generosity, are innate elements of the human constitution . . ." [7] But the important point, perhaps, is that he credited men with at least a capacity for goodness, and this capacity itself he saw as determining the nature of the social arrangements that men require. For he expected that rationality would bring men insight into the requirements of natural law which then they would honor in their relations with other men. The problem is substantially one of enlightenment.

Jefferson's perspective proposed, in other words, that since men are rational and capable of perfection, if they are given the proper conditions in which to live they can be trusted to act in a reasonable and "human" way. This optimism of the human capacity was not only characteristic of Jefferson but has been deeply influential in many of those who have shaped the later characteristics of the American tradition. It is the faith of the basic democrat. It is the faith of the Rousseauian, and perhaps even of the anarchist, who sees the predicament

---

[5] See above, chap. 2, esp. pp. 60–65.

[6] To Thomas Law, June 13, 1814, Lipscomb, *op. cit.*, Vol. XIV, p. 142.

[7] To Pierre S. du Pont de Nemours, April 24, 1816, Ford, *op. cit.*, Vol. X, p. 24.

of life not in the individuals who make up society but in the institutions with which the society has saddled men. It is the faith of those who believe that human lives can be and will be run in a better and more reasonable way if and when the world's "unnatural" influences on human life are put aside.

It is at this point that the great commitment to education fits into the larger Jeffersonian system.[8] Jefferson himself, it will be recalled, counted his establishment and early guidance of the University of Virginia as one of his greatest accomplishments, and he pushed for the extension of common public education in Virginia. Certainly his emphasis on education was one of his greatest contributions to the American heritage, for given Jefferson's perspectives on human and social life, it comes to seem possible through education to solve the problems of the world—a proposition that probably accounts for much of the American preoccupation with formal training for the young. Many of Jefferson's comments in this regard have not only a rationalistic cast but also a charming touch of the mystical about them, so deep-running was his belief in the beauty and power of education. "Enlighten the people generally, and tyranny and oppressions of body and mind will vanish like evil spirits at the dawn of day."[9] "Educate and inform the whole mass of the people. Enable them to see that is is their interest to preserve peace and order, and they will preserve them. And it requires no very high degree of education to convince them of this. They are the only sure reliance for the preservation of our liberty."[10] Highly similar and of the same general theoretical import are Jefferson's ideas about the relationship of the newspaper to politics, for he seems to have seen the newspaper as an educational medium. In one of his best-known statements, for example, he said,

The basis of our governments being the opinion of the people, the very first object should be to keep that right; and were it left to me to decide whether we should have a government without newspapers, or newspapers without a government, I should not hesitate a moment to prefer the latter. But I should mean that every man should receive those papers and be capable of reading them.[11]

The thrust of these basic Jeffersonian ideas is obvious. Man is fundamentally a good and simply rational creature inhibited by his social

---

[8] See James B. Conant, *Thomas Jefferson and the Development of American Public Education* (Berkley: University of California Press, 1962).
[9] To Pierre S. du Pont de Nemours, April 24, 1816, Ford, *op. cit.*, Vol. X, p. 25.
[10] To James Madison, December 20, 1787, the version quoted is that in Lipscomb, *op. cit.*, Vol. VI, p. 392.
[11] To Edward Carrington, January 16, 1787, Boyd, *op. cit.*, Vol. XI, p. 49.

condition from understanding the elemental laws of morality. Jefferson seems to have found that the scale of society, more than anything else, stands between man and his potential for living the good life. But this is anticipating a point discussed below. At any rate, man can be encouraged and educated to live in accordance with "natural" standards. The greatest problem is to induce him to believe this of himself, and thereby abandon the search for the good life in such things as the structures of authority which, in fact, stand between man and self-realization. In proper circumstances and in good time, the institutions of society—in themselves fundamentally a source of evil—can be swept away, and men can be left to their own devices and trusted to pursue a moral life. "I have no fear," Jefferson once wrote, "that the result of our experiment will be that men may be trusted to govern themselves without a master." [12] Perhaps, of course, "master" to Jefferson meant only king or despot. However, at about the same time, he wrote elsewhere that "among the former public opinion is in the place of law and restrains morals as powerfully as laws ever did anywhere." By "the former" he referred to "those societies (as the Indians) which live without government and enjoy in their general mass an infinitely greater degree of happiness than those who live under the European governments." [13] Jefferson's anthropology was dubious, but his belief is unquestioning. It would be captious to suggest that Jefferson was an anarchist in any real sense of the term, or to suggest that scattered comments like those quoted take one any distance toward proof of a case. Nonetheless, the tone of the comments is such as to provide interesting material for speculation. Perhaps it would be fair to conclude that while Jefferson did not hold that man can do without government, he seems to have been convinced that man could do with little. Along with the sociopolitical prescriptions this suggests about the importance of such things as education and a free press go some very fundamental and likewise familiar political prescriptions following in the train of Jefferson's assumptions that men are fundamentally capable of good and ought to be equipped by standards of morality and politics to seek the good.

Jefferson's theory of politics, then, follows inexorably and logically from his theory of human nature. Out of his faith in man springs a faith in the people, and from that faith in the people flows the view that government by the people is both basically right and basically rational. "I am not," Jefferson said, "among those who fear the peo-

---

[12] To David Hartley, July 2, 1787, *ibid.*, Vol. XI, p. 562.
[13] To Edward Carrington, January 16, 1787, *ibid.*, Vol. XI, p. 49.

ple."[14] Expressing clearly his commitment to the contract theory in such writings as the *Declaration of Independence* and the *Summary View of the Rights of British America,* he held that the just power of the government derives from the consent of the governed.

But his theory of political power goes much further in the democratic direction than this, for, as we have suggested above, the idea of consent can be a tenet of authoritarian liberalism like that of Hobbes or conservatism like that of Edmund Burke. To Jefferson, consent was an operating principle of government as well as a principle of ultimate justification. As a matter of prudence and basic right, Jefferson would extend the principle of consent as broadly and deeply as possible into control of the operations of political authority. He searched for ways, in other words, to make the voice of the people as continuously effective as it could be in the determination of public policy.

Jefferson recognized, however, an implication of rule by the people or self-government that not all basic democrats have been willing to admit. He recognized that *vox populi* can be made authoritative in its dynamic application to public policy only when it is linked to the principle of majority rule. He was explicit in his acceptance of majority rule as a fundamental principle of democratic government, even though the concept of majority rule implies that at any given moment in the determination of state policy, the will of one-half minus one of the people may be left without political effect. "Every man, and every body of men on earth, possesses the right of self-government. They receive it with their being from the hand of nature. Individuals exercise it by their single will; collections of men by that of their majority; for the law of the *majority* is the natural law of every society of man."[15] Though this view might be thought to be qualified when Jefferson says that "though the will of the majority is in all cases to prevail, that will, to be rightful, must be reasonable," the qualification is not fundamental. In expressing such a view, Jefferson might be restating for emphasis his plea for the enlightenment of the mass of the people, his hope that the voice of the people will be more moral as it is more enlightened, more humane as it is better educated.

His commitment to the rule of the majority is further reflected in his well-known belief in the right to revolution as a dynamic part of the people's equipment for political control. "The present generation has the same right of self-government which the past one has exercised

---

[14] To Samuel Kercheval, July 12, 1816, Ford, *op. cit.,* Vol. X, p. 41.
[15] Opinion on Residence Bill, July 14, 1790, *ibid.,* Vol. V, pp. 205–6.

for itself." [16] In other words, to be right, the majority must be a current one; one generation cannot commit others to systems of rules or institutions. Only as a majority commits itself in a dynamic and current sense does the authority of government comport with the principles of democracy which serve in the final sense to make it legitimate. Although it would be unfair to deduce from this proposition that Jefferson was in any real sense an anticonstitutionalist, his commitment to the moral immediacy of democracy was so deep-running as to imply a certain modification in the meaning of constitution. Even more than other theoretical systems, his seems to make a constitution a set of working rules rather than a set of ulterior standards for the exercise of power. Jefferson, of course, had explicit ideas about the kinds of working rules and institutions that must be utilized to make the dynamic principle of democracy operative in government, and these will be reviewed below.

Before we proceed to Jefferson's institutional embellishment of the idea of democracy, however, another basic element in the Jeffersonian view of society and state must be introduced. The foregoing paragraphs make Jeffersonian political theory sound almost entirely majoritarian. They suggest that in Jefferson's view, the will of the majority, particularly of the enlightened majority, is absolutely right and should be insulated from check and almost from criticism. This majoritarian theory in itself suggests some reasons and devices for checking the will of the majority, but the interplay of Jefferson's basic democratic commitment with another of his basic notions urges even more strongly the need for the limitation of the active political power of the democracy by suggesting certain countergoals or counterstandards of morality that are pertinent to political life. Jefferson, in other words, cannot be fairly interpreted as a pure democrat, for as the *Declaration of Independence* so clearly reveals, he also believed in fundamental and individualistic natural rights. Our previous consideration of the natural rights doctrine suggests that these rights, to be effective, must be regarded as limitations on the exercise of political power— that is to say, as delineations of the points in social relationships where political power may justifiably intrude.[17] If this is the case, natural rights must be taken in the extreme analysis as the denial of the legitimacy, at least in some instances, of the power of the majority. This, of course, is a problem that all liberal democratic theory has had to face in some form.

---

[16] To John H. Pleasants, April 19, 1824, *ibid.*, Vol. X, p. 303.
[17] See above, chap. 4.

Jefferson hoped that enlightened public opinion or the enlightened will of the majority would never cut across the basic rights of man. This, in some sense, is the main thrust of the doctrine of the Enlightenment as it related to the democratic political form. Such a hope, however, reaches much further than the standard expectation of liberal democratic theory, in which it is assumed there is enough badness in man to warrant the erection of checks between the will of the majority and the right of individual people. Perhaps the most standard liberal solution to the dilemma of conflict between majority will and minority rights is the approach which regards democracy in its dynamic and operating sense not as a right but as an instrumental procedure through which consent in the ordinary course of things can be elicited. The voice of the people then becomes not always right but in ordinary circumstances a convenient expression of legitimacy. It may be honored so long as it does not cut across reserved areas of individuality which in no case—with majority sanction or otherwise—may be justifiably violated. This is a solution which Jefferson himself does not seem to have fully appreciated, although, of course, this claim cannot be documented by reference to isolated statements or quotations in the Jeffersonian political writings. It is a generalization from what we might call the sense of the Jeffersonian position.

Nonetheless, Jefferson's works incorporate what must be regarded as a basic theory of natural rights which constitute limitations on the operation of political authority. Edward Dumbauld has compiled from Jefferson's works an interesting list which illustrates in detail what might be called the content of natural rights as Jefferson saw them. Among the items enumerated are: life, liberty, and pursuit of happiness; expatriation; self-government; freedom of religion; freedom from retroactive legislation; freedom from imprisonment for debt; freedom from perpetual obligation; freedom of communication between constituents and representatives; commerce with neighboring nations; innocent navigation; the right to labor for a livelihood; self-defense against wrong-doers and aggressors; coercion against the delinquent party to a compact; and the right to an impartial judge.[18] Some of these items, to be sure, could scarcely be called natural rights. Some would have been defined by Jefferson himself as civil rights, i.e., rights realized only under the protection of civil law. Others, such as self-government and freedom of communication between constituents and representatives, might be called instrumental rather than basic, and relate more clearly to the democratic procedure than to the

---

[18] Dumbauld, *op. cit.*, pp. xxviii–xxix.

limitation of that procedure. But the list would seem to indicate how deeply Jefferson felt about the need of the individual for protection from the arbitrary exercise of political power. The depth of this feeling is manifest in the fact that Jefferson sought protection for the individual both through individual-based devices for the determination of public policy and through the declaration of limitations on the substance and procedure of public policy, apparently without being bothered by deep appreciation of the potential contradiction between the two.

Given these basics of man, society, and government, we may now consider the Jeffersonian prescription as to the instrumentalities by which the basic aims can be realized. To a considerable degree, Jefferson was logically a believer in a "simple democracy" through which the consent of each citizen might be elicited in the validation of each policy decision. This is the end toward which the logic of moral democracy drives, the end which is sought through such institutions as the town meeting, the initiative and referendum, and the plebiscitary democratic voting exercise. But Jefferson did recognize that circumstances often dictate the impossibility of the use of direct democracy, and that representative institutions are therefore necessary.

> I will add . . . that a pure republic is a state of society in which every member of mature and sound mind has an equal right of participation, personally, in the direction of the affairs of the society. Such a regimen is obviously impracticable beyond the limits of an encampment or of a small village. When numbers, distance, or force oblige them to act by deputy, then their government continues republican in proportion only as the functions they still exercise in person are more or fewer and, as in those exercised by deputy, the right of appointing their deputy is *pro hac vice* only, or for more or fewer purposes, or for shorter or longer terms.[19]

In the face of this practical limitation on direct democracy, Jeffersonian theory from this point on is a search for (1) representative institutions which will provide the most accurate reflection and most efficient safeguard of the voice of the people, and (2) political arrangements which will preserve, insofar as possible, the conditions in which direct democracy can be made effective.

The first criterion suggests standards for two kinds of practices— those relating to the selection of agents of the people and those relat-

---

[19] To Isaac Tiffany, April 4, 1819; from *The Political Writings of Thomas Jefferson,* edited by Edward Dumbauld, copyright, 1955, by the Liberal Arts Press, Inc., and Reprinted by permission of the Liberal Arts Press, Inc., division of The Bobbs-Merrill Company, Inc., p. 55.

ing to control of such agents. As to selection, Jeffersonian theory relied primarily on a broad-based franchise and frequent elections of those who are instrumental in devising and executing public policy. In summary, Jeffersonianism argued here for an application of republican institutions as complete as circumstances make possible. Republicanism is, then, "government by the people, acting not in person, but by representatives chosen by themselves, that is to say, by every man of ripe years and sane mind, who either contributes by his purse or person to the support of his country." [20] The idea of extending the franchise to all who "fight or pay" is in itself an interesting formulation and a liberal one for Jefferson's day. Further, Jefferson stated that he wanted to see the republican principle "pushed to the maximum of its practicable exercise," [21] that is to say, extended as far as possible into every branch of government.

But control by election, even though frequent and broad in popular base, is an inadequate protection for popular rights and popular consent; indeed, it is from the practice of representation that despotism often arises, for the properly selected agents of the people are quite capable of abusing their power. Jefferson once wrote, "the evils flowing from the duperies of the people are less injurious than those from the egoism of their agents," [22] and in a famous phrase, quoted by Madison in *The Federalist* papers, said, "an elective despotism was not the government we fought for. . . ." [23] The problem, then, is not only to assure that the power of the agents arises from their selection by the people but also to contain that power as it is exercised by those thus selected.

Jefferson's answer to the power control problem lies in a formulation typical of his time, at least as far as its label and superficial terms are concerned, for he thought that such protection could be achieved at least in measure by the separation of powers. Thus, he advocated establishment of a system through which the departments of government exercised mutual checks on one another, and thus vitiated both individual and common abilities to exercise power in an arbitrary fashion. The Jeffersonian version of separation of powers, however, is interesting as it differed in form and reason from the familiar doctrine with which we have been dealing. As a commitment to the separation of powers is often not a complete commitment to the doctrine

---

[20] To Monsieur A. Corey, October 31, 1823, Lipscomb, *op. cit.*, Vol. XV, p. 482.

[21] To Isaac Tiffany, August 26, 1816, Lipscomb, *op. cit.*, Vol. XV, p. 66.

[22] To John Taylor, May 28, 1816, Ford, *op. cit.*, Vol. X, p. 31.

[23] "Notes on Virginia," quoted in *The Federalist*, No. 48, ed, Jacob E. Cooke (Middletown, Conn.: The Wesleyan Press, 1961), p. 335.

of mutual checking and often embodies implicit favor to the position of one department or another, so Jefferson's version of the separation of powers seems to have been somewhat equivocal. Here again, one feels the effect of the contradiction between his commitment to majority rule and his belief that somehow the voice of the majority must be checked in behalf of minority rights. Given his faith in the people, Jefferson leaned in the direction of majority rule, and in formulating prescriptions as to the institutions of government, he probably favored the position of the legislature as basic, as the most direct and, therefore, least suspect of the centers of governmental power.

Thus, in theory, Jefferson favored the legislature as the predominant power in government. Even in the Presidency he leaned toward legislative supremacy, and much of his initiative was exerted through the House of Representatives by use of his power as party leader. It is interesting to note in this connection the characteristics of two draft constitutions prepared by Jefferson for Virginia in 1776 and 1783. In both these drafts, the principle of separation of powers was explicitly stated. The second, for example, included a clause which read:

> The powers of government shall be divided into three distinct departments, each of them to be confided to a separate body of magistracy; to wit, those which are legislative to one, those which are judiciary to another, and those which are executive to another. No person, or collection of persons, being of one of these departments, shall exercise any power properly belonging to either of the others, except in the instances hereinafter expressly permitted.[24]

But by the terms of both drafts, the executive could only be called a weak department; each provided for the selection of the executive by the legislative body and neither for an executive veto. The earlier draft explicitly denied the executive a "negative on the bills of the legislature." In the executive articles of each, more emphasis was put on the limitation of executive power than on its positive abilities to participate in active fashion in the business of exercising authority.[25]

This qualification of Jefferson's commitment to the doctrine of separation of powers probably reflects both his strong reaction to the colonial experience with British government and his underlying theoretical reasons for advocating separation of powers at all. In the Hamiltonian theory, and to a considerable extent in Madison's state-

---

[24] "Proposed Constitution for Virginia," June, 1783, Ford, *op. cit.*, Vol. 111, p. 322.
[25] On the Jeffersonian view of administration, see Leonard D. White, *The Jeffersonians* (New York: Macmillan Co., 1951); Lynton K. Caldwell, *The Administrative Theories of Hamilton and Jefferson* (Chicago: University of Chicago Press, 1944).

ments on the subject, the motivation behind the separation of powers lay in the desire to check the power of the majority of the people. In the context of Jeffersonian theory, however, the separation of powers was intended rather to protect the majority than to check it. Jefferson was more concerned with the tyranny of the agents of the people than he was with the tyranny of the people themselves. Once more, his faith in human nature dictated the shape into which he believed political institutions should fall.

On the one side, Jeffersonian political theory sought means of containing political authority; on the other hand, it sought means of limiting as much as possible the necessity of delegating that authority. The main thrust of this aspect of Jeffersonian thought is toward a strong commitment to localism in politics. In general terms, Jeffersonianism dictated that government should be kept as close to the people as possible on the premise that in this fashion political power would be more responsive and responsible to the needs and demands of its constituents. As Jefferson would have left as much power as possible out of the hands of coercive authority, so he would have left as much power as possible out of the hands of distant authority—authority separated from the people by space and political perspective. This element in Jeffersonian thought is another of its tremendously powerful contributions to the American ideology and, of course, another place where it tended to clash head on with some of the prescriptions of Hamiltonian theory.

It was this aspect of the basic Jeffersonian outlook on government that gave meaning and content to his attitude toward federalism under the American Constitution. In general terms, Jefferson held that the states should be independent in respect of everything within themselves, and the power of the national government should be confined to things respecting the conduct of foreign relations. This tenet, in turn, became a theory of constitutional interpretation, a theory that would have greatly confined the ability of the national government to deal with a variety of problems that seemed to Hamilton and others to be national in scope. It was a part of the general Jeffersonian political posture to be skeptical of the exercise of national powers.

This perspective was reflected in Jefferson's position in some historic public controversies and in some of his well-known public acts. As Secretary of State in Washington's Cabinet, for example, he submitted on the President's request an opinion on the constitutionality of Hamilton's plan for a national bank. He held the establishment of such an institution beyond national authority, reflecting his "strict constructionist" approach to the meaning of the Constitution. Jefferson's position was fundamentally a simple one. He found nothing in the enumerated powers to enable the Congress to establish a bank, and he denied the doctrine of implied powers that in the Federalists' view permitted its establishment under the blanket of other specific enabling clauses. It was Jefferson's contention that necessary means necessary in the literal sense. That is to say, in the interpretation of the necessary and proper clause, the effect of necessary was to restrict rather than to expand the scope of national power. A necessary instrumentality, then, would be one without which the specifically enumerated powers of the national government could not be exercised. Jefferson felt that this could not be said for the national bank, and brought his influence to bear, though in vain, against the project.[26]

A similar Jeffersonian position may be noted in connection with the well-known controversy over the Alien and Sedition Laws passed by the Federalists in 1798. These restricted certain kinds of expression and activity thought to be deleterious to the maintenance of public order. It was the contention of Jefferson and his adherents that these laws lay beyond the legitimate exercise of national power. Among the responses were the Virginia and Kentucky resolutions, the Virginia drafted by Madison with Jefferson's advice, the Kentucky by Jefferson himself. The general theory suggested by these resolutions may be summarized as follows: The national Constitution is a compact among the states under which the national government is to exercise only certain delegated powers. The residuum lies with the states and with the people. Among the powers of the national government, none enable it to exercise authority like that typified by the Alien and Sedition Laws. Further, both the First and Tenth Amendments and their combined effects prohibit such authority to the nation as well as its exercise by the President, who under those laws might provide for imprisonment by his own order. Therefore, that the national government can undertake regulation like the Alien and Sedition Laws and that the national government alone can be the judge of its own powers are both ideas destructive to the system of government established by the Constitution of the United States. The response to the constitutional crisis proposed by the Virginia

---

[26] "Opinion on the Constitutionality of a National Bank," February 15, 1791, Ford, *op. cit.*, Vol. V, pp. 284–89.

and Kentucky resolutions was individual and concerted state action to nullify the effects of the laws.

It does not seem adequate to label this Jeffersonian position simply a crude defense of states' rights. It was, of course, influential in laying the groundwork for subsequent controversies in which that symbol became paramount, but the Jeffersonian position is deeper-rooted than one that would merely deny power to the national government for the sake of its denial, or than one that would deny power to the national government simply to give it to the states. The Jeffersonian position was informed first by his belief in devolution of the powers of government to the greatest extent; it does not seem to be based on the notion that state authority is political authority in the highest form. It should be seen as a specific reflection in a specific context of political controversy of the urge to localism, which would be carried by its adherents as far as feasible in terms of the social needs of the situation. It was, in other words, the legalistic and constitutional form of a basic Jeffersonian localism and not an end in itself.

This point is illustrated in that the prescriptions of Jefferson were not particularly generous in granting power to the state itself. These prescriptions reflect an almost Rousseauian nostalgia for the sociopolitical condition of the city-state in which power might be exercised on a direct and highly localized basis. Jefferson once proposed, for example, that Virginia (and, by implication, the country) be divided into tiny wards, each about six miles square, within which as much political power as possible would be exercised and political policy made. "Each ward," Jefferson wrote, "would thus be a small republic within itself. . . ." [27] The basic functions of government— education, policing, provision of militia, care of the poor, roads, administration of justice, etc.—would be carried on within these jurisdictions. In such near utopian formulations as this, the romantic Jeffersonian convictions about the decentralization of political power are strikingly manifest.

Another of the durable and powerful Jeffersonian bequests to American ideology, and yet another area of conflict with Hamilton, lay in his preference for the agrarian country and the agrarian way of life. This preference was again related to the structure of fundamentals of Jeffersonian theory with which we have been dealing. Jefferson distrusted cities and the manufacturing economy, because he feared it would disable people from developing and exercising the

---

[27] To John Cartwright, June 5, 1824, Lipscomb, *op. cit.*, Vol. XVI, p. 46.

rational control over political power which he thought was essential.[28] The rural culture, he thought, was a sociological requisite to the proper limitation and control of political authority. Here again, there is a touch of the romantic in Jeffersonian political ideas. "Those who labor on the earth," he wrote, "are the chosen people of God, if ever He had a chosen people." [29] In the nature of the society and economic enterprise of his time, the farmer of all people came closest to controlling his own destiny. He was, therefore, the best conceivable subject for self-government.[30] Further, the farmer's situation produced a spirit of independence and equipped him both ideologically and in a material sense to maintain his freedom from dependence on the secondary and ulterior society. Whether one agrees either with his political ends or prescriptions, this Jeffersonian diagnosis will likely be regarded as shrewd sociology by those who have observed the effects of urbanization on man's social and political condition. What Jefferson was describing is a favorite subject of contemporary sociology: the growth in interdependence and increase in social scale brought about by the rise of the industrial and urban society. Both the agglomeration of large numbers of people in the urban center and the specialization of the industrial worker have without doubt changed the conditions for the operation of political institutions. They have to a large degree separated man from the means of understanding and controlling his own personal life and its relationships with others. Whether, as Jefferson would have it, the loss outweighs the gain is a complex matter of social evaluation, but the diagnosis at least would seem to be an acute one.

The prescriptions that arose out of this element in Jefferson's thought are clear and predictable. Jefferson hoped that the people would spread out over the land and the center of life and politics would rest in small agrarian communities. As a result, he opposed and regarded as basically threatening such programs as those of Hamilton which would have ranged the power of the government behind the process of urbanization and industrialization. This program Jefferson regarded as a misapplication of usurped power. Thus, to his anticosmopolitan localism is added his antiurban agrarianism, both

---

[28] Morton and Lucia White, *The Intellectual Versus the City: from Thomas Jefferson to Frank Lloyd Wright* (Cambridge: Harvard University Press and M.I.T. Press, 1962), esp. pp. 12–20.

[29] "Notes on Virginia," Ford, *op. cit.*, Vol. III, p. 268.

[30] See A. Whitney Griswold, *Farming and Democracy* (New York: Harcourt, Brace & Co., 1948).

within the framework of a system of ends pointing to a measure of democratic self-determination as large as possible.

Much more in detail might be added, of course, about the nature and direction of Jefferson's political speculation and about his behavior as an important political actor in the development of the new American nation. His collected works are expected to fill 50 volumes; the best that can be hoped for a summary analysis of this sort is that it faithfully and suggestively reflects the major dimensions of the man's point of view. Before undertaking a summary of Jefferson's political ideas, it is interesting to take note of the peculiar relationship of theory, ideology, and practice in the interaction of what we have broadly called Jeffersonianism with the American political system. We have called Jefferson's ideas "theory," and they seem sufficiently generalized and sufficiently interconnected with logic to merit application of that term. At the same time, it must be granted that when engaged in political practice, especially when the weight of responsibility of national leadership was on his shoulders, Jefferson departed in significant degree from the prescriptions for political conduct he himself laid down. This is not, of course, a suggestion of impropriety or ineptitude in his conduct of public trust. On those questions there would seem to be no room for doubt. Jefferson has been and will be honored as one of America's most effective and skillful chief executives. But perhaps the point can be illustrated by Jefferson's theory and conduct with respect to two major American political institutions—the Presidency and the system of political parties.

As we have suggested above, his theory of separation of powers dictated weak rather than strong executive institutions together with a system of virtual legislative supremacy. In practice, he was a President of considerable accomplishments, and he is commonly classified as one of the strong and energetic incumbents of the presidential office. To some extent, he acted on policy through the intermediary of a House of Representatives which he controlled politically and thus was spared from the explicit need to modify his own theory to comport with his practice. His relationship with the House of Representatives, however, does not reveal the whole story of his conduct of the Presidency in an energetic manner. His purchase of Louisiana on his own initiative can scarcely be taken to be a weakening of the presidential prerogative.

Similarly, his attitude toward the political party system was one of distrust. In the fashion common for his time among the varieties of political liberals, Jefferson regarded parties as factious, divisive, and destructive of popular cohesion and political goodwill. But again Jefferson utilized political parties both in his ascent to the position of chief magistrate of the national government and in his conduct of the powers of office. He was the first successful party politician to hold the position of President of the United States. The party he led, developed during Washington's administration and held together to considerable degree by ideological cohesion, was to become a persistent and dominant force in American politics. More than anything else, Jefferson's party support made it possible for him during his Presidency to control national policy through legislative influence.[31]

These examples of disjunction between theory and practice suggest the difficulties of adhering to a rigid set of prescriptions in the face of a changing political and social situation. The relationship is even more curious, perhaps, when one considers that it is the theory more than the practice which has left the Jeffersonian imprint on the ideology of the American people. While specific influences on ideology are even harder to demonstrate than the content of the ideology itself, it would not seem unreasonable to say that Jefferson's heritage to the American folklore of politics has been decidedly Whiggish as respects the exercise of political power, and decidedly distrustful as far as partisanship and the party institution are concerned. This suggests that Jefferson is more remembered for what he said than for what he did, and raises interesting questions about the sources of folk attitudes toward politics.

JOHN TAYLOR OF CAROLINE

Before attempting to summarize Jeffersonian thought, we should, perhaps, add a note concerning the contributions of John Taylor. In a sense, the note is bibliographic, for Taylor's contributions were more expository than originally theoretical. But his works on government provide a sufficiently systematic and thorough analysis of the Jeffersonian ideas to make them worthy of mention. The ideas of Jefferson himself were so diffuse and widely scattered that it is useful to take note of Taylor's efforts to draw them together. Taylor, a gentleman farmer of Caroline County, Virginia, active in politics, was a friend of Jefferson with whom Jefferson himself said he "rarely if ever differed in any political principle of importance." Taylor was

---

[31] For an excellent account of the development and early character of the party system, see William N. Chambers, *Political Parties in a New Nation: the American Experience, 1776–1809* (New York: Oxford University Press, 1963).

often in correspondence with Jefferson and Adams on matters of political concern, and he produced a variety of writings, including scientific essays on agriculture. His most important political ideas, however, are to be found in four books published between 1814 and 1823: *An Inquiry into the Principles and Policy of the Government of the United States* (1814); *Tyranny Unmasked* (1822); *Constructions Construed and Constitutions Vindicated* (1820); and *New View of the Constitution of the United States* (1823).[32]

Taylor's works were fundamentally and thoroughly Jeffersonian, and while he had a considerable taste for abstract theory, a good many of his political writings were stimulated directly by the political controversies of his day. In succession, he took on the three main prophets of Federalism, Adams, Hamilton, and Marshall. On the basis of a humanitarian and optimistic fundamental democracy pervaded by the fear of political power, he reargued the laissez-faire, anti-monopoly, agrarian, localistic Jeffersonian outlook on governmental activity.

In his *Inquiry*, Taylor vigorously attacked Adams' theory of aristocracy. The publication of this book, incidentally, stimulated an instructive exchange of letters between Adams and Taylor in which the former suggested that Taylor had not fully understood his concept of aristocracy and in which he attempted to clarify his intended meaning.[33] Taylor did not call into question the concept of diversity of talents and interests nor the importance of that concept in shaping human relationships. However, he asserted that the idea of aristocracy connotes an artificial diversity that is man-made and not natural. Aristocracy, he thought, refers to groups set apart in terms of title or wealth and in terms of invidious and ritualistic distinctions. These distinctions, furthermore, stimulate those who benefit from them to attempt to maintain their positions of predominance through suppression and in contradiction to natural moral law. Thus, they come to be artificial and deleterious inhibitions on social justice.

The government of the United States, Taylor held, was founded on true moral principles—such principles as equality and consent. Its hallmarks are democracy, the minimization of political authority, and

---

[32] For commentary on Taylor, see E. T. Mudge, *The Social Philosophy of John Taylor of Caroline* (New York: Columbia University Press, 1939); Manning J. Dauer and Hans Hammond, "John Taylor: Democrat or Aristocrat," *Journal of Politics*, Vol. VI (November, 1944), pp. 381–403; Grant McConnell, "John Taylor and the Democratic Tradition," *Western Political Quarterly*, Vol. IV (March, 1951), pp. 17–31. McConnell discusses differences between Jefferson's and Taylor's theories.

[33] See above, chap. 5, pp.

the division of powers. This structure of government, though cast in the Constitution, is being perverted by men who use its instruments to attempt to make aristocrats of themselves. These are men, in other words, who would seize the influence of public office and attempt to turn it to their good without regard either to moral principle or to the public interest. Such motives Taylor found behind the broad range of Federalist social and political programs.

In *Tyranny Unmasked,* Taylor turned his attention particularly to Federalist economic proposals. In a broad sense, he objected to these as contrary to the principle of least government. Government intervention in the economic system or government sponsorship of particular kinds of economic activity could be no more congenial to Taylor's outlook than to that of Jefferson. Taylor's specific target in *Tyranny Unmasked* was the tariff, which, it will be recalled, was one of the Federalists' Hamiltonian instruments for promoting the growth of a manufacturing economy. Taylor considered the tariff an artificial restriction on competition, in a sense one of those artificial devices developed by the privileged to utilize public power in their own interests. Specifically, he regarded the tariff as a scheme to enhance the profit and power of the manufacturing class at the expense of other elements in the community, in violation of what he called "a natural right of free trade." On similar grounds, he attacked grants of charters of incorporation, which he felt were, likewise, manipulations of political authority by and in the selfish interests of those in power.

In *Constructions Construed and Constitutions Vindicated,* a pamphlet excited by Marshall's opinion in the McCulloch case, Taylor turned his attention to the specific device of judicial review. He, like Jefferson, regarded this as a questionable instrument for the exercise of illicit power by those of Federalist sentiments. The decision in McCulloch, it will be recalled, not only promoted the doctrine of implied powers but also validated a specific Federalist policy at the expense of a specific exercise of state power.

The doctrine of localism was very important in Taylor's thought, though more likely in his writings than in the writings of Jefferson to be cast in terms of states' rights. Taylor viewed the national Constitution as the creature of the states—a kind of compact between them. His interest in this matter foreshadowed the period preceding the Civil War when the problem of the nature of the federal system became the overriding concern in American thought. Like Jefferson, he regarded the powers of the national government as limited to those items specifically enumerated in the Constitution, and believed that in some basic sense the power of the national government would best be restricted to matters concerning foreign relations. The doctrine of implied powers seemed to him an abridgement of the terms of the contract, and he was dubious of those forms of exercise of national power which would bring it to bear directly on the people without the intermediation of the various states. Also, like Jefferson, Taylor favored going to lengths to defend the powers of the states and keep in check the powers of the national government. At the time of the Virginia resolution of 1798, he advocated nullification or even secession if those measures were necessary to maintain the proper distribution of powers between the two levels of government. Like Jefferson's, Taylor's localism was an integral part of a broader political system that reached to his interpretation of the nature of political society itself.

JEFFERSONIAN THOUGHT: A SUMMARY

We might now undertake a systematic summary of the main points of Jefferson's sociopolitical theory. Admittedly, what follows draws only on principal tenets and implications; as we pointed out above, taken as a whole, Jefferson's ideas miss by some measure the criterion of logical consistency. But seen in broad terms, the Jeffersonian argument developed somewhat as follows: First, its point of departure is an axiomatic belief about the nature of man—man's potential for rationality and morality is high and educable. Indeed, his penchant for sociability outweighs his penchant for unsociability. Second, the moral system of human society is regulated by a set of natural rights. Third, by deduction from the premises of rights and rationality, democracy is the only legitimate form of political power. This democracy, however, may be exercised when necessary through the agency of representative institutions. Fourth, in the nature of things, as long as power is necessary it is dangerous to human rights. Fifth, this danger implies two prescriptions for the organization of political institutions. These prescriptions are (a) keep the basis of power small, and (b) develop institutions that provide for the internal checking of the exercise of power among those in whose hands it is placed. The means for keeping power small include enlightment of the people so that they may be as self-reliant as possible, encouragement of an agrarian and localistic base for social life, and decentralization in the arrangement of the powers of government. Institutions or structural forms for alleviation of the threat of overweaning political power include functional separation of powers and the development of an explicit and strong federalistic arrangement of power distribution.

The problems of the Jeffersonian theory are to some degree both internal and empirical. Judged by the standard of common liberal theories of his day, Jefferson laid far greater emphasis on the democratic element in authority than he did on the limitation of that authority. His assumptions about the rationality and morality of man led him to the belief that man in the mass can be trusted to exercise power in a way that does not threaten the fabric of individual rights. True to the climate of opinion of his time, however, Jefferson did recognize that authority, even when vested in majorities, is subject to abuse. In a way, one senses two Jeffersons in his political thought— the Jefferson whose trust in the majority was complete, and the Jefferson whose trust in the majority could not outweigh his suspicion of all political authority. The implicit conflict Jefferson himself never seems to have resolved satisfactorily, but the central thrust of his theory was certainly toward the democratic as opposed to the constitutionalist view. Rather than trusting, like Madison, to the complexity of institutions to provide safety for human rights, he tended to look toward rational simplicity as the best repository of hope.

As we have often suggested, whatever the theoretical viability of Jefferson's ideas, their contribution to the ideology of American political tradition has been overwhelming. The points at which the influence of Jefferson ideas is patent in common American ways of looking at social and political matters might include the following: (1) the fundamental and overriding importance of consent, both original and dynamic, as the criterion of political legitimacy; (2) the importance of education, the ability of education to provide men with the means of improving their lot and protecting themselves; (3) the doctrine of natural rights against political authority; (4) freedom of religion, listed separately because Jefferson himself regarded his contributions to free religion as among his most important, and because he was instrumental in setting free religion not only into the theory of the American way of life but into the institutions of American practice; [34] (5) distrust of national government and of the concentration of political power, the perspective which suggests that bigness in itself is a thing to be feared, (6) localism in politics and social life,

---

[34] Thus, see Jefferson cited as favoring a "wall of separation between Church and State" in both majority and dissenting opinions in *Everson* v. *Board of Education, 330 U.S. 1.*

the ideal of the small society, of the near-medieval, face-to-face, highly integrated community, (7) agrarianism, the idea that the tiller of the soil has a special role in society, that agriculture is somehow the backbone of America. These ideas are somehow integral to American ways of looking at things, probably not because Jefferson said them, but because Jefferson expressed in good part the American spirit as it was then taking shape and as it has since endured.

It is interesting to reflect on the extent to which various of these elements of the Jeffersonian ideology persist in the United States. From an impressionistic point of view, it would seem they are all important in shaping our day-to-day perspectives. Take an isolated but important example. There would seem to be many ways in which the preferences and life-styles typified in suburbanization of the American culture reflect the Jeffersonian image of the good life. Suburbia is probably in part an attempt to recreate the localistic Jeffersonian community—the community where one's political destiny is in his own control.[35] The appeal of the grass and trees of suburbia, furthermore, may very well be agrarian in base, may very well reflect the American commitment to the idea that the good life requires man to get his hand in the soil. Even in the highly complex urban setting, which is itself the product of the triumph of un-Jeffersonian cultural modes, trees and grass maintain their status as goods in themselves. Furthermore, a look at the distribution of the suburban tax dollar suggests the extent to which education is regarded in characteristically Jeffersonian fashion. The ideal, the passion for education, indeed, permeates all American life, and has been at least partly instrumental in providing the moral base on which the world's largest, most complex, and most comprehensive educational system has been erected. We might also find traces of Jefferson in the arguments of the past half-century over the continual expansion of the national government's power. Jefferson would still seem to be apparent in the reflex responses of many Americans to the abstract ideas and concrete policies of "big government" at mid-twentieth century.

It is also instructive to consider another element in Jeffersonian thought, perhaps more apparent in the ideas of Taylor than in the ideas of Jefferson himself, that has been influential on characteristic political reactions. There is particularly in the ideas of Taylor a note of conspiracy, a tendency to find political ills the product of the manipulation of political enemies, particularly of "privileged ele-

---

[35] See especially Robert E. Wood, *Suburbia: Its People and Their Politics* (Boston: Houghton Mifflin Co., 1959).

ments in society." Even the occasions for Taylor's most important contributions to political thought were occasions when he felt it necessary to point out the effects of what he took to be Federalist manipulations of public policy. Some analysts of American society have professed to see this conspiracy outlook as one of the most characteristic of American political ideas—the tendency to structure society in terms of good guys and bad guys, the tendency to find the roots of social ills in plots and schemes, the tendency to suspect one's opponents of ill motives and assign to their actions the honor of overwhelming influence. Particularly, this orientation was manifest in the populism of the late nineteenth century.

While these suppositions about Jeffersonian imprints on American ideology are perhaps too broad to verify in any concrete fashion, the weight of impression is great. It is on this basis we have proposed the importance of the Jeffersonian version of the scope of political power as an influence on the development of American institutions and modes of behavior.

VII

BASIC DEMOCRACY:
RADICAL AND ROMANTIC VERSIONS

The period in American history extending roughly from the War of 1812 to 1850 was dominated ideologically by the reevaluation and reinforcement of certain basic American political commitments, particularly those having to do with democratic political procedures. In its last stages, stimulated by the controversy over slavery, the period also witnessed growing attention to the federal structure of American politics. But this is a problem with which we will deal in a later chapter. In the present chapter, our focus will turn to the growth of democracy as the central element in the American social consensus on political arrangements. Our analysis will deal successively with two of democracy's major phases, one principally political and sociological, the other principally philosophical and literary, the first centering around what might loosely be labeled Jacksonianism, the second most clearly identified with the ideas of transcendentalism.

JACKSONIAN POLITICS: IDEAS IN ACTION

Except as it deals with Tocqueville's treatment of American politics, our analysis of Jacksonianism must in large part draw on political history. The central figure of the Jacksonian period, Andrew Jackson himself, was almost purely a man of action. Indeed, the extent to which his ideas were instrumental in giving shape to Jacksonianism is a matter of question, though a question with which we need not deal, since our interest is in the shape of the theoretical model of Jacksonian politics and not in its specific sources. While we are dealing with the materials of political history here, it is not our purpose to reconstruct the events of the time. They are pertinent only as they serve as indicators of theory and ideology, and reflect the

impact of theory and ideology on political practice.[1] In very general
terms, Jacksonianism was the expansion and reinforcement of the Jeffersonian outlook on political means. The period has been described
as that which witnessed the arrival of the common man in American
politics. The effect of Jacksonianism was to erase in large part the
"Federalism" of Hamilton and John Adams from the ideology if not
from the political practice of the American nation. By Jackson's time,
of course, the Federalist party as a coherent political force had been
replaced by National Republicans and Whigs, neither an enduring
participant in the American political contest. The mainstream had
converged on some of the central elements of Jeffersonianism, and the
period of Jackson can be seen as a consolidation period for some of
those central tendencies, particularly the commitment to the democratic device. It also set the stage for the next major ideological
controversy, the most grave the American nation has ever faced. In
a loose sense, the slavery question and its companion problem of the
relative positions of nation, section, and state were internecine disputes among those who in a large degree had accepted the fundamentals of the Jeffersonian commitment.

Given the nature of the Jacksonian movement, we will treat its
political theory by examination of the implications of some broad
"practical" political developments of the period. In good part, the
theory of Jacksonianism is implicit in action. Three phases of the
politics of the Jacksonian era are particularly significant for what
they reveal about and have contributed to the American political
tradition. They are: (1) the movement toward the extension of the
suffrage, whose effect was to push further toward the consummation
of the democratic ideal; (2) the strengthening and, in some senses,
revision of two of the central political institutions of American society—the Presidency and the political party system; (3) the predominantly laissez faire tendency of public policy of the time. At
least the first two have left lasting imprints on the American political system; they explain in large part why the period of Jackson

---

[1] For commentary on the politics of the period, see Arthur M. Schlesinger, Jr., *The
Age of Jackson* (Boston: Little, Brown & Co., 1945); Marvin Meyers, *The Jacksonian Persuasion* (Stanford: Stanford University Press, 1957); Harold C. Syrett, *Andrew Jackson:
His Contribution to the American Tradition* (Indianapolis: The Bobbs-Merrill Co., Inc.,
1953); John W. Ward, *Andrew Jackson: Symbol for an Age* (New York: Oxford University Press, 1955). Representative source material is collected in Joseph L. Blau (ed.), *Social
Theories of Jacksonian Democracy* (New York: Hafner, 1947). Some of Jackson's political
ideas are to be found in a documentary collection, *The Statesmanship of Andrew Jackson as Told in His Writings and Speeches*, ed. F. N. Thorpe (New York: Tandy-Thomas
Co., 1909).

was crucial in the development of "mature" American modes of political action.

The Extension of the Franchise

The movement for extension of the suffrage in the United States is not attributable to Jackson himself, but to the spirit of an age which could make a Jackson the President. Indeed, it had, in large part, taken form during the decade of the 1820's before Jackson himself assumed the Presidency in 1828. But the democracy represented in the series of events which led to broadening of the franchise as well as in the election of the popular general from Tennessee to succeed an unbroken line of presidents from Virginia and Massachusetts is probably the most characteristic and important of the elements that made the period a distinctive juncture in American political ideas.[2]

The specific context of the movement to extend the franchise was one of widespread dissatisfaction with the obsolete state constitutions framed during the Revolutionary period. The adaptability of the American political temper is suggested in that by 1820 there was very considerable popular pressure to revise the old charters. These constitutions, though written only forty to fifty years earlier, had apparently come to seem like the products of another political era, inadequate to new needs. Liberal when they were written, they seemed conservative by the 1820's, primarily because of the extent to which they tied political power to wealth and assured to the "substantial" elements in the community the political instruments by which they could "balance" the demands of the democracy. This accumulation of dissatisfaction produced what was, except for the framing period of the federal Constitution, the most extraordinary manifestation in American history of the American penchant for constitution-writing. The issues were vital, and some of the finest minds ever engaged in American politics, including John Quincy Adams, Storey, Webster, Kent, Madison, Monroe, Randolph, and Marshall, participated in the redrafting of the various state constitutions. The three most significant conventions were those held in Massachusetts in 1820, in New York in 1821, and in Virginia in 1829 and 1830. The debates of these conventions contributed notably to the argument about the

---

[2] For discussion of the suffrage problem in general and the developments of this period, see Alfred De Grazia, *Public and Republic: Political Representation in America* (New York: A. A. Knopf, 1951); Kirk H. Porter, *A History of Suffrage in the United States* (Chicago: University of Chicago Press, 1918); Chilton Williamson, *American Suffrage from Property to Democracy: 1760–1860* (Princeton: Princeton University Press, 1960).

meaning and proper extent of the democratic suffrage.[3] The specific issue generally at stake was that of representation in the state senate, which had, up to this time, been the preserve of the people of property.

The Jacksonian arguments were based upon the literal reassertion of fundamental principles presumably already incorporated into the American political tradition. In a sense, the Jacksonian democrats argued that their demands merely looked toward realization of what the American political system had seemed to promise all along. American government was based on fundamental principles of equality, popular liberty, and natural rights; it was intended to be a government of the people, not a government of property. The restriction of the franchise, therefore, was simply the invidious denial of a right to consent, one of the basic rights of a free people. To extend the franchise would be merely to take seriously and to put into political practice commitments to established ideals.

It is most interesting to note that the arguments of these "radicals" were not arguments against property or the protection of property. They did not attack the validity of property rights and did not seek political power through the extension of the franchise in order to make inroads on the protection of property by the government.[4] This protection was granted to be essential and, indeed, defended by reference to the same set of commitments used in support of the case for broadening political participation. Indeed, these arguments illustrate the extent to which the right to property was fundamental to

-----

[3] See *Journal of Debates and Proceedings in the Convention of Delegates Chosen to Revise the Constitution of Massachusetts* (1820) (Boston: 1853); *Reports of the Proceedings and Debates of the Convention of 1821* (Albany: State of New York, 1821); *Proceedings and Debates of the Virginia State Convention of 1829–30* (Richmond: Ritchie and Cook, 1830). Illustrative selections from the debates in all three states may be found in A. T. Mason, *Free Government in the Making: Readings in American Political Thought* (2d ed; New York: Oxford University Press, 1956), pp. 382–428.

[4] Consider, for example, the following comments by David Buel, Jr., in the New York Convention:

I contend, that by the true principle of our government, property, as such, is not the basis of representation. Our community is an association of persons—of human beings—not a partnership founded on property. The declared object of the people of this state in associating, was, to 'establish such a government as they deemed best calculated to secure the rights and liberties of the good people of the state, and most conducive to their happiness and safety.' Property, it is admitted, is one of the rights to be protected and secured; and although the protection of life and liberty is the highest object of attention, it is certainly true, that the security of property is a most interesting and important object in every free government. Property is essential to our temporal happiness; and is necessarily one of the most interesting subjects of legislation. The desire of acquiring property is a universal passion. ... Property is only one of the incidental rights of the person who possesses it; and, as such, it must be made secure; but it does not follow, that it must therefore be represented specifically in any branch of government. (Quoted in Mason, *ibid.*, p. 407.)

classic liberalism, for the theory with which we are dealing characteristically combines a defense of individual rights with assertion of the fundamental importance of protecting private property through and from government. In a major sense, the right to property provided the impetus for those who advanced the case for a broader franchise; political power was seen as a means of facilitating mobility, and property ownership was an end for which mobility was sought. The notion that all men aspire to property, often heard in the conventions which reshaped state constitutions, suggests the motivation that lay behind the Jacksonian demand for the realization of a broader democracy.

The arguments of the democrats were not class arguments; in fact, they often denied class antagonism and, in a sense, repudiated the class interpretation of politics. They denied, as Taylor had denied in his arguments against Adams' concept of aristocracy, that differences among men should be sealed into the political arrangements by which the community governed itself. Their rhetoric was that of eighteenth-century individualism, not that of nineteenth-century class theory. It looked back to standards assertedly implicit or explicit in the historic American version of proper political arrangements.

It is interesting to set beside these democratic arguments the case of those who would have maintained a restricted franchise qualified by property ownership requirements. This group held that the control of political power by those who own property is a natural phenomenon, a phenomenon whose perpetuation by constitutional arrangement is in the best interests of the full society. On its descriptive side, this bit of theory is a reassertion of the Harringtonian proposition that political power necessarily flows into the hands of those who control the economic enterprise, particularly those who control the community's land resources. While a certain amount of industrialization had by this period begun to shift the emphasis from the position of the landed group to the position of those also who controlled financial and industrial resources, it still bore rather heavily on the real property factor. Regardless of this question, the theme of economic determinism was shared by the conservatives who used it to justify the predominance of wealth in the community, and by others who saw in it reasons for destroying the property system by peaceful or revolutionary means. The position advocating the system's destruction, incidentally, had few adherents in the America of Jackson's period. The conservatives, representing the claims of property in the debate over extension of the franchise, seem to have felt simply that the process of democratization was a rather foolish attempt to fight the inevitable. In the picturesque terms of John Randolph, "the two sexes do no more certainly gravitate to each other than power and property."[5]

More interesting, however, were two forthrightly prescriptive conservative arguments. Both are familiar; their significance derives largely from their implications when set beside the arguments of the democrats reviewed above. One ran to the age-old proposition that property and virtue tend to accompany each other. This is to say simply that property ownership is in itself a badge of virtue, that possession is an indication of the industriousness of the possessor, and that, generally, the poor are poor because they are indolent and wasteful. If this is assumed to be true, the implications for political power are obvious, as it is difficult to argue for constitutional arrangements that cast control of political authority in the hands of those whose incompetence is already demonstrated. The second prescriptive point was that the propertied have a greater interest in government, a greater stake in society. This argument is based on the view that influence in the political process should be proportioned to what one stands to gain in protection through the political process. It is closely allied to, though not identical with, the argument that the rich should pay more than the poor toward the support of political power, because they have more to gain by the maintenance of political power. These two basic ideas were accompanied by the corollary that the property system can best be preserved by checks on political power. In short, the entire line of argument runs something like this: Society as a whole will benefit by the rulership of those of demonstrated virtue; furthermore, the propertied have a higher claim on government by dint of the fact that they have more to gain from its effectiveness and more to lose from its ineffectiveness. Therefore, the property system deserves protection for the sake of the best interests of the entire society. This protection can be achieved (1) through institutional arrangements that recognize the propertied group's higher moral claims on political power by granting it disproportionate representation, and (2) by erecting formal and structural barriers between political authority and the "right" to property.

Basically, what the conservatives were stating was a class analysis of politics and society, an analysis founded on the fear that the poor would act as a class against the wealthy. From the conservative point of view, a realist outlook on political power must take account of this

---

[5] Quoted in *ibid.,* p. 425.

ever-present class conflict. In a strange way, these patrician arguments of the 1820's foreshadowed the Marxian analysis of politics that took shape a few years later. Marx's theory was not, of course, developed out of thin air. It was, as he and Engels suggested, part of his heritage from eighteenth-century liberalism and the primitive statements of modern socialism. In earlier American political thought, in the ideas, for example, of Madison and Adams, the relationship between property interests and political power had quite clearly been discussed. But the controversy over the extension of the franchise elicited a statement of the theory in specific terms, and its employment at this time in this context suggests the extent to which class relationships were being disturbed by the thrust toward democratization. In other circumstances, this argument might have been dangerous for those who propounded it when the battle was lost and suffrage became universal. For then, the conservatives would have been confronted with the necessity of persuading the poor not to act as a class and not to move against property ownership. The social and economic circumstances of the United States probably did this persuading for them, for threats to the basic values of property ownership were scarcely significant in the United States for at least a century after the Jacksonian period, and they are only doubtfully important even today.[6]

To a considerable extent in the conventions of the 1820's, and even more in the longer run, the radical position was triumphant. The extension of the franchise proceeded apace, and by 1850, the country realized nearly universal white manhood suffrage. Thus, it might be said that the age of Jackson brought about an instrumentation of one of the basic American values. Except for the persistently troublesome problems of the Negro suffrage in the southern states and the more easily handled question of woman suffrage, commitment to the standard of one man–one vote and equal access to the ballot box early became an almost unquestioned part of the American political tradition. Incorporation of this general value into the American tradition did not, of course, resolve all the problems associated with practical use of popular political power. Indeed, it created in itself further problems for the system to attempt to resolve, demonstrated currently not only in the move for racial political equality but also in the matter of reapportionment. But in both positive and negative terms, the impact on the American political system of the effectuation of the doctrine of political equality was staggering. Some of its effects can

---

[6] Cf. *ibid.*, p. 385.

be seen clearly in other structural and institutional developments of the Jacksonian age.

The Alteration of the Party System

The most striking institutional impact of the Jacksonian period of American political practice was felt through its contributions to the shaping of the political party system and the Presidency. Developments in both these fields were closely related to the Jacksonian passion for democracy demonstrated in the movement for revision of the suffrage.[7] Both were evidence of the depth and importance of that fundamental commitment. Though manifest more in action than in abstract idea, they were, probably, the best evidence of the predominant tendencies in American theory and ideology afoot during this period when so many of the aspects of the American political tradition were being given their contemporary form.

The theoretical and ideological implications of these changes in the American party system wrought by the Jacksonian period can be explained rather briefly. They were, in part, demonstrated by the very conditions under which Jackson was elected to the presidential office. His was the first election since Washington's in which the Congress did not either at the stage of nomination or at the stage of election have a hand sufficient to give it control over selection of the executive. It was also immediately preceded by three instances in which the Secretary of State of the outgoing President's Cabinet succeeded the chief executive. It indeed began to appear that the office of Secretary of State was coming to provide its possessor with a claim to automatic succession.

But more importantly, Jacksonianism also witnessed the breakup of established American party alignments and the development of a new basis and new roles for the political party within the system. Bitterness over John Quincy Adams' 1824 victory in the House of Representatives magnified internal divisions within the predominant Republican party. Even before 1828, competing groups had crystallized around opposing party leaders—Adams and Clay on the one hand, Jackson and Calhoun on the other. These groups came to be identified as National Republicans—shortly to be called Whigs—and Democrats, parties that in a very loose sense are the forebears of our

---

[7] For discussion of the historical backgrounds, see Claude Bowers, *The Party Battles of the Jacksonian Period* (Boston and New York: Houghton Mifflin Co., 1922); Wilfred Binkley, *American Political Parties: Their Natural History* (New York: A. A. Knopf, 1947), pp. 120–51.

major parties today, though there was, of course, no institutional continuity between the Whig party and the Republican party of 1856 forward. The division in the national party was reflected into local party arrangements and, to some extent, was also sectional in basis. It would seem fair to say, however, that the Whig–Democratic division was chiefly based on conflicts of interest rather than conflicts of class or section.

The key to the significance of this development lies in the growing extent to which the large body of the American people was being involved in the operation of the political system. It was during this period, for example, that presidential electors generally came to be chosen by popular vote rather than by state legislatures. It was also during this period that the nominating convention replaced the caucus of national political leaders as the mechanism for selection of party candidates for President. While today the convention may not seem the paragon of democratic devices for selection of candidates to public office, by comparison with caucus nomination, it represented a giant step toward democratization. It was also during the Jacksonian period that the political campaign itself came to be carried to the people, that the presidential election became an exercise in the elicitation of citizen approval on a mass basis.[8]

Thus, it may be claimed that during the period of Jacksonian democracy the American party system became one of the important things it is today, a connecting link between popular will and those who determine governmental policy. The development of the party was the development of a structuring device for political consent, the organizational vehicle for the principle of democracy. This is not to claim, of course, that the party immediately became an effective mediating device between public opinion and public policy. Political practices develop slowly, and the effectiveness of this one is still a matter of question. But the important point is that the institutional structure of the American Constitution was so importantly and permanently modified through the party system to accommodate and make meaningful the broadened concept of consent implicit in the Jacksonian version of democratic politics. It may also be noted that to an important degree the Jacksonian democratic movement represented the embellishment and institutionalization of Jeffersonian ideas and practice, for the development of the party, like the develop-

---

[8] Interestingly, Jackson himself suggested in his first Annual Message that the electoral college be eliminated so as to assure "fair expression of the will of the majority." Thorpe, *op. cit.*, p. 43.

ment of a broadened franchise, was the effectuation and refinement of basic Jeffersonian commitments. Jefferson himself was instrumental in, if not responsible for, the development of an earlier party schism within the American system. Jacksonian democracy in its political party manifestations may thus again be seen as the instrumentation of preexisting commitments and tendencies.

Jacksonian democracy contributed to the development of the American party device at its policy end as well as its popular end, i.e., added to the effectiveness of the party as a contributor to the policy process. Here, too, it drew on its Jeffersonian heritage, for Jefferson had used the party with some success as a sounding board for policy and an instrument for control of decision-making. Jackson did not have a free hand with Congress. But his party did serve him as a binding substance around and through which issues could be defined and promoted. While the conditioning characteristics of American society have prevented parties from being truly effective policy machines, they have become, thanks in part to the Jacksonian reinforcement, media for some communication between executive and legislative bodies. This development represents a further step in the adaptation of the system of separation of powers to the needs of positive government in a society of expanding scale. In this respect, Jacksonianism embraced a measure of Hamilton along with its core of Jefferson.

In summary terms, the period of Jacksonian democracy projected the American political party into its characteristic modern form. The main characteristics of this form may be described as follows: (1) The party system developed in the first place mainly because of the confrontation of the principle of consent with a society of such scale and complexity that popular government could not work without the mediating effects of the party. (2) The particular shape or configuration of the political party system—its structural and ideological characteristics—was influenced by both the constitutional characteristics of the society and the social characteristics of the community as respects such things as division and distribution of interests. (3) The function of the political party within the political system is fundamentally to provide a structure of consent or communication from populace to decision-makers. (4) Particularly as the society has grown more complex, the party has also come to play the complementary role of communicator in the reverse direction, from decision-maker to populace. (5) The motivating force in the party system has been neither ideological nor communicative, but has rested in the personal interests and power and career motivations of those who have assumed leadership in the party structure. (6) By virtue of its communicative role within a system whose formal, i.e., constitutional, communicative channels are limited, the party has become a device which knits the system together around its substantive policy on public issues.

Democratization of the Presidency

Very closely related both in source and impact to the development of political parties during the period was the Jacksonian contribution to the Presidency. Here again, Jacksonianism seems to have played the role of pushing to realization some of the early abstract commitments of the American nation. It appears that the Founding Fathers widely shared the Lockean–Jeffersonian view that the legislative department would become the forum of the people, particularly through its lower house, and that the executive would exercise a kind of balance on behalf of stability and substantiality. It was in extension of this principle that Adams developed his case for a strong executive power and Jefferson his case for a system of modified legislative supremacy. Thus, it seems to have been the expectation of most of the founders and most of the liberal theorists of the time that the executive would be a bastion of privilege, and it was the hope of some, most notably Jefferson, that for this reason the executive power would be restricted.

The political and social developments of the Jacksonian period stood this theory of institutions on its head. The main contribution of the period and of Jackson himself to American political ideas and practice was doubtless felt in the democratization of the American Presidency.[9] The Jacksonian change in modes of selecting the chief executive has been mentioned above. This change, of course, meant the executive was no longer reliant on the Congress for office or power, but owed his preference to the people. Thus, the President alone of all public officials came to represent a national popular constituency. The impact of changes in mode of selection and basis of power have made of the presidential office, to use the phrase of Henry Jones Ford, "an elective kingship."[10] More clearly than ever before, the President became not only a political actor but the American system's nearest thing to the embodiment of national will.

This development in the presidential office was closely related

---

[9] A classic analysis is found in Henry Jones Ford, *The Rise and Growth of American Politics* (New York: Macmillan Co., 1900). See also E. S. Corwin, *The President: Office and Powers* (3d ed.; New York: Washington University Press, 1948), pp. 22–28 and *passim*.

[10] Ford, *op. cit.*, p. 293.

both as cause and effect to the specific political controversies that flared around Jackson's Presidency as well as to his style in the conduct of the office. The Whig opposition, centering in the Senate, took on in the course of events the appearance of protector of certain special interests, and in contrast, Jackson came to seem the champion of the people. Jackson was an apt medium for the forces of change not only politically but personally. A popular hero and a product of the backwoods himself, his conduct and associations were flamboyant when compared to those of his predecessors, the Virginia gentleman politicians and the asture Adams. Even in appearance, he fit well the role of "democratizer." Whether self-conscious creator or unwitting vehicle (and he was surely some of both), Jackson's career in the Presidency illustrated well the potential impact of the political actor on the system in which he acts.

Three specific aspects of Jackson's approach to the office illustrate the thrust and content of his contributions. He was responsible for the revivification and redefinition of the veto power. In the message accompanying his famous veto of the bill recharting the Bank of the United States, he stated forcefully if not particularly clearly his conviction that the veto power was the weapon of an independent and coordinate executive branch, to be exercised in judgment on both constitutional and policy issues. The veto afforded an occasion for a show of force and an opportunity to formulate and articulate views about the nature and breadth of the presidential power. Jackson's pronouncements on the question dealt mostly with the matter of constitutionality, but its broader point was the independence of the President in participating in the policy-making process. Jackson left no doubt that he considered this participation a rightful part of the constitutional relations among the departments of government.

His handling of the question of the deposit of public funds in the Bank of the United States also demonstrated in rather dramatic terms his style and view of the presidential office. The fact that he removed two Secretaries of the Treasury because of their refusal to execute his order to withdraw the funds may seem extraordinary today when experience has accustomed us to such presidential power. The situation in Jackson's time, however, was a good deal different, in part because the Jacksonian precedent was not then available. The Treasury Department had developed and maintained a peculiar relationship with Congress, a relationship so strong and direct that Congress had come to view the operation of the Treasury as at least as much under its control as within control of the President himself. Such relationships between Congress and bureaucracy or bureaucratic agencies are not, of course, unheard of even today. But as Jackson's very election to the Presidency flew in the face of precedent, so did his dismissal of this Cabinet officer when his directions were refused. The dispute itself raises interesting organizational questions about the relationship of chief executive, bureaucracy, and legislative body, questions still pertinent to the conduct of government. Beyond this, the incident illustrates the lengths to which Jackson would go to impose his hand on the development and administration of national policy. The course of action he chose with respect to the Bank and the Treasury raised bitter outcries in the Senate. In the face of these, however, Jackson reasserted executive control and, in the process, further developed the tools of his office. The episode is significant both for its continuity with the Hamiltonian tradition and for its implications for subsequent administrative practice.

A third contribution of the Jacksonian Presidency to the institutionalization of American democracy lay in his use of the patronage device. Here again, the development of the political party and the development of the Presidency converged to establish a common stream of political action. Jackson did not invent the spoils system nor the patronage idea. Patronage is a term broad enough to refer to practices that have been used in politics since time out of mind. Jefferson, on his assumption of the Presidency, made some changes among federal jobholders to favor his own political supporters, but until the time of Jackson there was a striking continuity in the occupancy of federal office, even at the top levels. It was not uncommon even for Cabinet members to remain in office from one administration to the next. Jackson, however, effected a complete change in personnel in the upper echelons and replaced, an authority states, 252 of 612 presidential appointees.[11]

The full implications of Jackson's use of the patronage power may better be gauged by his rationalization of patronage and by its effects on the political system. Patronage is a device which interconnects the democratic idea, the power of the President, and the role of the party in the political system. Jackson defended on democratic grounds the idea of rotation in office, claiming also that this extension of the democratic principle helped to assure efficiency and honesty in the conduct of the public business. In his first annual message to Congress, he phrased his position as follows:

[11] S. E. Morrison and H. S. Commager, *Growth of the American Republic* (New York: Oxford University Press, 1942), Vol. I, pp. 472–73.

The duties of all public offices are, or at least admit of being made, so plain and simple that men of intelligence may readily qualify themselves for their performance; and I can not but believe that more is lost by the long continuance of men in office than is generally to be gained by their experience.

In a country where offices are created solely for the benefit of the people no one man has any more intrinsic right to official station than another.[12]

The idea is similar to one later stated by Karl Marx, namely, that the bureaucratic functions are sufficiently simple that nearly everyone in society is capable of undertaking them. It also suggests that rotation in office is not only good as a matter of principle, but protects the public from the deleterious effects of vested interest in public office, effects including both corruption and inefficiency.

Through the patronage power, the President also gained a tool for the assertion of his will on the bureaucracy and thus enhanced his equipment for playing an energetic role in the control of governmental policy. The extent of presidential control over the bureaucracy has been a persistent issue, illustrated in Jackson's own difficulties over the Secretary of Treasury, in a variety of later controversies over the Civil Service system, and in such recent Court cases as Myers, Rathbun, and Weiner.[13] On this matter again, the thrust of Jacksonian democracy was toward comprehensive presidential control. While the insulation of the bureaucracy from political influence was later to be an "ideal" of American politics manifest in civil service reform, the converse was the goal of Jacksonian democracy. One of its central aims was to render the civil servant responsible to political forces rather than keep him free of them.

Obviously, the development of the patronage system was also a step toward strengthening the political party in the American system. One of the ideas behind the patronage system is succinctly expressed in Senator Marcy's famous phrase, "to the victor belong the spoils," the assumption being that the victor will use these spoils to further enhance the political capital of his party or group. Historically, patronage has been one of the adhesive forces of the American political party, a source of reward for the party faithful, a stimulant to enthusiasm, a device through which leverage can be exerted to assure party political unity and further party policy. Some students have claimed that the development of the Civil Service system, destroying as it does the mag-

---

[12] Thorpe, *op. cit.*, pp. 44–45.

[13] All cases having to do with the removal power of the President: *Myers* v. *United States,* 272 U.S. 52 (1926); *Humphrey's Executor (Rathbun)* v. *United States,* 295 U.S. 602 (1935); *Weiner* v. *United States,* 357 U.S. 349 (1958).

nitude of the patronage power, has had greater negative than positive effects on the American political system because it has vitiated party effectiveness. However this may be, one of the substantial Jacksonian contributions to both the theory and practice of the American political tradition was the reinvigoration of the parties through the reassertion of patronage power.

Thus, Jacksonian democracy illustrated theory manifest in practice and practice manifest in theory. Its key lay in the development and refinement of the operating devices of government by consent. At this point in time, the democratic ideal was assured a payoff, for as it took institutional form in the party, the popular Presidency, and the controlled bureaucracy, it built the practices of large-scale democracy into the American tradition. While no political development is assured permanence, the impact of this one is still felt.

Jacksonian Public Policy

What has been said above about Jacksonianism gives little indication of its characteristic views about the scope of governmental power or the substance of public policy. On examination, these turn out to be the converse of what one might expect. In the light of the Jacksonian preference for basic democracy and an energetic executive, one might expect it to have produced an energetic and welfare-oriented public policy, but that was scarcely the case. The program of Jacksonianism had a utilitarian ring, an orientation similar to that of the English philosophical radicals. The crux of such a program lies in the theory that society is characterized by a harmony of interests through which conflict will resolve itself by natural means. Given this notion, the role of government lies merely in the protection of equal rights, except in those rare instances when the forces of natural harmony fail. Thus, government is only an artificial harmonizer for a residuum of rare situations. Its general maxim is: Leave society alone so the forces of natural harmony can do their work; tampering when unnecessary only disturbs the balance of things. The policy of government, then, is controlled by the attitude of laissez faire.

Translated into prescription, such an interpretation of society severely limits the role of government in the regulation and promotion of economic and social activities. In terms of actual policy, Jackson opposed high tariffs, spending for internal improvements, public indebtedness, and taxation beyond the minimum necessary for the support of legitimate public functions. As we have already indicated, he considered the national bank to be both unconstitutional and unwise. In more general terms, the Jacksonian orientation revolved around an attack on privilege and monopoly and on the variety of social forces whose effect was to limit freedom of action and restrict economic competition. If to the twentieth-century mind such an attitude toward government policy seems ill-suited to a political movement based on democratic appeals to the masses, the seeming dilemma can be resolved by considering the nature of the social forces that underlay Jacksonian democracy. The period really marked the beginning of rapid American social expansion upward. It was the period when new opportunities were sought on the frontier and when industrial revolution in urban areas began to suggest new possibilities for economic and social ascent. Jackson's political power rested in large part on small holders, mechanics, and frontiersmen who saw the future in terms of unfettered opportunities to improve their situations. Not yet jaded either by the closing of the frontier or by the realization of adverse effects and limited opportunities inherent in industrial enterprise, they wanted nothing more than competitive opportunity freed from and protected by the power of the state.

It cannot be argued that the economic attitudes described above were embraced by all "Jacksonians." American political movements are seldom as monolithic as they must be described in a treatment such as this. On the one hand, William Cullen Bryant, editor of the New York *Evening Post,* provided the laissez faire position with one of its more extreme statements. Bryant advocated free trade, doubted the legitimacy of granting corporation charters, and even went so far as to urge the abandonment of usury laws. On the other hand, Orestes Brownson dissented from the laissez faire doctrine and advocated a kind of mild Christian socialism through which control of the state by the workers could protect workers' rights and end the exploitation that accompanied the wage system. But the main policy and theoretical bent of Jacksonian democracy lay in the laissez faire principle. The acute analysis of Jacksonian American society provided by the works of Alexis de Tocqueville suggests some of the causes and effects of this ideological orientation in American society.

TOCQUEVILLE'S PERSPECTIVE ON JACKSONIAN AMERICA

Tocqueville's *Democracy in America,* published in 1835 as a result of a visit the young Frenchman paid to the United States earlier in the decade, is without doubt one of the most influential books on American politics ever written.[14] Its author was not only an astute observer

---

[14] Many English language editions of this great work are available, the most common

of social life, but also a keen analyst of what he saw. He combined the virtues of imagination, system, acute observation, and skillful and lucid writing to set forth a view of politics that has grown more impressive with age. Few books in the history of political writing demonstrate better the durability of perceptive political analysis; Tocqueville's themes and observations have a fascinating currency—their influence on political thinking is patent even down to the present day.[15]

Both Tocqueville himself and his work on America are complicated subjects to which we cannot do full justice in the course of a few pages. For our purposes, *Democracy in America* has two major values —its description of life and politics in the Jacksonian era, and its theory of politics, particularly its insightful treatment of the relationship of ideas to political structure and action. The two volumes of *Democracy in America* are filled with detail on the first, and this we must largely omit; what follows, then, will focus chiefly on the second. Basically, Tocqueville's contribution will be treated here as a general and profound model of politics with particular value for what it suggests about the important underlying characteristics of the American political system.

The primary problem in Tocqueville's theory had to do with the social effects of the broad democratic revolution of the modern world, a revolution of which the eighteenth-century American struggle was only one manifestation. More specifically, Tocqueville's question was: What had happened to political and social relationships under the impact of changes in fundamental modes of thought in the Western world? Perhaps the basic element in this change as he saw it was the breakdown of the "status" society of medieval Europe. This breakdown was a gradual process with differential rates and effects in various cultures. Overall, however, the political and social development of the modern world has been characterized by the evolution of society from a condition of simplicity, localism, and primary social relationships to a "contract" situation, a situation in which relationships have come to seem and be artificial rather than natural. Modern man,

---

being the Reeves translation, e.g., *Democracy in America* (2 vols.; New York: A. A. Knopf, 1945). Citations that follow are to this edition. Commentary on Tocqueville is sparse. See, however, J. P. Mayer, *Alexis de Tocqueville: a Bibliographic Essay in Political Science,* trans. M. M. Bozeman and C. Hahn (New York: The Viking Press, 1940); Jack Lively, *The Social and Political Thought of Alexis de Tocqueville* (Oxford: Clarendon Press, 1962).

[15] See, for example, William Kornhauser, *The Politics of Mass Society* (Glencoe: The Free Press, 1959), *passim;* S. M. Lipset, *Union Democracy* (Glencoe: The Free Press, 1956), pp. 74–76; S. M. Lipset, *Political Man* (Garden City: Doubleday & Co., Inc., 1960), *passim,* esp. pp. 24–28.

by the shift in the basis of social organization, has lost a good part of his attachment to society and the orientation provided him by traditional arrangements. In modern times, the formulation is a familiar one. Since Tocqueville, it has been stated and restated by countless social scientists and philosophers, perhaps most influentially in the works of Marx, Durkheim, Tonnies, and Simmel. Socially, Tocqueville suggested, modern men are shorn of the roots that formerly bound societies together.

They owe nothing to any man, they expect nothing from any man; they acquire the habit of always considering themselves as standing alone, and they are apt to imagine that their whole destiny is in their own hands.

Thus not only does democracy make every man forget his ancestors, but it hides his descendants and separates his contemporaries from him; it throws him back forever upon himself alone and threatens in the end to confine him entirely within the solitude of his own heart.[16]

Ideologically, the most significant symbol of this characteristic condition of modern man is the symbol of equality. Tocqueville emphasized the importance of equality in two senses, both as the "ideal and end" of the democratic society and as the fundamental fact of modern society. Equality, in other words, has become the key symbolic representation of the democratic social revolution. The ideal of equality, deriving its importance from the age of the democratic revolution, has drawn men to demand political, economic, and social controls over their own destinies. Its realization in political and economic upheaval has, in turn, created the conditions in which the politics and society of democracy must operate. The ideology of equality, then, has determined both the nature of social change itself in the modern world and the political alterations that change has brought in its train.

As to politics, the changes in individual life (and, hence, in social structure) brought about by the equalitarian revolution have caused the destruction of community and, with it, the destruction of the stabilizing effects of community authority. Modern society has witnessed the destruction of the old sources of stability, a situation which threatens to reduce the human condition to anarchy. A look at American society, where this equalitarian social revolution had gone furthest in Tocqueville's time, however, made it apparent that it had recreated the conditions for stability, viability, and progress. Despite its attachment to individualism and equality, it embodied many community characteristics that had disappeared. Tocqueville's question of Amer-

---

[16] Alexis de Tocqueville, *Democracy in America,* trans. Henry Reeve (New York: A. A. Knopf, 1945), Vol. II, p. 99.

ican institutions was: How can this phenomenon be explained—what it is that holds this artificial community together, makes living in propinquity possible, and provides mechanisms for the solution of the many kinds of problems and conflicts to which an individualist society must necessarily give rise?

Tocqueville took his cue from a general theoretical proposition that it must be authority of some kind which holds the community together and provides for the resolution of difficulties. With loss of the natural authority of the status society, the modern society of equality has developed an authority in its own characteristic mode, an authority adapted to the underlying ideological demands of the social revolution. Democratic man, said Tocqueville, has *created* the only authority tolerable in terms of his own ideology, namely the authority of himself en masse. He has substituted dependence on the majority of his equals for his lost dependence on the structure of the status system. He has created the political form to correspond to the social condition and the ideology of his age, the form commonly called democratic.

The real problem, however, arises from the implications and consequences of the democratic authority system. Tocqueville believed that the equalitarianism of modern democratic society may have either of two consequences, one of which he clearly valued over the other. It may lead, he suggested, either to the breakdown of liberty or to the development of a system of individual freedom and morality. He was, perhaps, most interested in pointing out the evil implication of equalitarianism, which he thought not so apparent as its good ones, and for this reason, he sometimes seemed to suggest that the development of democracy necessarily thrusts man in an illiberal direction. This interpretation however, seems to overstep Tocqueville's theory, for he postulated the possibility but not the necessity that democratic society and ideology precurse the development of a totalitarianism of the mass in which men are reduced to uniformity, conformity, and the mediocrity of a lowest common denominator.

The alternative he thought quite feasible: freedom may be substituted for servitude, knowledge for barbarism, and prosperity for wretchedness. The passion for equality may be accompanied by or perhaps even lead to the development of the values of the liberal society. Tocqueville concluded on the basis of his observation that America had to an extent achieved a more desirable liberal situation, for he recognized that to a considerable degree American political life had managed to preserve the individual freedom and privacy sought by the Founding Fathers. This conclusion, in turn, stimulated a further question: How has it happened that America has managed to maintain liberty in a situation where the passion for equality has burned bright and democratic revolution rather rapidly run its course? Tocqueville's analysis pointed out three liberalizing characteristics which, taken together, may provide the answer to this question. The first is historical. American society, developing from a colonial situation, had, in a sense, never been a status society after the fashion of the older European nations. Relatively speaking, America has always been equalitarian, devoid of the measure of class hatred and war that accompanied the democratic revolution in Europe. That the American Revolution could take the form of a revolution against an external oppressive power saved the American society from the trauma of deep internal dissension. It, of course, must be recognized that the American Revolution was accompanied by both social and political distinctions among groups, and that before and after the Revolution the country was the scene of some class tension. But these were indeed mild when compared with the similar difficulties of the continental countries. Thus, one might say that by heritage and historical situation the achievement of democracy by Americans did not bring in its wake so much of the need to level barriers and distinctions. The bitterness of the American Revolution was siphoned off in bitterness toward the English Crown and English Parliament, and thereby relieved of the need to find internal targets.

A second explanatory factor in the resistance of American democracy to the pull of totalitarianism might be found, Tocqueville suggested, in the forms of American politics. These forms, inherited and gradually modified from British usage, almost accidentally provided for checks on the authoritarian exercise of political power. In regionalism and localism and in such institutions as the separation of powers, America possessed a kind of built-in protection against some of the worst tendencies of authority resting in the hands of the mass.

The third factor, a sociological one, involved what is perhaps the best-known aspect of Tocqueville's work on politics. The presence of a network of voluntary associations affords social protection against arbitrary authority and provides a social corrective for some of the negative effects of the society of artificial social relationships. Tocqueville was struck, like many later students of American institutions, by the extent to which the people of the country were inclined to carry on activities through private groups. He wrote:

> Only those associations that are formed in civil life without reference to political objects are here referred to. The political associations that exist

in the United States are only a single feature in the midst of the immense assemblage of associations in that country. Americans of all ages, all conditions, and all dispositions, constantly form associations. They have not only commercial and manufacturing companies, in which all take part, but associations of a thousand other kinds, religious, moral, serious, futile, general or restrictive, enormous or dimunitive. The Americans make associations to give entertainments, to found seminaries, to build inns, to construct churches, to diffuse books, to send missionaries to the antipodes; and in this manner they found hospitals, prisons, and schools. If it is proposed to advance some truth or to foster some feeling by the encouragement of a great example, they form a society. Wherever, at the head of some new undertaking you see the government in France or a man of rank in England, in the United States you will be sure to find an association.[17]

These associations serve to fill the void between the weak individual and the overbearing mass. They provide an artificial attachment to substitute for lost ties both in "locating" the individual in the social world and in providing through numbers significant opposition to political tyranny. Tocqueville describes the social role of these associations as follows:

Feelings and opinions are recruited, the heart is enlarged, and the human mind is developed only by the reciprocal influence of men upon each other. I have shown that these influences are almost null in democratic countries; they must therefore be artificially created, and this can only be accomplished by associations.[18]

Tocqueville's position on the importance of the private group in a democratic society has been a subject of considerable attention and widespread agreement among later democratic theorists. It has often been broadened to the proposition that liberal democracy is impossible in the absence of a layer of free voluntary organizations. Its prescriptive implications are vast and have, without doubt, been influential both in American theory and in the development of American practice with its considerable emphasis on freedom of association. The position itself is not dissimilar from that of the later pluralists who posited for the group not only a personality and reality of its own, but *the* vital role in the preservation of liberal freedoms. While America is not unique in respect to this proliferation of private associations, it is interesting to note that a gross historical perspective on the development of modern democracy as well as a considerable amount of research on smaller scale organizations seem to provide some empirical validation

---

[17] *Ibid.*, Vol. II, p. 106.
[18] *Ibid.*, Vol. II, pp. 108–9.

for Tocqueville's position. Consider, for example, the fate of the
private association in those modern countries, most strikingly Germany and the Soviet Union, where the democratic ideology of equality
has been accompanied by totalitarian political and social forms. Consider, indeed, from the French Revolution to the present the un-
friendliness of totalitarian mass movements in general toward the
divisive effects of faction. The evidence suggests strongly the viability
of Tocqueville's position on the central importance of the private
group in the maintenance of liberty. It is incidentally interesting to
note how this portion of Tocqueville's theory cuts from the level of
individual psychology through the level of social structure and organization to the level of political authority and policy.

Tocqueville's writing also suggested that the social condition of
modern man, with its tension between equality and liberty, had certain identifiable effects on the American character. Several aspects of
the American style of life seemed to him unique and reflective of the
society's ideological structure. He thought, for example, that one effect of living in this type of society was the frantic release of energy
in economic activities. The American is typically a man constantly in
motion, endeavoring to achieve success and carrying on his struggle
within the context of a society where relative equality of condition
is typical. This equality of condition means that the attainment of distinction requires greater effort, and that a rather slight movement in
social position either up or down becomes rather obvious against the
background of the social setting. The economic life offers the most
obvious vehicle for both the release of pent-up energy and the achievement which may set one apart from his fellows. In this respect, it
might be well to recall that Tocqueville wrote during the era of laissez
faire.

The American society may further be described as apolitical, as
a society in which far greater attention falls to economic pursuits than
to the political sector. Politics is, after all, in itself an institutionalization of equality in a democracy. Political life, therefore, is not a particularly attractive arena for seeking distinction. In a situation in
which man's urge to differentiate himself runs against a politics ideologically committed to equality, politics as a career is likely to be rejected.

A similar set of considerations Tocqueville thought to condition
the American attitude toward change. Here, he found the typical disposition conservative, i.e., not resistant to changes incipient in eco-

nomic or social development, but deeply suspicious of change that threatens a major revision in relationships. This follows from the sensitivity of modern man, particularly modern American man, to changes in status. Thus, a radical readjustment in society is threatening because unpredictable in its effects on the status structure. Most people decline to take the risk: "[Americans] love change but they dread revolutions." [19]

Two aspects of Tocqueville's political work merit some further attention, if only to suggest their importance and implications for the study of contemporary politics. One has to do with the theoretical nature of Tocqueville's intellectual enterprise, the second with the modern implications of the substance of his theory. On the first, it will be clear that what has been said above represents a good deal of abstraction and considerable interpolation from Tocqueville's writings. But the author's own clarities make his work subject to the sort of systemization that yields contemporary empirical theory—indeed, almost invites it. With some imagination, Tocqueville's commentary on American politics may be seen to yield theory on at least three levels.

In the first place, it yields a general model of political relationships. The present interpretation has emphasized a model in which ideology is the central term and the causal progression runs from ideology to social structure to political forms and, in turn, loops back to ideology. This general description of the model, of course, neither defines variables nor characterizes the mechanisms, content, or strength of the relationships. An examination of Tocqueville's writings on politics suggests much of the way in which these aspects of the theory might be filled out.

On another level, Tocqueville provided a partial test of his model on a specific society, the society of American democracy in the Jacksonian period. Though in an impressionistic and rather unsystematic fashion, he did take his propositions about political relationships to the empirical materials of the American society of the time. It may be noted that to a striking degree the evidence both from that period and later suggests strongly the validity of many of Tocqueville's formulations. It should also be noted that while his theory and tests were broad and general in character, dealing with gross units of analysis, many of his propositions have since been refined and tested with simpler societies under better control.

At a third level, Tocqueville also dealt, though largely implicitly,

---

[19] *Ibid.*, Vol. II, p. 255.

in prescriptive theory. Though the foregoing paragraphs have not attempted in any broad way to characterize Tocqueville's political position, it doubtless conditioned both the nature of his theory and many of his specific observations about American politics. At the same time, Tocqueville's work suggests both the impact of a value position on what is fundamentally a descriptive framework and the extent to which it is possible to separate a descriptive theory from its value context. The work itself was vastly influenced by the climate of opinion in which it was written, in a broad sense substantially liberal in tone, and its major propositions—for example, its concern with the impact of equality on liberty—are propositions to which the value system itself no doubt gave rise. The entire framework, like most if not all frameworks for political investigation, demonstrates the constraints imposed on theory by the intellectual tradition in which it grows. Still, these are questions that can be stated in testable form and taken to test with empirical materials, where they may help to validate a theory which, however much its general shape is bounded by a system of preferences, still contains elements of experiential verity.

It is unnecessary to do any more than mention the contemporary implications of Tocqueville's political ideas as they have been adverted to in specific contexts in the foregoing paragraphs. But perhaps it is fitting to mention their particular applicability in an era when the mass society has become a reality and some of its political potential has been realized in the most brutal forms of totalitarianism. Tocqueville's theory was substantially a theory of the mass society that foreshadowed some of the threats to which liberal democracy has been subjected in the twentieth century. His experience with his native France made him no stranger to such threats, and his prescriptions may not be effective in an age when interdependence and fundamental democratization have gone much further than he in his day could have dreamed. But his warnings remain meaningful for those who would preserve liberal values and institutions, and are made particularly meaningful by the fact that they were developed as American democracy in the Jacksonian period brought a democratic ideology to its apex and provided such substantial impetus for the perfection of democratic institutions and structures. In the section to follow, we will review some characteristic American romantic and philosophical defenses of the Jacksonian revolution, and examine some statements on politics that pushed these preferences to their ulterior implications.

BASIC DEMOCRACY: ROMANTIC VERSIONS

Complementary to the political developments and accompanying commentaries of the Jacksonian period—i.e., of the period extending roughly from 1825 to the Civil War—was an outpouring of philosophical and literary works that caught the spirit of the age and provided both inspiration for and interpretation of the growing American democracy and maturing American nationhood. This period may be described as the great age of American literature. In addition to Emerson and Thoreau and Whitman, with whom we will deal at somewhat greater length below, the literary life of the time saw the publication of such essayists, poets, and novelists as William Cullen Bryant, Nathaniel Hawthorne, James Fenimore Cooper, and Herman Melville; such historians as Francis Parkman and George Bancroft; and in addition, such humanitarians and reformers as Lucretia Mott, Elizabeth Cady Stanton, Margaret Fuller, and Dorothea Dix. Out of the writings and other activities of this prodigious list of American greats came much social commentary.[20]

It cannot be said that there was philosophical, political, or artistic homogeneity among the intellectual leaders of the time. In interests, talents, and social attitudes, they exhibited substantial and significant differences. The period was characterized, however, like nearly any period, by certain fundamental themes that were broadly if not universally shared among its creative figures. In a quite general sense, most of the literature and reform of this period was pulled together in the individualism of Jacksonian democracy. The romanticism we are treating in the present section cannot be thought to represent the consensus of Jacksonianism, but rather to represent one form of the expression of Jacksonianism in the feeling of the time. It has certainly provided a major vehicle for the transmission of much that was unique and creative in the American spirit.

The term romantic is, of course, a very loose one. In the present context, we mean it to refer to the reemphasis within the liberal tradition of the impulse of religion, of optimism, and of reform. It was a reassertion of faith in the individual, captured in the reinvigorated use of such terms as spirit, nature, destiny, and faith. The impulse of romanticism was not entirely novel to the liberal tradition, not entirely the invention of the Jacksonian period. For certainly its over-

---

[20] For commentary and selected writings, see Van Wyck Brooks, *The Flowering of New England: 1815–1865* (New York: E. P. Dutton Co., Inc., 1937); Perry Miller (ed.), *The Golden Age of American Literature* (New York: George Brazillier, 1959).

tones may be detected in the works of such political humanists as Jefferson, and its spirit in some sense had infested the French version of liberalism as well as the questionably liberal doctrines of Rousseau. Whereas our examination of the Jacksonian period to this point has concentrated on the institutional meaning of democracy and its implications for political and economic policy, the romantic democrats of the Jacksonian period asked questions about the natural roots and individual implications of the Jacksonian attitude in politics, and found answers to their own satisfaction in speculation on the natural career of the human spirit.

Emerson: Politics and Transcendentalism

The idea of transcendentalism is likewise difficult to define; its use retains a certain fuzziness. As a label, however, it does suggest a general ideology, a posture toward the world and human life shared by many intellectual leaders of the period and particularly typified by Ralph Waldo Emerson.[21] Probably the basic underlying concept of the transcendentalist attitude is the idea of the "oversoul." The term itself suggests the touch of religious and metaphysical perspective that characterized transcendentalism as literature and social commentary. The idea of the oversoul is the idea of a fabric of nature into which all the higher elements of man's life are woven. In human life, it is realized in man's spirit, in his higher aspirations, in his realization of the interconnectedness of individuals' lives in the common bonds of human potential. It is an injunction to view human life not in terms of animal needs and desires but in terms of those higher products of the soul that demonstrate man's unique abilities and his unique relation with God. In a sense, it represents the reassertion of the Reformation notion of the direct and all-pervading relationship of every individual to Divinity. But it is also a rephrasing of that notion without the trappings of doctrine and ritual, and with a naturalistic cast substituted for the Reformation's theism. Its key might be said to be the God in man and nature, rather than the God in church and doctrine. Insofar as transcendentalism was reformist, its aim was to free man from the shackles that inhibit his realization of the incipient goodness and even Godliness of his own individual career.

Two central themes perhaps suggest best both the content of tran-

---

[21] There is an abundant literature of commentary on Emerson and transcendentalism. See, e.g., Perry Miller, *The Transcendentalists: an Anthology* (Cambridge: Harvard University Press, 1950); Ralph E. Rusk, *The Life of Ralph Waldo Emerson* (New York: Charles Scribner's Sons, 1949); Kenneth W. Cameron, *Emerson the Essayist* (Hartford: Transcendentalist Books, 1961).

scendental politics and the contribution of transcendentalism to the development of the American ideology. One of these is an idea of freedom, a high-minded individualism that insists on giving a free rein to the human spirit but finds its justification at a higher plane than utilitarian economic interest. A second theme is a spiritual nationalism. For while it showed certain traces of continental influence, transcendentalism was uniquely and emphatically American, the expression, it has been said, of America's coming of age. The theme of American destiny, of an American mission, of the peculiarly fortunate situation of the American nation found expression, often of a romantic sort, in the works of transcendentalists and others of the same period who made contributions to the development of the American culture. Brooks Atkinson has called Emerson "the first philosopher of the American spirit," and the development of the American spirit in this period was perhaps the first major excrescence of the nation's self-consciousness of its nationhood, of its community, and of its unique powers and opportunities.[22] The statement of this theme in the works of transcendentalists was not blatant as commitments to nationalism often go, but both as a form of nationalism and as an element in a humanistic world view, it is an interesting intellectual phenomenon.

The political ideas of Emerson himself are chiefly amplifications of these themes, particularly the theme of individualism. Though not a systematic thinker, Emerson did have an explicit interest in politics, and in one of his well-known essays set down some of his core thoughts on the subject.[23]

His emphasis fell, of course, on the role of the individual and his articulation with the transcendent spirit. This articulation is not, he thought, the articulation of interdependence among men, but individual articulation with the spirit of nature, cutting the person off from the encumbrances of tradition and institutions. Thus, Emerson's Phi Beta Kappa oration, "The American Scholar," (1837) urged that the scholar divest himself of the baggage of thoughtlessly accepted authority; indeed, the oration was a kind of intellectual declaration of independence from foreign cultures' ideas and habits of mind.[24] It is an example of that subtle transcendentalist nationalism of which we spoke above. The scholar, said Emerson, is "man thinking." The activity of scholarship and, indeed, all the valuable activities of the

---

[22] Brooks Atkinson, "Introduction," *The Complete Essays and Other Writings of Ralph Waldo Emerson* ("The Modern Library" [New York: Random House, 1950], p. xi.
[23] "Politics," in *ibid.*, pp. 422–34.
[24] See *ibid.*, pp. 45–63.

human life are the personal doings of what Emerson called "the active soul." They are human expeditions into intimate relationships with nature, unmediated except by inspiration.

Throughout, the emphasis falls on the individual and his relationship with God, a relationship far more personalistic than that postulated by early Protestantism. It rejected ritual and other forms of human intervention as artificial elements in what ought to be a natural spiritual association. Emerson himself left the Congregational pulpit out of distaste for administering the sacraments. The following passage from "Self Reliance" suggests the tenor of both the individualism and the religiosity in Emerson's philosophy:

> Henceforth, please God, forever I forego
> The yoke of men's opinions. I will be
> Light-hearted as a bird, and live with God.
> I find him in the bottom of my heart,
> I hear continually his voice therein.

What of the place of the state against this background? Emerson saw the state as a fact of life indicative of some of the major characteristics of the human condition. Reflecting on the elevated nature and God-relatedness of human life as Emerson pictured it, one may wonder how such an optimistic view could give rise to a theory of political authority at all. The answer is a curious and rather interesting one. He felt that the institutions of society, including those of the state, inhibit man from the development of his full personality and potential, stand between him and universality, confront him with irrelevant obstacles and distractions. At the same time, the state and society are reflections of what men put into them. They are products or representations of what man is. Man's need to lean on the institutions of authority is an index of his weakness. The answer to the dilemma posed by the question above would seem to be that man is perfectable but not perfected. The view of human nature we have attributed to Emerson is, in effect, a view of human potential, an ideal which man has not commonly realized but toward which his career can be pushed or can grow. Thus, the state represents man's deficiencies, but these are deficiencies which are not innate or inseparable from human life. In a sense, this is a modification of the Protestant–Christian view; it takes cognizance of the present sinfulness of man, but differs from orthodox Christianity on both the possibility of earthly salvation and the means by which goodness may be made to substitute for badness in human life.

Such a view raises questions about the means of rectification of a human condition in which man's potential is stunted. In dealing with this problem, Emerson rejected the two correctives most commonly promoted by the liberal tradition—government and organized religion. His cure was as personalistic as his diagnosis. The basic way to improvement of man's lot, he thought, lay in individual moral reform—the development of a moral strength which would not only permit but prompt people to throw off institutional interference with their individual lives. Emerson was extremely reluctant to join the common cry to approach the difficulties of social life through reform of social or political institutions. This he regarded as standing the proper order of things on its head. Such reform would be futile until individual moral reform was achieved. Tinkering with laws or with structures was of little use without the proper development of the individual personality. Despite his deep-seated aversion to slavery, he hesitated even to join the abolition movement, though finally he did so. But to him, the prior point of attack was on the consciences of those responsible for the perpetuation of social institutions.

Emerson did not look for human development to eventuate in the development of more sympathetic and bearable human institutions. Rather, he supposed that when human character improved, the need for civil law and the structures of government would melt away to a minimum. A better mankind would not need political authority, and in the absence of the need, the structure of consensus underlying authority would permit its disappearance. In Emerson's optimism, this idea seems to have been both a prescription and a hope, the sense of these being caught in the essay on "Politics":

> Hence the less government we have the better—the fewer laws, and the less confided power. The antidote to this abuse of formal government is the influence of private character, the growth of the Individual; the appearance of the principle to supercede the proxy; the appearance of the wise man; of whom the existing government is, it must be owned, but a shabby imitation. That which all things tend to educe; which freedom, cultivation, intercourse, revolutions, go to form and deliver, is character; that is the end of Nature, to reach into this coronation of her king. To educate the wise man the State exists, and with the appearance of the wise man the State expires. The appearance of character makes the State unnecessary.[25]

Emerson's faith that progress would come is further suggested in this sentence from the paragraph that follows the one above: "We think

---

[25] *Ibid.*, p. 431.

our civilization merits meridian, but we are yet only at the cock-crowing and the morning star." [26]

The course of human development implied in this formulation is an interesting one, one which the liberal tradition, given its ambivalent view of human nature, has often approached but seldom carried through. Indeed, even Emerson did not carry the implications of his supposition of human perfectability so far as he might, or even so far as they were carried by his friend Thoreau. Such sentiments took Emerson to the brink of a philosophical anarchism, but at the brink he drew back, for he did not really seem to believe that all political control could be abandoned. He, himself, found the atmosphere of the small New England town congenial, and perhaps felt that the context of the rural and localistic community would be optimal for human development. On this level, he participated in civic life even to the extent of serving as a minor public official. But insofar as the structure of the small town represented political authority, it was chiefly authority directed to the mutual sharing of talents for the provision of minimal services. Beyond such functions as these, Emerson seems to have felt that government expressed and brought out the worst in man and anticipated its replacement by the good will and individual efforts of men themselves. There was a great deal of the Jeffersonian and some of the Rousseauian in Emerson's ideas on politics. Perhaps they can be described as the full blossom in romantic form of the Jeffersonian–Jacksonian faith in the individual man. Emerson sublimated respect for the individual into a transcendent doctrine and drove democracy almost to its ultimate by rejecting political authority in favor of the democracy of human autonomy.

It might be inferred that Emerson's ideas could be fairly described as antisocial, but such an inference would rest on a misunderstanding of some of the subtleties of his social thought. It seems much fairer to say that his view of man was deeply and perhaps overly social, if by "social" one means able to get along with one's fellow man living in a common context. For it was Emerson's belief that when stimulated to reach their full moral stature, men were so social as not to require the intervention of arbitrary authority as a substitute for conscience. The morality Emerson sought was a natural social harmony for which the mediation of government was a mere shabby substitute. His "ideal society" would be one in which man was so at peace with himself, his God, and his fellow men as to never require either the protection or the control of government except in the most minimal and service-

---

[26] *Ibid.*, p. 432.

related fashion. Emerson stated the position Locke might have taken had he not been pessimistic about the difficulties that property ownership would engender in the human community. The difference between Locke and Emerson was, of course, substantial, for the property variable was a crucial one in the development of Locke's system of political theory. Still, the comparison is instructive.

The impact of Emerson's ideas and those of his contemporaries who shared his point of view was doubtless great, but it is difficult to gauge. Except for the relationship of transcendentalism to the abolition movement, its effects can scarcely be read in changes in American institutions, either social or political. The interests and ideals of Emerson, for example, were simply not programmatic in character, but he expressed a kind of exhilaration with the creed of individualism, an exhilaration that seems a part of the America of the nineteenth century, when optimism and faith in progress often held sway. Perhaps it is also not too far afield to suggest that Emerson and those who took similar positions on politics have made their influence felt in the apolitical and often antipolitical aspects of American ideology. The suspicion of politics Emerson expressed, a suspicion endemic to the liberal outlook, is still a real force in the American political scene. It is a reflection in part at least of the belief that man can and should be permitted to do for himself, that the state is unnatural and its activities somehow conducive to moral flabbiness. In terms of time, Emerson's statement of the creed of basic democracy, his version of its fundamental moral roots, fell between the rather crude frontiersmanship of Jacksonianism and the crass economic individualism of the social Darwinists. In terms of concept and influence, it probably modified and rationalized both. It provided a humanistic leavening in the loaf of American individualist ideology and, at the same time, a kind of hunting license for the later and less humanistic versions of limited politics and unlimited individual enterprise.

Transcendentalist Politics: Thoreau.

Henry David Thoreau, one of the most interesting figures in the history of American letters, was both personally and intellectually close to Emerson. He pushed a similar set of basic beliefs and commitments to more radical and perhaps more rigorous conclusions. Thoreau himself was on the fringes of society, a kind of eccentric without respect for the proprieties of life. His style of life and major interests are well known. He was not a political writer; indeed, he had rather little interest in and respect for politics as a subject of art or thought. He was pushed into writing *Civil Disobedience,* his only explicitly political tract, by mounting concern over the slavery issue. *Walden,* like all pieces of philosophy, may be read for hidden political or social meaning, but in this case, the meaning generally turns out to be both well hidden and negative in tone. Had it not been for the moral problem posed by the abolition movement, Thoreau might never have recorded in other than cryptic form his observations about the ills and limits of political authority.[27]

The main political theme of Thoreau's thought is much like that of Emerson's. On assumptions about individual conscience and a naturalistic relationship with God, Thoreau insisted that there was an absolute standard of morality accessible to the understanding of all men if they were prepared to seek it. There would be no conflicts among men, he thought, if only men could and would follow the dictates of conscience, and beyond that let each other alone. Like many another liberal, Thoreau saw government as the price of man's sins. "Thus, under the name of civil government," he wrote, "we are all made at last to pay homage to and support our own meanness." [28] Men are incipiently good and actively bad, and government is both an effect and a cause of the ill condition of the individual conscience.

Thoreau's perspective on politics and his hopes for mankind are neatly summarized in the following passage at the beginning of *Civil Disobedience:*

I heartily accept the motto,—"That government is best which governs least"; and I should like to see it acted up to more rapidly and systematically. Carried out, it finally amounts to this, which also I believe,—"That government is best which governs not at all"; and when men are prepared for it, that will be the kind of government which they will have.[29]

As this comment suggests, Thoreau shared Emerson's faith in human perfectability. But here again, improvement lay not in the direction of reshaping institutions or expecting politics to play a positive role in the congenial society of which mankind is capable. The basic good lies in men and not in institutions, and as men progress, institutions

---

[27] The general commentary on Thoreau is plentiful; specifically political commentary is more sparse. For the former, see Henry Seidel Canby, *Thoreau* (Boston: Houghton Mifflin Co., 1939); Joseph Wood Krutch, *Henry David Thoreau* (New York: W. Sloane & Associates, 1948); Mark Van Doren, *Henry David Thoreau: a Critical Study* (New York: Russell and Russell, 1961).

[28] Henry David Thoreau, *Walden, or, Life in the Woods, & On the Duty of Civil Disobedience* (New York: New American Library, 1956), p. 228.

[29] *Ibid.*, p. 222.

may disappear, since they will no longer be required in compensation for the deficiencies in human virtue.

Even Thoreau does not seem to have believed, however, that government could or would be abandoned entirely and right away. Its present necessity he recognized, but in the long run, he seems to have hoped for the entire withering away of political forms.

But the central and lasting thrust of Thoreau's political ideas was not really toward the elimination of political authority as a factor in social life. His chief contribution was an operating principle—the point that government may be wrong, often is, and even at the present stage of individual imperfection, must be watched by all. Though human conscience may be thin and underdeveloped, the basic presumption of goodness lies with individual man, and this is his license to constantly monitor the exercise of social authority through political power, even in a democratic polity. While the principle of majority rule is represented as a foundation of legitimacy, the majority rules not because it is right but because it is powerful and its dominion happens to be expedient.

To say, however, that men have a right or a license to monitor the actions of political authority does not do full justice to Thoreau's position on this matter. He holds the more extreme position that men have a *duty* to be watchful of political authority and, furthermore, a *duty* to disobey or to resist when the state is acting in a way that runs counter to good conscience. Note that Thoreau said *duty*—an obligation to conscience and standards of morality that outweighs the obligation to obey when the two come into conflict. Thoreau's principle was thus in his eyes a moral principle—a principle that not only requires vigilance but individual response to the organized immorality of political authority. It was the call of conscience responding to the slavery crisis and the Mexican War that finally prompted Thoreau to set down his thoughts on government in *Civil Disobedience*.

On the means of resistance to civil authority, Thoreau was explicit, and he himself was an exemplar of the techniques he advocated. By resistance, he had in mind only passive resistance, more specifically, disobedience to the commands of political authority, as the title of the essay suggests. Such measures as refusal to pay taxes and refusal to do military service for an unjust government are the kinds of passive antipolitical action of which he approved. With the development of moral sense among men and thus with the spread of resistance to authority, he thought the position of the state would be untenable and its authority not possible to maintain. He felt that a society could not long exist in a condition where all good men were prepared to accept jail rather than accept political command.

As has been suggested above, Thoreau's theoretical position is much like that of Emerson in terms of its relationship to the broad development of the liberal tradition. He, too, was a spokesman for that tradition's humanitarian wing. But Thoreau's impact may have been more specific and more direct than that of his transcendentalist colleague, for his doctrine of civil disobedience and the principle that lies behind it have had considerable effect on both idea and political practice in subsequent times. Passive resistance has, since Thoreau, often been a key weapon in struggles for political change, notably used, for example, in the struggle for Indian independence and in the American civil rights movement. Perhaps it would be most accurate to say that the position Thoreau took on the moral limits of political authority has stiffened the willingness of some Americans to criticize and resist government as they have seen fit in the light of good conscience. Thoreau rephrased and reemphasized the historic liberal injunction that government may be wrong, that majorities may be wrong, and that individuals must oppose them when the conscience is violated. The idea is very similar to Harold Laski's notion of contingent anarchy. Laski, in his early period, arguing in terms of natural rights, urged that political authority be confined in scope and made subject to the continual scrutiny of the men at whose behavior it is directed. Thus, he said, society is always in a state of contingent anarchy, a state where obedience is contingent on the acceptability of policy to the good conscience of the citizenry.[30]

Thoreau's ideas have seldom been carried to their ultimate implications by the American people, but his suspicion of government and politics, like that of Emerson, has come to be a traditional part of the American outlook. Thoreau's contribution to the American tradition has probably been merely to pique the American conscience. The structure of contemporary society is such that his general view of the scope of politics and perhaps even his hope for the moral improvement of mankind are difficult to take literally. But his political ideas were a subtle contribution to the American skepticism of governmental authority and even a guide to action through inaction.

Walt Whitman: Democratic and National Vistas

A short note might appropriately be added at this point about an-

---

[30] See, e.g., Harold L. Laski, *Authority in the Modern State* (New Haven: Yale University Press, 1919), pp. 55–57, and *passim*.

other romantic and literary nineteenth-century American democrat, Walt Whitman. Although Whitman's life (1819–92) spanned eras, he shared much with the outlook of the Jacksonian democrats and the transcendentalist philosophers. He was himself an early and vigorous exponent of many aspects of Jacksonian democracy, and published, in 1871, a forthrightly political work, *Democratic Vistas.* Basically, Whitman's contributions, both poetry and prose, were poetic expressions of the fundamental democratic ideology of nineteenth-century America.[31]

Undergirding Whitman's writings were abiding beliefs in the dignity of the common man and in the American mission. The first had its ramification in his commitment to equality and to the democratic community in which all men could live freely and play a part. He argued feelingly for the extension of the franchise, and seems not to have doubted the ability of men to provide singly and by collective action the rules for their own social lives. While his view of society and politics was highly individualistic, he placed more emphasis than Emerson and Thoreau on the community as a center of loyalties and mutual sympathy. But, like them, he put great stock in the importance of individual moral improvement. He is said to have been the first person to use the expression "democratic faith," a phrase now familiar but also revealing in the extent to which it deemphasizes institutions and authority and emphasizes individual relations and sentiments as the true sources of social control and morality. Real belief in the efficacy of the democratic faith gives evidence of an overriding optimism about the potentials inherent in the human community.

Like most publicists of his period, Whitman believed in the political and economic program of laissez faire. Here, he reflected what we described earlier as the core of the Jacksonian policy orientation. He attacked privilege, argued for opportunity for all men, and advocated a social system in which freedom from outside interference would lay open the opportunity to all for individual self-development. Like many another Jacksonian, he feared most the effects of restriction, either public or private, on the initiative of the citizen and on his changes to make his initiative effective. His conception of freedom was fundamentally a negative one; he did not see the government primarily as an instrument for the development of opportunity but

---

[31] For commentary on Whitman, see Van Wyck Brooks, *The Times of Melville and Whitman* (New York: E. P. Dutton & Co., Inc., 1947); Newton Arvin, *Whitman* (New York: Macmillan Co., 1938); Raymond C. Beatty, "Whitman's Political Thought," *The South Atlantic Quarterly,* Vol. XLVI (January, 1947), pp. 72–83.

rather as a protector of an opportunity he was inclined to regard as natural in the human situation.

In this respect, the ideas of Whitman when taken as a whole may seem somewhat peculiar from the perspective of current political ideas. His humanitarian spirit was strong, and he disliked and struck out at the social ills that dog humankind. But the times were not yet ripe, as they became early in the twentieth century, for this humanitarianism to become the basis of claims for positive economic and social reform. It might be said that Whitman and even the transcendentalists prepared the spirit by promoting sympathy for a state which would move toward the assurance of security for all. But the programmatic aspects of a political society such as that lay beyond either his tasks or his imagination and remained for later humanitarians to seek. In a fashion typical to his century, Whitman saw human good coming not from the positive action of the state, but only from minimal state protection of freedom for private action.

No less intense than Whitman's belief in the common man was his belief in his country. He saw America as a land of great natural endowment and of innate energy and vigor. The term destiny, an important concept in the politics and rhetoric of American nationalism, probably describes as well as any Whitman's concept of America. It often found expression in his poetry:

I heard that you ask'd for something to prove this puzzle a New World, and to define America, her athletic Democracy,
Therefore I send you my poems that you behold in them what you wanted.

I hear America singing, the varied carols I hear . . .

Whitman wrote of his travels up and down America, of the spectacular and the commonplace that all together made up the stuff of a dynamic democratic nation. He saw romance in city and countryside and wilderness and in the variety of activities, economic and otherwise, in which his countrymen engaged. Much of *Leaves of Grass* is a kind of poetic chronicle of Whitman's love of his country and its people.

Like Emerson, Whitman was impatient with reason and pedantry. He sought discovery and understanding through feeling and, to a large extent, rejected the intermediation of institutions and systems and books between man and nature. Through his poetry, he tried to convey the tranquillity and excitement of a growing and heterogeneous nation, not so much the America of statesmanship and organization as the America of common activity and simple sentiment.

The discussion of nineteenth-century views and versions of democracy could easily be extended. What we have said here only samples the range of contributions, though it samples at the most significant points. For the most part, however, the central themes are the same: America is the land of the integral individual freed from economic and social constraints and equipped to solve his political fate through the devices of democracy. Individual—opportunity—democracy: these were the keys to the times.

One strain of thought that represented a significant deviation in one respect deserves our passing attention. This is the utopianism that assumed some importance in the first half of the century.[32] Probably the leading theoreticians of American utopianism were Robert Owen (himself, of course, a Scotsman) and Arthur Brisbane (a disciple of the French political philosopher, Fourier). Beyond the theory, however, lay a large number of abortive attempts at practice, i.e., attempts to establish small societies guided by utopian principles. More than a hundred such communities were founded in America between 1825 and 1860, the best known being Owen's New Harmony, Indiana, and Brisbane's Brook Farm, Massachusetts.[33]

The range of ideas among these people and settlements was great; variation was so vast as to make it difficult to put them into a common general category. There were, however, two points of emphasis that set them off from the main flow of Jacksonian thought—emphasis on the predominant importance of economic relationships and emphasis on the potency of human sociability. Thus, for largely economic reasons, the utopians rejected existing society, rejected it as the source of man's misery. To a rather uncanny degree, Owen foresaw the ills the industrial system would spawn. These he believed increasingly responsible for the failure of people to live in social harmony.

The theme of sociability takes over from here. The idea of the utopia is that if disruptive institutions are destroyed, man's ability to live in natural harmony will fill the void. Thus, peace and order will grow out of institutional rearrangements, and community in its fullest classical sense will come to dominate the social world. Utopian communities were founded on the supposition that the effects of sociabil-

---

[32] See, besides the works of the principals themselves, Arthur E. Bestor, Jr., *Backwoods Utopias* (Philadelphia: University of Pennsylvania Press, 1950); Harry W. Laidler, *Socio-Economic Movements* (New York: Thomas Y. Crowell Co., 1945); Ernest Sutherland Bates, *American Faith, Its Religious, Political, and Economic Foundations* (New York: W. W. Norton, 1940); V. L. Parrington, Jr., *American Dreams; a Study of American Utopias* (Providence: Brown University Press, 1947).

[33] Bestor, *op. cit.*, p. 243.

ity could be made to work in the sequestered sub-society, and that its
success there would have the educational clout to convert the society
by example.

Utopianism is probably more significant as a curio than as a serious
contribution to idea and practice. Its "social" or "communitarian"
tone probably had little impact on the American tradition as compared with the individualism of frontier or urban Jacksonianism.
While it does partake of the romance and humanism of the transcendentalists, it seems a marginal part of the development of American life.
The central thrust of the period was the thrust of developing democracy against the background of developing industrialism and increasing scale.

VIII

THE BASIS OF POLITICAL POWER: NATION AND STATES

In this chapter, we will deal with two interrelated but distinct sets of problems—those arising out of slavery as an issue and those concerned with the distribution of political power between nation and states in the American union. Both questions were dramatically brought to the attention of the nation in the Civil War, but both were also embedded in the American political tradition and both are illustrative of basic aspects of the political process. Reflection on them suggests the extent to which no problem in politics is a novelty. The controversies over slavery and the federal system may both be interpreted as further explorations for the operational meaning of the basic American consensus. Though solutions were sought in the most traumatic experience through which the American body politic has been put, the problems were incipient in the system and culture at least since the framing of the Constitution and probably long before that.

The two political problems with which we are dealing are sufficiently different in basis to raise doubts about their treatment within a common context. The fact that both came to dominate national attention in the mid-nineteenth century, however, lends a certain historical weight to their consideration in this fashion. What follows should be seen as successive treatments of two conceptually distinct but historically intertwined problems. It must be emphasized that we are not interested in describing the Civil War as a historical phenomenon nor explaining the war itself in terms of social or other causes. In fact, the political–theoretical implications of the war, though they do raise interesting problems about the social and ideological conditions of revolution, will be touched on only incidentally in this chapter.

THE IDEOLOGY OF THE SLAVERY ISSUE:
ANTISLAVERY THOUGHT

In a formal sense, the issues raised by the slavery problem are not issues typical to the American political system. The holding of property in human beings is, indeed, a "peculiar institution," and one that, though not uncommon historically, certainly runs counter to the main tenets of the modern liberal tradition. It is also, on its face, a type of issue that, once settled, would seem to be settled with finality. However, the histories of the American Negro and the American South since emancipation strikingly illustrate how little of the problem was comprehended in the formal legal relationship.

Though we have been treating "the slavery issue" as if it were a singular thing, like most other social problems, it may be understood only as a complex bundle of factors.[1] The ideological–theoretical aspects of the slavery controversy may be divided into three categories: political–structural problems, concerning largely the question of relative power of nation and states; moral–political problems; and economic–social problems. Both pro- and antislavery thought played on variations of these three themes. The centrality of all three to the politics of the time can perhaps be illustrated by reference to the position of Abraham Lincoln, on whom they bore both personally and in his role as the predominant political figure of the time. Though not a radical abolitionist, Lincoln found the institution of slavery deeply repugnant and rejected it on moral and traditional grounds. He was also by geographic identification and sentiment attached to the interest and way of life of free Northern agrarianism, the expansion of which was threatened by the extension of slavery into the territories. At the same time, Lincoln was attached both by conviction and by political need to the desire to save the union. Indeed, this political commitment was perhaps the overriding one as he attempted to balance ideal and possible in the context of a divided society. Probably no single factor satisfactorily explains Lincoln's style and thought during the war. He felt the pressure of all three, exacerbated and com-

---

[1] There is a vast literature on slavery, the antislavery movement, and the relationship of the slavery problem to the Civil War. See, for example, Kenneth W. Stampp, *The Peculiar Institution: Slavery in the Ante-Bellum South* (New York: A. A. Knopf, 1956); Russel Nye, *Fettered Freedom: Civil Liberties and the Slavery Controversy, 1830–1860* (East Lansing: Michigan State University Press, 1949); Dwight L. Dumond, *Anti-slavery Origins of the Civil War in the United States* (Ann Arbor: University of Michigan Press, 1939); Kenneth W. Stampp, *The Causes of the Civil War* (Englewood Cliffs, N.J.: Prentice-Hall, 1959).

pounded in his case by the fact that as a political actor he had to make decisions and act on them.

On the moral–political level, the antislavery arguments focused largely on the literal reaffirmation and reassertion of the fundamental liberal creed. Toleration of holding human beings as property in a society whose fundamental constitutional commitments emphasized individualism and equality seems to be a strange contradiction in itself. This can hardly be an object of amazement, however, when we consider how far the practices implied in precepts of liberty, equality, and toleration ordinarily follow behind abstract social acceptance of the precepts themselves.

But the liberal doctrine provided ready-made rhetorical and moral leverage for the advocates of abolition. William Lloyd Garrison, one of the most militant of abolitionists, for example, often invoked the symbols of the Revolution, of the *Declaration of Independence,* and of the Founding Fathers in his writings on slavery:

More than fifty-seven years have elapsed, since a band of patriots convened in this place, to devise measures for the deliverance of this country from a foreign yoke. The corner-stone upon which they founded the Temple of Freedom was broadly this—"that all men are created equal; that they are endowed by their creator with certain inalienable rights; that among these are life, LIBERTY, and the pursuit of happiness." At the sound of their trumpet-call, three millions of people rose up as from the sleep of death, and rushed to the strife of blood; deeming it more glorious to die instantly as freemen, than desirable to live one hour as slaves.[2]

Garrison drew heavily on the fundamental values of liberalism and Christianity. Slavery he regarded as a simple violation of natural rights and freedom as meaningless when any men are deprived of it. No Christian could tolerate slavery, much less hold slaves, and remain true to the basic articles of his faith. While it would require a considerable stretch of the imagination to regard Garrison as a philosopher of the antislavery position, he reflected in skillful though bitter rhetoric the central moral arguments of the abolitionist movement, the call for the reaffirmation of universal values presumably embedded in the consensual American conscience and in its institutional representations.

More moderate and also more thoughtful statements of the basic moral position can be found here and there in the abolitionist litera-

---

[2] *Selections from the Writings and Speeches of William Lloyd Garrison* (Boston: R. F. Wallcut, 1852), p. 66. For a discussion of Garrison's ideas and role in the abolition movement, see Russel Nye, *William Lloyd Garrison and the Humanitarian Reformers* (Boston: Little, Brown & Co., 1955).

ture, in the writings, for example, of William Ellery Channing. Channing, a leading transcendentalist and Unitarian minister, was influential in the spread of abolitionism in New England, though he lived only until 1842. Channing's position, while it shared much with Garrison's, gave greater emphasis to the religious aspects and abstract ideals of abolitionism and less to their historical and nationalist roots. His arguments were those of the enlightened humanitarian.

Channing's basic claim was that a slave is a man and must be treated as man and not as property. Once this step is made, the rest is simple. Rights, equality, the essential notion of human justice were to Channing self-evident; they required no justification. The tone as well as the content of Channing's views on slavery are captured in the following quotation from his book, *Slavery*, published in 1841:

I come now to what is to my own mind the great argument against seizing and using a man as property. He cannot be property in the sight of God and justice, because he is a Rational, Moral, Immortal Being; because created in God's image, and therefore in the highest sense his child; because created to unfold godlike faculties, and to govern himself by a Divine Law written on his heart, and republished in God's Word. His whole nature forbids that he should be seized as property. From his very nature it follows, that so to seize him is to offer an insult to his Maker, and to inflict aggravated social wrong. Into every human being God has breathed an immortal spirit, more precious than the whole outward creation. No earthly or celestial language can exaggerate the worth of a human being. No matter how obscure his condition. Thought, Reason, Conscience, the capacity of Virtue, the capacity of Christian Love, an immortal Destiny, an intimate moral connection with God,—here are attributes of our common humanity which reduce to insignificance all outward distinctions, and make every human being unspeakably dear to his Maker. No matter how ignorant he may be. The capacity of Improvement allies him to the more instructed of his race, and places within his reach the knowledge and happiness of higher worlds. Every human being has in him the germ of the greatest idea in the universe, the idea of God; and to unfold this is the end of his existence. Every human being has in his breast the elements of that Divine, Everlasting Law, which the highest orders of the creation obey. He has the idea of Duty; and to unfold, revere, obey this, is the very purpose for which life was given. Every human being has the idea of what is meant by the word, Truth; that is, he sees, however dimly, the great object of Divine and created intelligence, and is capable of ever-enlarging perceptions of truth. Every human being has affections, which may be purified and expanded into a Sublime Love. He has, too, the idea of Happiness, and the thirst for it which cannot be appeased. Such is our nature. Wherever we see a man, we see the possessor of these great capacities. Did God make such a being to be owned as a tree or a brute? How plainly was he made to exercise, unfold, improve his highest powers, made for a moral, spiritual good! and how is he wronged, and his Creator opposed, when he is forced and broken into a tool to another's physical enjoyment! [3]

Though their rhetoric was florid, Channing and Garrison doubtless expressed the misgivings that piqued the common American conscience and came to serve as the ideological core of the abolition movement. The institution of slavery may seem strangely incongruent in a liberal society and it may raise doubts about the initial strengths and meanings of liberalism, but the development of abolitionism into a strong and powerful movement also suggests the strength and staying power of liberal values in the American society.

Agreement about the philosophical and religious repugnance of slavery was not necessarily accompanied by agreement about the political implications of and solutions to slavery. Indeed, the whole matter of a solution to the slavery problem was not so simple as it might seem on its face. For quite apart from the difficulty of imposing any change in the institution on the South, there were monumental questions about what solution might be practical and moral, and whether black and white races could exist in the same society on an equal footing. Equality is a question that we are still attempting to deal with, and it was a question that bothered thoughtful abolitionists long before the Civil War. Thomas Jefferson, who deeply disliked the institution of slavery, thought recolonization of the Negroes in Africa the only workable answer to the problem, and many others shared Jefferson's beliefs.

Among abolitionists, too, there were differences as to how and at what pace freedom for the slaves might be accomplished. It is important to recall that the positions to which we are referring here are positions taken long before the Civil War and not, therefore, positions conditioned by tactical considerations. Among many prominent in the abolition movement also, these positions were not much affected by deep fears for the preservation of the union. That is to say, abolitionists as abolitionists were somewhat inclined to seek single-mindedly their objective of ending chattel slavery. Garrison at one end of the continuum advocated immediate abolition. His absolutist position on the wrongs of slavery vitiated his ability to accommodate to the idea of a gradual solution. "There must be no compromise with slavery—none whatever," and further, "Slavery cannot be dethroned by flattery and stratagem." He also found a source of frustration in the

---

[3] William Ellery Channing, *Works* (10th ed.; Boston: George G. Channing, 1849), Vol. II, pp. 26–27.

Constitution and the structure of the union, since the effects of these institutions was to mediate political demands and apply a brake to precipitate action. He cared little for the union, whose existence stood in the way of correcting the wrongs of slavery. This attitude, indeed, extended to the whole of the Constitutional structure, which he once described as "an agreement with hell." [4] So firm was Garrison in his activism and so committed to the notion of the duty of the conscience to oppose wrongs to humankind that he exceeded Thoreau's position of civil disobedience as the proper course for abolitionism. He thought it impossible to support in good conscience a structure of government that promoted, protected, or even permitted such a gross violation of natural moral standards.

Channing, on the other hand, was more moderate in his prescriptions for abolition if not less convinced of the rectitude of his own view of right. He was among the abolitionists who felt that immediate and complete emancipation would create an injustice hardly less than that of the slavery institution itself. He hoped his ends could be accomplished through moral suasion which might enlist the South in the voluntary abandonment of its injustice. He foresaw a period of tutelage for the slaves during which they would be prepared to support themselves and assume their roles as free men in the free society.[5] The differences between abolitionists like Garrison and abolitionists like Channing on these matters reflects an age-old problem in political thought. It is a problem of priorities among values. The question is whether one must sacrifice social stability, to most men a value of high priority, if the sacrifice is necessary to achieve or preserve freedom, also a value of high priority. This was, perhaps, the most important question of political philosophy raised by the entire Civil War controversy. It occurred for Lincoln; it occurred for the statesmen of the South. There must, indeed, have been few actively engaged in political thought or practice for whom it did not represent a difficult choice. It continues in a variety of forms to be an important problem today. Only those like Garrison who can be described, to use Eric Hoffer's phrase, as "true believers" can free themselves from the effects of this moral dilemma.

Complementing the moral antislavery arguments of those like Garrison and Channing were near-utilitarian arguments directed at the economic and sociological effects of the slavery institution. Perhaps

---

[4] The earlier quotations are found in *Selections, op. cit.*, pp. 140–41; on the Constitution, the union, and related matters, see "The American Union," *ibid.*, pp. 116–19.

[5] Channing, *op. cit.*, Vol. II, pp. 110–11.

the best known of those who publicized the case against slavery from this point of view was Hinton R. Helper, a resident of North Carolina who, in 1857, published a book, *The Impending Crisis of the South: How to Meet It.*[6] The position of Helper and others who shared his point of view was that slavery sapped the economic and cultural vigor of the society. Helper amassed statistics to support his thesis. The empirical evidence showed, he held, that though the states of the South had started with the formation of the union on a substantially equal or perhaps slightly superior level of development to the Northern states, they had steadily fallen behind in nearly every important respect. With the institution of slavery making labor and production appear degrading rather than virtuous, the South, Helper claimed, had lost its impetus to create. This led to the decline of economic position as well as to cultural impoverishment, and made the South dependent on the North for the processing of goods, the improvement of life, and the development of leadership. By vesting social control and initiative in the hands of a very few, the social condition of the slave society was such as to prevent it from tapping much of the creative and productive talent within itself. Furthermore, the argument ran, the institution of slavery is such that it distracts attention from the other problems and potentialities of the culture. In these various ways, slaveholding, according to Helper, had robbed the South of what had once been its position of vigorous leadership in the American nation, and only the complete abolition of slaveholding could bring about conditions in which the South could find and reassert itself. Helper himself, incidentally, advocated complete and immediate abolition and Negro colonization.

It is interesting to take note of the nature and method of Helper's argument against slavery. He did not, by any means, ignore the religious and moral arguments against the institution. But the significance of his case rests on its empirical basis. What he did fundamentally was to examine the consequences of a given course of social action. The relationship of a set of consequences to a set of values is an important one for political science, since a large measure of the controversy over policy and structure is, in effect, the examination of relationships of this kind. From the standpoint of most contemporary social science, empirical evidence does not and cannot prove or disprove a value. It can, however, presumably demonstrate whether a

---

[6] Hinton R. Helper, *The Impending Crisis of the South and How to Meet It* (New York: A. R. Burdick, 1860); also published in Harvey Wish (ed.), *Ante-Bellum* (New York: Capricorn Books, 1960).

given course of action or policy is conducive to the realization of values of a stated sort. At bottom, the procedure resolves to an investigation of the relationship between instrumental and ultimate values. A course of action, a policy, or a structure ordinarily represents a value commitment of an instrumental type, i.e., commitment to a means not valued for itself. The logical form of the problem, then, is as follows: If this type of instrument is used, then will this more ultimate goal be either realized or destroyed? Helper treated slavery as an instrumental institution and questioned whether in its presence a higher value for American political society is attainable. As the higher value, Helper postulated a goal generally identified by the concept of progress.

Actually, there are two empirical elements involved in the application of this form of thought to a given social situation. One is the operationalization of the fundamental values and measurement of the realization of these values in the society in question. Helper, for example, did this in part systematically and in part impressionally by comparing the economic and social conditions of the South with those of the North. Such a procedure might be carried out with any assumed value; it does not, in fact, depend on whether the value is actually held in the society or regarded as valuable by the researcher. The second empirical element in this type of procedure is substantiation of the researcher's estimate about the commitment of the society in question to the basic values he has postulated. It is this procedure which establishes the relevance of the investigation to the specific society. One might undertake, for example, elaborate investigations of whether the policies and structures of the society were conducive to the realization of values that are not sought by members of the society at all; in most circumstances, such investigations would be pointless. The question of relevance is simply the question whether a value whose institutional aspects are to be examined is salient to the operation of the social system being studied.

Helper's approach to his time assumed that progress is a more viable and consensual end than slavery or any end toward which slavery might be instrumental. Without doubt, the idea of progress has been a central element in the American tradition, and Helper's appeal to it was sound and sensible. The obscurity and equivocation inherent in "the American consensus" is apparent, however, in the catastrophic consequences of the attempt to destroy the slavery institution. Thus, it may be supposed that even if Helper's arguments had unmistakably established the higher utility of abolition for social progress, the development of consensus and action would have been slow and expensive, if possible at all. As things did go, a century has gone by without national agreement.

A few miscellaneous comments should be added about Helper's work and his place in the antebellum society. First, what goes above should not be taken to suggest that his use of empirical methods was impeccable or his case necessarily convincing. What is intended is to call attention to the interesting use of empirical tools in the context of an important value dispute. Second, it is important and instructive to note that Helper's antislavery argument and his general orientation to the problem differed in some integral respects from those of the abolitionists we have treated above. He was not an apostle of tolerance between races, but rather, in a pattern not exceptional for the people of the Southern Appalachians, bitterly anti-Negro in his sentiments. In works published after the Civil War, he adopted a quite explicit racist philosophy. Further, it should be noted that Helper's position can seemingly be explained in terms of his geographic and class origins, and that his ideas gave voice to the position of a considerable segment of Southern society opposed in interest to the slaveholder and, at the same time, fearful of the Negro. Historically, Helper's role was of considerable importance in stimulating abolitionist agitation. His work was praised by abolitionists like Greeley and Garrison, and *The Impending Crisis* had substantial circulation in the North, particularly in a compendium edition sponsored by abolitionist Republicans. His ideas illustrate one aspect of the mounting contention of values that brought about the breach of national consensus and the breakdown of the mechanisms of peaceful problem-solving.

PROSLAVERY THOUGHT

By the outbreak of the Civil War, there had accumulated a substantial body of proslavery thought in the United States, a body of thought particularly interesting for the fact that it embodied the most direct challenge to basic American value and institutional commitments the nation has ever experienced on a major scale. While a good part of antislavery thought was clearly rooted in the American tradition and built on that tradition through invocation, elaboration, and interpretation, proslavery thought, except in its political–structural forms—i.e., except insofar as it was debated on the basis of sectionalism and states' rights—reached beyond the American tradition for its intellectual roots and authority. It went, in effect, to the classical framework of Aristotle and Aquinas for fundamental assumptions and

prescriptions. Considering the nature of the cause it fought, the proslavery position was surprisingly creative and positive in tone, although inevitably a good deal of it was devoted to denial, disaffirma-
tion, and negative critique. The major contribution to political
theory of this period was undoubtedly that of John C. Calhoun. As
Calhoun's position was not really stated in terms of the slavery question, we will put aside discussion of his ideas to the later pages of the
chapter. There remains a body of proslavery theory sufficiently original and significant to merit our passing attention.[7]

As proslavery thought did not find its intellectual roots in the
American tradition, it did not develop in a significant way until the
slavery controversy itself had nearly reached maturity. It should be
noted that from the early 1800's and to some extent before, there had
been real doubt in South as well as in North about the economic and
social viability of the slavery institution. The doubts based on
economics had certainly been reinforced by the cultural accumulation of equalitarian liberal doctrines, and more specifically by the
democratic equalitarianism of Jeffersonian and Jacksonian movements. It appears to have been assumed during the early years
of the century that the South itself would work out a gradual
and satisfactory solution, probably eventuating in some form of
recolonization of the Negroes. With the development of the cotton
economy, however, the institution began to appear in a new light
economically, and as abolitionist pressure mounted in the North, the
development of ideology as a weapon of defense became more and
more a part of Southern response.

The Southern intellectual defense of slavery took shape largely—
though not entirely—in the 1850's. The pages that follow will be
directed chiefly at the ideas of one of the best-known publicists of
the proslavery cause, George Fitzhugh, author of two leading and
influential works, *Sociology for the South* (1854) and *Cannibals All*
(1856), and of numerous articles on the slavery question.[8] Whether
Fitzhugh's position was "typical" we will not debate; it was influential
and central in the development of the Southern posture.

Proslavery theory can be analyzed in categories similar to those

---

[7] See William S. Jenkins, *Pro-Slavery Thought in the Old South* (Chapel Hill; University of North Carolina Press, 1935); also Louis Hartz, "The Reactionary Enlightenment: Southern Political Thought before the Civil War," *Western Political Quarterly*,
Vol. V (March, 1952), pp. 31–50.

[8] Both books are published in Wish (ed.), *op. cit.* For commentary see Harvey Wish,
George Fitzhugh: Propagandist of the Old South (Baton Rouge: Louisiana State University Press, 1943).

used above—moral–political, economic–social, and structural–political. On the moral–political level, Fitzhugh rejected the entire individualistic and mechanistic structure of Anglo-American liberalism in favor of an Aristotelian organic theory. In *Cannibals All,* he acknowledged the similarity of his theory to that of Aristotle, commenting that after the publication of *Sociology for the South,* "To our surprise, we found that our theory of the origin of the society was identical with his, and that we had employed not only the same illustrations, but the very same words." [9] The basis of this organic theory is a social view of human nature. It finds morality and productiveness inherent in the association of men in the human community, not in their individualities. It emphasizes the importance of differentiation, distinction, and division of labor in giving structure to the community. The good for the individual lies in his articulation with the larger whole in terms of which his life takes on meaning. Man is born to status, i.e., to a series of social relationships, and the preservation and appreciation of these relationships is the requisite of social stability. It is man's nature to be submerged in the social organism, and the destruction of the organism, particularly of institutions proved by use, is the destruction of what is worthwhile in human life. Fitzhugh identified his perspective as a form of socialism in terms of its emphasis on the social dimension as the source of social good, but he differentiated it from the equalitarian socialism that had begun to make itself felt in Europe. The keynotes of this theory were sociability, differentiation, and human interdependence.

From this basis in organic theory, Fitzhugh proceeded to a bitter attack on the moral, political, and economic tenets of liberalism. The doctrines of equality and natural right were, from his perspective, simply wrong—simply misunderstandings of the social nature of the human being. He wrote:

It seems to us that the vain attempts to define liberty in theory, or to secure its enjoyment in practice, proceed from the fact that man is naturally a social and gregarious animal, subject, not by contract or agreement, as Locke and his followers assume, but by birth and nature, to those restrictions of liberty which are expedient or necessary to secure the good of the human hive, to which he may belong. There is no such thing as natural human liberty. . . . Modern social reformers, except Mr. Carlyle, proceeding upon the theory of Locke, which is the opposite of Aristotle, propose to dissolve and disintegrate society; falsely supposing that they thereby

---

[9] Wish (ed.), *op. cit.,* p. 108.

follow nature. There is not a human tie that binds man to man that they do not propose to cut "sheer asunder!" [10]

The entire doctrine of consent, furthermore, seemed to him a shibboleth, as human communities are held together by natural ties, not by artificial agreement, and human lives require direction.

The very term, government, implies that it is carried on against the consent of the governed. Fathers do not derive their authority, as heads of families, from the consent of wife and children, nor do they govern their families by their consent. They never take the vote of the family as to the labors to be performed, the monies to be expended, or as to anything else. Masters dare not take the vote of slaves, as to their government. If they did, constant holiday, dissipation and extravagance would be the result. Captains of ships are not appointed by the consent of the crew, and never take their vote, even in "doubling Cape Horn." If they did, the crew would generally vote to get drunk, and the ship would never weather the Cape. Not even in the most democratic countries are soldiers governed by their consent, nor is their vote taken on the eve of battle.[11]

By dint of the natural differentiation of human talents, some men are qualified for rulership, some are not, and the effect of the doctrine of consent is to destroy the natural and sensible bonds of communal authority.

In similar terms and at some length, Fitzhugh attacked the doctrine of laissez faire. Principles of free trade and economic liberty, he held, also run contrary to the natural basis of social life. Their effect is to make the weak prey to the strong and to destroy the social responsibility of one element of the community to the other, indeed to destroy the social responsibility of all elements of the community. Laissez faire cuts man free from his essential ties and casts him adrift in a hostile world.

Fitzhugh also examined in semi-sociological fashion the consequences of organization of the human community along liberal lines. The insecurity and exploitation of the free industrial system has led, he held, to a degradation of the Northern worker that is worse in terms of individual happiness and welfare than that of the slave in the South. The slave, indeed, as part of the genuine community has more freedom than the worker in a capitalist society, the free labor system being, in effect, a form of slavery without the virtues and advantages of the slave system. Fitzhugh discussed at length the condition of the workingmen of the Northern states and England,

---

[10] *Ibid.*, p. 139.
[11] *Ibid.*, p. 151.

concluding inevitably that their life situations were poor and the societies in which they lived morally degenerate. Such societies, he felt, were inevitably doomed to breakdown because man by his nature will seek the security of a closed social system. The danger in modern society, therefore, is not that the "free" society will persist but that a closed society based on the false premises of equality will replace it. At any rate, slavery in some form is sought by all men, and its best form is to be found in the "humanitarian" chattel slavery system of the South. Fitzhugh frequently made reference to the peaceful, serene, and easy life of the Southern slave, contrasting it with the ill condition of what he called the "so-called free worker." He also held, as might be anticipated, that the Negro was unsuited for freedom, and the white race was superior and uniquely suited to rule.

Historically, the type of theory which Fitzhugh's represents came to be of considerable significance in the United States not only as ideology for Southern resistance to abolition but also as a leavening in the liberal loaf, a leavening of importance in later times. Though he was extreme in his position on the policy question of slavery, Fitzhugh's type of thought provided a center pin for conservative critique of American institutions. Its debt to the classics is clear. It also bore a relationship in similarity to some of the communitarian thought prominent both in Europe and America in the middle and late nineteenth century. The theoretical basis of Fitzhugh's position, though not necessarily its implications and prescriptions, was shared by later American nationalists and by such European political philosophers as Carlyle, Hegel, and the English idealists.[12] What he shared with these thinkers was primarily an anti-individualist organicism—that is, an emphasis on the differentiated community as the locus of meaning and morality in human life.

It is also interesting to note the extent to which Fitzhugh's critique of capitalist society shared perspectives with the developing ideas of Marx and Engels. The implications they drew and the prescriptions they made, of course, were quite different, but both saw in capitalism the basis of exploitation and alienation. To a considerable extent, too, ideas of the type Fitzhugh expressed have continued to have an influence in the United States on racial ideologies as well as the growth of consciousness of the importance of the human community, especially the national community, in providing political and social attachments for modern man. Although now we might con-

---

[12] Fitzhugh acknowledged his debt to Carlyle as he did his debt to Aristotle. See, e.g., the introduction to *Cannibals All, ibid.,* pp. 106–7 and *passim.*

sider Fitzhugh's sociology to be moral philosophy, his emphasis on
the examination of life in terms of social context was symptomatic
of the turn in philosophy which doubtless gave rise to a mounting
scholarly interest in sociology as a field for study.

The implications that the American slavery controversy has for
the relationship between political theory and political practice are
many and varied, but perhaps they can be adequately summarized
in two general comments. First, the slavery controversy would seem
to demonstrate some things about political consensus and its relation to political practice. At least for a good part of the nation, the
slavery controversy pointed up the disparity between public belief
and public practice, and illustrated the difficulty of bringing the two
into line. In the chapters above, we have described the American
tradition in terms of its liberal postulates, but the defense of slavery
and the need to reaffirm those postulates in the attack on slavery
suggests the extent to which the liberal tenets inadequately described
American pre-Civil War consensus. Perhaps the problem is primarily
one of whether there can be consensus in a large and heterogeneous
nation. In such a society, it may be that consensus can at most be a
kind of negative thing, i.e., not agreement around a central set of
beliefs to which everyone makes a positive commitment, but rather
a comity which depends on all elements in society being not forced to
make a positive commitment to any set of beliefs. When, however, a
social crisis forces examination of this comity, and consensus is, therefore, invoked as a positive force, it fails to correspond to private belief
and, therefore, fails to hold the society together. The slavery crisis
also suggests the intractability of the socioeconomic structure when
that structure, as in the case of the South, carries within it reasons
for resistance to a change in ideology.

To put the matter in a slightly different way, examination of the
slavery controversy illustrates the extent to which the core liberal
tradition of the American nation has failed to dominate either the
ideology of subcultures or the operating norms of those subcultures
when it has been brought to a test. In general terms, we have treated
the tradition as a set of limits within which particular ideological
variants and operating institutions have developed. In the case of the
slavery controversy, the tension between those limits and social needs
was so great that the limits failed to hold. Therefore, action moved
outside the limits imposed by the ideology in the resort to violence
for the solution of problems, and thought moved outside the limits
in the development by Fitzhugh and others of a counter-ideology op-

posed to the liberal tradition at the basic level. Thus, finally, all down the continuum from pure thought to pure action, the slavery controversy brought about the rejection of the liberal tradition. Though this rejection appears to have been widespread in the sub-culture—the slaveholding South—the foregoing analysis should not, of course, be seen as completely adequate historical description of all aspects of Southern attitudes and actions.

Secondly, the slavery issue and its attendant problems illustrated the slowness and painfulness of the process of constitutional adjust-ment when an established practice lies outside presumed constitu-tional norms for conduct. The holding or staying power of the basic liberal norms is suggested by the fact that the attempt to eliminate chattel slavery for the sake of the ideals of equality and liberty was pushed steadily forward even at great cost. But the period of negotia-tion between the norm and the discrepant institution was a protracted one, and progress toward realization of the norm was often halted and sometimes reversed. Only reluctantly and in the heat of armed con-flict could even so convinced an advocate of the liberal norm as Abraham Lincoln be induced to strike the blow that brought the legal end of the slavery institution. The American constitutional sys-tem does not permit precipitate action even in defense of its most fundamental tenets.

The difficulty of constitutional solution of a problem of this sort is further illustrated in the fact that by-products of slavery are still in some senses alive; even a century after the war they constitute what is, perhaps, our most troublesome internal problem. The process of establishing Negro freedom as a social, political, and economic reality has persisted far beyond the point where slavery was ended. The response of the social institutions of the South, and to a con-siderable degree of the North, to the formal constitutional adjust-ment was to develop a rigid and pervasive caste system to replace the system in which the Negro was held as property. And once again, progress in the adjustment of social practice to liberal norms has been piecemeal and halting. In the field of segregation of public facilities, including schools, for example, it has tortuously evolved from general disregard for equality before the law through a period of presumably equal but separate public facilities to the point where, at present, general racial integration is in process but far from realized. And even the achievement of institutional adjustments that will satisfy present definitions of equal protection of the laws will leave vast gaps between the liberal norms literally interpreted and social and economic practice in both South and North.

The general problem is the problem of the adjustment of practice, both personal and public, to proclaimed public belief. Public policies are the political mechanisms used for this adjustment. They account for only a fraction of social change, though in many circumstances that fraction is doubtless critical. How large the fraction really is in particular circumstances poses a difficult and intriguing question for gross political analysis. It is interesting to speculate about the ways and extent to which sociocultural changes condition a society's ability to make these adjustments, and the rapidity with which adjustments are accepted. It may be supposed, for example, that development of the high degree of interdependence that creates what we now call mass society has sped up the process of adjustment. Here, as elsewhere, questions raised by the examination of gross phenomena and stimulated by attention to political thought are related to and may perhaps be partially answered by research on political phenomena at more micro-levels.

NATION AND STATES: JOHN C. CALHOUN

In the preceding section of this chapter it was suggested that the period of mid-nineteenth century in America, the period dominated by the Civil War, gave rise to three fundamental types of issues in American politics—economic–social issues, moral–political issues, and political–structural issues. The first two of these were primarily excited by the slavery controversy and primarily directed to the controversy itself. The last, which is fundamentally a question of the relationship between the nation and the states, was somewhat broader in source and considerably different in implication. Because of these differences and because of the significance of theory on this issue, we have separated it for treatment in the remaining pages of this chapter.

For analytic purposes, we will treat this issue in terms of the two sides of the controversy, dealing first with the position of those who stated the case for sectionalism and states' rights, then with those who argued from the position of American nationalism. Of the first, the leading theoretician of the period was undoubtedly John C. Calhoun. Indeed, the political theory set forth by Calhoun stands as one of the most cogent and thoughtful of all American contributions to political thought. Calhoun was perhaps par excellent a combination of statesman, ideologist, and theorist, and whatever might be thought of the position he took, few Americans have combined these roles so well. It is important that Calhoun's ideas not be seen simply as rationalizations of the slavery institution. While his death in 1850 did not predate the slavery controversy, that controversy was in an early stage. Other sectional problems, particularly the tariff and general economic relationships, probably had as much effect as slavery in stimulating Calhoun's formulation of an outlook on the matter of distribution of power. Furthermore, while Calhoun's work may be a defense of the South, it may also be seen as a general theory of American politics or even of political systems. His importance in this last respect is suggested both by the content of the theory itself and by the extent to which his ideas have frequently been invoked not only in defense of Southern sectionalism but in explanation of the political process.[13]

The analysis that follows is based largely on the succinct and broad-gauge statement of political ideas to be found in the *Disquisition on Government,* published after Calhoun's death. In a sense, his theory sought means to the same end served by classic liberalism—the limitation of government on behalf of minority rights. Its differences from the classic Lockean position, however, were substantial. As against the basic liberal assumption that man's life by nature is individualistic and antisocial, Calhoun began with the Aristotelian assumption that man is by nature a social being. At this level, his position was like that of Fitzhugh. Man's inclinations and wants impel him to social life, and he is never found and cannot exist in any other than a social condition. The sociality of human life makes man what he is—a moral and intelligent creature:

His inclinations and wants, physical and moral, irresistibly impel him to associate with his kind; and he has, accordingly, never been found, in any age or country, in any state other than the social. In no other, indeed, could he exist; and in no other,—were it possible for him to exist,—could he attain to a full development of his moral and intellectual faculties, or raise himself, in the scale of being, much above the level of the brute creation.[14]

Thus, there is no basis, historical or natural, for considering the life of man outside its social context.

But while man is naturally social, he is also possessed with self-interest. While his sociability is high, it is not ". . . so great as to over-

[13] For biography and commentary see Charles M. Wiltse, *John C. Calhoun* (3 vols.; Indianapolis: Bobbs-Merrill Co., Inc., 1944–51); August O. Spain, *The Political Theory of John C. Calhoun* (New York: Bookman Associates, 1951); Margaret L. Coit, *John C. Calhoun, American Portrait* (Boston: Houghton Mifflin Co., 1950).

[14] John C. Calhoun, *Works* (New York: D. Appleton & Co., 1853), Vol. I, p. 2.

power this all-pervading and essential law of animated existence." [15]
Man feels his own needs most directly, and in situations where these
conflict with the needs of his fellows, self-interest predominates. In
human societies there arises, therefore, the need for an external
controlling power, a power which, when necessary, can articulate
individual and community interest. It is this need which gives rise
to government.

Thus, government is a natural concomitant of the human condition
—natural in a sense more basic than for the main stem of the liberal
tradition. Though Calhoun drew a distinction between society and
the government, both are within the bundle of necessary relationships that make up the human community. Both are aspects of the
situation within which men must live to develop their full capacities
as men. Both are aspects of what the Greeks called the "constitution"
in its broadest sense. The following comment, heavily Aristotelean
in tone, illustrates the point:

To the Infinite Being, the Creator of all, belongs exclusively the care and
superintendence of the whole. He, in his infinite wisdom and goodness,
has allotted to every class of animated beings its condition and appropriate
functions; and has endowed each with feelings, instincts, capacities, and
faculties, best adapted to its allotted condition. To man, he has assigned
the social and political state, as best adapted to develop the great capacities
and faculties, intellectual and moral, with which he has endowed him; and
has, accordingly, constituted him so as not only to impel him into the social
state, but to make government necessary for his preservation and well-
being.[16]

However, despite his belief in the essentially sociable character
of man and the corollary natural basis of human society and government, Calhoun affirmed that men living in society are subject to
abuse from political authority. The reason for this is simply that
governments cannot make themselves go, they must be administered
by men. As all men, including those who occupy political office, are
frequently inclined to pursue their own interests, political power may
be turned away from its proper public objects and utilized in the private interests of those who hold it. In the nature of things, then, the
need arises to protect men from government.

It might be supposed by those accustomed to think of political
relationships in terms of the assumptions and norms of liberal democracy that the need to limit government arises out of sacrosanct in-

---

[15] Ibid., p. 4.
[16] Ibid., pp. 6–7.

dividual human rights threatened by arbitrary political power. Indeed, Calhoun sometimes wrote of injustice and oppression as though individual rights were his initial point of reference. But the threat of abuse posed by government must finally be a threat to society, since the fundamental values of human life lie in society; the society, not the individual, is the locus of ultimate value in human life. Individuals have neither rights nor characteristics as human beings independent of their social situations. The threat, then, that is posed by the abuse of political power is not a threat to individuals but a threat to society, more particularly to the stability of the society and to its ability to preserve itself. On social stability depend man's chances of exercising capacities and fulfilling potentials. The very maintenance of society, in other words, is the first condition for the development and realization of human life. Without stability, society dissolves, there is no community with which people may articulate their lives, and men are robbed of the opportunity to live in the ways of men.

On the basis of these assumptions, Calhoun erected a simple and compelling prescriptive theory about the organization of political power. The first consideration at this level is how the power of government may be limited for the sake of preserving society. Here again, Calhoun's formulation sounds much like that of the liberal tradition. At the first step, he prescribed democracy, the use of machinery by which those who wield political power are required to elicit the consent of the governed. Calhoun expressed the idea in these words:

Such an organism, then, as will furnish the means by which resistance may be systematically and peaceably made on the part of the ruled, to oppression and abuse of power on the part of the rulers, is the first and indispensable step toward *forming* a constitutional government. And as this can only be effected by or through the right of suffrage,—(the right on the part of the ruled to choose their rulers at proper intervals, and to hold them thereby responsible for their conduct)—the responsibility of the rulers to the ruled, through the right of suffrage, is the indispensable and primary principle in the *foundation* of a constitutional government.[17]

Thus, through the exercise of the suffrage "systematically"—i.e., regularly and through established institutions—the community is provided with the means for peaceably circulating elites, thereby assuring political responsibility to the majority. This formulation of the democratic principle is unusually simply stated and phrased in realistic and modern terms.

---

[17] *Ibid.,* p. 12.

It also follows from Calhoun's basic assumptions, however, that democracy alone is not sufficient protection from the abuse of political power, at least not in a complex society. The reason for the inadequacy of democracy lies in natural differentiation among men, for society, though a whole, is composed of many parts, the health of each integral to the health of the larger entity. The health of society cannot, therefore, be seen only in terms of the interests of the whole but also requires attention to the differential needs of the parts. A system of majority rule provides the response of politics only to the preponderant proportion and not to the whole of the body. Were a body composed of parts whose interests could be common each with the others, protection of the majority would be adequate to provide for the interests of the society. But such is not the nature of the human community. If such homogeneous societies do exist, they exist only on a small scale and probably only in a relatively primitive condition.

Thus, the nature and needs of society itself dictate that means be found to protect the interests of all its various parts, that is to say, to protect the interests of social minorities. It must be emphasized that this protection is, finally, not protection of the minorities as such but of minorities as integral parts of the entire social structure. In what amounts to a class interpretation of politics, Calhoun suggests that there is inevitably conflict among the interests of society.

If the whole community had the same interests, so that the interests of each and every portion would be so affected by the action of the government, that the laws which oppressed or impoverished one portion, would necessarily oppress and impoverish all others,—or the reverse,—then the right of suffrage, of itself, would be all-sufficient to counteract the tendency of the government to oppression and abuse of its powers; and, of course, would form, of itself, a perfect constitutional government. The interest of all being the same, by supposition, as far as the action of the government was concerned, all would have like interests as to what laws should be made, and how they should be executed. All strife and struggle would cease as to who should be elected to make and execute them. The only question would be, who was most fit; who the wisest and most capable of understanding the common interest of the whole. This decided, the election would pass off quietly, and without party discord; as no one portion could advance its own peculiar interest without regard to the rest, by electing a favorite candidate.

But such is not the case. On the contrary, nothing is more difficult than to equalize the action of the government, in reference to the various and diversified interests of the community; and nothing more easy than to pervert its powers into instruments to aggrandize and enrich one or more interests by oppressing and impoverishing the others; and this too, under the operation of laws, couched in general terms;—and which, on their face, appear fair and equal. Nor is this the case in some particular communities only. It is so in all; the small and the great,—the poor and the rich,—irrespective of pursuits, productions, or degrees of civilization;—with, however, this difference, that the more extensive and populous the country, the more diversified the condition and pursuits of its population, and the richer, more luxurious, and dissimilar the people, the more difficult is it to equalize the action of the government,—and the more easy for one portion of the community to pervert its powers to oppress, and plunder the other.[18]

Thus, the peace and progress of the whole community require not only that conflicts be settled but that they be settled without vital damage to any of the community's subparts. Democracy itself is an instrument of political control that conduces to the advantage of a subpart, which happens in itself to embody the majority, i.e., more than half of the entire community. In imposing limits on democracy out of fear of its effect on minor elements in the community, Calhoun's theory adopted, although for somewhat different reasons, the liberal tradition's important distinction between democracy and constitutionalism, and like liberalism, too, its major thrust was as much toward the protection of minorities as toward providing the instruments of majority rule. While the distinction between Calhoun's concern for minorities as parts of the organic social body and classical liberalism's concern for the individual as an integral moral being is an important one, the institutional implications of the two positions were highly similar.

Somewhat different, however, was Calhoun's formulation of the means by which constitutional protection can be given minorities within the democratic society. In his answer to this problem lay Calhoun's most interesting and significant contribution to American political thought—the principle of the concurrent majority. Government must be provided, he said, with structures that assure that public policy comports to the needs and desires of all the community elements on whom it will have an effect. The end of affording adequate protection in minorities, he wrote,

. . . can be accomplished only in one way, and that is by such an organism of government,—and, if necessary for the purpose, of the community also,—as will, by dividing and distributing the powers of government, give to each division or interest, through its appropriate organ, either a concurrent voice in making and executing the laws, or a veto on their execution.

---

[18] *Ibid.*, pp. 14–16.

It is only by such an organism, that the assent of each can be made necessary to put the government in motion; for the power made effectual to
arrest its action, when put in motion;—and it is only by the one or the other
that the different interests, orders, classes, or portions, into which the community may be divided can be protected, and all conflict and struggle
between them prevented,—by rendering it impossible to put or to keep it
in action, without the concurrent consent of all.[19]

Thus, Calhoun drew a distinction between the numerical and the
concurrent majority, the concurrent being the true voice of the
people, the voice of the entire body and not of a part. The principle
of the concurrent majority requires the subjection of the seeming or
immediate needs of the parts on behalf of the real needs of the whole.
Immediate and particular needs are most obvious as, for example,
democracy reveals the immediate and particular needs of the majority.
These, however, must be put in the perspective of their relationship
to the long-term interest of the whole. In a sense, the idea of concurrent majority is the idea of constant compromise for the sake of
the entire social community.

In Calhoun's view, however, mere exhortation is insufficient to
provide proper protection for minority interests. Pious paper inhibitions on the exercise of majority power, while they may have some
persuasive effects, must be complemented by institutional checks that
assure the operation of the veto principle. An advantage of absolute
government, including absolute democracy, Calhoun wrote, is its
simplicity of structure. Indeed, this may be its only advantage. But
a constitutional democracy, to fulfill the criteria Calhoun's prescriptions would impose, would have to be complex. It must incorporate
a variety of procedural brakes on the development of public policy so
that the numerical majority, in whose hands overwhelming power
tends to rest naturally, will find its latitude for decision-making
effectively limited. Calhoun cited examples of political systems in
which complexity of structure had made the principle of concurrent
majority work, describing the Polish constitution, the Iroquois
federation, the Roman republic, and the British constitutional structure as among those that had met the test. Systems like these have
found, he thought, means by which the accommodation of majority
power to minority needs is achieved.[20]

The diversity of implication and purpose in Calhoun's political
writings makes their interpretation a difficult job, just as his role

---

[19] *Ibid.*, p. 25.
[20] *Ibid.*, pp. 71–73, 92–107, and *passim*.

in American political history obscures somewhat his stature as a statesman. The problem with his theory does not lie in its elegance or complexity. Its argument, in fact, is extraordinarily neat and simple. The difficulty arises from two sources. One was the compulsion, inherent in the circumstances, to make the theory serve as ideology as well as theory. While it is doubtless true that any commentator on political matters must write in a social context and, in some sense, play an ideological role, Calhoun's position in his society and the nature of his society itself forced him to write of political phenomena in terms of a political program. The second source of difficulty in interpreting his political ideas lies in his equivocal relationship to the American liberal tradition—that is to say, in the extent to which he arrived at liberal conclusions from divergent premises. We will return to this second matter in a few paragraphs. Our evaluation of Calhoun's political ideas will deal with them on three levels—the level of political program, the level of descriptive interpretation of the political system, and the level of prescriptive theory.

Actually, an evaluation of Calhoun's political program must be made in terms of the substance of the political dispute of the times, in terms of his ideological position in that dispute, and in terms of its workability in the framework of American political life. As we suggested above, Calhoun's program offered a way of resolving sectional disputes, including slavery, on political–structural grounds. He advocated a way of arranging the institutions of political decision-making that, in effect, would have excluded the issues at stake from resolution by national political authority. The problem of slavery would not, so to speak, have been subject to authoritative decision. For the device of the concurrent veto would assure a Southern negative on national policy on slavery or tariff or other economic and social questions at issue in the tendentious relationships between South and North, and thus they would have been neutralized as national issues. In terms of practical mechanisms, the logical ulterior of the concurrent veto would be the device of nullification, and Calhoun himself was prepared to push the idea this far. The structure of his theory provided ready grounds for rationalization of even such extreme action as this in terms of the good of the larger society. Without arguing the virtue of the Southern cause either as respects slavery or economic problems, the difficulty of his position would seem to lie in its failure to accommodate to changes in social scale, and in its deemphasis of the need for sustained and broad-reaching social authority. The clear effect of the operation of the concurrent veto doctrine would be to inhibit the application of political power to social problems. The question, then, is whether this inhibition can be afforded in a society whose scale is so large that the consequences of failure to take action are spread immediately throughout society, transcending the interests of those sections or groups which could veto public action. The consequences of such a deadlock might be the quick destruction of the social system within which and for whose preservation the concurrent veto is expected to operate.

At the second level, Calhoun's theory offers the outline of a descriptive theory of American politics. In recent years, his ideological reputation having been somewhat neutralized by the passage of time, his works have come to be highly regarded by some as descriptions of the fundamental tendencies in the American political system.[21] From this point of view, it can be argued that whatever the underlying assumptions of Calhoun's theory, he caught the inner sense of American politics by emphasizing its tendency to grant virtual veto power to the wide variety of forces operating in the system. Though the constitutional structure was in its inception influenced more by the individualistic orientation of the Founding Fathers than by a view directed to the overall good of the social whole, it nonetheless came out providing minorities with a wide range of protective devices. It is a set of institutions constructed so as to complicate rather than simplify the process of public decision-making. Its major overall effect is to limit democratic authority through both procedural and substantive restrictions, while vesting final choice, where choice can be made, in popular consent.

The doctrine of the concurrent veto is given contemporary effect in a range of institutional devices. These include the variety of mechanisms built into the governmental structure to limit the scope and application of authority: a legislative branch with two houses different in social basis, an executive veto, judicial review, federal division of powers, diverse terms of office and electoral bases among the three branches, filibusters, elaborate parliamentary procedures, senatorial participation in appointment and treaty-making, and others. The effect of these is to make decision virtually impossible without wide concurrence among participating groups. While the formality of concurrent veto is not written into the American Constitution, the nature

[21] See, for example, Peter F. Drucker, "A Key to American Politics: Calhoun's Pluralism," *Review of Politics*, Vol. X (October, 1948), pp. 412–26; John Fischer, "Unwritten Rules of American Politics," *Harper's Magazine*, Vol. 197 (November, 1948), pp. 27–36; Ralph Lerner, "Calhoun's New Science of Politics," *American Political Science Review*, Vol. LVII (December, 1963), pp. 918–32.

of the system is such as to make concurrent majorities nearly requisite for authoritative decisions.

Calhoun's interpretation of American politics also does more than most to take account of the importance and role of the functional "interest" group. Along with Madison and Tocqueville, he can be regarded as a precursor of the group theory approach to politics. While Calhoun himself treated interests in terms of their sectional bases and thought of them as being differentiated geographically, there would seem to be no reason why interests held together not by geography but by function cannot be treated in the same way for the same reasons. Why should such minorities not have the same type of negative on public policy as he would accord to the interests of states and sections? The social and economic structure of the country has to some extent tended to neutralize the internal homogeneity and external heterogeneity of the nation's geographic areas. At the same time, with the development of a national culture and national economy, and with the heightened social and economic differentiation brought about in the society by industrial specialization, identifiable and important interests have come to extend across geographic bounds and serve as a popular basis for conjoint political action. In some fields and through some mechanisms, these interest groups have, indeed, developed influence of veto proportions. To cite some examples, the functional dominance of congressional committees, the influence of the regulated on regulatory and licensing agencies, and the supposed strong ties between certain functional groups and the political parties afford these interests strong bases for asserting their views if not imposing their vetoes on the policy-making process. Such influences are also operative in important ways in the administration of public policy.

At a third level, Calhoun's political ideas may be seen as a neat network of prescriptive theory. It marches in orderly fashion from assumptions to prescriptions, lays its basis in values clear, and even incorporates some evidence from comparative politics in behalf of its major propositions. Assuming that a recapitulation of the theory is unnecessary, we will confine our discussion here to two general observations. The first, already mentioned above, is the extent to which a comparison of Calhoun's theory and the main tenets of American liberalism demonstrates how theories divergent in basic assumptions can converge at the level of institutional prescription. Although he wrote in a cause that proved to be the source of the most difficult experience ever suffered by the American political system, the kinds of institutions Calhoun advocated and the spirit of his discussion of the American Constitution were certainly not foreign to the American tradition. If the threat of nullification should be deemed extraordinary and extreme, it might be recalled that such American luminaries as Thomas Jefferson and John Taylor were largely responsible for the Kentucky and Virginia resolutions, and that, in more recent times, the theory of interposition popular among some southerners has drawn on Calhoun for its posture of opposition to federal policy. But short of this extreme, Calhoun's emphasis on the protection of minorities and his disposition toward the complexity of political institutions are within, not beyond, the common American attitudes. Yet, Calhoun's organic interpretation of society and state is quite at loggerheads with the assumptions of the *Declaration of Independence* and the Constitution on these matters. Perhaps the contrast can be emphasized by pointing out that Calhoun's fundamentals lie very close to those of Fitzhugh, whose attack on the *Declaration of Independence,* with its doctrines of rights, contract, and equality, was downright venomous.

In sum, Calhoun worked with two kinds of political theory. On the one hand, he was a conservative in the great tradition of Aristotle, St. Thomas, and Edmund Burke. Like them, he emphasized the health of the social whole, the natural sociability of man, the differentiation of human talents, and the importance of mediating devices in the development and validation of public policy. While his contributions to this point of view were not original, they constitute one of the few important American statements of the conservative position. On the other hand, Calhoun may be seen as a contributor to the theory of institutional pluralism, to the point of view most highly developed in England but very influential in the shaping of American attitudes. Pluralists found the basic unit of social life to lie in the voluntary group that they assumed to have a real moral personality. From their perspective, the group, not the society as a whole, was organic. Working from this foundation, they questioned the legitimacy of the power of the centralized state and prescribed political forms that would afford groups the power to defend their own interests. In this respect, their notions about the proper basis of political organization were not unlike those of Calhoun.

From an abstract point of view, the principal question raised by Calhoun's theory is whether it provides with sufficient certainty an adequate basis for the exercise of political authority. Its thrust is toward the limitation of political power, perhaps without sufficient concern for the problematic aspects of large-scale social relationships.

The counterargument, developed during the same period and reinforced by the experiences of the Civil War, lay emphasis on the primacy of nation to states and on the need for adequate provision for the exercise of power on a national basis. The fundamentals of this position are the subject of the section to follow.

AMERICAN NATIONALISM: THE CASE FOR
NATIONAL SOVEREIGNTY

Juxtaposed to the case for the sovereignty of states or sections typified here in the ideas of Calhoun is a case for the sovereignty of the nation. Nationalism in the United States, the development of a feeling of American nationhood, was a movement that cut across eras and specific conflicts.[22] We treat it here because the controversy over national sovereignty reached its highest pitch at the time of the Civil War, and because in America, as elsewhere, the political theory of nationalism was brought to its most refined state, during the middle and late nineteenth century. It is probably unnecessary to emphasize, however, that American nationalism was not strictly a Civil War-related phenomenon.

By nationalism, we basically mean a self-conscious sense of unity, identity, common fate.[23] This self-consciousness may be ethnic, geographic, or political in base. It may embrace the inhabitants of a state or a politically dependent ethnic minority. Its ideological manifestation is often the belief that obligation to the nation-state transcends all other loyalties, and it usually utilizes a variety of symbols that appeal to the emotions. In any case, nationalism tends to militate against loyalties both broader and narrower in base, to submerge these in an overriding tie to the nation. It attacks those perspectives that find in either individual or mankind a locus of rationality or morality. It is the national group that defines value in human life from this point of view, the group that has some particularly potent appeal to primary identification.

Nationalism is usually treated as a modern political phenomenon, and in a real sense, it is. Although there was, perhaps, a tone of nation-

---

[22] See esp. chaps. 3 and 7, above.

[23] For general commentary on nationalism in history and theory, see Hans Kohn, *The Idea of Nationalism: a Study in Its Origins and Background* (New York: Macmillan Co., 1944); Carleton J. H. Hays, *Essays on Nationalism* (New York: Macmillan Co., 1926); Carleton J. H. Hays, *Nationalism: a Religion* (New York: Macmillan Co., 1960); Louis L. Snyder, *The Meaning of Nationalism* (New Brunswick: Rutgers University Press, 1954); Boyd C. Shafer, *Nationalism: Myth and Realty* (New York: Harcourt, Brace & Co., 1955); on American nationalism specifically, see Hans Kohn, *American Nationalism: an Interpretative Essay* (New York: Macmillan Co., 1957).

alism in the classical Greek view of the city-state, something different
is required to focus loyalty on the large and complex modern national
society than is necessary to find it in the primary society of the small
city. Nationalism, as we indicated above, experienced a slow growth
both in organizational fact and in ideology during the Middle Ages. It
has been suggested that in Machiavelli is to be found one of the early
statements of the nationalist political prescription. French nationhood
seems to have been sealed by the politics of Richelieu early in the
seventeenth century, by the political impact of the Thirty Years' War,
and later with the influence of Louis XIV. The English sense of nationhood grew under the Tudors and profited from the centralization
of political control they managed to achieve. The mercantilist economics of the seventeenth and eighteenth centuries was nationalistic
in thrust. The rationalism of the Enlightenment and the individualism of English liberalism were to a degree countertrends to the development of the nationalist perspective, but the growth of the nation-
state as a political fact from the sixteenth to the eighteenth century
laid the groundwork for the flowering in the nineteenth of the mature
political thought of nationalism. The nineteenth century saw the
nation-state's development embellished with elaborate philosophical
systems that rationalized its fundamental characteristics and alleged
functions.

We have noted, at various points above, signs of the development
of American nationalism. It was certainly a part, though a relatively
undeveloped part, of the ideological syndrome that made the American Revolution a political possibility. It was also, as we have noted,
apparent in the ideas of American transcendentalism, though perhaps
not so much in its political as in some of its cultural and intellectual
aspects. It was certainly active as popular ideology in the Mexican
War, the controversy over the boundaries of the Oregon Territory,
and the movement toward rapid Western expansion. The question of
nationalism was also latent in the development of the federalistic
structure of American government and in such political controversies
as the Jeffersonian–Hamiltonian dispute over the extent of national
power. Thus, both structurally and ideologically, the basis was pre
pared early for the introduction of the symbol of nationalism into
controversies about sectional economic differences and the slavery
problem. It was out of these disputes that coherent statements of the
theory of American nationalism arose.

American nationalism is unusual but not altogether unique. It is
unusual because (1) its object, the American nation, was a recent and

"artificial" phenomenon, and (2) it was directed toward an extremely heterogeneous ethnic, social, and geographic national unit. The idea of an American people does not have ancient roots like the idea of a French, a German, or an English people. America's beginnings are not lost in the mysteries of antiquity, but are apparent in recent history. Her nationalism, therefore, has, in a sense, been a manufactured thing, its growth and struggle for survival almost parts of the current scene. This is not to say the impact of American nationalism is any less real for that reason, but only to say its conditions are different and, perhaps, somewhat more tendentious than those of many of the nationalisms of Europe. In these respects, many contemporary nationalist movements are more firmly established on historical and ethnic grounds than America's has ever been.

Another interesting aspect of American nationalism and an aspect that will be emphasized in what follows is its structural character. During the Constitutional Convention, for example, when the emotional symbols of nationalism were little in evidence, the question of nationalism is found in discussion of the structure of the federal system. In the Civil War controversy, the nationalism dimension also hinged on the structure question. The meaning and implications of nationalism for America, in other words, have been discussed largely in terms of the relative powers of nation and states. This may reflect what seems to be a tendency in American politics to place more emphasis on structure than on policy content.

The nationalist position and its alternatives were generally argued around a formalistic but venerable question: Where is the sovereignty? This problem has been a favorite in political theory since the beginning of the modern period. Simply put, the classical idea of sovereignty was a conception of a supreme power unrestrained by laws. In its specific application to American politics, the question was whether the sovereignty lay with the whole or with the parts, with the union or with section and state. The sectionalists emphasized the sovereignty of the several states. In doing so, they did not question the reality of the union but maintained that when the problem is driven to its ultimate, when some specific political issue poses a head-on and irreconcilable conflict between interests of nation and of states, legitimacy finally lies with the states. Thus, in the extreme case, the states might legitimately reject the authority of the national government through an ordinance of nullification, and interpose themselves between the national authority and the people. Behind this position lies the claim that the union is a compact of states and not a direct creation of the people of the nation. This interpretation of the constitutional basis of national government had been pressed by many people since the time of the framing. It is also important to note that although this legalistic problem was, in a sense, the fulcrum of the dispute, the nationalist case ordinarily embodied not only these arguments of reason and history but also arguments rooted in mystery, in sentiment, and in tradition.

In the remaining sections of this chapter, we will treat two distinguishable if not entirely distinct types of American nationalism—what might be called the political nationalism of such figures as Webster and Lincoln and of the Supreme Court in the post-Civil War period, and the idealist nationalism, largely academic in origin and mostly a restatement in American terms of the Hegelianism then so great a force in Europe.

Political Nationalism

One of the earliest and most compelling defenses of the national sovereignty was that of Daniel Webster. Webster's overriding commitment to national sovereignty was apparent in a good many of his political acts and statements. Perhaps as a practical politician he fell somewhat short of single-mindedness on the question, but his nationalism overrode even what might have been anticipated of his sectional view on the slavery issue. Perhaps Webster's best-known statement on the subject is to be found in a speech of three days' duration, delivered in the Senate in 1830 on an issue (Foote's Resolution) involving inquiry into speculation in the sale of Western lands. Webster's principal adversary in the debate, Senator Hayne of South Carolina, turned the debate to the general question of states' rights.

Webster's argument was a blend of the legalist and romanticist elements of nationalist theory mentioned above. In its legalist aspects, it was first a search for the occasions and forms in which opposition to national authority might be justifiable. Webster granted that in extreme circumstances, i.e., those enumerated by the *Declaration of Independence,* there is a legitimate right of revolution against government. But as the Constitution is a framework for the peaceable solution of social conflict, resort to revolutionary violence or even nonviolent denial of the bonds of political obligation put one outside the Constitution and dissolved both its ties on him and the protection he might expect to derive from it. There is, however, no right of revolution *within* the Constitution. It prescribes arrangements for the settlement of disputes along agreed lines, and embodies a promise and an obligation to undertake only prescribed forms of political action. Nullification is not such a prescribed form and, therefore, not defensible within the Constitution.

The case may be elaborated by reference to the question of sovereignty. The sovereignty matter was traditionally (and logically) treated in terms of search for a *single* locus of power, the very idea of divided sovereignty being self-contradictory. Webster used the concept to attack the case for nullification and to bolster the case for national authority. His exploration of constitutional theory led him to the conclusions that sovereignty lies with the people, and national and state governments alike are creations of the people acting in their sovereign capacity. On this ground, Webster rejected the contention that the union is a compact of the states. "We are all," said Webster, "agents of the same supreme power, the people." [24] This does not mean, however, that one national and twenty-four state constitutions are all of equal standing. It is absurd to think that there can be twenty-five sovereigns. The sovereignty by definition is indivisible, and the practical results of divided sovereignty would be grave.

The question of priorities among constitutions may be answered by reference to the terms of the national charter itself. ". . .[T]he people have wisely provided, in the Constitution itself, a proper, suitable mode and tribunal for settling questions of Constitutional law." [25] The answer is found in the supreme law clause of Article VI that states, "This Constitution, and the laws of the United States which shall be made in pursuance thereof . . . shall be the supreme law of the land . . . anything in the Constitution or laws of any State to the contrary notwithstanding." Thus, national supremacy is clearly established. Furthermore, the national Constitution goes even further, for in establishing a framework for judicial review, it provides a particular structure for giving finality to decisions about the distribution of power between levels of government. The judicial branch, being a coordinate part of the national structure of power, serves as an organ for the imposition of national sovereignty in cases where conflicts arise. The very function of validating national authority or granting to the states permission to act on a specific problem is in the hands of the federal judiciary exercising the national sovereignty. The intent of the people to provide for the active handling of the problem of sovereignty in this way is expressed simply in that clause of the Con-

---

[24] *The Writings and Speeches of Daniel Webster* (Boston: Little, Brown, 1903), Vol. VI, p. 55.

[25] *Ibid.,* p. 67.

stitution which declares, "The judicial power shall extend to all cases
. . . arising under this Constitution [and] the laws of the United
States . . . ." [26]

Webster thus held that the question of sovereignty in both its theoretical and practical reaches could be resolved by a clear reading of
the Constitution. Though the people have a right to revolt, a nullify-
ing act by a state government means nothing. The peaceful resolution
of social problems within the framework of established institutions is
fundamentally to be sought by the people through the organs of the
national government in the ways clearly provided by the Constitution.
"It is, Sir, the people's Constitution, the people's government, made
for the people, made by the people, and answerable to the people." [27]
Webster thought the authority of the nation seen in these terms was
clearly paramount.

To say this is not to say, however, that the law of the nation is unchecked by the sovereign people. This was not, in other words, an
authoritarian theory but one that took account of the American commitment to limited government. Webster enumerated five safeguards
of the power and rights of the people: first, "the plain words of the
instrument"; second, frequent elections in which the people may hold
their "servants and agents" responsible; third, a "respectable," "disinterested," and "independent" judiciary; fourth, the power "to alter
or amend the Constitution, peaceably and quietly, whenever experience shall point out defects or imperfections"; fifth, a denial of power
to the states to construe or interpret "*their* high instrument of government, or to interfere, by their own power, to arrest its course and
operation." [28]

To this constitutional argument, Webster added a note of emotional appeal to the rising tide of American nationalist sentiment.
The following quotation illustrates that side of the nationalist case
and constitutes, furthermore, an impressive example of the high political rhetoric of a bygone day:

I have not allowed myself, Sir, to look beyond the Union, to see what
might lie hidden in the dark recess behind. I have not coolly weighed the
chances of preserving liberty when the bonds that unite us together shall
be broken asunder. I have not accustomed myself to hang over the preci-
pice of disunion, to see whether, with my short sight, I can fathom the
depth of the abyss below; nor could I regard him as a safe counsellor in

[26] Article III, sec. 2.
[27] *Ibid.*, p. 54.
[28] *Ibid.*, p. 73.

the affairs of this government, whose thoughts should be mainly bent on considering, not how the Union may be best preserved, but how tolerable might be the condition of the people when it should be broken up and destroyed. While the Union lasts, we have high, exciting, gratifying prospects spread out before us, for us and our children. Beyond that I seek not to penetrate the veil. God grant that in my day, at least, that curtain may not rise! God grant that on my vision never may be opened what lies behind! When my eyes shall be turned to behold for the last time the sun in heaven, may I not see him shining on the broken and dishonored fragments of a once glorious Union; on states dissevered, discordant, belligerent; on a land rent with civil feuds, or drenched, it may be, in fraternal blood! Let their last feeble and lingering glance rather behold the gorgeous ensign of the republic, now known and honored throughout the earth, still full high advanced, its arms and trophies streaming in their original luster, not a stripe erased or polluted, nor a single star obscured, bearing for its motto, no such miserable interrogatory as "What is all this worth?" nor those other words of delusion and folly, "Liberty first and Union afterwards;" but everywhere, spread all over in characters of living light, blazing on all its ample folds, as they float over the sea and over the land, and in every wind under the whole heavens, that other sentiment, dear to every true American heart,—Liberty *and* Union, now and forever, one and inseparable! [29]

In dealing with American political nationalism of the mid-nineteenth century, a few comments must be added about the contributions in idea and action of Abraham Lincoln. Lincoln was without doubt the greatest of the American nationalist statesmen. While the idea of nationalism does not exhaust the full scope of his political position, it does seem to have constituted a kind of primary point of reference for him in the determination of his course of action. Thus, as we have suggested above, his dedication to the cause of saving the union probably overrode his dedication to the cause of abolition or the cause of a free Western agriculture. In 1854, he declared, "Much as I hate slavery, I would consent to the extension of it rather than see the Union dissolved, just as I would consent to any great evil to avoid a greater one," the greater one being the destruction of the American nation in its larger entity.[30]

In his first inaugural address, delivered in March, 1861, Lincoln set forth in summary terms his position on the nationalist question. First, he held that the union is necessarily and by definition perpetual,

---

[29] *Ibid.,* p. 75.
[30] Quoted in A. T. Mason, *Free Government in the Making* (2d ed.; New York: Oxford University Press, 1956), p. 520.

perpetuity being "implied, if not expressed, in the fundamental law of all national governments." [31] The Constitution, in other words, cannot be destroyed from within itself. It can be destroyed, as Webster suggested, only by some force from outside the framework of government it established. Furthermore, even if the government of the United States were but a contract among states and, as Lincoln put it, "not a government proper," it could still be legitimately destroyed only by mutual consent of the parties. The notion of a contract is the notion of an agreement binding on both sides, an agreement from which one side cannot arbitrarily release itself of obligation. Lincoln also asserted that there is in the union a perpetuity and historical meaning that extends even beyond its instrument, the federal Constitution. The union, said Lincoln, "is much older than the Constitution." [32] It dates to the Articles of Association of 1774, and its principle is restated in the *Declaration of Independence* and in the Articles of Confederation. Lincoln noted that, according to the Preamble, one of the purposes of the union was "to form a more perfect union." Each of these stages in the natural history of the union represented a step in its perfection, none of them an act of artificial creation. Thus, the union must be treated like a growing, living thing, not a mechanical contrivance.

To these arguments in legal and political philosophy, Lincoln added a kind of sociogeographic argument in defense of the union. The respective sections, he said, cannot divorce themselves from one another, but must remain in propinquity; in the nature of things, they must remain connected. The disputes giving rise to the threat of secession and resort to arms would not be concluded by a contest of violence, whatever its outcome. They would remain to chafe relations between the sections even if they were separated, until some mutually satisfactory basis for their resolution was found. [33] The later history of relations between North and South tends to demonstrate Lincoln's insight.

The first inaugural address, like most of Lincoln's public pronouncements, was directed primarily toward the preservation of the union. Lincoln's priorities at this point as at the point of emancipation were governed by his regard for the union as the primary political and moral structure. "I have no purpose," he said, "directly or indi-

---

[31] *Inaugural Addresses of the Presidents of the United States* (House Document No. 218, 87th Cong., 1st sess.) (Washington, D.C.: U.S. Government Printing Office, 1961), p. 121.

[32] *Loc. cit.*

[33] *Ibid.*, p. 124.

rectly, to interfere with the institution of slavery in the states where it exists. I believe I have no lawful right to do so, and I have no inclination to do so." [34] He sought above all to hold the nation together and to preserve for the national government the power he believed rested rightfully with it. He concluded the address with this symbolic appeal: "The mystic chords of memory, stretching from every battlefield and patriot grave to every living heart and hearthstone all over this broad land, will yet swell the chorus of the Union, when again touched, as surely they will be, by the better angels of our nature." [35]

A further statement of the nationalist point of view, similar in tenor to the position of Lincoln and interesting chiefly as an endorsement by the legalistic and otherwise not particularly nationalistic Supreme Court is to be found in the Court's decision in *Texas* v. *White*.[36] It is unnecessary here to go into detail about the nature of the legal dispute, but its substance can be presented in a few sentences.

In 1850, the United States had given Texas 10 million dollars in bonds in settlement of boundary claims. Texas law had, in turn, provided that these bonds should not be placed in private hands unless endorsed by the governor of the state. In 1862, the secessionist government repealed this law and put a million dollars worth of bonds in the hands of a military board empowered to use them without the governor's endorsement for the purchase of supplies for prosecution of the war. Thus, White, the defendant in the case, came into possession of unendorsed bonds. After the conclusion of the war, Texas brought an orginal action in the Supreme Court to recover the bonds from White on the ground that he held them illegally. The questions raised were twofold: first, whether Texas, at that time unreconstructed (unrepresented in Congress), could still bring suit before the Supreme Court as a state; second, whether redemption of the bonds by private parties should be enjoined and recovery by the state approved by the Court. The Court answered yes to both these questions, but it is the first that is of interest to us here.

The Court's approach to this problem was based on the grounds that the act of secession is illegitimate under the Constitution and that Texas, by taking part in the rebellion, had not, therefore, legitimately taken herself outside the Constitution. This being the case, the state retained its legal standing and, the war being concluded, could bring original action before the Court. Mr. Chief Justice Chase, writ-

---

[34] *Ibid.*, p. 119.
[35] *Ibid.*, p. 126.
[36] 7 Wallace 700 (1869).

ing for the majority, simply denied that it was within the power of a state to take herself out of the constitutional relationship at her own election. "The Union of the States," wrote Chase, "never was a purely artificial and arbitrary relation. It began among the Colonies, and grew out of common origin, mutual sympathies, kindred principles, similar interests, and geographic relations." [37] Like Lincoln, Chase cited the Articles of Confederation and the Constitution as instrumentalities designed to strengthen and perfect the union already in existence. "What," he asked, "can be indissoluble if a perpetual Union, made more perfect, is not?" [38] This does not, he thought, render the states entirely subservient to the will of the national government, for under the Constitution they retain a fair measure of autonomy. Here, the inherent conservatism of the Court as an institution obliged to live with its own precedent as well as some of the political tastes of its membership probably shows through. But the nationalist thrust of the opinion remains.

The ordinance of secession and the acts taken under it were declared by the Court to be null and without effect. The state remained in the union; her citizens remained citizens of the United States. The ties, the vitality of the nation override the transitory desires of one of her parts. "The Constitution, in all its provisions, looks to an indestructible union, composed of indestructible states." [39] "Our conclusion therefore is, that Texas continued to be a State, and a State of the Union, notwithstanding the transactions to which we have referred." [40]

American Idealist Nationalism

A second set of ideas contributory to the development of nationalism in American ideology is found in a largely academic group of German-influenced philosophical nationalist idealists. Though to an extent the implications of their position were similar to those of the political figures discussed above, their sources, inspirations, and philosophical roots were substantially different. American idealism was not the direct outgrowth of the Civil War. It seems probable, however, that the Civil War and the historical events and ideological conflicts that surrounded it prepared the American ideological soil for statements of an idealist nationalism relevant to the American condition and American problems. The westward movement and the indigenous

---

[37] *Ibid.*, pp. 724–25.
[38] *Ibid.*, p. 725.
[39] *Loc. cit.*
[40] *Ibid.*, p. 726.

sense of manifest destiny probably were equally instrumental in preparing the culture for such ideas.

Here, we shall only summarize briefly the idealist nationalism found in the ideas of two prominent academics, John W. Burgess and Francis Lieber. Both these men were heavily influenced by continental Hegelianism, both having studied in Germany at centers of Hegelian philosophy. The Hegelian influence on American thought is not by any means exhausted by the ideas of these two scholars, nor does their nationalism fully reflect the political implications of the Hegelian system. Thus, we are not claiming in this section to do full justice to Hegelianism as a set of political ideas, nor even to the complex and articulated Hegelian ideas of Lieber and Burgess themselves. It is important, however, to see their formulations in the context of the entire philosophy to gain some insight into the roots and characteristics of this version of the very influential Hegelian system.

Hegel postulated an absolute, universal truth or reality with which the individual life is articulated through the medium of the state. The life of the individual, he thought, can best be understood as a system of internal tensions between conscience on the one hand and material needs on the other, a tension absorbed into a larger ethical life. In the ethical life, in itself a higher level of reality than individual life, there are correspondent tensions between the family—the social representation of conscience—and the institutions of civil society—social instruments for securing and protecting material needs, that is, property. This tension is resolved in the phenomenon of the state, a temporal representation or extension of the larger flow of history or dynamic reality. The state is the march of history or, as Hegel said, "the march of God in the world." It is the place where the tensions of individual and social life are resolved in common dedication to an overriding order.

The end of human life, Hegel suggested, is "perfect freedom." This freedom implies self-consciousness and knowledge of the truth, that is to say, realization of one's relationship to his larger context. The only complete freedom, however, is that which is whole in itself, which can itself embody reality and, therefore, true self-consciousness. Hence, only the social whole can be truly free. The individual man, however, can share this freedom to the extent that he can find his place and live his life as a part of the larger, self-conscious whole. In sum, the answer to the problem of freedom for the individual lies in articulation, in the realization and enactment of his role within the society, the nexus between him and reality. The "complete" or "real" society is the nation-state. The state is man transcending the particular history of the moment. The highest goal in man's life is to integrate himself with the world spirit manifest in the state, and the free man is the man who does this. Politics is the reconciliation of the particular with the universal, of the individual with the world spirit incipient in the state. On the basis of this cursory and partial description of a complex social philosophy, it is not hard to see how it prescribed strength in the nation-state and induced a commitment to nationalism. Hegel's account of historical development interpreted the modern nation as the highest expression of man's social character.

We will review only very briefly the ideas of the American Hegelian nationalists; their significance lies not so much in their original contributions to Hegelian theory as in their addition of an organic Hegelian flare to American ideology and to American social science and historical scholarship. Francis Lieber, a German immigrant who taught at Columbia, published two leading works before the Civil War period, *Manual of Political Ethics* and *On Civil Liberty and Self-Government*.[41] Lieber's work focused on repudiation of the mechanistic constitutionalism of the liberal tradition. He rejected the contract theory and its implications as inadequate to explain the nature and mission of the organic national community. Although like the English Hegelian, T. H. Green, he lay great emphasis on civil liberty, he interpreted liberty as an aspect of men's lives within the state, neither against the state nor transcendent to it. Like Hegel, he held that the potential of man's life is realized only within the context of the community and in terms of a relationship to or articulation with the community. The nation, Lieber urged, has a moral mission. It is not the fortuitous juxtaposition of private interests, and its role in human society is neither accidental nor marginal; it is, rather, the source of the most elevated and human aspects of man's life, those things that elevate the life of man above that of the brute. From this perspective, the nation rather than the individual life is the integral unit, the whole moral thing. Such a view cut across the established tenets of liberal individualism, but in America, it complemented the long-developing consciousness of nationhood.

A somewhat more conservative nationalism is to be found in the works of John W. Burgess, who also taught at Columbia and held the first American chair in political science. His best-known writing was a

---

[41] Francis Lieber, *Manual of Political Ethics* (2 vols.; Boston: Little, Brown, 1838–42); *On Civil Liberty and Self-Government* (Philadelphia: J. B. Lippincott, 1859).

two-volume work, *Political Science and Comparative Constitutional Law,* published in 1891.[42]

Like Lieber, Burgess attacked the mechanistic orientation of modern liberal theory and decried its hegemony in American social thought. Adequate appreciation of the nature of the American nation, he felt, depended on realization of the nation's character and role as the independent and dynamic force in social life. The nation-state embodies the highest form of human existence, and without it or in its less developed forms, the life of man has less meaning and less moral standing. In comparison with Lieber's, Burgess' focus shifted from the role and freedom of the individual within the state to the nature and role of the larger whole itself.

He drew an important distinction between nations and states. A nation, he wrote, is "A population of an ethnic unity, inhabiting a territory of a geographic unity. . . ."[43] But a nation does not necessarily possess the political or moral attributes of statehood. It is the characteristic of statehood, i.e., realization of the fact and implications of its unity, that may give a nation articulation with reality, appreciation of its role in human life, and, therefore, the will to fulfill its mission. All nations do not become states. Burgess felt that a systematic examination of comparative political practices and institutions would reveal important distinctions among the nations of the world. "Not all nations, however, are endowed with political capacity or great political impulse."[44] These do not fulfill the higher functions of the state form of association. The highest talent for politics is to be found, Burgess thought, among the Aryan nations, and even among these there are significant differences: ". . . the Teuton really dominates the world by his superior political genius."[45] The historical evidence suggests, according to Burgess, the overriding political ability and, therefore, in effect, morality of Teutonic nations. He further believed that ". . . the fact that [the national state] is the creation of Teutonic political genius stamps the Teutonic nations as the political nations *par excellence,* and authorizes them, in the economy of the world, to assume the leadership in the establishment and administration of states."[46] Thus, this formula for understanding politics supposedly reveals not only the internal mission of the political organ-

---

[42] John W. Burgess, *Political Science and Comparative Constitutional Law* (2 vols.; Boston and London: Ginn & Co., 1891).

[43] *Ibid.,* Vol. I, p. 1.

[44] *Ibid.,* Vol. I, p. 3.

[45] *Ibid.,* Vol. I, p. 4.

[46] *Ibid.,* Vol. I, p. 39.

ization to set in historical order the lives of citizens, but also its mission in the world at large. The second mission is to provide political leadership for those nations less fortunate in natural moral endowments. This formulation was not so much an exhortation to political domination as a rationalization of the role certain nations were then playing and would come to play in the historical development of nineteenth and twentieth centuries, an attempt to demonstrate that the dominion of certain states is not only morally right and understandable but also inevitable in the nature of things.

In Burgess' view, the United States was a Teutonic nation with a mission, destined to be a great power and take her place among the predominant forces in the shaping of world history. His position counseled boldness in dealing with the rest of the world as well as in educating citizens in their relationship to the nation and in the duty, obligations, and potentials of citizenship.

In the ideas of Burgess as they have been explained here, the theory of nationalism is carried perhaps not to its ultimate but to relatively harsh terms. It was given the racist overtones that in the late reaches of the nineteenth century came to be very heavily associated with nationalist symbols and goals. It was also given its later "power politics" connotations. While American nationalism has rarely been carried to such theoretical lengths, there can be no question that in both nineteenth and twentieth centuries, the American people have often thought of an American destiny justifying their rise to predominance in the world. So firm, however, has been the counterweight of American liberalism that the harshness of Hegelian nationalism has never gained a powerful place in the American ideology. Neither internally nor in its relations with the external world has the American nation characteristically reacted like a nation completely convinced of the moral predominance of her national mission.

IX

LIMITS ON POLITICAL POWER: ECONOMIC INDIVIDUALISM

With this chapter, we step out of the period when American political thought and controversy centered around the complex of issues that gave rise to the Civil War. In this specific transition, American political thought entered the contemporary period. Its problems, no longer those of slaveholding, no longer in a central sense those of sectional economic conflict, and no longer really those of distribution of power between federal government and state, moved to the sphere of the meaning and consequences of modes of economic organization and action. This was the period, ranging roughly from the end of the Civil War to World War I, when the implications of laissez faire and its impact on the society came to be fully realized. Though, previously, laissez faire had been a characteristic American economic posture, the scale of the society and the maturing industrial system now confronted it with new issues. In terms of social organization and impact, laissez faire came to mean something different in this period than it had earlier when opportunity was sought in small economic units or on the frontier. America was still a dynamic society, but its dynamism was expressed in vertical rather than horizontal expansion. With the closing of the frontier and the ripening of the economic system came industrialization, the rise of the large corporation, and the quickening of the pace of urbanization.

Old questions assumed changed meanings, and new ones arose. Social and economic relationships manifest in complexities of urban residence and the depersonalization of work prompted new reflection on the character of the capitalist society. Not the least of the problems raised by these changes were political, for changes in the conditions of social life tended to put new content into established American political forms and styles. Universal suffrage, for example, came to mean voting by the industrial worker in the large urban center as well as by the yeoman on the frontier.

The core problem for political thought was how the condition of the maturing industrial society was to be interpreted by and made congenial with American political tradition. Again the political tradition was put to the test of facing the consequences of social change, in this case, perhaps, the most deep-running change the American community had ever confronted. Particularly, the social conditions of industrialization forced confrontation of the problem of the grounds and extent of justifiable political intervention in the arrangements of economic and social life. The development of the capitalist system evoked again but in even more stark terms the Hamiltonian–Jeffersonian problem of the proper scope of political power in dealing with the social situation. In good part, therefore, controversy moved to questions about the substance of policy. Preoccupation with the substance of policy is, as we have suggested elsewhere, not characteristically American; the American political tradition has tended to focus its attention on questions of form or structure rather than those of substances. But the needs and the ills of capitalist industrialization forced matters of substance to the top of the national political agenda.[1]

The ideology of the period was typically progress-oriented. Whatever their commitments on the appropriate means and institutions for achievement of progress, nearly all social philosophies of the time took progress to be an ultimate goal, and in this way carried forward one of the fundamental symbols of the American tradition. Social and political prescriptions for progress, however, were widely divergent. On the one hand stood a group which bolstered the claims of laissez faire, particularly through the application of some biological concepts to human relationships. On the other hand stood a group which sought political power as an instrumentality for the restructuring of social relationships, hoping to use government to guide development toward the realization of values embedded in the political tradition, particularly the value of equality. In this chapter, we will analyze a representative statement of the first point of view, and briefly examine some of the mechanisms and rationalizations through which it was given effect on public policy. In the chapter to follow, we will analyze some

---

[1] For history and commentary, see especially Henry Steele Commager, *The American Mind: An Interpretation of American Thought and Character since the 1800's* (New Haven: Yale University, 1950); Eric Goldman, *Rendezvous with Destiny: a History of Modern American Reform* (New York: A. A. Knopf, 1952). On urbanization, see Blake McKelvey, *The Urbanization of America: 1860–1915* (New Brunswick, N.J.: Rutgers University Press, 1963).

of the alternative approaches. As in the preceding chapters, our approach will be highly selective rather than comprehensive.

WILLIAM GRAHAM SUMNER: THE CASE FOR LIMITED POLITICS

William Graham Sumner, a Yale sociologist and economist, was probably the leading American figure in publicizing and developing the theory of economic individualism, often called social Darwinism. In its terms, the case for political nonintervention in economic and social relationships was most prominently stated during the period. Sumner, a vigorous teacher and prolific writer, published between 1883 and 1910 a vast number of books, essays, and articles in which the evolutionary interpretation of laissez faire comprised the central theme.[2] At its roots, Sumner's statement of social theory was not particularly original. Behind it lay the moral and psychological individualism of the liberal tradition, the promotion of laissez faire by the economists and philosophical radicals, the commitment to progress inherited from the eighteenth century, and the American social and environmental setting that made it almost a natural ideological posture. Further, Sumner's theory owed much to the ideas of Herbert Spencer, the Englishman whose *Social Statics*, published in 1850, nine years before the publication of *Origin of Species*, spearheaded the application of biological concepts to human social relations. While Sumner's work was not simply a copy of the ideas of Spencer, it was so similar in its theoretical basics as to be considered mainly adaptation and publicity. It should be noted that Sumner provided not only a rigorous and scholarly statement of the case for laissez faire but also an important early influence on the development of sociology as a scholarly discipline in America. For a considerable period of time and to some extent down to the present day, his orientation dominated a good deal of writing and teaching of academic sociology in the United States. Especially well known and influential in this respect was a volume called *Folkways* in which he stated the case for a relativistic perspective on human culture. In this chapter, our attention will be di-

---

[2] For Sumner's political and social thought, reference is particularly made to *Essays of William Graham Sumner*, ed. A. G. Keller (New Haven: Yale University Press, 1934); *The Challenge of Facts and Other Essays*, ed. A. G. Keller (New Haven: Yale University Press, 1914); *Folkways* (Boston: Ginn & Co., 1907); *What Social Classes Owe to Each Other* (Caldwell, Idaho: Caxton Printers, 1954). The last work was first published in 1883, but page references that follow are to the edition cited. For commentary on Sumner, see Richard Hofstadter, *Social Darwinism in American Thought* (rev. ed.; Boston: Beacon Press, 1955); and Robert G. McCloskey, *American Conservatism in the Age of Enterprise* (Cambridge: Harvard University Press, 1951).

rected chiefly to the sociopolitical position set out in *What Social Classes Owe to Each Other,* a comprehensive treatment of the problem of political intervention.

It seems most useful to start our analysis of Sumner's ideas with reference to his view of sociology and sociological method. His perspective on the nature and task of sociology shared much with the development of modern science and the views developed a few decades earlier by August Compte. It also told a great deal about his conception of the nature of society itself and the basic assumptions from which his theory derived. Simply stated, Sumner's professed position was that sociology should be an impartial, objective science of society, descriptive of the facts and free from moral preference. It is as important for the social scientist as for the natural scientist to divorce himself from advocacy for the sake of advocacy, as important that he free himself in his work from the influence of personal values. In the same way that a natural scientist who passed judgment on natural forces would make himself look ridiculous, "Just so a sociologist who should attach moral applications and practical maxims to his investigations would entirely miss his proper business." [3] "Nature's forces know no pity. Just so in sociology. The forces know no pity." [4] It is beyond the purview of sociology to attack or defend nature. The job of the sociologist as Sumner saw it is to understand the operation of social forces and, one may assume from his own sociological style, to promote the spread of that understanding. Essentially, he saw himself erasing the traces of evaluative natural law thinking from social science.

Sumner's social science was not, however, an inductive science, nor was he, apparently, much interested in problems of verification. His system was fundamentally deductive, devoted to the development of lawful statements of the general principles that regulate the universe. He was committed to the idea that society and its human life run according to certain universal principles that can be rationally understood. The process of sociology, then, was for him a process of finding those principles and deducing from them observations about the characteristics of social behavior. As we shall see, this procedure, in Sumner's hands, came to have the tone of moral exhortation, despite his rejection of such exhortation as part of the proper business of the sociologist.

In its most basic elements, Sumner's theory of society was not unlike Thomas Hobbes' theory. Its first principle, its basic assumption, is

---

[3] *What Social Classes Owe to Each Other, op. cit.,* p. 133.
[4] *Loc. cit.*

human individuality, and this idea of individuality, both physical and psychological, gives shape to the rest of the theoretical system. It sees each man as a thing unto himself, a cluster of powers ranging about in an atomistic social world, a world of aloneness, a world without natural ties or bonds. Sumner wrote,

> A human being has a life to live, a career to run. He has a centre of powers to work, and of capacities to suffer. What his powers may be— whether they can carry him far or not; what his chances may be, whether wide or restricted; what his fortune may be, whether to suffer much or little—are questions of his personal destiny which he must work out and endure as he can . . .[5]

This is the elemental law that gives shape to human life, and only the conjunction of these human lives makes up the social world.

Having begun with this general assumption, Sumner could proceed to ask what things about human life make the social world the way it is. Then, the theory moves down the ladder of deduction toward more specific statements. Thus, certain regularities of human nature, i.e., certain natural human characteristics, combine to create specific patterns of man's social life. Fundamentally, that life grows out of "the vices and passions of human nature—cupidity, lust, vindictiveness, ambition, and vanity. These vices are confined to no nation, class or age." [6] They are, in other words, the common stuff of life. Human nature being motivated by these passions underlying the basic drive for existence, there is no end to the unceasing struggle of man for existence, and this struggle inevitably brings him into vital conflict with his fellows, as in Hobbes' state of nature. To carry the analysis further, the social world, like the animal world, is characterized by inequality. This inequality gives form to the human struggle, for it means that some are able by their natural endowments to rise above others. If nature is allowed to run its course, it will bring about a society of natural differentiation, a society in which inequality of condition comes to reflect inequality of ability. Those with high natural endowments will succeed in accumulating the objects of human desire; they will succeed in the struggle for things, for power, sometimes for existence itself, while others will fail. In the social world, he said, those of "energy, courage, perseverance, and prudence," will come out on top.[7]

Sumner insisted that equality in the descriptive sense has no mean-

---

[5] *Ibid.*, pp. 30–31.
[6] *Ibid.*, p. 27.
[7] *Ibid.*, p. 68.

ing. There is no equality in fact, and nature being what it is, there is no properly prescriptive meaning to the ideal of equality. In this respect, Sumner stepped outside the basic tenets of the liberal tradition or, as some might prefer to put it, took a more realistic view of them. It is at this point that he abandoned the Hobbesian perspective, and in doing so, he committed himself to a different interpretation of the conditions underlying the development of civil government.

From this picture of the basics of human nature, Sumner developed his concept of social class. His use of the concept of class is, in a sense, foreign to the general thrust of his theory, but it can probably be explained in terms of intellectual fashion. Sumner wrote in the period of great blooming of class theory and class ideology. The meaning of the concept class to Sumner was, however, substantially different from the meaning given it by Marxian theory. His class was not an organic thing, nor an overriding historical force, nor was it in itself related to some ulterior developmental social pattern, since his radical individualism would scarcely accommodate such usages. Rather, he used the term class simply to describe categories of men, classified according to their differential abilities and their differential successes at acquisition. The basis of his concept lay in the inequalities characteristic of the human world, reflecting that as they live their lives, men sort themselves out as their careers take them in different directions of style and accomplishment. Sumner summarizes the class idea in the following terms:

If words like wise and foolish, thrifty and extravagant, prudent and negligent, have any meaning in language, then it must make some difference how people behave in this world, and the difference will appear in the position they acquire in the body of society, and in relation to the chances of life. They may, then, be classified in reference to these facts. Such classes always will exist; no other social distinctions can endure.[8]

Thus, Sumner's class does not have the overtones of metaphysical reality given to the concept in Marxist thought, nor is its defining characteristic in consciousness of distinction and social position, as some classical and medieval formulations suggested. Its mark does not lie in the trappings of aristocracy but rather in accomplishment and, finally, command of the means of survival. It is not, in fact, entirely different from the class concept of John Adams, though it is distinguished from Adams' by its emphasis on economic rather than political power. From the standpoint of its political significance, Sumner's class concept did

---

[8] *Ibid.*, p. 144.

not yield a principle of obligation. He denied that differentiation creates an obligation for the successful to take care of the unsuccessful or for the unsuccessful to obey the successful. The fortunate need not concern themselves over the plight of the unfortunate. He specifically renounced the efforts of those who would restore the obligational characteristics, the *noblesse oblige*, of the status society. Such desires, he suggests, are sinister in motive and contraventory of the natural forces of nature. For the other part of the class relationship, the obligation of the unprivileged to respect the privileged, one may suppose Sumner thought "natural" command by the privileged of the instruments of power would take care of that. Thus, class to Sumner was a set of categories into which men could be sorted in the interests of theoretical and descriptive convenience.

These basic perspectives on man and society and on the function and method of sociology comprise the framework within which rested Sumner's attitudes on political organization and public policy. There lay in his approach to social and political life an interesting dualism. On the one hand, in describing his sociology he professed and insisted on objectivity and moral neutrality. As we noted above, he proclaimed that a social scientist must not pass judgment on the forces of nature. Yet, on the other hand, his deductive system was such that the laws of nature themselves came to sound like moral principles and his social theory became the basis for moral critique and exhortation. The first principle implicit in his discussion of social and political arrangements would seem to be that men ought to live according to nature; he made "follow nature" a moral imperative. Men ought, in other words, to let nature take its course, and their doing so will yield good social and personal policy.

At this point, Sumner's analysis is often stated in terms of the well-known analogy to biological evolution, i.e., in terms of social Darwinism. While the label is most often associated with the ideas of Spencer, it is about as apt when applied to Sumner. The basic notion is simple. In social as in biological phenomena, nature permits the fittest to survive. The survival of the fittest is "the way it should be," i.e., the forces of nature should be allowed to have their way. The peculiar aspect of this formulation is that it appears to concede that the forces of survival in the social world are not equally natural. In general terms, only those are natural and, therefore, to be defended that are manifestations of the atomistic individualism which underlies the proper perspective on the natural world. In this way, the theory offered both a basis for an evolutionary "description" of the development of social life and a basis (indeed, perhaps two bases) for judgment of the forces at work in the world.

An important element in this conflux of description and valuation is the commitment of Sumner and others who thought in similar ways to the idea of "progress." Progress they saw as a basic good, perhaps the ulterior good in the judging of social arrangements. Evolution, development, improvement, progress—all are terms that suggest the proper framework for the evaluation of society, all terms that suggest a "natural" movement toward "better" and "higher" conditions. Those modes of conduct that make possible the betterment of the human situation are interpreted as conducive to evolution, and these are the forces to be maximized. Evolution is instrumental to development, and development to progress, and progress, being the demand of nature, constitutes the key to moral judgment. Whatever really is, then, is what contributes to human development in terms of the most fundamental natural laws, and it is this which deserves to be maximized.

This relationship is illustrated by Sumner's interpretation of and posture toward the modern contract society. The virtue of the industrial society of artificial relationships, the society that has replaced status with contract, is that it enhances freedom of economic and social movement and, by removing fixed barriers to mobility, offers people *chances*. Rights and liberties pertain only to chances—that is, to the opportunity to improve one's position in the world. There are no rights to conditions, but only rights to opportunities to improve. Liberty is the situation in which each man may make maximum use of his powers exclusively for his own welfare. The world owes men this much but no more. "All institutions," wrote Sumner, "are to be tested by the degree to which they guarantee liberty." [9] Thus, by this test, the freedom of opportunity promoted by the laissez faire industrial system is to be praised and preserved, because it gives man the chance to use his powers, and the use of his powers as an individual is natural. Hence, nature, the particular nature of Sumner's radical individualism, again dictated the standards for good personal behavior and social organization. The relationship of nature to standards of morality will be further apparent as we turn in the following paragraphs to Sumner's perspectives on and prescriptions for political and social organization and policy.

The existence of political authority in society, according to Sumner, is dictated by the fact that some men are criminals who, in effect, seek

---

[9] *Ibid.*, p. 30.

to destroy or pervert the operation of nature. These are men who seek
to acquire the gains of others or who rob others of their rightful
chances for the sake of their own gains. Given his view of human nature, it is not surprising that Sumner would anticipate the presence of
some in the human community whose greed motivates them to seek
their own benefits without paying the appropriate price. Industry and
economy are the means by which men naturally seek their own survival, and the presence in the community of those who seek to substitute their own standards by preying on the industry of others compels
the development of the institutions of authority. The function of the
organs of authority, then, is to preserve (or enforce) natural relationships.

While certain implications of this position are clear, it is not clear
how it distinguishes defensible from indefensible sorts of human endeavor. Thus, the state is supposed to be able to distinguish industry
from robbery, but without clear guidelines as to what makes the essential difference. Except by resort to the "feelings" about such things
that the culture stuffs into us, how are we supposed to know the one
from the other? Surely, the problem is not solved by saying robbery
is done in a black mask and industry in a top hat.

A further difficulty in his formulation was, however, understood by
Sumner—the problem that the control of political power itself is a
weapon for plunder. In some sense, the exertion of authority is an
exertion against "natural" forces. Bentham, for example, called the
function of the state the "artificial" harmonization of interests. Hence,
the state authority begins with a sort of presumptive case against it.
But the problem extends even further, because it is clear that some
exertions of state power are of one sort and some of another so that,
from whatever point of view, some acts of authority are "corrupt,"
"overbearing," and "illegitimate." Moreover, the state not only confronts society with potential threats, but those threats are the most
portentious of all because they are organized on the largest scale. Government in the wrong hands, guided by the wrong prescriptions, in
other words, is in a position to plunder on a society-wide basis and to
make its threats effective by the use of a power that comes, through
force of habit, to be regarded as legitimate.

Sumner's response to this problem goes no further than to suggest
that risks be cut by the limitation of the scope of power. The idea is
that if authority cannot be used, it cannot be used for ill. Basically, its
function is to be confined to the preservation and protection of
chances. Sumner once wrote that government should deal with only

two things—the property of men and the honor of women.[10] Elsewhere, he said that ". . . liberty for labor and security for earnings
are the ends for which civil institutions exist. . . ." [11] His fundamental demand, then, was that government simply create the conditions
under which nature can take its course. When government extends
the scope of its authority beyond the promotion of chances, it is en-
gaging in the kind of organized plunder which lies beyond legitimacy.
The implications of this position for the variety of governmental welfare programs developed in recent years are clear.

Political forms, in turn, can be judged in terms of their tendencies
either to stay within or to exceed these boundaries of proper political
action. Sumner expressed the point in terms of rights and duties, the
rights referring to chances, the duties to men's obligation to contribute
to the maintenance of the political system. The good political system keeps rights and duties in equilibrium; the bad system imposes
duties on some and gives rights to others, or gives rights to all and
duties to only some.[12] Evaluated in these terms, democracy is a dangerous though not necessarily bad system. The tendencies of human nature are likely to impel the mass who control the political authority
in a democracy to take advantage of those who are better off, and to
use the instrumentalities of politics to redistribute goods in accordance with the criterion of equality of condition. Those who have
labored industriously and lived prudently may find themselves vic-
timized by the large class of the indolent and spendthrifty. If man
realized that his and his alone was the responsibility for his own welfare, democracy would be a safe system—might, in fact, be the system
best adapted to honor the conditions of real liberty in society. The
problem with democracy, however, is the problem with human nature, namely, that men are unlikely to take seriously their responsibilities for themselves, particularly when they are confronted with the
opportunity for insuring their survival in other ways. Thus, democracy may be a system that impedes progress or natural human development by offering men easy and unnatural devices for fulfilling their
needs.

Sumner, however, was not much concerned with the details of political organization. He looked more to the substance of political policy than to the mechanisms and structures by which policy is made for
the fundamental answers about how preferred goals might be sought.

---

[10] *Ibid.*, p. 88.
[11] *Ibid.*, p. 31.
[12] *Ibid.*, pp. 31–32.

His policy preferences are easily deduced. He was laissez faire to the nth degree, holding that government should let the economy alone, that the society should be permitted to run its natural course and find its natural level without "artificial" restriction or promotion. He had no patience with social and economic programs, which he described with such terms as "meddling" and "tinkering." Those who advocate social reform through political welfare programs, Sumner thought, are either fools or rogues. They are fools insofar as they are motivated by desires to change things that cannot be changed, rogues insofar as they are out to upset the proper balance between rights and duties. The drive for equality, the would-be humanitarian urge to provide socially for the deficiencies in some men's moral characters, flies in the face of nature and upsets the progressive and orderly development of the society. The fittest will and should survive, the incompetent will and should perish. Men should not and cannot in the name of democracy change this inexorable operation of the world's natural forces.

Many of the ills of society, Sumner thought, are the products of such unnatural intervention in social relationships. They are the results of bad advice and self-delusion, of "all the tinkering, muddling, and blundering of social doctors in the past. These products of social quackery are now buttressed by habit, fashion, prejudice, platitudinarian thinking, and new quackery in political economy and social science." [13] Ultimately, they spring from the tendency of men to adopt goals out of harmony with natural reality. Reform movements are mistaken in their fundamental conceptions of what can happen, and because of these mistakes, they create the ills of disadjustment and impose impedimentia to progress. Sumner described the process of reform as follows: "All this mischief has been done by men who sat down to consider the problem, (as I heard an apprentice of theirs once express it), What kind of society do we want to make? When they had settled this question *a priori* to their satisfaction, they set to work to make their ideal society, and today we suffer the consequences." [14]

"Society," said Sumner, "does not need any care or supervision." [15] In other words, things if permitted will take care of themselves naturally. Society particularly does not need the protection of would-be welfare legislation. It does not need and cannot afford legislation whose purported purpose is to protect the weak and unprivileged, for these elements in society by their very lack of privilege demonstrate

---

[13] *Ibid.*, p. 102.
[14] *Ibid.*, p. 103.
[15] *Loc. cit.*

their unfitness to survive. The effect of welfare legislation is to upset the natural social balance. It forestalls the operation of the natural social forces and, in doing so, places a burden on those whose ability should make them the bearers of the natural forward thrust toward social progress. Thus, those very people whom nature would reward for their diligence are penalized through social legislation for their virtue. Sumner was particularly concerned about this penalty levied on the upright and industrious, whom he called "the forgotten man," who is, he thought, forced by the society, particularly the democratic society, to pay the price for the failure of others.

To him, the defensible approach was to let the processes of nature eliminate the incompetent. "Nature's remedies against vice are terrible. She removes the victims without pity. A drunkard in the gutter is just where he ought to be, according to the fitness and tendency of things." [16] Men (and governments, too) should become accustomed to letting the drunk lie. Picking him up is a useless expenditure of energy on behalf of a useless cause, its effect being to perpetuate the burden on society of those who make no contribution themselves. The rule by which a government should live is "mind your own business." [17] Minding the business of others out of humanitarian sympathy, however noble and altruistic it may seem in terms of "platitudinarian thinking," does not comport with a "scientific understanding," as Sumner would have it, of the forces of the natural world. Again, his basic maxim would seem to be, do not fool around with the forces of nature.

On these grounds, Sumner defended a policy of minimal government activity and maximal freedom for individual enterprise. He was especially bitter against the tariff and, indeed, became a leading publicist of the free trade position. The tariff he interpreted as a grand scale scheme for the sponsorship of those too incompetent to survive in a competitive situation. It was in his eyes an impressive illustration of the modes in which the organized power of government could be mobilized in the interests of public plunder by a small and special group in society. His view of the tariff as a wasteful anachronism in a competitive society is perhaps best and most succinctly expressed in the title of a pamphlet he published on the subject, *Protectionism: the Ism That Teaches That Waste Makes Wealth.*[18]

Sumner's position on labor organization, however, might surprise

---

[16] *Ibid.*, p. 114.
[17] *Ibid.*, p. 104.
[18] New York: Henry Holt & Co., 1885

those who are accustomed to thinking in terms of the categories and slogans of present-day society. While labor unionism is now commonly associated with welfare programs and even with governmental intervention in economic affairs, it should be recalled that American trade unions have historically been highly voluntaristic and free-enterprise in orientation. Sumner, reflecting a similar view of the very early American labor organization, felt it fair and legitimate that employees should form unions as vehicles for common action. Unions, he thought, might serve valuable functions in furthering the natural development of the society, particularly stimulating enterprise as they formed media for spreading information, raising worker morale, and elevating public opinion. Moreover, they might perform functions in the industrializing society that were increasingly being fulfilled by the government. The fact that unions might be, in effect, bulwarks against the expansion of government control may in itself go a long way toward explaining Sumner's generally favorable treatment of the labor organization movement. Such functions as the inspection and policing of industry might very well, he felt, be worked out in private and thus natural ways, if trade unions were able to develop and maintain strength. There are, he granted, some features of labor activity that are negative in effect. Among these, he saw the limitation of apprentices as the deprivation of chances. Another, the strike, is inevitably wasteful and, therefore, difficult to regard in a favorable light. But the strike is a legitimate weapon for use at last resort in the competition between capital and labor, and if it is won, it may be thought to demonstrate that in reality it served the promotion of natural law. On balance, and given the various difficulties apparent in collective labor action, Sumner seems to have felt the trade union to be a defensible social institution. He saw it as one of those few devices by which the person who labors, the forgotten man, is able to defend himself against the rapacious greed of privilege.[19]

Sumner's social ideas are simple enough and systematic enough as not to require any extended summary. As ideology, they represent a very important attempt to rationalize the laissez faire system in a society where it cut across some rather well established equalitarian and humanitarian values, particularly the values inherent in the democratic system. Economic individualism is, however, a type of thought that has had a powerful hold on the American mind, and indeed, still does. Its appeal can probably be explained in terms of social dynamics, particularly the drive, energy, and opportunity represented

---

[19] *Ibid.*, pp. 71–87.

in the conquering of the frontier and the rapid expansion of business enterprise. It should be noted that Sumner's was far from being the only notable expression of the laissez faire point of view. The hegemony of this outlook was evident in a great many fields of action and idea in the late nineteenth and early twentieth centuries. It found expression in a great variety of forms: in folk thought and maxims, in Horatio Alger stories, in the predominant themes of organized religion, and, of course, in many aspects of the institutional development of the business and political systems.[20]

It is important to stress, at the same time, that Sumner was much more than an uncritical apologist for the business community. He not only sought theoretical integrity but dissented in substantial measure at several points from the common practices and theories of the business ideology of his time. His attack on the tariff and his willingness to defend the role of organized labor are illustrative. He had no more patience with the stifling of independence and initiative by business combination than he had for political combination. In this respect, he was more than a publicist, though perhaps no more than an ideologist.

Some of the philosophical and theoretical problems with Sumner's system have been mentioned above in passing. Principal among them is the discrepancy between his claims to objectivity and the highly moralistic character of his deductive system. While he disclaimed judgment, his system developed along highly judgmental lines. Thus, "natural" became not a descriptive term, but a metaphysical standard by which human actions are to be judged. There is in Sumner a strong element of the idealist's distinction between reality and seeming reality, and while it is not historical, Sumner's reality is not unlike the transcendent reality-in-idea expounded by Hegel. Although perhaps the analogy involves a far reach, it might even be suggested that, like Marx, Sumner stood Hegel on his head, substituting the realization of order in the world through the actions of individual men for Hegel's realization of individual fulfillment through the action of the social order.

In any case, the position of Sumner and of those who thought like him has been vastly influential in the development of American political, economic, and social practice. Some of the ramifications of this

---

[20] The breadth and character of individualism as an ideology is, to a degree, suggested by the commentaries cited in notes 1 and 2, above. For interesting reading in some prominent original sources, see Andrew Carnegie, *The Gospel of Wealth and Other Timely Essays*, ed. Edward C. Kirkland (Cambridge: The Belknap Press, 1962); Russell H. Conway, *Acres of Diamonds* (New York: Harper & Bros., 1915).

posture in public policy and in political institutions will be suggested in the paragraphs to follow. The rest of the chapter will be devoted to demonstrating what doubtless requires little demonstration—namely, that economic individualism has had a substantial impact on the action of the American political system. A further effect might be suggested at this point. Individualism has also provided a popular, respectable, and integral rebuttal to the case for change, for humanitarianism, social welfare programs, regulatory legislation, and so on. This fact in itself has probably helped improve the quality of public action and helped preserve a measure of theoretical liveliness in a nation otherwise highly oriented toward material development.

ECONOMIC INDIVIDUALISM, PUBLIC POLICY AND THE SUPREME COURT

The ideology of economic individualism made itself felt in many reaches of American life, serving for an extended period as the predominant theme in the American social outlook. As such, its influence on the course of the public policy of the nation was overwhelming. There have been few periods when the correlation of social conditions, ideology, and political action has been more obvious. Perhaps the most notable and at least the most identifiable ramifications of economic individualism in policy were to be seen in the decisions of the courts, especially the Supreme Court during the period from the Civil War to the middle of the New Deal in the 1930's. The Court of this era has been called a bastion of social Darwinism, sometimes a bastion of privilege. To be sure, the form of American political institutions is such that the role of the Court in promotion of a point of view is easy to identify and observe, and for this reason, the influence of the judiciary relative to that of legislative bodies and executives may appear out of proportion to reality. There can be no doubt that the spirit of economic individualism often hampered the chances of regulatory and reform legislation in legislative bodies and at executive levels. In the nature of things, however, the Court's perspective is explicitly stated, and when it acts, even in the negative, it usually gives its reasons for behaving as it does. Not only does the Court itself play a central role in public policy, but its work provides us with frequent checkpoints on the ideological profile of the changing nation. During the period of economic individualism, the judicial process was one of the main settings in which ideological antagonists clashed.

In response to the social and economic problems created, exacerbated, and made evident by industrialization and urbanization in

American society, political authorities at both state and national levels moved toward regulation of the economy on a number of fronts. As we shall have occasion to observe in detail in the next chapter, the maturing of the Industrial Revolution resulted in stimulation of demands for a counterrevolution in public policy. Similar demands had been in evidence in England at a much earlier period. Most notably, the American states and the national government began gradually after the Civil War to undertake regulation of certain types of business activity and regulation of wages, hours, and conditions of labor. As might have been expected, the convergence of the work situation of the industrial system, the compacting of population in the cities, the growth of interdependence, and American values of equality and opportunity generated considerable pressure for regulatory political activity.

Selectively and intermittently over the period mentioned, the Supreme Court adopted the position of economic individualism to strike down various of the reform measures developed by legislative bodies. Care must be taken not to suggest that the central trend of Court opinions was the exclusive judicial attitude. While individualism tended to dominate the perspective of the courts, regulation was permitted to stand in a substantial number of cases dealing with both national and state legislation. However, the presumption ran heavily against regulatory and welfare legislation. Courts, and particularly the Supreme Court, relied heavily on two devices to rationalize restrictions on legislative freedom to deal with the problems spawned by industrialization. With respect to federal legislation, the Court emphasized restrictive interpretation of the enumerated powers of the national government, particularly the commerce and tax clauses, on which most federal attempts at regulation were hung. In doing so, the Court, in a sense, revived the Jeffersonian view of the necessary and proper problem, and brought into prominence the inhibitory effect of the Tenth Amendment. This has sometimes been called the period of dual federalism, an interpretation of federalism in which the national and state governments are seen as competitors for a limited fund of power, with the national government's grasp restricted by the literal interpretation of its substantive terms of reference. Still, one should not assume that the period marked a retrogression of national power in absolute terms, for despite the somewhat unfavorable atmosphere of public jurisprudence of the period, the scope of national power expanded steadily if somewhat slowly.

With respect to state legislation, the courts' main weapon was the complex and interesting doctrine of substantive due process of law. This doctrine found its entrée into constitutional interpretation through the adoption of the Fourteenth Amendment following the Civil War. This Amendment, it will be recalled, forbade states to "abridge the privileges or immunities of citizens of the United States," "deprive any person of life, liberty, or property, without due process of law," and "deny to any person within its jurisdiction the equal protection of the laws." Though the question of intent in framing the Fourteenth Amendment is still debated, at least overtly it appeared to have been added to the national Constitution to provide the legal framework for protection of the rights of newly freed Negroes. Its utility in this respect was severely limited in its early years, but its provisions, particularly the one respecting due process of law, were seized on to buttress economic activity against state interference.[21]

One of the steps in this set of developments made it possible for the courts to consider corporations as "persons" in legal standing, a step not really extraordinary in view of the long-standing tendencies of legal theory in dealing with corporate bodies. A second step was to broaden the meaning of the "due process" concept. Due process had ordinarily been regarded as a requirement pertaining to the procedures by which laws are passed by political authorities and enforced by police and courts. To this denotation of due process, the courts now added a "substantive" side by virtue of which they looked at due process as restricting not only the modes of legal action but also the content of the social behavior the law prescribes. That is to say, due process became restrictive not only of the ways in which things were done by political authority but also of the things which authorities might do. Thus, the due process clause of the Fourteenth Amendment was used to restrict the sphere or scope of state interference with economic activities.

At both the national and state levels, the variety of cases and substantive issues that demonstrated the courts' commitment to the principles of economic individualism is such as to preclude any but a selective and illustrative treatment. Perhaps it is best to begin with a discussion of the courts' treatment of regulatory legislation on the

---

[21] On the problem of intent, see Jacobus ten Broek, *The Anti-Slavery Origins of the Fourteenth Amendment* (Berkeley: University of California Press, 1951). On the general orientation of the Court during this era, see Benjamin R. Twiss, *Lawyers and the Constitution: How Laissez Faire Came to the Supreme Court* (Princeton: Princeton University Press, 1942); E. S. Corwin, *The Twilight of the Supreme Court* (New Haven: Yale University Press, 1934).

national level, and in this connection we should note again that during the period with which we are dealing, very substantial expansion of the economic regulatory activities of the national government was brought about. But it occurred, one might say, in spite of the generally negative tone of American ideology in respect to such matters. For example, passage of the Sherman Act, 1890, provided legislative and policy grounds for regulation of interstate business activity held to be in restraint of trade. The attitude of the courts, however, severely restricted application of the Sherman Act and its later supplement, the Clayton Act, passed in 1914. In the "Sugar Trust Case," for example, the Court adopted a narrow view of the meaning of interstate commerce and, in effect, circumscribed its applicability to manufacturing or processing enterprises.[22] That is to say, in denying applicability of the antitrust act to companies engaged in the processing of sugar, the Court maintained the position that commerce must mean transportation or trade in goods in a fairly narrow sense and that the power of the national government to deal with the economic affairs through the commerce clause is thus circumscribed. This inhibition was a crucial one in terms of the ability of the national government to undertake effective and broad-gauge regulation. The point is further illustrated in *Hammer* v. *Dagenhart,* in which the Court considered the merits of a congressional attempt to regulate child labor on commerce clause grounds.[23] The crux of the decision in this case was its denial that the conditions of labor under which a piece of goods is made may properly be construed as a part of the interstate commerce in the goods. On the ground of this denial, the Court was able simply to prohibit this manner of congressional regulation. A similar position was adopted early in New Deal days in the Schecter case that invalidated certain provisions of the National Industrial Recovery Act.[24]

Somewhat similar results followed congressional attempts to regulate social and economic relationships through the exercise of its enumerated power to tax. While the tax power was successfully used in some few cases for patently regulatory purposes, in other cases, when the regulatory intent of Congress was manifestly too blatant in the eyes of the courts, congressional uses of the tax power, too, were struck down. Here again, illustrations may be drawn from congressional attempts to regulate child labor and from the experience of the early

---

[22] *United States* v. *E. C. Knight Co.,* 156 U.S. 1 (1895).
[23] 247 U.S. 251 (1918).
[24] *Schechter Poultry Corp.* v. *United States,* 295 U.S. 495 (1935)

New Deal period. When its attempts to deal with child labor on the basis of the commerce power failed, Congress resorted to the use of the tax clause, levying a tax that would make production by child labor uneconomic. In *Bailey* v. *Drexel Furniture Co.,* the Supreme Court refused to permit Congress the exercise of this power in this way on the ground that the power to tax was fiscal rather than regulatory and the legislation in question had clearly regulatory ends.[25] The Court's position was substantially the same when it invalidated the Guffy Coal Act in *Carter* v. *Carter Coal Co.* and the first Agricultural Adjustment Act in *United States* v. *Butler,* both decided in 1936.[26]

Because of the structure of the national Constitution, each of these cases concerning the national economic regulatory power was decided on grounds other than those concerning the proper scope of political authority as such. The courts, seeking the minimum grounds necessary to forestall government interference with economic life, were able to handle these problems on the basis of what in this framework might be called technicality—most particularly, the specific meaning of the commerce and tax clauses. As instructive as these cases are about the Court's view of the distribution of power under the federal system, it is more the decisions than the opinions that hint at the Court's attitude toward exercises of political power that contravene the laissez faire doctrine. However, because the constitutional framework for handling state economic and social legislation precluded retreat from the policy question itself, cases contesting exercise of state power in these fields yielded much more than hints of the substance of the courts' thinking.

The fashion in which the courts dealt with state attempts to regulate business competition and rates, for example, is instructive. The decision in the Granger cases of 1877 opened the way for state regulation of rates charged by such "utilities" as grain elevators and railroads.[27] Particularly in the western states, this decision was the signal for development of vigorous legislative regulatory policies. The impact of these, however, was vitiated by subsequent decisions which required states to set rates in such fashion as to assure regulated industries a "fair return on a fair value," and to confine regulation to such types of business as could be demonstrated to be "affected with

---

[25] 259 U.S. 20 (1922).

[26] *Carter* v. *Carter Coal Co.,* 298 U.S. 238 (1936); *United States* v. *Butler,* 297 U.S. 1 (1936).

[27] *Munn* v. *Illinois,* 94 U.S. 113 (1877).

the public interest." *Smyth* v. *Ames,* 1898, not only enunciated the doctrine of fair return but assured business the further protection of judicial review of the "reasonableness" of rates established.[28] The holding in this case, in other words, not only imposed the requirements of substantive due process (i.e., limitation on the content of state rate-fixing policy) but also those of procedural due process on state attempts at regulation.

Thus, so far as regulation of business rates and practices is concerned, the courts on behalf of economic individualism limited legislative authority through the due process clause to (1) those regulations that would not deprive enterprise of a fair return and (2) those regulations that were applied only to peculiarly "public" types of economic activity. In definition of the second point, we can do no better than quote the words of Chief Justice Taft in *Wolff Packing Co.* v. *Industrial Court:*

(1) Those which are carried on under the authority of a public grant of privileges which either expressly or impliedly imposes the affirmative duty of rendering a public service demanded by any member of the public. Such are the railroads, other common carriers and public utilities.

(2) Certain occupations, regarded as exceptional, the public interest attaching to which, recognized from earliest times, has survived the period of arbitrary laws by Parliament or Colonial legislatures for regulating all trades and callings. . . . (3) Businesses which though not public at their inception may be fairly said to have risen to be such and have become subject in consequence to some government regulation. They have come to hold such a peculiar relation to the public that this is superimposed upon them. In the language of the cases, the owner by devoting his business to the public use, in effect grants the public an interest in that use and subjects himself to public regulation to the extent of that interest although the property continues to belong to the private owner and to be entitled to protection accordingly.[29]

While this doctrine was so interpreted as to facilitate the extension of public regulation to a variety of public utilities-type enterprises, at the fringes the rule was as much used to prohibit public regulation as to permit it. A series of decisions in the 1920's and 1930's, for example, found businesses such as meat packing, theatre ticket brokerage, employment agencies, gasoline sales, and ice sales not affected with the public interest and, hence, not subject to regulation.[30] Perhaps it can

---

[28] 169 U.S. 466 (1898).

[29] *Wolff Packing Co.* v. *Court of Industrial Relations,* 262 U.S. 522, 535 (1923).

[30] See, e.g., *Tyson and Bros.* v. *Banton,* 273 U.S. 418 (1927); *Williams* v. *Standard Oil Co.,* 278 U.S. 235 (1929); *New State Ice Co.* v. *Liebmann,* 285 U.S. 262 (1932).

be fairly said that the substance of the courts' position was that in the interests of free competition, public regulation is to be avoided except in those cases when the risks of damage to the interests of the community are overwhelming. This laissez faire doctrine was a severe inhibition on the development of protective and reform legislation.

The courts' insistence on maximum economic freedom from social interference is even more dramatically illustrated in cases dealing with state labor legislation. Here again, the cumulative impact of the decisions was not monolithic. In some instances, protective legislation was permitted to stand, and some court prohibitions against regulation lacked real effect. *Holden* v. *Hardy* and *Muller* v. *Oregon,* for example, sustained state laws limiting hours of employment in mines and smelters and of women in laundry establishments.[31] Other decisions of the Court during the same period, however, struck down state maximum hour laws and child labor laws.

Among the most forthright and instructive statements of the opposing doctrines represented on the Supreme Court at this time are the opinions in *Lochner* v. *New York*.[32] The Lochner case involved a New York statute restricting to ten the legal hours of employment in bakeries. Mr. Justice Peckham, speaking for the majority, denied that the conditions of bakery employment were such as to validate an extraordinary exercise of the police power to protect employees' health or the health of the consumers of bakery products. He interpreted the issue as one of liberty guaranteed by due process of law, and on this ground found the state act to be in contravention of the Fourteenth Amendment. "The general right to make a contract in relation to his business," he wrote, "is part of the liberty of the individual protected by the Fourteenth Amendment of the Federal Constitution. . . . The right to purchase or to sell labor is part of the liberty protected by this amendment, unless there are circumstances which exclude the right."[33] While the police power of the state may prohibit certain types of contract in certain circumstances, those circumstances are not reached in the case in question, "The question whether this act is valid as a labor law, pure and simple, may be dismissed in a few words. There is no reasonable ground for interfering with the liberty of person or the right of free contract, by determining the hours of labor, in the occupation of a baker."[34] Rejecting contentions that the

---

[31] *Holden* v. *Hardy,* 169 U.S. 366 (1898); *Muller* v. *Oregon,* 208 U.S. 412 (1909).
[32] 198 U.S. 45, (1905).
[33] *Ibid.,* p. 53.
[34] *Ibid.,* p. 57.

nature of the baking business puts it in a special position as respects the need for state protection of employees' health, the Court held rigidly to its comprehensive interpretation of liberty under the due process clause and seemed to destroy the possibility of general state regulation of hours and conditions of employment as well as state regulation in many of the specific kinds of industry which the states might wish to reach through the police power. The majority opinion continued,

It seems to us that the real object and purpose were simply to regulate the hours of labor between the master and his employes (all being men, *sui juris*), in a private business, not dangerous in any degree to morals or in any real and substantial degree, to the health of the employes. Under such circumstances the freedom of master and employe to contract with each other in relation to their employment, and in defining the same, cannot be prohibited or interfered with, without violating the Federal Constitution.[35]

In 1923, in *Adkins* v. *Children's Hospital,* the Court adopted a similar position as respects minimum wage legislation.[36] The legislation in question in this case established a board to fix the terms of compensation for employed women and children in the District of Columbia. Once again, the freedom of contract position was the heart of the Court's majority argument. The Court took pains to distinguish the minimum wage regulation from regulations of hours of labor, although it did quote at length and with approval from the Lochner opinion. The wage relationship, it held, is "the heart of the employment contract," and, therefore, even further removed than other aspects of the relationship from state interference. It seems to have regarded wage legislation as a thrust to the heart of the rational economic system of the laissez faire society. In *West Coast Hotel Co.* v. *Parrish,* 1937, the Adkins holding was explicitly overturned by the Court, as many of the other individualist-oriented decisions were overturned, implicitly or explicitly, during the late 1930's and early forties.[37]

We have already noted that the individualist outlook on business and labor legislation did not completely dominate the picture during the period in question, for some regulatory acts were permitted to stand. We should also take note of the tone and content of some of the dissents and counterstatements to individualism made within the

---

[35] *Ibid.,* p. 64.
[36] 261 U.S. 525 (1923).
[37] *West Coast Hotel Co.* v. *Parrish,* 300 U.S. 379 (1937).

framework of the legal process. In a few of the labor cases, for example, including *Muller* v. *Oregon* and *Bunting* v. *Oregon,* the Court was presented with arguments of a kind it had seldom been asked to consider.[38] These briefs, prepared by Louis Brandeis assisted by Felix Frankfurter, Josephine Goldmark, and others, presented systematic sociological, medical, and economic evidence on the consequences to society and individuals of the employment of women. They added a new dimension to the Court's consideration of social legislation by introducing considerations other than abstract legal doctrine. In the Muller and Bunting cases, both of which upheld Oregon labor laws, the majority opinions of the courts cited in evidence the materials that Brandeis had presented. They represent a significant step (1) toward use by the Court of empirical data in weighing the consequences of public policy, a procedure still in the developing stages;[39] and (2) toward understanding of the process of judicial review as a part of the political framework for the development of policy. By emphasizing the entire social context of labor and welfare legislation, the Brandeis briefs put the litigation part of it in perspective and perhaps helped remove some of the mystique from a process that is often seen in strictly legalistic and abstract terms. Thus, the decisions of the courts may have come to seem a part of the general human process for solving concrete, on-going social problems.

A similar impact on American political and social thought was probably made by some of the dissents presented from the high Court's ideological minority during the era of individualist predominance. The best known and perhaps the most consistent of these were the products of Holmes during the early period and of Holmes and Brandeis later. In a subsequent chapter, we will briefly consider the central tendencies of Holmes' jurisprudence. The vigor with which he attacked the individualist position, however, should be noted here, and perhaps it can be summarized most succinctly in a few sentences from his famous dissent in the Lochner case:

This case is decided upon an economic theory which a large part of the country does not entertain. If it were a question whether I agreed with that theory, I should desire to study further and long before making up my mind. But I do not conceive that to be my duty, because I strongly believe that my agreement or disagreement has nothing to do with the right of a

---

[38] On Brandeis' ideas and contributions, see Louis Brandeis, *The Social and Economic Views of Mr. Justice Brandeis* (New York: Vanguard Press, 1930); Alpheus T. Mason, *Brandeis, a Free Man's Life* (New York: The Viking Press, 1946).

[39] See, for example, the use of social science data and theory in the school desegregation problem. Especially see *Brown* v. *Board of Education of Topeka,* 347 U.S. 483 (1954).

majority to embody their opinions in law. . . . The liberty of the citizen
to do as he likes so long as he does not interfere with the liberty of others
to do the same, which has been a shibboleth for some well-known writers,
is interfered with by school laws, by the Post Office, by every state or municipal institution which takes his money for purposes thought desirable,
whether he likes it or not. . . . The Fourteenth Amendment does not
enact Mr. Herbert Spencer's Social Statics. . . . [A] constitution is not intended to embody a particular economic theory, whether of paternalism
and the organic relation of the citizen to the State or of laissez faire. It is
made for people of fundamentally differing views, and the accident of our
finding certain opinions natural and familiar or novel and even shocking
ought not to conclude our judgment upon the question whether statutes
embodying them conflict with the Constitution of the United States.

. . . I think that the word liberty in the Fourteenth Amendment is perverted when it is held to prevent the natural outcome of a dominant opinion, unless it can be said that a rational and fair man necessarily would
admit that the statute proposed would infringe fundamental principles
as they have been understood by the traditions of our people and our law.[40]

Although the effects of war and depression have forced abandonment of many aspects of laissez faire policy in the United States, elements of the ideology of economic individualism certainly remain
prominent in the American scene. It has, without question, served as
a brake on a society that has been driven by circumstances to lean
more and more toward the evaluation of social policies in terms of
social responsibility and welfare. Probably no major step in the extension of welfare orientation on state or national levels is taken without the invocation and consideration of its effect on the values of
economic independence. It seems safe to suggest that the element of
economic individualism in the American ideology is now much more
specific than general. That is to say, for the many who make the argument to laissez faire on specific policy proposals, few either among
the theorizing intelligentsia or among the populace at large take seriously and consistently the natural law and evolutionary fundamentals
of the Spencer–Sumner position. Some would say few ever did, but
without arguing the merits of this sweeping proposition, we may propose that leavening the consistency of the laissez faire position with
characteristically twentieth-century American pragmatism has made
possible on peaceable and widely accepted grounds the development
of the public welfare policies with which the nation now lives.

---

[40] *Lochner v. New York*, 198 U.S. 45, pp. 75–76, (1905).

X

GROUNDS FOR POLITICAL INTERVENTION

If the theories discussed in the preceding chapter may be seen as rationalizations of the free-wheeling development of the American society in the later 1800's, those we are about to review are counter-responses. The identifying theme of these theories is protest—protest not so much against the ideas of laissez faire as against the conditions of the American society of the time. The underlying force was rapid change, with its accompanying discordances and maladjustments. It is not surprising that a society that expanded as rapidly as America's did between the Civil War and World War I should have experienced a variety of social frictions. Population, industrial enterprise, agriculture, technology, commerce, the city—all grew and with growth brought varieties of social problems that were, in turn, reflected in discontent. This discontent found its reflection in political ideas, a surprising amount indigenous and some imported from Europe where the ideology of discontent flourished in societies without the safety valve of the frontier.

The sets of ideas, the theories, the ideologies we will lump together in this chapter are diverse. Though joined by the common theme of protest and the common appeal to reform, in underlying diagnosis and prescription they represent a fairly wide spectrum of social thought. Some were the products of systematic social philosophers and social scientists. Some were the ideas of publicists who addressed themselves to the ills of the industrial society and to its reform. Yet others were the ideologies of social movements, sometimes ill defined, sometimes inconsistent or inarticulate, that, nonetheless, embodied important approaches to the problems of large-scale society.[1]

---

[1] For general treatments of the period and its main figures and movements, see Richard Hofstadter, *The Age of Reform: from Bryan to F. D. R.* (New York: A. A. Knopf,

It is difficult to subclassify the theories that come within the subject matter of this chapter, but they can to some extent be distinguished by focus. On the one hand, we might place those whose description and diagnoses were fundamentally economic, and on the other hand, those whose emphasis ran more to the political aspects of the social situation. This division is not, of course, completely satisfactory, for in some sense, those who dealt with politics must also have dealt with economics, and vice versa. But it will help achieve some order in our account of this period of rapid theoretical development and change. In the first category, we will place Henry George, Edward Bellamy, and the variety of American socialist ideas more or less influential in the period around the turn of the century. In the second category, we will place the ideas embodied in two American political movements of the period—populism and progressivism.

HENRY GEORGE: THE CASE FOR LAND REFORM

One of the most interesting figures in the movement for social reform and author of one of its most influential statements was Henry George. During his young manhood, George traveled about both in the United States and abroad and worked at a variety of manual jobs. As a result of his personal experiences and observations, he grew upset with the conditions of life that seemed to accompany industrial development. His ideas apparently were in the first instance more the outgrowth of direct personal impression than of an abstract or scholarly interest in the working of the social system. In 1871, he published a pamphlet, *Our Land and Land Policy,* setting forth the outlines of a position that he never abandoned, a position tracing social ills to land policy and arguing that through land reform the entire answer to social problems might be found. Though the original pamphlet was limited in circulation, a much expanded version published in 1879 under the title *Progress and Poverty* became tremendously popular and made of George one of the central figures of American social reform.[2]

1955); Henry Steele Commager, *The American Mind: an Interpretation of American Thought and Character since the 1880's* (New Haven: Yale University Press, 1950); Eric Goldman, *Rendezvous with Destiny: a History of Modern American Reform* (New York: A. A. Knopf, 1952); Daniel Aaron, *Men of Good Hope* (New York: Oxford University Press, 1951).

[2] Henry George, *The Complete Works of Henry George* (New York: Doubleday, Page, & Co., 1904). *Progress and Poverty* is Vol. I of *Works; Our Land and Land Policy* may be found in Vol. 8, pp. 1–131. For a biography of George by his son, Henry George, Jr., see Vols. 9 and 10 of *Works.* For commentary, see Charles A. Barker, *Henry George* (New York: Oxford University Press, 1955); Raymond G. George, *The Philosophy of Henry George* (New York: Macmillan Co., 1933).

The so-called single tax movement stimulated by his formulations attracted thousands of adherents and developed hundreds of local study groups pushing the cause of land reform. It is estimated that the world-wide circulation of *Progress and Poverty* in all languages exceeded two million copies, and probably more than half this number were in circulation in the United States.[3] Certainly few American political tracts have received as much attention from the American people, and while his influence cannot be measured, his stature as a contributor to the nation's political ideology must be called substantial. After the publication of *Progress and Poverty*, George himself was active in the movement, spreading the doctrine of the single tax through lectures and travels and entering the arena of active politics by twice running for mayor of New York City. Though unsuccessful in both attempts at public office, the size of his vote was substantial and reflects in another way the prominence of his contribution to the cause of social reform.

Our purposes here, of course, are not historical. We are interested rather, in examining George's ideas as a structure of political theory. He did not deal merely in the polemic of social reform, but also in systematic analysis of the social situation, particularly through reexamination of the tools and concepts of classical economics. The greatest share of *Progress and Poverty* is devoted to a critique of certain elements of the classical theory, some of it fairly technical in nature. It should be emphasized, however, that running through the framework of his economic analysis is a strong ethical thread stemming from his reaction to widespread poverty. He assumed that poverty is bad, that it degrades society, that steps ought to be taken to eliminate it. He took as a prime commitment the humanitarian belief in a good life for all men. His economics were in the last analysis tied to a moralistic rejection of the existing order and a set of prescriptions based on distinctly nonrationalistic, nonclassical social values.

The doctrine of *Progress and Poverty* can be separated into three parts, consisting of: (1) an economic analysis of the causes of poverty and the explanations of poverty found in the classical formulations; (2) a prescriptive formulation of the single tax idea as the palliative for the social ills of industrial society; (3) the formulation of a "law of progress" through which George provided a social justification for his prescriptive doctrine. In other words, the line of development of the book proceeds as follows: What is the cause of poverty? The ex-

---

[3] Henry George, Jr., "How the Book Came to Be Written," in *Progress and Poverty* (Fiftieth Anniversary Edition; New York: Robert Schalkenbach Foundation, 1942), p. xii.

planation of classical economics fails to answer the question. An examination of the theoretical problem locates the cause of poverty in the industrial society's land policy. How can poverty be cured? Poverty can be cured through the revision of land policy, particularly through the revision embodied in the idea of the single tax. Why should poverty be cured? The latent explanation lies in the plain fact that the life of poverty is a "bad" life for the individual human being. The manifest answer is that poverty impedes social progress, and since, as everyone knows, progress is good, poverty as an impediment to progress must be eliminated. We will examine the three major elements in George's theory in this order, looking more, however, for political implications than for the technicalities of economic analysis. Behind the entire structure of the argument runs the question stimulated by George's observation of industrial society: Why does poverty accompany progress?

In his search for an explanation of the coincidence of progress and poverty, George first examined two doctrines of classical economics which purported to offer an explanation of this curious and contradictory phenomenon. One classical explanation rested on the "wage fund" theory. This theory held that wages are paid from a fixed amount of advanced capital, an amount set aside not by a whim of the capitalist but by the inexorable operation of the laws of the economic system. That is to say, the system, according to this interpretation, operates in such fashion that only a given share can be devoted to the reimbursement of the laboring force. The role of the capitalist is not that of decision-maker but that of mechanism carrying out decisions inherent in the organization of the system. Allocations for rent and for investment are determined by the supply–demand relationship for land and for capital respectively. What remains constitutes the wage fund. Thus, the total amount of wages available is not subject to alteration. Individual wages, in turn, are determined by the number of workers among whom the wage fund is to be divided. The larger the working population, the lower the individual wage level. The nature of society is such that the competition for wages is intense, and these tend to move, therefore, toward the subsistence level. In view of the "fact" that the total sum available for wages is fixed, artificial attempts to raise wages are useless or harmful. All they can possibly achieve is some redistribution of income among the labor force, thus driving the wages of some workers even lower. The effect of trade unionism, for example, must be to raise the wages of those who are in stronger bargaining positions and depress the wage levels of the weaker, especially the unorganized. In any case, the answer of this theory to George's major question is that the expansion of the working force brought about by industrialization inevitably brings poverty in the train of progress.

A second and complementary line of analysis in classical economic thought explained poverty through the population theory of Thomas Malthus. Briefly summarized, Malthus' ideas suggested that an increase in population necessarily pressed against the food supply, population growing geometrically while the food supply expands only in arithmetic progression. For this reason, the large portion of men are to be found at or below subsistence level. Although exogenous to the theory proper, sociological observation of the shifting patterns of life-style on human reproduction brought about by the Industrial Revolution probably magnified the nineteenth-century conviction that population in and of itself is a prime cause of the miserable condition of human life, especially in the industrial city.

George's attack on both these aspects of classical economic theory centered on the role of production and productivity. He rejected both wage-fund and population theories as wrong and deceptive. As to the wage level, he insisted that wages must be seen not as advances from capital but as payments for production. "Production," he wrote, "is always the mother of wages." [4] The level of wages is dependent on the amount produced and not on the size of a fixed wage fund, and thus the level of wages may be improved by increases in production. As productivity rises with the growth of skill, the introduction of machines, and the rationalization of the process of production, the wage situation of the worker may improve in like amount. It does not and will not improve, however, when the psychology of the society is dominated by the classical notion that workers cannot share in the improvement because of the operation of an inexorable natural law. To state the matter in a different way, George charged that the psychological effect of the classical theory was to rationalize payment of workers at the subsistence level, whatever the magnitude of their productive contribution, and that poverty was partly caused by the impact of psycho-ideological manifestations of the classical economic theories.

George's answer to the Malthusian explanation of poverty was somewhat similar. He claimed that increases in population bring increases in productivity in sufficient amount to feed additional people. More men create more production, and evidence indicates that Malthus' formula for this relationship was grossly in error. The historical

---

[4] *Works, op. cit.*, Vol. I, p. 55.

experience of the United States in this respect, where the production of food has habitually outrun need and the social problem has been not so much subsistence as surplus, would seem to suggest that George's insights into the factors of production were much more penetrating than those of Malthus.

From the standpoint of George's overall approach, the difficulty with the classical theories was that they made poverty seem intractable—not subject to attack or amelioration. He was interested not only in finding an explanation for poverty but also in devising the means for an attack on social and economic injustice. Such classical doctrines as the wage fund theory and the Malthusian formulation, if widely accepted, destroyed any possibility of alleviating the effects of poverty in a sustained way. They made poverty appear to be the inevitable result of the operation of natural forces. In fact, both theories suggested that social attempts to alter the relationships of production would have the effect of magnifying rather than ameliorating the maladjustments of modern society. They tended to support the Sumnerian position that the effects of tinkering with the socioeconomic system were worse than the effects of the system itself. Thus, the classical formulations dictated laissez faire—let the system alone—and argued vehemently against "artificial" attempts to improve the condition of society through the intercession of social reform.

Accordingly, George sought an alternative explanation of poverty that would yield to social attack, and he found his answer in yet another of the classic formulations; his search for an alternative theory came to rest on the classical law of rent. He defined rent as follows: "The rent of land is determined by the excess of its produce over that which the same application can secure from the least productive land in use." [5] This law presumably applies to land in all kinds of economic use, not simply land in agricultural production, and since any form of economic activity requires some use of land, the effect of the law of rent is felt everywhere in the system. The rent relationship, George felt, was the basic element in explaining the distribution of rewards in the economy, particularly those rewards garnered as a result of increases in productivity. The excess value created by capital and labor is reaped by the owner of land, however much effort might be put into the improvement of production. Furthermore, as civilization expands and populations increase, poorer and poorer land will be put into production. When this occurs, rent rises even further, rent being, according to the law, that surplus over and above the productive capacity of

_____
[5] *Ibid.*, p. 168.

the poorest land in use. The landlord, then, reaps the entire benefit of progress, the entire benefit of the improvement of production methods and of the expansion of civilization.

The classical economists, whatever their implicit Spencerian commitments to living according to nature, did not attach moral connotations to their formulation of the result of the law of rent. George, on the other hand, considered it to be the explanation of injustice in society and found in it an aspect of the economic system subject to adjustment through a fairly simple reform measure. In effect, he accepted the analysis of the classical economists but found through their formulations that point in the economic system subject to social attack. The basic cause of the failure of progress to beat poverty, he said, lies in the fact that the landlord who exerts no effort reaps all the benefit of progress.

The reason why, in spite of the increase of productive power, wages constantly tend to a minimum which will give but a bare living, is that, with increase in productive power, rent tends to even greater increase, thus producing a constant tendency to the forcing down of wages.[6]

As the margin of production increases, the landlord appropriates all the reward. "The fundamental law of nature," George wrote, "that her enjoyment by man shall be consequent upon his exertion, is thus violated."[7] His reaction to this arrangement was not unlike Marx's moralistic reaction to the idea of the expropriation of surplus value by the capitalist, except that in George's analysis the bête noire is landlord rather than capitalist. Analyses that find the cause of social injustice in conflict between capital and labor, he thought, miss the real point. For conflicts between capital and labor are minor compared to the conflicts between capital and labor on the one hand, and landholders on the other. The landholders are the real recipients of the unearned increment of economic progress.

Not only, in fact, is the landlord without an active role in the productive process, his land itself is imparted value by the society. At least in substantial part, the value of land is created by social location; for example, a piece of land in the heart of a big city where rents are at their social highest assumes its extraordinary value merely because the society happens to cluster about it in a pattern that enhances its use value. Rent, therefore, is payment to someone entirely without relationship to his contribution to the ongoing pattern of social progress.

---

[6] *Ibid.*, p. 280.
[7] *Ibid.*, p. 339.

George reached the conclusion that the answer to the problem of poverty lay in land reform. He wrote:

There is but one way to remove an evil—and that is, to remove its cause. Poverty deepens as wealth increases, and wages are forced down while productive power grows, because land, which is the source of all wealth and the field of all labor, is monopolized. To extirpate poverty, to make wages what justice commands they should be, the full earnings of the laborer, we must therefore substitute for the individual ownership of land a common ownership. Nothing else will go to the cause of the evil—in nothing else is there the slightest hope.[8]

The answer to the basic question of progress and poverty lies in the rent relationship, and the solution to the social problem of poverty is obvious in the diagnosis—the solution is to expropriate rent. To achieve social justice in the distribution of rewards, it is not necessary to undertake some such cumbersome step as confiscation of land. The effect can be secured by a rather simple fiscal device, the "single tax." "It is not necessary to confiscate land; it is only necessary to confiscate rent." [9] George believed that all desirable social reform would follow in train from this single step, the levying of a tax equal to the full rent value of all property in land. It is important to note that his single tax would have fallen only on the rent value of land itself and not on the value of improvements, the improvements being the product of the owner's exertion. But the full value of the land itself would accrue to the state.

The effects of this step on the redistribution of rewards in society would, George felt, be severalfold. In the first place, the confiscatory tax on rent would make possible repeal of all other taxes, including those that are restrictive of trade, of production, or of improvement in the economic processes. Thus, laborers and capitalists would reap the full value of their contributions to the productive process rather than surrendering some of it to the state to maintain the functions of government. Second, the land tax would support the government well enough that it could maintain a high level of services beneficial to the whole community.

That is to say, the wealth produced in every community would be divided into two portions. One part would be distributed in wages and interest between individual producers, according to the part each had taken in the work of production; the other part would go to the community as a whole, to be distributed in public benefits to all its members. In this all would

---

[8] *Ibid.*, p. 326.
[9] *Ibid.*, p. 403.

share equally—the weak with the strong, young children and decrepit old men, the maimed, the halt, and the blind, as well as the vigorous. And justly so—for while one part represents the result of individual effort in production, the other represents the increased power with which the community as a whole aids the individual.[10]

Third, the single tax would aid fair distribution by reducing the speculative value of land. This, in turn, would cause rents to decline and leave more to reward those who contribute to the productive process. "Labor and capital would thus not merely gain what is now taken from them in taxation, but would gain by the positive decline in rent caused by the decrease in speculative land values. A new equilibrium would be established, at which the common rate of wages and interest would be much higher than now."[11] Furthermore, the expropriation of rent would encourage further expansion of production by turning the uses of land to the most fruitful possible pursuits. Thus, George felt the advantages of common ownership could be achieved without the inconvenience of socializing the titled property. Finally, he felt that since the moral title of landholders to their possession in land is questionable, expropriation need not be compensated through outright governmental purchase. His overall expectations of the primary and secondary effects of this reform were immense. "What I, therefore, propose," he wrote,

as the simple yet sovereign remedy, which will raise wages, increase the earnings of capital, extirpate pauperism, abolish poverty, give remunerative employment to whoever wishes it, afford free scope to human powers, lessen crime, elevate morals, and taste, and intelligence, purify government and carry civilization to yet nobler heights, is—to appropriate rent by taxation.[12]

The third and final step in George's case for social reform was his analysis of the "law of progress." Here again, he adopted and modified a classical concept and turned it to purposes quite different from those of its classical use, although the reference in this case is not so much to classical economics as to the progress orientation of Spencerian liberalism. By George's time, the concept of progress had wide currency as a central element in the explanation of the onrush of human development. Progress had become a kind of moral ultimate or ideological kingpin in terms of which arguments for social action and inaction were commonly phrased. Thus, it was on behalf of progress, for example, that those who thought like Sumner were able to advocate

---

[10] *Ibid.*, pp. 438–39.
[11] *Ibid.*, p. 440.
[12] *Ibid.*, pp. 403–4.

letting natural social forces run their course. George, too, adopted progress as an ultimate point of reference but rejected existing formulations as to its content and method. It was, however, to further the cause of progress that he sought a means to extirpate poverty from the human community. Thus, the cure of poverty was to be instrumental to progress as land reform was to be instrumental to the cure of poverty. It was in this way, among others, that George's ideas were articulated with the general flow of ideology of his time.

In terms of the broader framework of his inquiry, George sought to show that poverty was not the inevitable accompaniment of progress, but that, on the contrary, it depended on the elimination of poverty. Social Darwinism found the mechanism of progress in the struggle to survive, the results of the struggle being the substance of progress—survival of the fittest. George, on the other hand, thought this a mistaken understanding of progress, and shifted attention from social struggle to the social cooperation that, he claimed, creates the conditions that make progress possible. The key to improvement of the human situation, then, is the process of building on the knowledge and techniques of a culture handed from generation to generation and from man to man. Progress occurs only in the situation of sustained social interaction, the human community.

Into this web, woven by each society, or rather, into these webs, for each community above the simplest is made up of minor societies, which overlap and interlace each other, the individual is received at birth and continues until his death. This is the matrix in which mind unfolds and from which it takes its stamp. This is the way in which customs, and religions, and prejudices, and tastes, and languages, grow up and are perpetuated. This is the way that skill is transmitted and knowledge is stored up, and the discoveries of one time made the common stock and stepping stone for the next.[13]

Although progress depends on cooperation rather than competition, the powers men develop in association may be used in either constructive or destructive ways, depending on the setting in which they are exercised. That is to say, interaction in itself is not enough to assure the constructive use of human powers. In certain conditions, the interaction of the human community, or, rather, the energies that constitute the interaction in the human community, may be siphoned off into destructive or useless conflict.

The key source of such conflict in the human community, George

---

[13] *Ibid.*, p. 502.

suggested, is inequality. Inequality lays the basis for those jealousies and frictions that cause the potentially productive association of the human community to turn away from its potential. Progress depends on (1) community, the systemic condition for productive human inter-action, and (2) equality, the social condition in which that interaction can be turned in productive directions.

Thus association in equality is the law of progress. Association frees mental power for expenditure in improvement, and equality, or justice, or freedom—for the terms signify the same thing, the recognition of the moral law—prevents the dissipation of this power in fruitless struggles.

Here is the law of progress, which will explain all diversities, all advances, all halts, and retrogressions. Men tend to progress just as they come closer together and by cooperation with each other increase the mental power that may be devoted to improvement, but just as conflict is provoked, or association develops inequality of condition and power, this tendency to progression is lessened, checked, and finally reversed.[14]

The law of progress is the converse of what the times represented it to be. The law of progress, indeed, demands and the character of the economic system permits social action through economic reform. Progress and poverty need not go hand in hand. In fact, on clear analysis they may not. Progress depends on reform that is not only possible but potentially simple of application.

This truth involves both a menace and a promise. It shows that the evils arising from the unjust and unequal distribution of wealth, which are becoming more and more apparent as modern civilization goes on, are not incidents of progress, but tendencies which must bring progress to a halt; that they will not cure themselves, but, on the contrary, must, unless their cause is removed, grow greater and greater, until they sweep us back into barbarism by the road every previous civilization has trod. But it also shows that these evils are not imposed by natural laws; that they spring solely from social maladjustments which ignore natural laws, and that in removing their cause we shall be giving an enormous impetus to progress.[15]

The principal significance of George's theory probably lies in its exemplification of the push toward social reform. It was, as we shall see, one of a variety of single-cause, single-nostrum approaches to the problems of a complex society. In terms of the internal structure of the theory, many questions can be raised about George's approach. It is interesting, for example, to set his analysis beside that of Marx and note that they explain the same general phenomenon, namely poverty,

---

[14] *Ibid.*, p. 505.
[15] *Ibid.*, p. 541.

by reference to the same general cause, namely expropriation of value, but that they differed radically in their identifications of the expropriators. It may be questioned whether one was any more convincing than the other in ascribing social problems to the economic role of a particular class. Further, one may wonder why George was convinced that elimination of the conflict of both capitalist and worker with the landlord would necessarily allay the conflict between these two groups. His argument on this point, though vital to his analysis and to his scheme of reform, is inadequate. Further, these comments do not touch the more difficult though probably irrelevant problem of the practicality of the single tax solution.

Despite its wide distribution and considerable popular appeal, *Progress and Poverty* does not seem to have had much specific impact on political or economic policy. As part of a movement, however, and in terms of the kind of aims and techniques it represented, its indirect influence on the course of American development may have been great. It was representative of those kinds of thought which held reform to be possible and which pointed the direction of development toward socialization in its broadest sense. It was an antidote not only to the laissez faire and Darwinistic tendencies of economic individualism, but also to their anticommunitarian orientation. Perhaps the main message of those who, like George, advocated social reform is that common action in pursuit of values is not only a possibility but a necessity. Once again, we may see in George the selective playing on the fundamentals of the American political tradition—in this case, particularly equality and welfare—to argue for new adaptations of social policy and structure.

EDWARD BELLAMY: AN ALTERNATIVE ECONOMIC FORMULATION

An alternative statement of the case for social reform, contemporary with that of Henry George, is to be found in the works of Edward Bellamy, particularly in his utopian novel, *Looking Backward*.[16] While not so scholarly or programatic as the ideas of George, Bellamy's social critique reflects in its fundamentals a similar analysis

---

[16] Published in 1887. Citations in the pages that follow are to Edward Bellamy, *Looking Backward: 2000–1887* ("The Modern Library" [New York: Random House, 1951]). For commentary, see Robert L. Shurter, "Introduction," in *ibid.*; Arthur E. Morgan, *Edward Bellamy* (New York: Columbia University Press, 1944); Arthur E. Morgan, *The Philosophy of Edward Bellamy* (New York: King's Crown Press, 1945); Sylvia E. Bowman, *The Year 2000: a Critical Biography of Edward Bellamy* (New York: Bookman Associates, 1958); Sylvia E. Bowman, *Edward Bellamy Abroad: an American Prophet's Influence* (New York: Twayne Publishers, 1962).

and evaluation of the ills of the industrial society. Bellamy had been a writer of stories, and whether his passion for social reform grew out of the novel or the novel out of the passion seems to be a matter of some dispute. In any case, his major book caught and articulated the tone of the reform, and, like *Progress and Poverty,* was widely distributed and influential in stimulating attention to the needs and possibilities of reconstruction in the society and the economy.

Like George, too, Bellamy undertook to disseminate and promote the spread of reformist ideas. After the publication of *Looking Backward,* he lectured widely and was influential in the establishment of a series of "nationalist clubs" which, though short-lived, were said to number more than 150 at the height of their popularity. The very development and existence of the single-tax and nationalist groups in the 1880's and 1890's suggests very strongly the appeal of the reform ideology to the American populace in that era. In view of the importance of the "movement" phenomenon, it seems reasonable to propose that the American consensus was again disrupted during the period, as it had been at mid-nineteenth century, though the stimulus for this disruption was in new causes, particularly the conditions created by the maturing of the industrial society.

The serious content of Bellamy's novel is simple and easy to summarize, and it shares much with the ideas of George and the American socialists whom we will discuss below. It might be noted that in 1897, nine years after publication of *Looking Backward,* Bellamy published *Equality,* an attempt at scholarly economic analysis of the industrial society.[17] The scholarly volume added little of interest or significance to *Looking Backward,* and failed to excite the attention and attain the influence of the novel.

The social commentary of *Looking Backward* had two central themes: first, an overriding conviction of the fundamental goodness of man, out of which grew an ultimate norm of equality; second, an economic interpretation of history similar to much of the politico-social writing of the time and often suggestive of the major ideas of Marxism. The basic idea is probably Bellamy's optimistic interpretation of human nature, a perspective widely shared by social reformers, though doubtfully compatible with the Marxist perspective. In any case, Bellamy thought man to be fundamentally good. The disruptions and injustices of modern society, he felt, rest in morally destructive forms and institutions with which men burden themselves and through which they destroy their own capacities for living up to their

---

[17] *Equality* (New York: Appleton & Co., 1897).

innate moral abilities. The path to social reform, given such a view, lies in the rearrangement of institutions, basically the economic institutions of production and distribution. In this respect, Bellamy's ideas were similar to those of the nineteenth-century European philosophical anarchists whose fundamental belief was that man is good but institutions are evil. To be sure, they went further than Bellamy in suggesting that complete destruction of the institutions of authority will permit man to live in comity without the interference and the incident negative effects of the state.

The fundamentally economic character of Bellamy's analysis of society is revealed in his explanation of how the new society of *Looking Backward* came about. The book is based on the story of a nineteenth-century man who finds himself in the American society of the year 2000, a society whose organization is entirely foreign to his expectations. The evolution from one era to another, it develops, was determined by changes in economic relationships which, in turn, had caused a whole range of social and moral adjustments.

Capitalism, said Bellamy, had begun in the small, personally run enterprise. That, in turn, gave way to larger aggregations of capital and productive power. Concentration of enterprise proceeded rapidly during the late nineteenth century, and by the early twentieth century the economy was controlled by a few large corporations. The fact of concentration of capital, in turn, stimulated labor combination as a means of protest and resistance. The end of the evolutionary process was, as Bellamy described it, inherent in the logic of development: final combination into one huge, all-inclusive national business. "The epoch of trusts," he wrote, "had ended in the great trust." [18]

This evolution in economic development was the dynamic that brought about the novel social arrangements in all the reaches of the society Bellamy described in fanciful terms in *Looking Backward*. But it was economic change that was the motivating factor behind progress, with other adjustments coming in its wake. And it was a new economic system that made possible the salubrious and unfettered life of the society of 2000. Likewise, it was the corrupt economic system of the nineteenth century that, in Bellamy's view, was responsible for the social ills of that age. His picture of his own age was described by means of an allegory that is worth quoting at length:

By way of attempting to give the reader some general impression of the way people lived together in those days, and especially of the relations of

---

[18] *Looking Backward, op. cit.,* p. 41.

the rich and poor to one another, perhaps I cannot do better than to compare society as it then was to a prodigious coach which the masses of humanity were harnessed to and dragged toilsomely along a very hilly and sandy road. The driver was hunger, and permitted no lagging, though the pace was necessarily very slow. Despite the difficulty of drawing the coach at all along so hard a road, the top was covered with passengers who never got down, even at the steepest ascents. These seats on top were very breezy and comfortable. Well up out of the dust, their occupants could enjoy the scenery at their leisure, or critically discuss the merits of the straining team. Naturally such places were in great demand and the competition for them was keen, every one seeking as the first end in life to secure a seat on the coach for himself and to leave it to his child after him. By the rule of the coach a man could leave his seat to whom he wished, but on the other hand there were many accidents by which it might at any time be wholly lost. For all that they were so easy, the seats were very insecure, and at every sudden jolt of the coach persons were slipping out of them and falling to the ground, where they were instantly compelled to take hold of the rope and help to drag the coach on which they had before ridden so pleasantly. It was naturally regarded as a terrible misfortune to lose one's seat, and the apprehension that this might happen to them or their friends was a constant cloud upon the happiness of those who rode.

But did they think only of themselves? you ask. Was not their very luxury rendered intolerable to them by comparison with the lot of their brothers and sisters in the harness, and the knowledge that their own weight added to their toil? Had they no compassion for fellow beings from whom fortune only distinguished them? Oh, yes; commiseration was frequently expressed by those who rode for those who had to pull the coach, especially when the vehicle came to a bad place in the road, as it was constantly doing, or to a particularly steep hill. At such times, the desperate straining of the team, their agonized leaping and plunging under the pitiless lashing of hunger, the many who fainted at the rope and were trampled in the mire, made a very distressing spectacle, which often called forth highly creditable displays of feeling on the top of the coach. At such times the passengers would call down encouragingly to the toilers of the rope, exhorting them to patience, and holding out hopes of possible compensation in another world for the hardness of their lot, while others contributed to buy salves and liniments for the crippled and injured. It was agreed that it was a great pity that the coach should be so hard to pull, and there was a sense of general relief when the specially bad piece of road was gotten over. This relief was not, indeed, wholly on account of the team, for there was always some danger at these bad places of a general overturn in which all would lose their seats.

It must in truth be admitted that the main effect of the spectacle of the misery of the toilers at the rope was to enhance the passengers' sense of the value of their seats upon the coach, and to cause them to hold on to them more desperately than before. If the passengers could only have felt assured that neither they nor their friends would ever fall from the top, it is probable that, beyond contributing to the funds for liniments and bandages, they would have troubled themselves extremely little about those who dragged the coach.

I am well aware that this will appear to the men and women of the twentieth century an incredible inhumanity, but there are two facts, both very curious, which partly explain it. In the first place, it was firmly and sincerely believed that there was no other way in which Society could get along, except the many pulled at the rope and the few rode, and not only this, but that no very radical improvement even was possible, either in the harness, the coach, the roadway, or the distribution of the toil. It had always been as it was, and it always would be so. It was a pity, but it could not be helped, and philosophy forbade wasting compassion on what was beyond remedy.

The other fact is yet more curious, consisting in a singular hallucination which those on the top of the coach generally shared, that they were not exactly like their brothers and sisters who pulled at the rope, but of finer clay, in some way belonging to a higher order of beings who might justly expect to be drawn. This seems unaccountable, but, as I once rode on this very coach and shared that very hallucination, I ought to be believed. The strangest thing about the hallucination was that those who had just climbed up from the ground, before they had outgrown the marks of the rope upon their hands, began to fall under its influence. As for those whose parents and grand-parents before them had been so fortunate as to keep their seats on the top, the conviction they cherished of the essential difference between their sort of humanity and the common article was absolute. The effect of such a delusion in moderating fellow feeling for the sufferings of the mass of men into a distant and philosophical compassion is obvious.[19]

This is not, it is true, a systematic economic theory of cause, but rather a piece of moral rhetoric. Bellamy did not set out in sophisticated fashion an account of the mechanisms through which the economy would break down and yield to new forms. He did not, indeed, write to that purpose. The closest he came to it in *Looking Backward* was in comments on the inefficiency of the capitalist system—on the wastes entailed in lack of information, competition, economic crisis, systemic friction, and so on. "Their system of unorganized and antagonistic industries," he wrote, "was as absurd economically as it was morally abominable."[20] But even the point of this criticism, it will

---

[19] *Ibid.*, pp. 3–6.
[20] *Ibid.*, pp. 198–99.

be noted, was finally moral. Bellamy did not seem to be saying that the inefficiency of the economic system caused the downfall of capitalism in the sense that Marx, for example, predicted the downfall of capitalism because of internal tensions. Bellamy was content with suggesting that inefficiency is wasteful and waste is bad, a proposition not adequate as an explanation of change unless one believes that the good will inevitably win. Inefficient systems of various kinds not only may but have sustained themselves over long periods of time, and, indeed, the inefficient sometimes give weight to the more inefficient. This criticism is serious, however, only if one were to regard *Looking Backward* as a genuine effort at prediction. If its impact is to be seen in terms of its moral effect, its gaps in explanation are only problematic insofar as they vitiate the effects of the hortatory effort.

There is no need to discuss in detail the nature of Bellamy's utopian society except insofar as it is indicative of the kind of social arrangements he thought desirable. The industrial enterprise was controlled through a set of guilds under which all labor was organized. Unskilled services were rendered by an industrial army to which each citizen contributed three years of service. After this service, people were allowed free choice of trades and professions. Before it, that is, until age twenty-one, everyone was given a common education. The efficiency of the system permitted universal retirement at age forty-five, pay was equal for all, and the supply of labor for various economic enterprises was altered by manipulation of the hours of work and conditions in which work was done. Money as a medium of exchange was eliminated and replaced by only credit on the common stock of goods—credit which could not be saved. As to style of life, Bellamy put great emphasis on conveniences, leisure, and cultural opportunities. He saw his ideal society as one in which people could be freed in great part from the drudgeries of life and in which social responsibility replaced individual responsibility. Men would willingly undertake the performance of social tasks, he thought, when the artificial institutions of compulsion were eliminated. His great faith in human reasonability was reflected not only in his notions about the operation of the economic system, but also in his supposition that the sanctions of political authority could be much reduced.

Bellamy's description of politics in the new society followed closely in the train of his ideas about the new economic system. Again reminiscent of Marx, he treated politics as reflective of the modes of production, with the condition of society intervening. Thus, when the economic system is changed so as to eliminate frictions, society will throw off the obsolete sanctions of political authority. Behind the conflicts which politics must needs settle, and behind the established modes of settlement, lie the inequities and frictions of economic life. When these disappear, so will politics as it was known in Bellamy's nineteenth century. Bellamy did not suppose that the state would wither away entirely, but for that matter, neither did Marx. Government would, however, take on a fundamentally different role in the society; in this respect, Bellamy's formulation is suggestive of Marx's proposition that the state would turn from the administration of men to the administration of things. The function of the state, it might be said, would change from sanction to organization. Once the system were established, furthermore, it would pretty well run itself. While political position would be honorific, it would no longer be coveted for its power. In Bellamy's utopia, political office would be held by those who had retired from the active work force, a kind of hobby for the elderly unemployed.

The major points were that change in social institutions would bring about change in individual attitudes and behavior—or perhaps better, realization of the social inclinations of the individual—and that this change would effectively eliminate the need for the kinds of social control necessary in nineteenth-century society. The basic idea, which we met before in Jefferson and Thoreau, is that men are all right but their institutions are bad. In Bellamy's utopian society there was no need for lawyers and little need for courts and other institutions of punishment, retribution, or correction. The economic sources of crime removed, social aberrations could be understood as pathological manifestations and accordingly handled as psychomedical problems. Bellamy also extended his approach to relations among nations, developing a picture of a world-system in which relatively wealthy national units would live together in comity, aware of the wastefulness of aggression and conflict.

An interesting and significant element in Bellamy's account of the place of ideals in the social system is nationalism, a label which, as we noted above, became the public symbol of the social movements inspired by his work. Throughout his account of the development and character of the utopian society, the idea of nationalism is very much in evidence. He saw the nation rather than the class, group, or individual as the basic unit of social life, the unit through which the amelioration of social conditions would proceed. Thus, he achieved a rather strange but not wholly novel formulation which combined the passion for individual welfare and equality with the often emo-

tional and group-oriented ideal of self-realization through the sub-
mergence of individual need in the national state. He did not reject
the nation to embrace the universalistic symbols inherited from classical liberalism, as social reformers commonly have. His nationalism
is nowhere better depicted than in the passage when he discussed the
evolution of the society of the nineteenth century into the utopia of
the year 2000. In this passage he described the National Party, the
mechanism of the change that brought about the ideal society. In the
words of the character describing the social evolution:

The labor parties, as such, never could have accomplished anything on a
large or permanent scale. For purposes of national scope, their basis as
merely class organizations was too narrow. It was not till a rearrangement
of the industrial and social systems on a higher ethical basis, and for the
more efficient production of wealth, was recognized as the interest, not of
one class, but equally of all classes, of rich and poor, cultured and ignorant,
old and young, weak and strong, men and women, that there was any prospect that it would be achieved. Then the national party arose to carry it
out by political methods. It probably took that name because its aim was
to nationalize the functions of production and distribution. Indeed, it
could not well have had any other name, for its purpose was to realize the
idea of the nation with a grandeur and completeness never before conceived, not as an association of men for certain merely political functions
affecting their happiness only remotely and superficially, but as a family, a
vital union, a common life, a mighty heaven-touching tree whose leaves are
its people, fed from its veins, and feeding it in turn. The most patriotic of
all possible parties, it sought to justify patriotism and raise it from an in-
stinct to a rational devotion, by making the native land truly a father land,
a father who kept the people alive and was not merely an idol for which
they were expected to die.[21]

The evaluation of Bellamy's work requires an appreciation of some
of the roles ideas can play in the political picture. It hardly contains
all the elements of a serious system of political theory; it is fraught
with gaps and inconsistencies and irrelevancies. It captures, however,
some of the flavor and ambiguity of the social reform of his period.
Basically, his ideas were expressive of the moral problems of politics
in an age when the tension ran high between inherited liberal values
and the consequences of social change, an age when society groped
desperately for solutions to problems it had not yet come to understand. This is not to speak, of course, about the further problem of the
"practicality" of Bellamy's solution or the accuracy of the assumptions
about human nature on which his entire system was based. Indeed, it

---

[21] *Ibid.*, pp. 206–7.

may be doubted whether comments about practicality are pertinent at all, i.e., whether Bellamy himself expected *Looking Backward* to be taken seriously as a program of reform.

In a sense, Bellamy's work makes interesting reading today, because one senses in it a certain flair for prediction, though it is the prediction of fancy and not of science. There is even a touch of the Jules Verne in his description of the accoutrements and conveniences of the utopian society. Perhaps more interesting from the standpoint of the contemporary society, however, are Bellamy's suppositions about social tendencies. Like most of the commentators of his age, he was concerned about bigness, monopoly, and concentration of social control. His answer to these tendencies was off-beat, because he suggested not simply that we reject them but that they constituted in themselves keys to social reform. Thus, his utopian society was the product of the tendency to concentration running its full course. Bellamy's work might also tend to remind us of contemporary concern with the elimination of conflict in society. In some sense, Bellamy's utopia was a society of conformity, a society in which, since there was no conflict and no aspiration, men would willingly live the lives of "organization men." Bellamy himself, in his description of the popular novel of the utopian society, seemed a little puzzled about what a novel about life without conflict might be like. While he described it as a great and stirring and revealing piece of literature, he gave little clue to the nature of such a literary masterpiece. Whether, as many contemporary critics suggest, a society of uniformity would be deadly and stultifying or whether it would be conducive to the realization of human potential, as Bellamy would have it, his work raised moral questions about social organization that are still of considerable interest and power.

AMERICAN SOCIALISM

American socialism is difficult to treat in the context of a study of this kind because of its special and limited influence and character. The student who would understand socialism as a system of political thought or as a series of action-related systems must reach beyond American materials to grasp his subject with any degree of comprehension, even if he identifies socialism in the broadest possible terms. American contributions to theoretical socialism have not been significant. While some earlier thinkers like Brownson, the Owenites, and Brisbane, developed socialist systems of sorts, and while the ideas of Bellamy and George are sometimes considered representative of a kind of socialist thought, these are marginal exceptions beyond which have been no significant major American social theorists. In large part, American socialism has reflected the socialism of Europe, even in terms of the divergent commitments of schismatic groups that have always characterized such American socialist movements as have existed.

This is not to say that socialism has contributed nothing to American political development. As social movements, some of the outcroppings of socialism in America added significantly to the thrust for social reform, especially in the period from the turn of the century to the outbreak of the World War and to a lesser degree into the thirties. In 1904 and 1908, Eugene Debs, presidential candidate of the major American socialist groups, won more than 400,000 votes, and in 1912, almost 900,000. In 1920, Debs went over the 900,000 mark, and in 1924, the American Socialist Party participated in the LaFollette campaign, which drew almost five million votes to its candidate, though doubtless only a small portion of these were socialist in origin or identification. Such records do not, of course, depict by any means the full measure of the socialist impact on American politics. For as it has often been noted, the policies advocated by the socialist groups, particularly the moderate socialist groups of the early decades of this century, have found their way into public law through sponsorship of the major parties. Thus, through the mechanism familiar in American politics by which the major parties maintain their majority status by co-opting the programs of minority groups, socialism has, in a sense, been an active element in the shaping of policy. Even this case, however, can easily be overstated, for similar policy positions were shared by non-socialist movements that carried the main thrust of the campaign for social reform—populism, Theodore Roosevelt's progressive movement, and Woodrow Wilson's new freedom. There is, finally, no way of measuring the socialist contribution to the reshaping of American policies and institutions. Even such socialization of enterprise as has occurred—in education and public utilities, for example—has been rationalized by pragmatism, defended with characteristic American symbols like equality, and set aside as special and practical problems of democratic governance.

The major point for our purpose is that American socialism is not the best representation of the theory of reform, not even to the extent that the Sumnerian restatement of Spencer's ideas is the best representation of the ideology of social Darwinism. Thus, we are suggesting that the chief role of socialism in the United States has been to serve as a minor variable, influencing the general course of public policy.

The reasons for the failure of socialism as an organized movement even to approach political control in the United States have to do largely (1) with the existence in America of "frontier" opportunities, enabling men to improve without resort to the political system; (2) with the rapid pace of industrialization and urbanization; (3) with the relative liberalism of the political system; and (4) with the looseness and separatism (and, hence, uncontrollability) of the system itself. In point (4) we are simply suggesting that Madison was indeed right in *Federalist* No. 10 when he suggested that in the "extent and proper structure" of the union, American politics would be protected from the impact of faction, even majority faction. The mere dispersal of political power in America has made it difficult for the forces of socialism to gain a widespread handhold on authority. We would also suggest that the existence of the Jacksonian and Jeffersonian traditions, the firmly rooted element of equality, the extension of suffrage, and the persistent and successful operation of democratic political mechanisms have provided some safety valves for American proletarian discontent, obviating in large measure the drive for working class political action. The combination of these forces would seem to have kept the balance of American politics fairly near to the middle and the policy framework a moderate one.

Our analysis of American socialist doctrines will proceed largely through variations on the fundamental Marxist themes. Though we will not stress this point in detail, the internal doctrinal differences in American socialism paralleled the familiar shadings of socialist thought of the same period in Europe. The spectrum of American socialism has been a broad one, reaching from positions on policy similar to those of the major American parties to the doctrinal and action extremes of revolutionary communist anarchism. As one might expect from a general knowledge of American politics, the most prominent elements in American socialism have been at the moderate end of the spectrum. This socialism, led by Debs and later by Norman Thomas, was closely related to populism; it grew somewhat out of the early Populist movement in which Debs himself was active.[22] It drew for support on a fair-sized segment of American labor, as the extent

---

[22] On American socialism generally, see Donald D. Egbert and Stow Persons (eds.), *Socialism and American Life,* (2 vols.; Princeton: Princeton University Press, 1952); and Hofstadter, *op cit.* On Debs, see *The Writings and Speeches of Eugene V. Debs;* introduction by Arthur M. Schlesinger, Jr. (New York: Hermitage Press, 1948); Ray Ginger, *The Bending Cross: a Biography of Eugene V. Debs* (New Brunswick, N.J.: Rutgers University Press, 1949); Howard W. Morgan, *Eugene V. Debs; Socialist for President* (Syracuse: Syracuse University Press, 1962); Irving Stone, *Adversary in the House* (Garden City: Doubleday & Co. Inc., 1947).

of Debs' appeal as a presidential candidate suggested. It was never, however, either the organizational or the ideological vehicle of the American labor movement, though in some industries, socialist spokesmen gained considerable union prominence and power. In terms of political position, Debs' socialism was not unlike British Fabian socialism—programmatic but not doctrinaire, gradualist, committed to political action through established democratic institutions, and founded ultimately on a moral commitment to equality. It saw in socialist programs for welfare and nationalization of economic enterprise the logical means for realization of venerated American and Christian ideals, and emphasized little the technical economic problems and historicist philosophy of "scientific" socialism. Its approach to economic reorganization was piecemeal, with emphasis falling on the need for public control of utilities and a few basic industries like railroads. But its demands were more directed to such proximate ends as freedom for labor organization and action, employment security, minimum welfare guarantees for the working man, and extended programs of public assistance and welfare of various sorts.

In contrast to the position of Debs was that of Daniel de Leon, who for years headed the Socialist Labor party in the United States.[23] De Leon, an able thinker and vigorous leader, stayed much closer to the orthodox Marxist line and devoted a good deal of his attention to attacking revisionist tendencies in American socialism. The explicit basis of his doctrine put more emphasis than did Debs on "scientific" Marxian economic analysis and less on ethical problems. De Leon expected that the structure of American capitalism would fall because of its internal contradictions and that history would bring in its train a socialist society corrective of the ills of capitalism. The role of the proletariat and of proletarian organizations, he thought, was to speed the coming of collapse of the capitalist economic structure.

De Leon waged a particularly vigorous attack on American trade unionism, which was content with achieving accommodation within the confines of capitalism and which limited its program to economic ends such as wages, hours, and conditions of work. His critique of this "voluntaristic" approach to labor organization and action was in some respects reminiscent of Lenin's comments on what he called the "trade union mentality," an ideology that assertedly obscures the workingman's vision of the full measure of his rights and of the only effective

---

[23] Much of the flavor of De Leon's doctrine can be distilled from *As to Politics* (New York: New York Labor News Co., 1935), a collection of newspaper columns written in 1906–7.

means for their realization by granting him piecemeal and insignificant gains in the distribution of social goods. Thus, trade unionism of the traditional American "business" type was from this perspective more negative than positive as a force in the long-run improvement of the workers' condition. De Leon's answer to social problems, of course, lay in a restructuring of society which would change the locus of economic control.

At the same time, De Leon did not advocate, because he did not deem necessary, the use of violence in the overthrow of capitalism. He did not, that is to say, claim that the only means of achieving a new society was a cataclysmic social upheaval that would end it at one stroke. His position was not, however, a council of gradualism in the Fabian sense, for like Marx he had little faith in the efficacy of parliamentary action to achieve reform. He felt, rather, that militant, uncompromising socialism and militant industrial unionism could exert such pressure on the system that it would not be able to save itself. Thus, his prescription was unceasing pressure on the capitalists through primarily economic means, with political action being primarily a device for recruitment of workers to the socialist cause and for peripheral harassment of the capitalist society.

De Leon's notions about the organization of the society of the future resembles somewhat those of the syndicalists and guild socialists. He struck the familiar Marxist chord in deemphasizing the administration of men and suggesting that government could focus on the administration of things. This, he thought, could be properly organized on an industrial basis, with workers controlling the economic enterprise through their own industrial unions and the rest of society falling into order as a result of the achievement of economic justice.

Between the mild reformist socialism of Debs and the more doctrinaire position of De Leon (and De Leon did not represent the far left end of the spectrum) one may find a variety of alternative statements. One of the important theoreticians who stood somewhere in the middle of this continuum was Lawrence Gronlund whose book, *The Cooperative Commonwealth,* published in 1884, apparently had considerable theoretical impact. The central elements in Gronlund's theory were orthodox Marxist in nature. His analysis of modern society was conceived in terms of the determinative role of the relationships of production; through a theory of surplus value he predicted the inevitable failure of the capitalist system. In the fashion of the orthodox European Marxists, he viewed parliamentary activity and democratic trade unionism as being substantially negative in its effects on the efforts of the proletariat to achieve the kind of change that would provide real amelioration of their condition. His position was the simple one that real change can take place only through and following the destruction of institutions controlled by the bourgeois society. Thus, trade unions designed to operate within the bourgeois framework are in effect and often in intent devices to prevent the mobilization and assertion of working class power.

In terms of prescription and expectation as to the shape of future society, however, Gronlund abandoned the orthodox formulation in favor of one closer to the central tendencies of the American tradition. The title he gave his major book is revealing in itself, for he anticipated that society might evolve through peaceful means into a commonwealth of cooperation in which the interests of all its members would be served equally. Behind this notion lay a fundamentally organic concept of society. Gronlund suggested that men are naturally bound together in the common associations of which society is composed. The problem is to achieve an arrangement in which they are disposed to appreciate the natural cooperative basis of social life and structure their lives according to natural principles. Gronlund's attitude toward the institutions of society of his time was one familiar to us—they operate to inhibit and stultify men's interrelationships and their capacities for sociability. The solution, therefore, is to destroy the institutions of conflict and substitute for them institutions that make natural human cooperation possible. Such institutions, he thought, would eventuate when the class basis of social conflict is eliminated and the state becomes an arm of society and a mechanism of progress turned to the interests of the entire community. Gronlund's scheme would not even entail the abolition of private property but only the abolition of exploitation. Production might be organized so as to eliminate the unjustified profit of those who make no active contribution to it. This conception is not unlike the guild principle, which found in mutual control of enterprise by the workers the answer to exploitation and inequitable distribution. Thus, Gronlund's ideas combined some of the elements of orthodox Marxism with some fundamentals of a nearly Aristotelian communitarianism, and came down finally to a rather mild set of prescriptions and expectations.

Two radical variants of socialism—anarchism and syndicalism—were sufficiently prominent in the America of the late nineteenth and early twentieth centuries to merit our passing attention, though neither appears to have had a major impact on American ideology or political practice nor even on the mainstream of American socialist thought. They do, however, help to illustrate and clarify some of the more subtle aspects of socialist thought, dramatizing these by showing the extremes to which they can be pushed. Their principal tenets can be summarized in a few paragraphs.

The term anarchism has been rather loosely used to mean a number of discrepant things. Its popular connotations are almost nihilistic; anarchism has often been confused with anarchy and, therefore, seen as a state of chaos or disorder. Even in the scholarship of political theory, anarchism has referred to at least two widely divergent views of society, one extremely individualistic and the other extremely communitarian. In the nature of things, the commutarian view has had more prominence as an inspiration for organized political action. Both individualistic and communitarian (commonly called communist) anarchism found vocal adherents in nineteenth-century Europe. The American anarchism with which we will deal here, however, is of the communist variety. Probably its three foremost theoretical contributors were Benjamin Tucker, Emma Goldman, and Johann Most. Though the three differed on some significant points of doctrine, we may be content with a summary of their general areas of agreement.[24]

In its basics, communitarian anarchism closely resembles Marxism. Its theoreticians interpreted society in terms of economic relationships and class conflict, and expected that the internal tensions of the capitalist society would bring about its breakdown. They also shared with Marxists and with many other reformers the highly moralistic revulsion at what they took to be the social inequities of the capitalist system. Their differences with Marxism lay in two points—one the form of social change and the other the form of society that would follow the breakdown of capitalism. On the first matter, the anarchists held that the violent destruction of the capitalist system was essential, not compromising even so far as Marx and Engels had in anticipating that some societies might achieve revolution without the agony of violence. The anarchists tended to see the capitalist society as intractably capitalistic and felt, therefore, that it would yield only to a stroke of force. They were, hence, even less likely than orthodox socialists to participate in or attempt to use the established forms of conflict resolution such as parliamentary devices. So, in theory if not in personal life they seemed to move entirely outside the established web of social relationships, to be foreigners to the whole extant social system; and since they sought the complete destruction of that system, their doctrine

---

[24] For a systematic if rather archaic analysis of anarchist theories, see Paul Eltzbacher, *Anarchism,* trans. S. T. Byington (New York: Benjamin R. Tucker, 1908).

seemed to threaten all the various devices of social control that hold society together. It is little wonder, therefore, that anarchists have commonly been considered society's worst enemies and pictured as devious-looking characters with long beards, carrying bombs, and prepared for any sort of wanton destruction.

The second point mentioned above, however, is a more interesting distinction between anarchists and socialists. The anarchists maintained that the key to fair and peaceable social relations lay in the destruction of existing institutions of social coercion, and that with the destruction of these institutions, society could *immediately* assume a peaceable form in which no sanctions of authority would be necessary. The traditional socialist formulation has been that at least during a transitional period some form of transitional state would be necessary to provide for reeducation of people and restructuring of the social situation. The most extreme and perhaps the most widely known variation of this position is the Leninist idea of the dictatorship of the proletariat, which maintained that once the capitalist system had been destroyed, the proletariat would have to use state power to prepare an ill-defined future classless and stateless society. The anarchists saw no need for such transitional coercive institutions.

It seems strangely contradictory yet true that the key to the anarchist position lies in their overwhelming faith in human nature, a faith that far outran that of the liberal. For the liberal saw the need for the indefinite maintenance of political authority to provide inhibitions on potential human wrong-doing. The anarchist, however, believed man is so good that he needs no threat from coercive institutions if only he is freed from the artificial restrictions of the state. Natural human sociability would provide plentifully adequate sanctions for the prevention of social wrong, and human relationships would fall into place in a natural social order. The need for a transitional state, then, simply does not exist, for the social conscience of human nature will "naturally" do its functions. Hence, this type of anarchism may be called communitarian. It viewed the community as a natural aspect of human life and the restraints of community consciousness alone as adequate restraints on human behavior. It pushed to their extremes the ideas of human perfectability and the rejection of existing social institutions.

Except in a negative way, anarchism probably had little influence in American life. In small degree, it may have had the effect of keeping the mainstream of American socialism as leftward as it managed to be, but for reasons that are obvious, anarchism failed either to gain a substantial mass following or to exert pressure in any major way on American institutions. From time to time it has been a sort of spectre to the American political community, and this phenomenon, too, is not had to understand. But even in this respect, anarchism is now obsolete, for it has been replaced by the "international Communist conspiracy" as the symbol of the radical threat to American social arrangements. This conspiracy is not only vastly different from anarchism in theory and organization but also much more real as a threat to the established web of social institutions.

Syndicalism had much in common with anarchism, particularly in its popular image. However, it can be differentiated on several grounds. It was not so well articulated theoretically as anarchism, but experienced somewhat greater organizational success and effect on ideology and political action. The syndicalist approach to society and social change was predominantly French in origin, and syndicalism has long been a major ideological element in the French trade union movement. Its prominence in the United States came mainly through the Industrial Workers of the World, the so-called Wobblies of American industrial unionism.[25]

The I.W.W. was founded in 1905, chiefly under the sponsorship of the Western Federation of Miners. Though rent by internal faction and never imposing in size (it is probably impossible to establish the precise size of its membership), it did achieve some measure of strength and considerable notoriety, especially in the mountain and Pacific states. Its main force lay in the mining, lumbering, maritime, and agriculture fields, where radical traditions had taken hold at an earlier period, where the unionizing efforts of the craft unions of the American Federation of Labor had notably failed, and where the work force included many transient or relatively rootless workers. To a large degree, the aims of the I.W.W. grew out of the failure of the institutions of society, and particularly those of established trade unionism, to express and protect the needs of employees in these unskilled and hard-to-organize industries. Probably the most important identifying mark of the I.W.W., however, and the crux of the syndicalist idea, lay in the rejection of the tactics of political reform in favor of direct economic means, particularly of the general strike. At an early stage, the I.W.W. experienced a bitter contest for organizational control between those who advocated exclusively economic

---

[25] See Paul F. Brissenden, *The I.W.W.: a Study of American Syndicalism* (New York: Russell and Russell, 1957); John G. Brooks, *American Syndicalism: the I.W.W.* (New York: Macmillan Co., 1913).

means and those who wished to orient the union to politically active socialism. The first group came to dominate the structure, and the I.W.W. took its character from this commitment to means.

Thus, syndicalism was noted for its militance and its advocacy of strike and sabotage as the means to overthrow of the bourgeoisie and capture of society by the workers. It was the position of the I.W.W. that a general strike would be the appropriate final blow. Before this capitalist finale, however, the ground would be prepared by sabotage and piecemeal strikes that would both weaken the capitalist resistance and spread the syndicalist message to workers through "the propaganda of the deed." Syndicalism was not a future-oriented or utopian-type movement, but its aims were clear. It anticipated that society would and should be organized and controlled by workers through national industrial union combinations. After destruction of bourgeois control, the workers could seize their industries and run them in terms of common needs and mutual aid, eliminating the exploitation inherent in the capitalist system. The syndicalist society, however, would be highly decentralized, with the threads of mutual cooperation and brotherhood of the workers holding the structure together at the center. In this respect, the syndicalist prescription is a rather extreme form of the guild idea, i.e., social organization and control according to function.

Theoretically, syndicalism adds rather little to our picture of American socialism, its main contribution lying in its advocacy of direct economic action as the means of reform. In terms of political impact, syndicalism and the ideology it represented may have had some effects on American trade unionism, particularly for its insistence on the industrial principle of organization. The problem of industrial unionism is one that has continued to plague the American labor movement, and the Wobblies helped bring it into focus, perhaps even toward solution. Like the anarchists, the Wobblies had a certain negative effect in American politics because of their pervasive attack on established institutions. During and after the First World War, they were an important focus of fear, especially for local civil authorities, and they were often subject to violence. Like the anarchists, too, their importance as a target of fear dwindled with the Bolshevik victory in Russia and the development of an international communism.

POPULISM

At the beginning of this chapter, it was suggested that the social ideas of the period of protest and reform could be categorized as predominantly economic and predominantly political. The distinction is not an easy one to maintain, for much of the protest and the friction that stimulated protest was, of course, economic in nature. But still, the diagnoses and prescriptions of the period varied. Those we have described above were analyses in which social ills were found to be rooted in economic relationships and prescriptions were largely for restructuring of systems of production and distribution. In those to follow, economic factors are important but not ultimate, and primary alleviation is thought to lie in the restructuring of political rather than productive and distributive power.

In the second category, we are lumping together two broadly related but not highly articulated perspectives on society and politics— the Populist and Progressive movements. As movements, they contributed much to American political ideology and practice, and as movements their boundaries are somewhat obscure and their relationships to each other and to several other points of view not easy to handle precisely. Furthermore, neither was identified so clearly with a leading spokesman that they received neat and definitive theoretical treatments. Therefore, in discussing them, our points of reference must be somewhat vague and our description subject to the qualifications necessary when one generalizes a theory out of a variety of events, statements, suppositions, and literary sources.

American populism is perhaps best characterized as a set of attitudes that found organizational expression in the agrarian protest movement of the 1890's, though it cannot be wholly identified with this movement.[26] In American experience, its beginnings are indistinct, but it certainly bore decided traces of Jeffersonian and Jacksonian democracy. It also carried the imprint of some European patterns of thought, most particularly of Rousseauian and French Revolutionary doctrine. Furthermore, some elements of the Populist syndrome were apparent in American politics throughout the nineteenth century, and some are quite distinctly still effective in the American political ideology in the middle of the twentieth. With its boundaries uncertain and no identifiable major philosophical spokesman, populism is extraordinarily difficult to handle in a sure and definitive fashion. We will try here, acknowledging the risks involved, to pull the main themes out of a variety of sources. It is worth reemphasizing, however,

---

[26] On populism generally, see Hofstadter, *op. cit.*, esp. chaps. 1, 2, 3; John D. Hicks, *The Populist Revolt: a History of the Farmer's Alliance and the People's Party* (Minneapolis: University of Minnesota Press, 1931); Norman Pollack, *The Populist Response to Industrial America* (Cambridge: Harvard University Press, 1962).

that populism has been an interesting, powerful, and persistent ideological force in American culture.

The proximate sources of populism lay in the western agrarian protest movements that became important in the decades following the Civil War. During this period, despite the persistence of opportunities on the frontier and the rapid development of the American industrial economy, the farmers of the West experienced mounting economic difficulties. In part, these were the result of the rising cost of money accompanying the growth of farm indebtedness. Thus, the farmer, heavily dependent on borrowed capital, found his debts increasingly difficult to pay. It is said a loan taken in 1870 that could be retired at that time with the proceeds from 1,000 bushels of wheat required 2,000 bushels worth of repayment by 1890. Another part of the problem lay in the decline of agricultural prices. Thus, as the supply of capital became scarce and part of it was channeled into new industrial opportunities, the farmer found it more and more difficult to meet the inexorable financial demands of his business. In some portions of the country, too, the agricultural economy was beginning to suffer the wearing out of land and the attacks of insects and drought.

In the face of such adversities, American farmers were surprisingly slow to organize and seek relief through politics. The Grange, organized in the 1860's, was and remained largely a fraternal and social organization rather than a militant vehicle of protest. It did establish cooperatives and undertake political action to promote some state economic regulation, but its main function seems to have been to bring social content into rural life. Some agrarian discontent was expressed through the ill-organized and unsuccessful Greenback party, which contested a few national and state elections between 1876 and 1884. More successful were the Farmers' Alliances of the 1880's and early 1890's. During these years of agricultural depression, they claimed a membership of 1 million, distributed chiefly in wheat and cotton belts. In 1892, the Alliances combined with the Knights of Labor and some other dissident groups to form the Populist party, whose presidential nominee, James B. Weaver, captured more than a million votes out of 11 million cast. In 1896, the spirit of populism was in good part absorbed by the Democrats with the nomination of William Jennings Bryan, and the Populist party ceased to be an important independent force in American politics. Populism as a movement and a set of ideas, however, did not become merely an appurtenance of the Democracy, for much of its thrust lay in its independence, and much of its spirit made itself felt through the western wing of the Republican party. As its party form disappeared, populism remained a powerful force.

The program of populism was a mixed bag of political and economic reform, with emphasis falling on the use of political power as the principal means. Perhaps the most known of the programmatic elements of the movement was the demand for free coinage of silver. The Populists also advocated such measures as government ownership of railroads, tighter government control of other utilities, abolition of national banks, reduction of tariffs, and various political devices to improve the credit position of farmers.

To assume that this program of political reforms of the economic system represents the full depth of the Populist point of view however, would fail to plumb some of populism's most interesting depths. The program was doubtless important in an organizational sense, and in both ends and means it tells a good deal about the Populist social point of view. But behind it was a more basic set of moral attitudes and a more basic interpretation of society's ills. One of its components was a literal reading of and emphasis on the American commitment to equality, an inheritance from Jacksonian democracy. At least in part, however, the Populist ideology turned away from Jacksonianism, particularly abandoning the Jacksonian prescription of laissez faire in favor of a prescription of active governmental reform.

In political terms, the thrust of Populist equalitarianism was much like that of Jacksonian equalitarianism. The symbol of democracy has probably never been taken so literally nor pushed to its logical extreme so firmly in American politics as it was in the ideology of populism, which tended to see in democracy both a moral principle and an instrument for the accomplishment of the various kinds of reform for which the movement stood. There is in populism a distinct overtone of the organic democracy more often identified with the tradition of Rousseau than with the tradition of Locke, being both egalitarian and without a theory of limits. In other words, the Populists tended to see the voice of the sovereign people as truly sovereign and just, to see it as a general will to which, when it is clearly discerned, no exception may legitimately be taken. Hence, the phrase "populistic democracy" has come to mean democracy based on undifferentiated and unchecked popular will; it has also come to be identified with the Bonapartistic type of democracy in which factionalism is not tolerated and the will of the nation is delivered to a demagogic leader skilled in the elicitation of mass consent. Many, though not all, of the leaders of populism projected the charismatic style implied in Bonapartism—Ignatius Donnelly, Mary Ellen Lees, Tom Watson, Sockless Jerry Simpson. Bryan himself had something of the style of the leader who sees himself vested in a semi-magical way with the will of the whole people. But the role of the charismatic leader, while perhaps even an inevitable concomitant to the Populist democracy, is only corollary to the central proposition that the voice of the people is truly the voice of God. "The common average judgment of the community," said the elder Robert LaFollette, "is always wise, rational, and trustworthy." [27]

From this ground, the Populist movement launched its attack on the established American democracy as the artificial facade of privilege. The American constitutional system it saw not as a framework for the expression of popular will but as a framework for keeping that will hidden or perverting its intent. The trouble with the country is that the voice of the people is kept from being heard, kept from being heard by an intricate network of political, economic, and social devices that exclude, manipulate, and misinterpret the most truly popular elements in the national personality. Most of the devices of the political and economic system as it functioned in late nineteenth-century America came under Populist attack for this reason.

Behind the attack on privilege and central to the Populist mentality lay a rather paranoid tendency to see the social system in terms of plots and conspiracies. The appeals of the Populist movement were shot through with the shadows of accusation; they persistently sought those who plotted against the virtues that Populists thought embodied the true American spirit and morality.

Populism had its great strength on the Main Streets of the small towns and on the farms of the Midwest and the South, and its virtues were particularly those of the heartland Americans. More than all else, populism feared the dark, foreign threat of cosmopolitan influences in the "outside" world, forces that sought to rule the activity of true Americans. Thus, it blamed hardship on New England, New York, Wall Street, bankers, Jews, Catholics, foreigners, internationalists, and various other elements of "Eastern" culture with its European tones. They tended to be suspicious of the ways and channels of commerce, the money market, the intellect, aristocratic manners and speech. They expressed the long-standing frustration of the West with its domination by the "effete," urbane society of the East. Vachel Lindsay caught the sense of the movement when he wrote:

> Bryan, Bryan, Bryan, Bryan
> Smashing Plymouth Rock with his boulders from the west.

---

[27] Quoted in Peter Viereck, *The Unadjusted Man: A New Hero for Americans* (Boston: Beacon Press, 1956), p. 179.

The impact of populism on American politics had both short- and long-run aspects. In the short run, as part of the reformist push of its time, it contributed to the broadening and strengthening of dissent in American society. It would indeed be surprising if the growth of social and economic institutions of the industrial society had not given rise to counterideologies, and populism provided one of the most effective vehicles of ideas. Its symbols gave focus to a great deal of mass discontent. The extent to which populism was movement rather than theory suggests the extent to which its importance lay in its penetration of the popular mind and of some of the geographic nooks and crannies of America. In this way, populism helped make reform a prime American agenda item. Thus, it helped stimulate change in institutions as well as in policies, and, as we noted before, forced new ideas and propensities for change on the political parties.

More specifically, the short-run impact of populism, mediated by progressivism, was manifested by a variety of procedural and substantive changes in American institutions and policies which were thought to promise relief from the disadjustments of social and economic change, largely by providing for the redistribution of political and economic power. Many of these reforms were concentrated at the state and local levels, and many were pushed furthest in the geographic areas where lay the strength of populism. Some, however, were realized at, or extended to, the federal government. A somewhat more detailed treatment of them will be offered in the section on progressivism to follow.

The long-run impact of populism, though even more difficult to gauge, would seem to lie in its reinforcement and reinterpretation of the American democratic spirit. Here, it took the basic democracy embedded in the American tradition by Jefferson and Jackson and pushed it a step further in its logic. Thus, in the "pure theory" of populism, democracy was identified with the public good and shorn of the traditional limits on popular power. One finds in populism a suggestion of the potential hardness of fundamental democracy. It assumed that the people could do no wrong and stimulated a search for other sources of ill which, in turn, led to the conspiracy mentality—the tendency to seek a scapegoat. It may be doubted that these attitudes made a constructive contribution to social problem-solving or to the articulation of the social force of mass democracy with other structural elements of the society.

Hence, populism may be seen as a force leading to experimentation with one of the central elements of the American political tradition. It grew within that tradition, comprises one of its most peculiarly native versions. Even though it emphasized one aspect—popular rule—at the expense of the rest and, hence, lay at one edge of the flow of American political development, it represented an attempt to bring such central concepts as democracy and equality to their full practical fruition. Like any ideology set on a fairly narrow set of assumptions, however, populism had some negative implications for broad political and social values. Broadly speaking, the heritage of populism may have made American outlooks on politics more susceptible to two tendencies. First, its overweaning commitment to the principle of popular rule may, perhaps, have led to inordinately high expectations of democratic forms. Social experience and the expansion of social–psychological knowledge suggest strongly the limitations of man's ability to cope with his environment in a complex society. The danger inherent in the juxtaposition of high faith and modest or negative results is the danger of disillusionment if the forms collapse or fail to live up to expectations. While such disillusionment has not run its full course in American society, it has on occasion led to a loosening of the grip with which Americans have held to democratic values.

Second, its combination of democratic and conspiratorial qualities and its susceptibility to Bonapartism, to demagogic leadership claiming legitimacy from the consent of the mass, suggest that populism has been one of the sources of extremist manifestations on the American political scene. Leaders of both right and left have sometimes successfully played the Bonapartist game, claiming communion with the popular will and at the same time heaping accusations on scapegoats. So far, such success has not lasted long, and the organizations and persons that have used it have not merged into a united front. Their scapegoat targets and policy goals have varied from group to group. But the point is that the spirit of populism has facilitated such irrationalism in American politics. It is not unique to America, nor has it gone to its harshest extremes here. Populism, however, has provided precedent for these dual mechanisms for escape from responsibility. In isolationism, for example, some Americans have long found a simple we-they conspiracy answer to the problems of a complex, ambiguous, demanding universe.[28]

PROGRESSIVISM: MODERATE REFORM IN
PRACTICE AND THEORY

Contemporaneous with the reform ideas we have been describing were theoretical and institutional developments commonly lumped under the term progressivism. The differences between progressivism

---

[28] For an interesting analysis of the matter of heritage, see *ibid.*

and populism are not stark, and we need make no attempt to draw clear distinctions. Ordinarily, progressivism refers to a more moderate political reform, more involved with institutional change and less involved with the psychological set described in the last few paragraphs. As it was more moderate in theoretical core and practical demand, progressivism was the real political cutting edge of the reform movement. Its message was reflected in the positions of members of both major parties, most notably though perhaps not most typically in the Theodore Roosevelt and Woodrow Wilson administrations. The imprint of its practice and theory was so deep as to leave impressions on the American political culture clearly discernible down to the present day. Its reforms are an integral part of present-day American commitments, and the weight of its scholarship is still significant.[29]

The political effects of progressivism were felt both in substantive policy and in structural and procedural change. In the first category, legislation like the income tax amendment, the Sherman and Clayton Acts, the Federal Reserve Act, the Federal Trade Act, the Lafollette–Seamans Act, and the Adamson (eight-hour day) Act as well as development of the conservation movement were largely Progressive contributions. These were, it may be noted, mostly efforts to extend economic regulation or redistribute economic power. The states during this period developed legislation on such matters as wages and hours and regulation of businesses affected with the public interest, discussed from the "negative side" in the preceding chapter.

In the area of structural and procedural reforms, the list of Progressive accomplishments is equally impressive, though here, too, the assignment of responsibility to a movement or a force is a little oversimple. On the level of the national government, Progressive procedural reform extends perhaps as far back as passage of the Pendleton Act in 1883, establishing a federal civil service system. Other notable federal accomplishments in this category might include passage of the Seventeenth Amendment, providing for direct election of senators; the movement for women's suffrage, which reached its goal with the ratification of the Nineteenth Amendment in 1920, can also be called an indirect if not the direct issue of the Progressive movement. In the

---

[29] The literature of progressivism, primary and commentary, is nearly endless. As the following pages suggest, it influenced vast areas of social thought, social science, public policy, journalism, letters, morals, manners, etc. Helpful historical accounts and interpretation include Commager, *op. cit.*; Goldman, *op. cit.*; Hofstadter, *op. cit.*; Russel B. Nye, *Midwestern Progressive Politics* (East Lansing: Michigan State College Press, 1951); Robert H. Wiebe, *Businessmen and Reform: a Study of the Progressive Movement* (Cambridge: Harvard University Press, 1962); Gabriel Kolko, *The Triumph of Conservatism: a Reinterpretation of American History, 1900–1916* (New York: The Free Press, 1963).

states and cities, progressivism brought with it even more structural and procedural change. The development of civil service systems and the progression of municipal reform generally—perhaps most notably typified by establishment of the New York Bureau of Municipal Research in 1910—proceeded apace with or ahead of developments in public personnel administration at the federal level.[30] Also at the state level, the institution of the direct primary nominating procedures, of devices for direct popular legislation, the initiative and referendum, and the recall also took place during this period, as did the passage of widespread corrupt practices and ballot and campaign reform legislation. In local government, progressivism brought some of the early impetus for manager and commission forms, for short ballots, and others. These reforms did not, of course, spread evenly throughout the country. For example, the statutory initiative and referendum have been used in only about twenty states, and only in 1955 did all the states make some use of the direct primary election for nominations to public office.

The other aspect of the Progressive reform movement with lasting ramifications in American society was the revision of social theory brought about by the scholarship of the period.[31] After the Civil War, scholarship in the social sciences and social philosophy had largely been dominated by classical economics, Spencerian sociology, and Hegelian–Germanic idealism. From about 1890 onward, America witnessed the growth of an indigenous scholarly reevaluation of American institutions which was influenced by and helped to shape the Populist–Progressive point of view. Notable contributions to the new scholarship were made by such economists, sociologists, political scientists, and historians as Lester F. Ward, Edward A. Ross, Richard T. Ely, John B. Clark, Simon Patten, J. Allen Smith, Charles Beard, Woodrow Wilson, Vernon L. Parrington, and Thorstein Veblen. Much of the movement's popular currency was developed by such journalists as Lincoln Steffens, Ida M. Tarbell, Upton Sinclair, Herbert Croly, and Walter Weyl. The list, of course, is only partial, but a moment's reflection on its breadth will suggest the importance of the impact of this scholarship on contemporary and later American perspectives.

---

[30] For a discussion of the impact of progressivism on public administration, see Dwight Waldo, *The Administrative State* (New York: Ronald Press, 1948).

[31] A highly critical commentary on progressive scholarship is found in Bernard Crick, *The American Science of Politics* (Berkeley and Los Angeles: University of California Press, 1959), esp. chap. 5. See also Morton White, *Social Thought in America: the Revolt against Formalism* (Boston: Beacon Press, 1957).

Progressive political theory is at once so diffuse in scope and so similar in fundamentals to what we have already discussed that it seems unwise and unnecessary to attempt a detailed treatment of it here. Its basic framework is much like that of populism. What the Progressive scholars did was to bring the scholarly analysis of industrial society to the service of radical Populist democracy. In premises, though often not in prescriptions, their theories revived the radical democracy of Jefferson, John Taylor, and the Jacksonian period.

Much of Progressive political science was devoted to reanalysis of the constitutional history and institutions of the United States. This enterprise rested on three critical assumptions. First, it took the assumption of basic democracy that choice by the masses is a moral good that must yield good results. In this aspect of their work, the Progressive scholars reaffirmed in more radical form the historic American commitment to democracy. Second, they assumed that the key to the realistic understanding of political relationships could be found in the identification of conspiracy, in the discovery of groups whose self-interest reflected into policy had determined the shape of American institutions. Third, they adopted an economic interpretation of political relationships, that is to say, found the basic motivations of political activity in the drive to satisfy material needs. This theme is strongly associated with Charles A. Beard, but it is also apparent in most of the other scholarly works on politics of the Progressive period, either implicitly or explicitly. Beard's famous work on the economic interpretation of the Constitution is probably the most durable and perhaps, too, the most careful contribution to this perspective. The works of many of his contemporaries, however, conveyed a similar orientation.[32]

Turned toward constitutional interpretation, these assumptions suggested that the American system, probably in its origins and certainly in its developed form, was an economic instrument wielded by privileged classes at the expense of the interests of the great body of the people. Thus, politics was fundamentally a conspiracy of the privileged class to deny the rest of the community its moral–political rights.

It may be said without exaggeration that the American scheme of government was planned and set up to perpetuate the ascendancy of the property

---

[32] Here again, the literature is too large to cite. Beard's work, *An Economic Interpretation of the Constitution of the United States* (New York: Macmillan Co., 1914), has been the object of sustained scholarly controversy. See esp. Robert E. Brown, *Charles E. Beard and the Constitution* (Princeton: Princeton University Press, 1956).

holding class in a society leavened with democratic ideas. . . . The Constitution was in form a political document, but its significance was mainly economic. It was the outcome of an organized movement on the part of a class to surround themselves with legal and constitutional guarantees which would check the tendency toward democratic legislation.[33]

The democratic elements in the political system are to be seen as sops to demands of the modern political ideology. They have been so hedged, however, with the balances of privilege as to render their effectiveness nil. The aims of the privileged classes have been so cleverly promoted that they obscure the true character of their manipulation.

For notwithstanding the overwhelming proof of the aristocratic origin of our constitutional arrangements accessible to the unbiassed student, the notion has been sedulously cultivated that our general government was based on the theory of majority rule. Unfounded as an analysis of our political institutions shows this belief to be, it is by dint of constant repetition come to be widely accepted.[34]

This self-delusion has been brought about by several influences, including indifference to politics founded on "material prosperity." At the heart of it, however, lies conspiracy: "The desire of the conservative classes to preserve and perpetuate the system by presenting it in the guise of democracy, and their influence generally must be regarded as the chief factor. . . ."[35] Smith follows this comment with a quotation from Woodrow Wilson on the establishment of a "constitution fetish" in the United States.

Many of the Progressives felt, however, that the time had arrived for the full assertion of the democratic system. The closing of the frontier and the magnification of social injustice with the rise of the urban industrial society had brought a situation where democracy might assert itself against privilege. Thus, Smith was able to write, "In the United States at the present time we are trying to make an undemocratic Constitution the vehicle of democratic rule."[36] The supposition of the Progressive political scientists and historians was that the democracy of the United States was prepared to assert itself against the domination of the manipulative element of society. They also ex-

---

[33] J. Allen Smith, *The Spirit of American Government* (New York: Macmillan Co., 1907), pp. 298–99.
[34] *Ibid.*, p. 184.
[35] *Ibid.*, p. 185.
[36] *Ibid.*, p. 31.

pected, as those committed to democracy might be counted on to expect, that once the mass was shorn of political impedimentia it would rearrange social and economic institutions and, in turn, create a policy in the common interest.

The prescriptions of the Progressive were basically political despite the underlying economic determinism of their thought. For the most part, they were prepared to defend the capitalist economic system, though some embraced a mild reformist socialism. But they hoped to rely on reforms in the institutions and procedures of government to bring about the more just world of which intellectual and technological progress seemed to bear promise. Thus, the emphasis on "popularizing" democracy through the use of such devices as initiative, referendum, and recall. Where economic policy was a focus in Progressive demands, it was policy aimed chiefly at remedying the balance of social interests. Those deemed unable to protect themselves given the standing distribution of power were to be afforded the leverage of governmental intervention: antitrust programs to protect the position of the small entrepreneur, labor legislation to compensate for the weak bargaining position of the worker, regulatory legislation to protect the diffuse and unorganized consumer interests. Such programs as these formed the heart of Progressive economic and social legislation.

The legacy of Progressive political action should be amply clear from what has already been said. Progressivism was, in a sense, the funnel through which the entire reform movement we have been discussing in this chapter was poured into the mainstream of American political development.

The legacy of Progressive scholarship was largely a strong infusion of what has been called "realism" into American social science and history. Progressivism fostered the empirical examination of social institutions to find out what society is "really" like, to find out what makes society take the form it does. Thus, this scholarship was followed by and invigorated attention to such elements in the political system as pressure groups, political parties, and political bosses. Even with its emphasis on "constitutions," it rejected the formalism and rationalism of classical economics, social Darwinism, and Hegelian metaphysics.

These highly developed theoretical systems tended to give way to the examination and description of mundane day-to-day affairs. In a way, then, progressivism was antitheory in its effect on social science, its product an array of careful accounts of the workings of politics. It was not, of course, entirely untheoretical, for underneath it lay the set of assumptions outlined above, but this theory was in good part covert and intended for the tests of experience rather than the tests of reason. It was, in a sense of the term, "pragmatic." Indeed, many of the themes of Progressive thought were restated and systematized in pragmatism, the subject of the chapter to follow.

XI

COMMUNITY AND CHANGE: PRAGMATISM

The analysis of the theory and politics of pragmatism illustrates once again and exceptionally clearly the processes of formulation, exposition, and action that characterize the relationship of thought and practice in American political life. The term pragmatism is ordinarily used in reference to the philosophical system developed by William James, but we shall use it here in a broader sense, as no other term seems to capture as well the general thrust of American ideas, including political ideas, in the first half of the twentieth century. Hence, the reader should be warned that the label we use is a nontechnical one referring to an interlocking and developmental set of philosophical and political contributions.

The social setting that underlay pragmatism was basically that reviewed in the preceding chapter. Its predominant themes were those of industrialization, urbanization, technological advancement, and the resultant growth of both personal and societal interdependence. Like populism and progressivism, pragmatism was the outgrowth of accumulating doubts about the shape of the social and economic systems. As the last chapter suggested, the social forces at work in America in the late nineteenth and early twentieth centuries gave rise to a variety of theoretical and practical responses, several of which we have already reviewed. It is interesting to note, however, that those closest to the mainstream of the American tradition tended to be less systematic in theoretical formulation and more piecemeal in practical proposal. To state the matter in the converse way, the most systematic and deep running of responses to the inequities and disadjustments of the growing industrial society were the ones that lay furthest from established American patterns of thought and action. Thus, what we have called progressivism—the movement through which the ideas of reform were injected into political structure and policy—was theoretically diffuse and undefined. It was through pragmatism that the urge to systematization, synthesis, and formulation of many of these fundamental theoretical attitudes made itself manifest. This synthesis found its first major expression in the work of William James, and was reformulated and given social content and action orientation in the works of John Dewey. At the same time, the pragmatist ideas had action implications of several kinds, the most significant being those of a new jurisprudence and the New Deal. What we shall review here, then, is how pragmatism grew out of discordances in the social structure, found articulation in philosophy, and fed back to action in politics.

THE MAJOR IDEAS OF WILLIAM JAMES

It is in the ideas of William James that the indigenous social and philosophical tendencies of the America of his period found a point of convergence.[1] James himself built heavily on the ideas of Charles Sanders Peirce, one of the most original of all American contributors to philosophical analysis.[2] We shall deal with James rather than with Peirce primarily because of the temporal proximity of his work to the application of pragmatism in social and political analysis and affairs. While James dealt little either with the social system or with politics as a manifestation of that system, he clarified the fundamental concepts of pragmatism which were later synthesized into social theory.

James's stimulus to the development of pragmatism appears to have come from philosophy in the broadest sense, that is to say, from the ideas he used to structure knowledge of the world. Where most systems of political theory seem to take their original impetus from urges to attack or defend existing arrangements, James's stimulus seems to have rested chiefly in his dissatisfaction with the world views proffered by the philosophy of his time. This is not to say, however, that James's work, therefore, needs to be seen as esoteric or abstracted from the issues then current in political theory, for in good part his system was a

---

[1] See esp. William James, *Pragmatism: a New Name for Some Old Ways of Thinking* (New York: Longmans, Green & Co., 1907). For commentary on James and pragmatism, see Ralph Barton Perry, *The Thought and Character of William James* (2 vols.; Boston: Little, Brown & Co., 1935); Lloyd Morris, *William James* (New York: Charles Scribner's Sons, 1950); Edward C. Moore, *American Pragmatism: Peirce, James, and Dewey* (New York: Columbia University Press, 1961).

[2] On Peirce, see Charles Sanders Peirce, *Values in a Universe of Chance: Selected Writings of Charles Sanders Peirce,* ed. Philip P. Weiner (Garden City: Doubleday & Co., 1958); for commentary on his contribution to pragmatism, seee esp. W. B. Gallie, *Peirce and Pragmatism* (London: Penguin Books, 1952); Moore, *op. cit.*

reaction from the philosophical framework of Spencerian individualism on which, as we have seen, the defense of the early industrial system rested.[3] Early in his life, James had been much attracted by the
Spencerian natural law interpretation of the world. He moved away
from it both rapidly and far, and developed a framework of ideas specifically responsive to some of the Spencerian notions that he found
unattractive. James saw in pragmatism an antidote to the determinism, the fatalism, and the metaphysical mystique of the classical liberal
philosophy.[4]

Spencerian liberalism, like classical economic theory, was built on
a framework of natural law. It viewed the world as operating in a
rigidly mechanistic way, the phenomena of society, like the phenomena of nature, being bound together in tight causal relationships predictable by rational deduction. What is to happen in society is to
happen, and it cannot and should not be inhibited by the intercession
of human activity. Thus, social life is not a process of dynamic human
adjustment but the playing out of combinations of forces determined
in the nature of things, toward results beyond the power of human
engineering. In a sense, this system was coldly indifferent both to human suffering and to human creativity.

The emphasis in pragmatism, on the other hand, fell on the practical, on the useful, on the everyday stuff of experience. It substituted
flexibility for the rigidity of the classical position and made its test
of truth the test of workability. Rather than a world whose relationships are defined by abstract laws, it postulated a world whose reality
is the reality of dynamic and immediate interactions. Perhaps more
importantly, it postulates a human role that is not the role of pawn
of forces but a role that is in itself creative, a role, in short, based on
the potential of human will. It is in a real sense this human will and
its potential that lies at the core of the pragmatic social theory.

Pragmatism has an empirical bias, a primary focus on the revela-
tions of sense experience. Human experience for pragmatism is reality; reality is defined and limited by the experience of the individual.
Experience is not atomic, not a simple collection of discrete events or
stimuli or the ideas engendered by events and stimuli. It is rather a continuous, flowing affair of interrelatedness between what is experienced
and man, a flowing dialogue between act, object, and subject. Man is
a part of his experience, and his reality is the interplay of his consciousness with the world of which it is a part. The world has no meaning

---

[3] Discussed above, chap. 9.
[4] See James's comments on Spencer in *Pragmatism, op. cit.,* pp. 39–40.

apart from or outside human consciousness, and human consciousness flows on in continuity as long as the organism maintains its vitality.

The experience in which the human life and the world share, however, is not even, nor is it a pattern. Though the analogy is far from a perfect one, experience is a little like a river in which the human being floats at an uneven pace, washed occasionally by ripples and foams, creating, in turn, its own troughs and furrows and splashes as it interacts with its environment. The career of the floating particle is the reality in which pragmatism is interested. Thus, experience is not only the condition of, but it is also affected by the life of the individual, a point which reemphasizes the central role of human will.

The concept of idea adds further texture to the pragmatic interpretation of the world of sense experience. Ideas, indeed, are the means by which human consciousness transcends the immediate sense experience to build a picture of the events of the past and expectations of the future. Ideas are the materials of human memory and imagination, the practical manifestations of the ongoingness, the dynamism, the interrelatedness of the experience of human life. They are, it may be added, the materials out of which experience gains intersubjective meaning through communication and, hence, through which human life takes on its social meaning. This addendum, however, reaches somewhat beyond the highly individualized tone of James's pragmatic theory.

The nexus between pragmatism's interpretation of the nature of reality and the emphasis on practicality and workability that James suggests may perhaps best be seen in the pragmatist's interpretation of truth. Though not always explicitly, the nature of truth is a central problem for all philosophy, inasmuch, at least, as philosophy is concerned with the expansion of permanently meaningful knowledge about the world. The substance of the truth for the pragmatists is not something to be judged by absolute fixed standards. The truth of an idea is really a matter of its relevance to future situations in which it may be used. An idea is true, in other words, if it leads us to accurate expectations about the world in which it is applied; an idea is true if it works, if it helps the individual in adjusting his life to the contingencies encountered in the ongoing processes of living. There is no final truth, for nothing is final, everything is a part of the flow of world experience. Truth, then, is the expedient in the best sense of that easily misunderstood word; it is that which proves useful in an ever-changing, ever-surprising human situation.

The fixed propositions of rationalism are from this point of view misleading and therefore disuseful. The entire framework of rationalism merely leads man to a false expectation of certainty where certainty cannot exist. This is not to say that the pragmatists saw life as being entirely unpredictable, for they believed experience and the ideas experience engenders to be valuable equipment in the mobilization of life against the future. It must also be noted that the utility or practicability against which pragmatism would test ideas is not the material utility of the utilitarians, for the pragmatists, most notably James, saw religious and esthetic beliefs as playing very important roles in preparing man to meet his life experiences. In its emphasis on verification as a process, pragmatism interprets truth not as a set of strictures on human activity but as something to be tested, reused, and reformulated in the creative role of the human will.

Pragmatism's rejection of absolute concepts calls into question the place of religion in the world of experience. James's work reveals the depth of his concern for the religious aspect of human life. Pragmatism's rejection of the absolute does not necessarily entail rejection of the idea of the absolute. Religion and the idea of God are parts of human experience which play vital roles in the process of man's confrontation of the universe. Indeed, religious beliefs are, in a sense, useful and practical and, therefore, pass the pragmatic test: ". . . the use of the Absolute is proved by the whole course of men's religious history."[5] In understanding the role of religious belief in human life, it is essential to grasp that men's religious experiences take on variety and that, therefore, their beliefs play various parts in the total picture of human experience. But the idea of God is so indigenous to the human spirit that it is one of the most ubiquitous organizers of meaning for the world. God is not omniscient and omnipotent as some theologies would have us believe, but the idea of God is a kind of partner in the creative struggle of the will with the world.

The existence of God cannot be verified by sense experience. But His existence is reasonable in terms of that experience, and, more importantly, experience proves the belief to be often useful. For the will to believe is a fundamental stimulus to human creativity. It provides an impetus to the exercise of will by suggesting that there is some ulterior, overriding purpose in a universe whose events may seem discrete and disconnected and whose experiences may sometimes seem overwhelming. Thus, man's inclination to develop theologies is something the pragmatists can well understand. It makes sense, it serves, it comes

[5] *Ibid.,* p. 273.

close in itself to playing a universal part in man's quest for meaning. It keeps him from developing the belief that the world is futile, that life is something simply to be lived out rather than to be fought out by an active and vigorous will. Thus, religion is truth in the pragmatist's sense of truth.[6]

Several of the central themes in James's pragmatism are themes that have informed contemporary and subsequent systems of political thought. James himself could scarcely be called a social thinker. He did not emphasize the interaction of human beings, the parts human beings play in one another's experiential environments, nor the patterns or institutions through which men move in concert to handle certain environmental tasks or challenges. Thus, his philosophy is not explicitly social or political in content. Its stimulus, as we noted above, seems to have derived from problems with ideas rather than from problems with social circumstances.

However, it does not take much imagination to see some of the ways in which the James's interpretation of the world can be given political meaning. The notions of creative will, the onflowingness and interconnectedness of human experience, and the meaningfulness of process but not of final ends—all have major implications for political theory. Many of these implications were developed in the work of John Dewey. Some have been developed in the common experiences of American political life. Pragmatism tended to bring a new kind of test against which the institutions and practices of politics were to be tallied often during the period in which its influence was at its zenith.

JOHN DEWEY: PRAGMATISM AND SOCIAL ACTION

The implications of pragmatism for political philosophy and political action were made much more explicit in the works of John Dewey than in those of William James. Indeed, if one is interested in the relationship between ideas and political practice, he can find few more subtle, more interesting, more important materials for study than Dewey's works. Dewey was a philosopher, doubtless the most influential American philosopher of his age, with an overt concern for politics and with a handhold on the social problems of the period in which he lived. He caught the sense of its major problems and reflected both its desperation and its optimism. In spirit and technique, Dewey seems

---

[6] See "Pragmatism and Religion," in *ibid.*, pp. 273–301; the title essay in James, *The Will to Believe and Other Essays in Popular Philosophy* (New York: Longmans, Green & Co., 1897), pp. 1–32; James, *The Varieties of Religious Experience: a Study in Human Nature* (New York: Longmans, Green & Co., 1902).

to have represented better than any other figure in American philosophy, or perhaps in all American scholarship, the major elements in American politics from the close of the progressive period to the middle of the twentieth century.[7]

The discussion of Dewey projects our commentary almost to the contemporary scene. He died in 1952 at the age of 93; the scope of his interests swept nearly the whole of the contemporary scene. His impact on academic philosophy was great, especially in turning the attention of professional philosophers toward primary concern with the philosophy of science. His ideas, too, were of great influence in psychology and the theory and practice of education. There can be no doubt that his influence in the educational field far outstrips that of any of his American contemporaries. He was also a man of action in political, social, and educational reform. Our commentary on Dewey must focus on his political theory, and we will make no effort to treat systematically his epistemology, educational theory, and so on. It is not possible, of course, to completely dissever the political ideas from ideas about other reaches of human experience, but it should be kept in mind that our main effort is the effort to understand Dewey as a political theorist and consider the probable impact of his political theory on the ways of political practice in American society.

A few comments on fundamentals must preface our attention to Dewey's specific political ideas. Philosophically, Dewey borrowed heavily from William James, among others. While there are important points of divergence between the two, Dewey's political and social theory can be meaningfully seen as having been built upon the foundation of James' pragmatism. Indeed, it should be noted that the influence between the two men was mutual, for James acknowledged a debt to some of Dewey's early writing. For our purposes, probably the two principal distinctions between James's and Dewey's work that need be noted are Dewey's "socialization" of James's highly individualistic interpretation of pragmatism, and Dewey's explicit emphasis on scientific method as the systemization of pragmatism's search for truth in experience.

From a broad perspective, however, it is certainly the similarity between the ideas of the two men that is the more intriguing. The-

---

[7] Selections and commentaries are too numerous to cite. Among the former, see *Intelligence in the Modern World: John Dewey's Philosophy*, ed., with introduction, Joseph Ratner ("The Modern Library" Random House, [New York: 1939]); *The Philosophy of John Dewey*, ed. Paul A. Schilpp (Evanston: Northwestern University, 1939). See also Sidney Hook, *John Dewey: an Intellectual Portrait* (New York: Day & Co., 1939); George R. Geiger, *John Dewey in Perspective* (London: Oxford University Press, 1958).

matically, Dewey, like James, began in a critique of contemporary philosophy's search for absolutes. Man, he suggested, falls short of understanding and control, and thus fails his potentiality by assuming a fixed order in the universe. This he found to be the result of the dominion of fatalistic rationalist thought in philosophy and in every-day perspectives. Thus, man's first need is to break the bounds of absolutism and to realize a new epistemology that can show him the way to control over his social and natural environment. On this development in the utilization of intelligence, all else is dependent. In *The Quest for Certainty*, Dewey took note of the consequences on human life and understanding of man's propensity to seek absolutes. It has resulted, he wrote, in the distinction of ideas from activity, with invidious results for activity, the essential stuff of life.

Hence the quest for certainty has always been an effort to transcend belief. Now since . . . all matters of practical action involve an element of uncertainty, we can ascend from belief to knowledge only by isolating the latter from practical doing and making.
. . . Experience cannot deliver to us necessary truths; truths completely demonstrated by reason. Its conclusions are particular, not universal. Not being "exact" they come short of "science." Thus there arose the distinction between rational truths or, in modern terminology, truths related to the relation of ideas, and "truths" about matters of existence, empirically ascertained. Thus not merely the arts of practice, industrial and social, were stamped matters of belief rather than of knowledge, but also all those sciences which are matters of inductive inference from observation.
One might indulge in the reflection that they are none the worse for all that, especially since the natural sciences have developed a technique for achieving a high degree of probability and for measuring, within assignable limits, the amount of probability which attaches in particular cases to conclusions. But historically the matter is not so simple as to permit of this retort. For empirical or observational sciences were placed in invidious contrast to rational sciences which dealt with eternal and universal objects and which therefore were possessed of necessary truth. Consequently all observational sciences as far as their material could not be subsumed under forms and principles supplied by rational science shared in the deprecatory view held about practical affairs. They are relatively low, secular and profane compared with the perfect realities of rational science.[8]

The Quest for Certainty was an appeal for a reorientation of philosophy and for an end of the false dichotomy between thought

―――――
[8] John Dewey, *The Quest for Certainty* (New York: G. P. Putnam's Sons, 1960), pp. 26–27.

and action. Its larger meaning lies in its appeal to society to abandon "its guardianship of fixed reality, of values and ideals" and to see in life an interconnected whole in which action and thought are interconnected and integral parts. Thus, for Dewey as for James, the emphasis in understanding and dealing with the world lay in experience and in the action that experiencing entails. But again as in James, Dewey's experience was not the passing by of discrete events. It was, rather, to be seen as a dynamic, flowing, continuous thing in which the mind of man plays an active part. Among the most notable elements in the world of total experiences is the participation of man himself. Man interacts with his environment and may effectively deal with the world in a creative fashion, if he understands the world properly and uses his intelligence in the light of what that understanding tells him. Most of all, his ability to deal with the world lies in his appreciation of the nexus between thought and action and his refusal to separate thought and action one from the other. Dealing with social experience is, like dealing with the materials of natural science, a continual testing, experimenting, and adapting to a subject that is not static but filled with contingencies. Indeed, the physical and social worlds are really but different-seeming aspects of the same totality. Finality and certainty are impossible, and life is ever changing, dynamic, always onflowing.

Dewey did, however, place much more emphasis than James on the social aspects of human experience. This heightened sense of the social nature of man's life has two important ramifications. On the one side, it emphasizes the role of other men in the individual person's environment, and on the other side, it emphasizes the potentiality of common creative action in dealing with experience and environment. Thus, human interaction becomes a major part of the picture of the world Dewey developed, as experience is both shared and interactive in itself, and as interactive creation becomes a central theme in dealing with the common world.

In this philosophical setting, the social sciences come to assume a central role in human experience, for it is through these sciences that the human portion of the environment comes to be understood and modes of common action come to be developed. Thus, in the light of its promoting an understanding of the consequences of human acts, social science may promote more effective individual and social activity, including more effective and more just methods of social control. The test of human activity always lies in its practical consequences, and social science at best would be the ordered and unfettered means of understanding what those consequences are.[9]

Closely related to the functions of social science in society are the functions of education. Education, in effect, is the means of translating the findings of social science, among other things, into the experience of the individual.[10] It does not seem extreme to say that Dewey invested his greatest hope in the potentials of education for social reconstruction. In its broadest sense, education is the sharing of society's experience and formal knowledge of ways of living with the total environment. The formal educational system is simply an unusually effective tool for transmission of this societal experience—unusually effective because, in some sense, it lies under the control of the entire community and also because it introduces the human being to its materials in the receptive and formative stage of his life experience.

Thus, education is to be directed toward enabling the individual to understand and deal with his experience, and, in consequence, if properly conceived, it will equip society in the same way. It must be experimental both in its own approach and in the attitudes and habits of mind it gives to the individual. It must prepare the individual to experiment with his life experiences, not to be afraid to create, to try to take the tentative view. The "progressive education" strongly influenced by Dewey put its emphasis on learning by doing and on educating the whole person. It was most notable perhaps as it directed the educational enterprise away from what it took to be the rigidities of classical instruction and directed them toward preparing the individual to handle his physical experience. Behind the attempt to build into education the goal of individual adjustment to the group lay the philosophic consideration of the overriding importance of the social environment.

One finds in Dewey in these ways the basis of an action- and society-oriented political theory. Its truth was not the immutable but the workable and practical in the immediate situation. Its world was the complete world of natural and social environment. Its action was the action of a creative and powerful human will with potential for dealing in common with the needs and strains of human experience. Its values were the values of the human community, conditioned by what is possible but always with ultimate reference to the consequences of social activity. In the light of these fundamentals, we may now turn to

---

[9] Thus, see John Dewey, *Reconstruction in Philosophy* (New York: Henry Holt & Co., 1920).

[10] Dewey's works on education were many. See esp. John Dewey, *The School and Society* (Chicago: University of Chicago Press, 1900); John Dewey, *Democracy and Education* (New York: Macmillan Co., 1916).

a somewhat more specific exploration of the political aspects of Dewey's thought, after which we may attempt some commentary and evaluation, some analysis of relationships with the antecedent American political tradition, and exploration of some of the consequences of pragmatism on American political practice.

POLITICAL THEORY: *THE PUBLIC AND ITS PROBLEMS*

Most of Dewey's work was heavily laced with political commentary. His overweaning concern with the social aspects of the human environment quickened his realization of the fundamental place of social and political relationships in the general scheme of things, an appreciation never realized in the pragmatism of James. The following excursion into Dewey's political ideas, however, will draw primarily on *The Public and Its Problems,* Dewey's best-known and most important extensive treatment of politics.[11] In this book, Dewey undertook a thoughtful reformulation of the basic problems of political theory. Like his work in philosophy, it was aimed at what he considered to be shibboleths of the classics. Interestingly, it came to a climax with a grand prescription that differed little from the classical view. It did, however, provide a direction and a rationalization for the loosening of some of the ideational bonds within which the American political system had long been constrained.

The fundamental element on which Dewey's political system was built is the fact of human association. As it applies to politics, this postulate is simply a representation of the belief in interconnectedness of all aspects of the world attributed to him in the preceding section. Thus, he began with a kind of organicism in which, in the final analysis, everything takes its meaning from its relationship to the totality. The social significance of this assertion really lies in its fundamentality, or, to put the case differently, in cutting off political theory from its relationship to other assumptions that might be ascribed a higher order of priority and might, in turn, impinge on one's prescriptive understanding of the political process. Thus, Dewey assumed at the outset the fallacy of political ideas based either on a metaphysic or on a mechanistic individualist analogy. As we will have occasion to remark again below, he attributed to these positions much of the confusion in which the contemporary political community finds itself.

---

[11] John Dewey, *The Public and Its Problems* (Denver: Alan Swallow, n.d.). Other important political works include especially John Dewey, *Liberalism and Social Action* (New York: G. P. Putnam's Sons, 1935); and John Dewey, *Individualism Old and New* (New York: Minton, Balch & Co., 1930).

Political theory may begin then with this axiom of association:

There is no mystery about the fact of association, of an interconnected action which affects the activity of singular elements. There is no sense in asking how individuals come to be associated. They exist and operate in association. If there is any mystery about the matter, it is the mystery that the universe is the kind of universe it is. Such a mystery could not be explained without going outside the universe. And if one should go to an outside source to account for it, some logician, without an excessive draft upon his ingenuity, would rise to remark that the outsider would have to be connected with the universe in order to account for anything in it. We should be just where we started, with the fact of connection as a fact to be accepted.[12]

The assertion of interconnection, however, falls far short of exhausting the important and interesting political problems, for, as Dewey pointed out, there still remain to be explained the particular characteristics of political association and the difficulties experienced by political associations in contemporary society in attempting to fulfill their special functions. Dewey did not attempt to differentiate association from interaction, but he did point out the great variety of levels and kinds of associations, each characterized by a shared interest and by particular characteristics. "Each form of association has its own peculiar quality and value, and no person in his senses confuses one with another." [13]

The unique quality of the political association lies in the *public* nature of the shared interests that hold it together. State and public are, therefore, in a sense identical, as it is the public character of human interconnections that marks the state as the genus of political association. In using the term public, Dewey has reference to the extensity of the interconnections among people. To put the matter more simply, all behaviors have consequences; when those consequences extend to people beyond those directly involved in the activity in question, they may be said to have a public character. As the consequences of such types of behavior come to be realized, the public takes form, and that form is identified as a state, through which political activity is generated and channeled. The function of politics thus is control, i.e., accounting for the consequences of behavior with extensive social or interactional ramifications. In Dewey's words:

The characteristic of the public as a state springs from the fact that all modes of associated behavior may have extensive and enduring conse-

---

[12] Dewey, *The Public and Its Problems, op. cit.*, p. 23.
[13] *Ibid.,* p. 27.

quences which involve others beyond those directly engaged in them. When these consequences are in turn realized in thought and sentiment, recognition of them reacts to remake the conditions out of which they arose. Consequences have to be taken care of, looked out for. This supervision and regulation cannot be effected by the primary groupings themselves. For the essence of the consequences which call a public into being is the fact that they expand beyond those directly engaged in producing them. Consequently special agencies and measures must be formed if they are to be attended to; or else some existing group must take on new functions. The obvious external mark of the organization of a public or of a state is thus the existence of officials.[14]

These officials, i.e., the government, are charged with monitoring and controlling acts whose consequences are widespread.

In general, then, the public is a particular type of interaction, and the state is its corporate expression. Actual states, Dewey suggested, have four characteristics, each of which demonstrates the viability of the concept as he developed it. These are: (1) temporal and geographic localization; (2) a functional need for organization generated out of the quantity of common interactions; (3) a concern with "modes of behavior which are old and hence well established, engrained"; [15] and (4) a particular guardianship of children and other dependents. One of the implications of Dewey's conceptualization of politics in this manner is, as we have pointed out above, that it totally identifies the state with the functional needs of society. Thus, it cuts off politics from absolutes, which Dewey maintained had no place in the shaping or judgment of political institutions and policy. He did not see his theory as being without a standard of judgment, for the theory is prescriptive in the final analysis. One of his main aims, however, was to shift the terms of judgment of politics to standards rooted in social needs and away from standards dictated by fixed principles inherited from the past.

. . . [O]ur conception gives a criterion for determining how good a particular state is: namely, the degree of organization of the public which is attained, and the degree in which its officers are so constituted as to perform their function of caring for public interests. But there is no *a priori* rule which can be laid down and by which when it is followed a good state will be brought into existence.[16]

In politics as elsewhere, Dewey was concerned with eliminating what

---

[14] *Loc. cit.*

[15] *Ibid.*, p. 58.

[16] *Ibid.*, p. 33.

he thought were the ill effects of blind adherence to fixed standards.

Out of this position grew, in turn, Dewey's assessment of the condition of contemporary government, his analysis of the situation of "the public and its problems." Democracy, he said, developed as one organizational form of public authority. Its particular characteristic is that it is so designed to secure the dominance of public over private interests. The prime problem of the public is to achieve and assure recognition of this political criterion, to assure this dominance. In the contemporary situation, however, a common confusion has shrouded the roles and characteristics of government, a confusion that is the outgrowth of the hegemony of the absolutes that Dewey felt were so threatening. Through a series of steps, the functional character of democratic government came to be forgotten, and through the doctrine of natural rights, democracy came to be linked with property rights and laissez faire. Government took on a negative form unresponsive to social needs and concerned chiefly with making property rights secure. The results of this situation are twofold: Government uses the common power to enhance the interests of some at the expense of the interest of the public; and government is foreclosed from fulfilling the function for which it grows, because its energies are diverted and its goals misinterpreted. It thus fails its most crucial test— the test of dominance of the public interest.

The question remains how this situation has come about. Dewey did not attempt to account for it solely by ascribing power to outworn absolute ideas, though this represented a major part of his concern with the contemporary situation. The other side of the diagnosis, however, points the way to the prescriptions and therapies Dewey finally promoted. The problem of the public, he said, arises out of the inability of the community to protect itself against the depredations of private interest. The result, Dewey said, has been the "eclipse of the public."

By the eclipse of the public, Dewey referred to the result of the process by which the society has undergone basic changes in the last few hundred years, changes that have been the subject of our discussion at various other points in the preceding analysis. They may be described as changes in social scale, as changes from status to contract or from small to great society, changes in social organization which reflect new ways of production, distribution, communication, and consumption. In rapid order, the face-to-face society of an earlier time has disappeared to be replaced by a society of tenuous, extended, and complex interrelationships. For our present purposes, the significant aspect of this change lies in its political effects.

One of these effects is the projection of increasing numbers of problems into the political process. For even as interactions became more extended in character, they have increased in rate in what Karl Mannheim has called the phenomenon of increasing interdependence. As expanding technology has required ever more intricate interrelationships, the entire society has become more sensitive to disturbance in any of its parts. On the commonplace level, for example, consider the elaborate network of people on whom the "average" man is now dependent just to travel to and from his place of employment. With this growth of social sensitivity and complexity, the public consequences of what were once private acts become vastly increased. The worker who goes on strike or the entrepreneur who closes down his plant is pursuing actions that were once thought to be clearly and strictly private; these are now actions that reverberate throughout the entire social system. In this way the demands on government as the orderer of interactive relationships with public consequences grow ever more intensive, complex, and greater in quantity.

The other side of the political picture of modern times lies in the impact of social change on the public's ability to organize itself for the identification and handling of social problems. A part of the difficulty grows out of the advanced nature of the problems themselves. Another part comes from the fact that political institutions took root in the society of a different character and were designed to handle problems of a different sort.

American democratic polity was developed out of genuine community life, that is, association in local and small centers where industry was mainly agricultural and where production was carried on mainly with hand tools. It took form when English political habits and legal institutions worked under pioneer conditions. The forms of association were stable even though their units were mobile and migratory.[17]

As our society has grown in geographic and social scale, however, political arrangements have failed to keep pace. "Political and legal forms have only piecemeal and haltingly, with great lag, accommodated themselves to the industrial transformation." [18]

The failure has by no means been absolute, as Dewey was quick to point out. Speaking primarily though not entirely to American polit-

---

[17] *Ibid.*, p. 111.
[18] *Ibid.*, p. 114.

ical experience, he took note of the measure of success with which American institutions have adapted themselves to new social and geographic conditions. Against great odds, the political system has expanded to embrace an entire nation, but while government has grown and the nation has managed to sustain itself, the public to a large degree has disappeared. "In spite of attained integration, or rather perhaps because of its nature, the Public seems to be lost; it is certainly bewildered." [19] The people in their corporate political capacity have lost the ability to articulate themselves, to recognize and give voice to their needs, and to control their supposed governmental agents. True government requires a truly articulated public, an organic, unified popular base. It is interesting and significant to note that Dewey takes as evidence of the dissolution of the public the flourishing of secondary and intervening associations. He seems to suggest, for example, that the development of political parties takes the truly public character from popular government.[20] At any rate, it is in this social setting that the purpose and structure of democratic government has disappeared and private interests have found it possible to prevail over public ones. The forces of the industrial era have disintegrated the historic social bases of government, and the public has disappeared to be replaced by factional groups unconcerned for the common interest and oriented only toward their own partial problems. As we will have occasion to note again later, there is a decided ring of organic communitarianism about this analysis, reminiscent of the demand of Rousseau for a politics of the "General Will."

In sum, Dewey's analysis of the condition of contemporary society may be described in terms of the loss of community. At a further step, the loss of community may, in turn, be attributed to failures in social communication. He epitomizes what is needed in the social situation as "the search for the great community." "Till the Great Society is converted into a Great Community, the Public will remain in eclipse." [21]

The great community will be the community where men realize the common interest, a social community in the classic sense of the concept, a community with many of the qualities of the Greek *polis*. It is only in this social environment, Dewey suggested, that individualism can reach fullness of meaning.[22] Perhaps Dewey's meaning and his

---

[19] *Ibid.,* p. 116.

[20] *Ibid.,* p. 119.

[21] *Ibid.,* p. 142.

[22] See *Individualism Old and New, op. cit.*

expectations for the great community can best be illustrated by his reformulation of some of the long-standing liberal concepts:

In its just connection with communal experience, fraternity is another name for the consciously appreciated goods which accrue from an association and which all share, and which give direction to the conduct of each. Liberty is that secure release and fulfillment of personal potentialities which take place only in rich and manifold association with others: the power to be an individualized self making a distinctive contribution and enjoying in its own way the fruits of association. Equality denotes the unhampered share which each individual member of the community has in the consequences of associated action.[23]

In communication lies the means for the transmission of common social needs and also the means for the dissemination of information about how to meet them. Only through communication can a society either understand or mobilize itself to handle its common social problems through common action. Indeed, said Dewey, knowledge itself is a social thing. "Knowledge cooped up in a private consciousness is a myth, and knowledge of social phenomena is peculiarly dependent upon dissemination, for only by distribution can such knowledge be either obtained or tested. A fact of community life which is not spread abroad so as to be a common possession is a contradiction in terms."[24] We have already noted Dewey's propensity to believe that through inquiry and experimentation, human societies could move to meet their problems, but such action, he maintained, is contingent on shared understanding.

Dewey took note of the ambiguous fact that techniques of communication are reaching ever-higher levels of development. "We have the physical tools of communication as never before. The thoughts and aspirations congruous with them are not communicated, and hence are not common. Without such communication the public will remain shadowy and formless, seeking spasmodically for itself, but seizing and holding its shadow rather than its substance."[25] There are, in short, massive obstacles to the full use of such devices of communication as are readily available to modern man. Among these obstacles are the institutional forms of control over communication media. Dewey had in mind here private rather than public orientation of institutions that provide the dissemination of ideas on a mass basis, particularly, of course, the press and electronic media.

---

[23] *The Public and Its Problems, op. cit.,* p. 150.

[24] *Ibid.,* p. 177.

[25] *Ibid.,* p. 142.

Unlike those who find in such institutional arrangements and in the economic motivations lying behind them the definitive answer to society's contemporary problems, Dewey seems to have regarded the institutions as secondary causes of the massive social problems of contemporary times. For these institutions seemed to him "merely . . . overt forces," merely reflections of the deeper patterns of thought which give shape to man's life in the modern age. Behind them lies the old bugaboo—abstract assumptions and understandings irrelevant to and untested by current political experience. "Emotional habituations and intellectual habitudes on the part of the mass of men create the conditions of which the exploiters of sentiment and opinion only take advantage." [26] These "habituations and habitudes" not only close off new modes of inquiry and render impossible the questioning of established ways of doing things, but also foreclose developments in the very media of communication themselves. They are deep-set fears "covered up and disguised by all kinds of rationalizations." [27] Much of philosophy and political theory has these characteristics and effects.

One of its [i.e., political theory's] commonest forms is a truly religious idealization of, and reverence for, established institutions; for example in our own politics, the Constitution, the Supreme Court, private property, free contract and so on. The words "sacred" and "sanctity" come readily to our lips when such things come under discussion. . . . . There is a social pathology which works powerfully against effective inquiry into social institutions and conditions. It manifests itself in a thousand ways; in querulousness, in impotent drifting, in uneasy snatching at distractions, in idealization of the long established, in a facile optimism assumed as a cloak, in riotous glorification of things "as they are," in intimidation of all dissenters—ways which depress and dissipate thought all the more effectually because they operate with subtle and unconscious pervasiveness.[28]

These, in compressed scope, are the fundamentals of analysis and prescription that formed John Dewey's political theory. Before commenting on some of its implications, we can probably best summarize by turning again to the words of Dewey himself. He wrote,

We have but touched lightly and in passing upon the conditions which must be fulfilled if the Great Society is to become a Great Community; a society in which the ever-expanding and intricately ramifying consequences of associated activities shall be known in the full sense of that word, so that an organized, articulate Public comes into being. The highest

---

[26] *Ibid.*, p. 169.
[27] *Loc. cit.*
[28] *Ibid.*, pp. 169–71.

and most difficult kind of inquiry and a subtle, delicate, vivid and responsive art of communication must take possession of the physical
machinery of transmission and circulation and breathe life into it. When
the machine age has thus perfected its machinery it will be a means of
life and not its despotic master. Democracy will come into its own, for
democracy is a name for a life of free and enriching communion. It had
its seer in Walt Whitman. It will have its consummation when free social
inquiry is indissolubly wedded to the art of full and moving communication.[29]

Many aspects of Dewey's work in political thought merit comment.
In some respects, it can be seen as a complement to or even a part of
the fundamental strains of progressive thought with which, indeed, it
was nearly contemporary. Like pragmatism, progressivism eschewed
absolutes, was experimental with institutions, and did not shrink from
innovation. Both have done much to make the American political
scene look the way it does today.

In terms of contribution to social theory, perhaps Dewey's prime
offering was his emphasis on attention to the social context as an integral part of the world with which man must deal. His political
and educational theories both stressed the proposition that interaction
among human beings is the central element in the life process. The
importance of this contribution was enhanced by the fact that Dewey
wrote at a time when the problems of the social context were beginning to be more acute than the problems of the physical environment.
That is to say, by Dewey's time men had come far toward control over
natural phenomena, but with development of the interdependent industrial and urban society, control over the social setting lagged ever
farther behind. In such a context, it is little wonder that Dewey's
heavy emphasis on social interaction should have become influential
on ways of thought.

In consequence of his orientation to the social environment and his
experimentalist orientation, his work also did much to promote attention to the methods of social science. This contribution has been
felt in the development of research in the academic social science disciplines and in ever-increasing influence of social research on social
decision-making. As we have seen, Dewey assumed that the accumulation and communication of systematic knowledge was the key to improvement of the social situation. In a sense, his entire set of prescriptions for social and political improvement is a plea for the development and dissemination of social science research.

---

[29] *Ibid.*, p. 184.

Dewey also contributed to the developing propensity of his time to see politics as an appropriate sphere for action. Here again, he added momentum to a major intellectual theme, urging abandonment of the tendency to see society in terms of abstract absolutes impermeable to the force of human will. The key to his position lay in his belief in the creative potential of human beings acting singly or in concert. With knowledge, he insisted, man can act to reshape the conditions of his life. Insofar as man can create social effects, politics is a worthwhile social pursuit. While few social philosophies have denied man some efficacy in dealing with social problems, few, too, have insisted as convincingly as Dewey on the potentials of common action. In this fashion, Dewey and his ideas probably contributed much to the "politicization" of American society by interpreting politics as significant activity.

From the standpoint of the content of theory, perhaps the most interesting and significant aspect of Dewey's work was its basically communitarian orientation. Such a perspective is not typical of American thought about politics, yet the "use" Dewey made of it did not take him outside the American tradition. Like T. H. Green had done in England, Dewey put communitarianism to work for some of the characteristic ends of liberal individualism.

By communitarian we refer to the perspective that interprets the community collectivity as the fundamental building block, the primary unit of theoretical analysis of the social world. Such theories posit a higher rationality, an integrity, and/or a higher value to the community than to individual men. Such a belief has been common in political thought since the days of Plato and Aristotle. Perhaps its leading modern exponents were Rousseau and Hegel, both of whom found echoes in Dewey's theoretical system. Like Rousseau, Dewey emphasized common action and found legitimizing force in the will of the community; his standard for political judgment was not unlike Rousseau's General Will. Further, both emphasized the distracting qualities of "civilization" and decried the intrusion of partial interests into the community arena. Dewey's theory resembled Hegel's not only in its adherence to community needs as political standards but also in its more fundamental emphasis on the onflowingness of human experience. Dewey did not, like Hegel, formally write history into the communitarian formula, but his development of that formula projects a more dynamic note than does the work of Rousseau.

The communitarian quality of Dewey's theory typifies one of the tendencies, indeed, perhaps one of the dilemmas, of modern liberal theory. For the roots of liberalism, as we have seen above, lay in the development of the individualist interpretation of rationality, morality, and political system. The individualist strain in the liberal tradition is apparent from an early time, but it reached its zenith with the development of social Darwinism. A variety of practical and philosophical answers to social Darwinism developed out of reaction to its theoretical and political implications, and Dewey's was one of these. But the individualism traditional to the liberal posture is not easily forgotten, and its tension with the community orientation of liberalism like Dewey's has brought an element of ambivalence into liberal thought and action. Hence, liberalism has tried to preserve a variety of symbols and commitments, some of them mutually contradictory. Pragmatism, emphasizing tests of policy consequences rather than tests of philosophical content or logical consistency, provided grounds for ignoring this problem. It did not, however, indicate clearly how the discordances in ideology produced by inconsistency were to be handled in a polity in which expression of preference has policy importance.

A further question arising out of Dewey's communitarianism is whether it implies an illegitimate leap from fact to value. More specifically, the question is whether it imputes value to the community from the fact that human beings live in the community situation and find in interaction the means of fulfilling needs that outrun individual abilities. It may be somewhat unfair to insist flatly that Dewey found the locus of value in the human community. He was, as we have already pointed out, attempting to find a *modus vivendi* between a theory based on common needs and a theory deriving its substantive values from classic liberal individualism. It seems even more difficult to deny, however, that his communitarianism has the upper hand and that his system finally resolves to standards of judgment that give priority to the welfare of the larger whole. Underneath seems to lie a naturalistic assumption that because human beings are grouping creatures, the value of grouping and the values asserted by the group must, therefore, have priority; hence, the suggestion that standards of value grow out of what is found to exist in the experiential world. The problematic aspects of such a position are several: it intermingles fact and value and assumes that propositions of the one type can be derived from propositions of the other; it destroys the possibility of developing standards of judgment independent of those predominant in the existing human community; it reverses the traditional priorities of liberal theory, making the needs of the individual subservient—logically totally subservient—to the needs of his society.

A final theoretical implication in Dewey's work is closely related to the one just mentioned. From the standpoint of traditional categories of analysis, he does not resolve the problem of the standards to which the judgment of actions can finally be referred. On the one hand, his work seems to imply that these standards of judgment are entirely relative to the informed wishes of the public. Both the moral and the psychological implications of such relativism are vast. On the other hand, it may be argued that instead of leaving values in this relativistic situation he simply substituted new absolutes for the old ones or merely found a way of restating traditional liberal absolutes in new and disguised forms. His insistence, for example, on the fundamental place of free inquiry in communication lies close to a traditional and basic liberal postulate. So strong is his case for free communication that he seems to be saying that it is a universal good requisite to the subsistence and development both of individual and of society. If this interpretation is fair, Dewey's position differs but little from the absolutism he was wont to attack. Those looking for political–moral guidance and not simply for explanation may thus find in Dewey some confusion as to the ultimate postulates of value to which his prescriptive theory may be driven.

What can be said, finally, of the implications of Dewey's political thought for political action? Much is explicit and much implicit but apparent in what has already been said, but a few points merit further emphasis. Perhaps the most significant is the impulsion Dewey's philosophy gave to experimentation in political policy and practice. As we have noted before, Dewey would make workability the practical guide to program- and structure-building, and abandon standards of policy or structure that are simply attempts to apply rigid abstract ideas. He was deeply concerned with the adverse effects on the community of reverence for the dead hand of the past. He saw the political structure as a dynamic outgrowth of changing community characteristics that, to be successful in performing its function, must stay on top of social change. Thus, political affairs, too, must be susceptible to change, must be susceptible to remolding in response to the appearance of new social needs and forces. Dewey did not fear change but embraced and promoted it. In this respect, he was the inheritor of the progressive tradition as well as many of the tendencies of Jeffersonianism. To be more specific, Dewey's thought can be seen as injunction to bold political experimentation.

It is also a theory heavily democratic in the Rousseauian sense, a theory that finds the source of political power in the community and legitimacy in common expressions of human needs. Dewey did not leap to the defense of the mechanisms of American democracy. If anything, he was doubtful about the defensibility of many of these. But his insistence on the position of the public as the final reference for political actions is democratic in a fundamental sense. What he called for was a freeing of the public from the chains in which the culture had wrapped it. There is a romantic tone in his faith in the ability of the public to rule in a fashion that must be deemed just by external standards.

We should also take note at this point of the important political role that Dewey's theory assigned to the function of education, though we need only reiterate what was said above about the nature of the educational function in retooling society to handle its problems in legitimate ways. Like Jefferson, Dewey would have invested most heavily in the educational process as therapy for the public's ills. In Dewey's formulation, education became the basic task of the state, a task that draws its importance from the standard of community well-being. Though different in underlying goals, Aristotle's insistence on education as a key to the solution of community problems is much like Dewey's in practical thrust. The difference lies in Aristotle's feeling that the function of education was to reinforce the polity by providing a socializing nexus between past and future, whereas Dewey saw in education the means by which ongoing social problems could be uncovered and methods for their solution devised and communicated. That education is a process on which a satisfactory politics is contingent is an age-old theme and one to which Dewey made an important contribution both in terms of its preservation and elaboration and in terms of its impact on real political processes. The American nation has been innovator and pioneer in the development of public education for public responsibility. While ambivalence between individual right and community responsibility has kept some ambiguity around the political role of education, the commitment to education as a public function has been firmly established both in institutions and in ideology.

In its implications for political action, Dewey's political thought was not programmatic, did not propose substantive measures for the improvement of the political system or the social situation. Its major proposals were procedural, and even those were, by and large, of an abstract and generalized type. Practically speaking, the im-

portance of pragmatism for politics has probably been in its rationalization of and influence on the reshaping of political institutions.
Thus, in an era of radical social change, ideas like Dewey's lay the
groundwork for accompanying political alterations. Something in the
American situation has made it possible for the nation to test and
revise political practices, even those of the most basic sort, during the
past fifty years. We might cite as examples such things as alterations
in the distribution of powers within the federal system, the expansion
of the public power in many spheres heretofore reserved for private
action, and the shifting relative roles among the institutions of the
American national government. To this we might add a staggering
list of political and economic innovations of substantive and procedural sorts. This complex of changes can be summarized as the
formal and informal revision of the American Constitution accomplished through courts, executives, legislatures, private groups,
and popular action. These changes have been accomplished at an
increasing rate as the American political system has learned to accept change. While the abstract symbols still remain strong, the recent
history of American politics would seem to reflect something like the
pragmatists' injunction: try it and see if it works. Thus, in a major
sense, perhaps Dewey grasped, explored, and articulated an important
aspect of the ideology of his age.

PRAGMATIC POLITICS

Articulation of the spirit and theory of pragmatism into the on-
flow of American political action is both difficult and easy to explain.
It is easy because the penchant of the American nation to experiment
in political matters in recent years has been so obvious, and because
pragmatism itself is so flexible as to permit a variety of action interpretations. It is difficult because the variety and flexibility of both
ideas and action in recent years may well make one wonder whether
anything definitive can be said about their interrelationships. For
these reasons, what is said below about pragmatism in American politics should be read as a set of questions, propositions, and tentative
inferences. But despite all these qualifications, it seems safe to say
that the political punch of pragmatism was immediate and strong.
One indeed has the feeling that its influence has been ubiquitous,
that it has been an important part of the stream of American life
in a multitude of unsuspected and undetected ways.

We have had occasion to comment above on the experimentalist
atmosphere of American progressive politics in the early twentieth

century. Progressivism and to a degree the other isms that accompanied it were founded on the rejection of the sort of absolute assumptions that had come to dominate much of American political ideas. In measure, Dewey's work represented a systematic restatement of many of the propositions on which progressivism was based. Thus, pragmatism drew on progressivism and vice versa; perhaps it might better be said that both represented a political syndrome that took hold of much of American politics during the twentieth century and that itself grew out of reaction to the shape of the American political tradition in the late 1800's. At any rate, it cannot be doubted that there is a close relationship between the two.[30]

In terms of our overall thesis, it is not extraordinary that such an orientation as pragmatism should have grown out of the social situation in the early half of the twentieth century, for, as we have pointed out above, this was the period in which the frictions and inadequacies created by advancing urbanization and industrialization made themselves felt in major ways. It became growingly apparent that the laissez faire policies of rationalistic liberalism would neither sustain the system itself nor prevent the system's doing vital damage to socially entrenched humanitarian values. At the same time, there are evident reasons why a piecemeal and nondoctrinaire approach to social problems, like pragmatism, held much attraction in American society. The heterogeneity and diffuse experience of the American people made widespread acceptance of doctrinaire answers to social problems improbable, and the society had shown itself tough and tenable even in the face of disruption. Hence the choice of adjustment to rather than substitute for the existing system, and the nation groped in its own experimental way for a variety of innovations and revisions through which to respond to social needs.

Where domestic problems were concerned, i.e., problems internal to the American society, the dilemmas of the urban industrial age were most forcibly brought to attention by the Great Depression of the 1930's. Amidst a nation still young and vigorous, with vast unexplored economic and social potential, the machinery of control and distribution failed, and American life was brought close to a standstill. The test was probably about as severe, excepting the destruction

---

[30] Histories of the period are many. See esp. Eric Goldman, *Rendezvous with Destiny: a History of Modern American Reform* (New York: A. A. Knopf, 1952); Richard Hofstadter, *The Age of Reform: from Bryan to F. D. R.* (New York: A. A. Knopf, 1955); and Arthur M. Schlesinger, Jrs.' series, "The Age of Roosevelt": *The Crisis of the Old Order* (Boston: Houghton Mifflin Co., 1957); *The Coming of the New Deal* (Boston: Houghton Mifflin Co., 1958); *The Politics of Upheaval* (Boston: Houghton Mifflin Co., 1960).

of physical war, as a social system and its economic and political elements can endure. The American polity's response to this challenge was not monolithic, nor did it take shape at any given place or time. The polity certainly does not speak with a single voice. But perhaps no other single term describes better than "pragmatic" both the spirit and the policy with which the American nation confronted the depression situation. In using this term, we have predominant but not exclusive reference to the postures and programs of the New Deal.

The New Deal was many things to many people, and many still see it as having been everything from too far left to too far right and from too doctrinaire to too expediential. Furthermore, the New Deal in itself, as a movement made up of men and their policies, was far from univocal. It combined the perspectives of people who differed among themselves as to proper methods of finding solutions to social problems. Too, the New Deal changed by periods and did not maintain a steady course over the eight years between Roosevelt's succession to office and the opening of the American participation in the Second World War. Subjected to analysis, the New Deal seems to bear traces of Jeffersonian basic democracy, Hamiltonian mercantilism, Keynesian economics, social pluralism, syndicalism, and perhaps other strains of thought. It sought in part to administer a controlled economy and in part to restore the free controls of the marketplace. It is marked by nothing else so much as the variety of possibilities it saw for sociopolitical action against the crisis.

The problem remains what can be said about the simple tendencies of a political movement that can be so described. To say that the New Deal was eclectic is true but not very helpful. The description offered above, however, itself suggests a somewhat more definitive line of interpretation, for the incorporation of such a variety of differing and sometimes even contradictory policies and positions within the framework of one movement would seem to indicate that the movement proceeded, whether by design or otherwise, through processes of trial and error. It suggests, in other words, that the New Deal was experimental, that it was committed to movement or creation, i.e., the activity of the creative political will, that it eschewed rigid doctrine in favor of a pragmatic approach to immediate problems. "This nation," Franklin Roosevelt said in his first inaugural speech, "asks for action, and action now!" [31] Perhaps the experimental, pragmatic nature of the New Deal philosophy is nowhere more clearly

---

[31] *Inaugural Addresses of the Presidents of the United States* (Washington, D.C.: U.S. Government Printing Office, 1961), p. 236.

conveyed than in the following comment of Roosevelt's: "The country needs . . . bold, persistent experimentation. It is common sense to take a method and try it: if it fails, admit it frankly and try another. But above all, try something." [32]

It would be out of place here to attempt to summarize in any detail the content of the New Deal program. That program moved on a broad front in both short- and long-run measures, hopefully designed to propel the country toward recovery and institutional reform. Hardly any major aspect of the social and economic life of the country remained untouched. In the field of monetary and related policies, measures ranged from such emergency steps as declaring a bank moratorium, taking the country off the gold standard, and devaluing the dollar, to such long-run steps as establishment of the Federal Depositors Insurance Corporation and the Securities Exchange Commission to provide investment security and some public control over capital finance. In the industrial and commercial field, the most spectacular New Deal measure was the National Industrial Recovery Act, which, among other things, provided public sanction for efforts to establish common business prices and industrial practices. Through the NIRA, the business community participated in the development of detailed codes for the regulation of basic aspects of the important subeconomies. In the labor field, New Deal measures meshed with those for the regulation of industry. The earliest of these were established as part of the general NIRA program. After judicial nullification of the NIRA, many of the same ends were sought through other legislation, including the Wagner Act, which dealt with labor organization and bargaining; the Fair Labor Standards Act, providing for minimum wages, maximum hours, and protection for child and women labor; and acts to establish programs for workmen's compensation, unemployment compensation, and old age and survivor's insurance. The New Deal also developed a complex set of policies in an attempt to meet the persistent depression in American agriculture through measures to increase farm credit and control prices by limiting supply. Both resource programs and unemployment problems were approached through such projects as the Tennessee Valley Authority and construction of vast hydroelectric facilities in the Pacific Northwest. At the same time, a variety of relief programs sought to provide for the fulfillment of fundamental human needs,

---

[32] *The Public Papers and Addresses of Franklin D. Roosevelt* (New York: Random House, 1938), Vol. I, p. 646.

improve and extend public facilities, and turn a part of the unemployed labor force to productive activity.

The economic system was brought into bold relief by the problems
of the Depression, and this aspect of the New Deal has tended to
dominate a great proportion of the commentary of the times. From
this perspective, much emphasis has been put on the contributions
of Keynesian economics, and probably properly so.[33] The central
contention of the Keynesian theory is probably the proposition that
the path to economic recovery lies in the policy of deficit spending,
that nothing else matters so much as increasing purchasing power that,
in turn, can stimulate production and bring about an increase in
prices. It would be pushing the point too far, however, to say that the
New Deal operated on the prescriptions of the Keynesians. When
New Deal policy coincided with these prescriptions, the coincidence
was probably as much fortuitous as planned. Furthermore, vast
reaches of New Deal policy were either irrelevant or contrary to
their ideas of effective policy.[34]

In its economic policy, the New Deal embraced a strange combination of pragmatism and conservatism. While it rejected laissez
faire, it aimed at preservation of the capitalist system through administrative decision that would control the distribution of resources
without taking distribution out of private hands. It advocated the
managed capitalist economy, a form that has come to all major
capitalist systems since the 1920's. It was pragmatic in the sense that
its technique was the technique of engineering existing institutions
and interposing will into the operation of "natural" forces in the
interests of the community welfare. Thus, the New Deal, with its

---

[33] The leading theoretical work of Lord Keynes was John M. Keynes, *The General
Theory of Employment, Interest, and Money* (London: Macmillan & Co., Ltd., 1936). See,
also, Alvin Hansen, *A Guide to Keynes* (New York: McGraw-Hill Book Co., Inc., 1953);
Seymour E. Harris, *John Maynard Keynes, Economist and Policy Maker* (New York:
Charles Scribner's Sons, 1955); H. L. McCracken, *Keynesian Economics in the Stream of
Economic Thought* (Baton Rouge: Louisiana State University Press, 1961).

[34] The Keynesian influence, through Keynes himself and through such New Dealers as
Tugwell and Frankfurter, apparently did, however, provide a prod as well as a theoretical
direction to some Roosevelt policies. Schlesinger quotes the following from a Keynes letter to the President, written in 1933:

You have made yourself . . . the trustee for those in every country who seek to mend
the evils of our condition by reasoned experiment within the framework of the existing
social system.

If you fail, rational choice will be gravely prejudiced throughout the world, leaving orthodoxy and revolution to fight it out.

But if you succeed, new and bolder methods will be tried everywhere, and we may
date the first chapter of a new economic era from your accession to office.

The Politics of Upheaval, op. cit., p. 656.
On the personal level, see *ibid.,* pp. 405–8 on Roosevelt's reaction to Keynes.

Keynesian theoretical accoutrements, proposed at the same time to take action to meet the desperation of a catastrophic social situation and, while doing so, to preserve the broad sweep of cherished American institutions. It was neither doctrinaire nor revolutionary in the sense that socialist theories are such. Even in the depths of crisis, the American polity turned back the appeals of the doctrinairies and sought its solution in piecemeal alterations of institutions and policies. Though the case is perhaps a strained one, what we are suggesting is that the extent to which the American polity could receive (not to say understand) this orientation is indicative of the pragmatic, tentative, testing attitude that characterizes the main force of American political ideology, even during the crisis period.

It is small wonder, then, that the New Deal was both so successful and so controversial. It drew on tendencies of thought well established in American political life. Its heritage from the progressivism of Theodore Roosevelt and Wilson was clear. It had, furthermore, two qualities that have great ideological appeal—it was experimental and conservative. It was experimental in the sense that it used politics as a mechanism for the exercise of human will in its willingness to try something and see if it works. It was conservative in the sense that its innovations were framed by the network of existing institutions, both political and economic. In effect, it rejected the abstract scheme and the all-pervasive palliative, even at a time when widespread social and economic disorganization might have been thought to make welcome such a scheme or palliative.

While the propensity to experiment and the conservative commitment to preservation might be thought mutually contradictory, they mesh in the overall attitude toward politics we have been describing as pragmatic. For while pragmatism is overtly experimental, it is also overtly opposed to the grand plan. Its experimentation is, therefore, perforce based in practice on retention of the existing broad scheme and many of the particulars of social organization. It is a theory of change, but a theory of change mediated by context and even perhaps by realization of the limitations imposed on change by possibility. Even Dewey was deeply committed to the preservation of existing values and instrumentalities whose abstract bases he rejected. And, seen in perspective, even the most dramatic of New Deal proposals for change—for example, the proposal to expand the size of the Supreme Court—were minor given the broad historical sweep of institutional development. Perhaps it is too much to say that such proposals and the attitudes behind them are palatable to conservatives; it is not too much to say that both their intent and their effects were conservative if conservatism is understood as a theory of change and not as a theory of statics.

NEW ORIENTATIONS IN AMERICAN JURISPRUDENCE

Correlative with changes in American philosophy and politics over the first half of the twentieth century were changes in jurisprudence, reflected both in the formulations of legal scholars and in the work of legal institutions. The tenor of this reorientation was suggested earlier in our discussion of Holmes' dissent in the Lochner case.[35] While we will not at this point attempt a thorough analysis of the highly technical and controversial issues raised by developments in this field, a few comments will help to lay clear some of the intellectual thrust and practical effect of new ways of understanding the nature of law and the functions of the courts.[36]

We are not dealing here with any single movement or any single school of thought tightly bound together in a common intellectual position. New orientations were the products of a variety of people in a variety of roles and of a variety of types and tastes. On the high Court, the influence of new modes of thinking about the law developed over a long period, particularly in the fields of economic relations, social reform, and civil liberties. New views did not dominate the Court in any consistent way at least until the middle 1930's, and then only dubiously so. The leading figures in the Court's reorientation were Justices Holmes, Brandeis, and Cardozo, each of whom expressed a philosophical point of view somewhat different from the others. Outside the Court, the most notable voice in this development was probably that of Dean Roscoe Pound. We will not try in the paragraphs that follow to treat separately the distinctive contributions of all of them, but will, instead, attempt the more difficult tasks of summarizing some of their common tendencies and indicating particularly the positions they share with the political theories we have reviewed in this and the preceding chapter.

Like so much of what we have discussed in the preceding pages, these developments in jurisprudence can be described as reaction— reaction against the predominant social forces of the late nineteenth

---

[35] *Lochner* v. *New York*, 198 U.S. 45 (1905), 74; see above, pp. 313–14.

[36] The literature dealing with the jurisprudence and public law of this period is vast. For discussion, see Edgar Bodenheimer, *Jurisprudence, the Philosophy and Method of the Law* (Cambridge: Harvard University Press, 1962); Wolfgang Friedman, *Legal Theory* (4th ed.; London: Stevens & Sons, 1960); Edwin W. Patterson, *Jurisprudence: Men and Ideas of the Law* (Brooklyn: Foundation Press, Inc., 1953).

century and against the ways of thought that had provided their rationalization. The tendencies to see the world in terms of absolutes, to regard these absolutes as having fixed social and economic relationships, and to determine policy chiefly through fear of violating the order of nature stimulated response not only among philosophers and political activists but also among those who worked with the law. In general terms, the core of the new legal scholarship lay in the tendency to see law as a part of the social fabric rather than as an imposition from outside. The law, in other words, came to be seen as a part of a system of social controls, devised by a society to assure itself an order and determined by the disposition of needs and forces in the social system. Thus, both the philosophy of law—the search for its metaphysical sources and meanings—and legal analysis—the examination of law in terms of its internal logic—came to seem irrelevant to both the jurist and the scholar. What was relevant was its social sources and, even more importantly, its impact on social relationships, its consequences for human behavior and the social system.

With this reorientation to the basic characteristics of law, new material became pertinent to the activities of judges, lawyers, and students of the legal system. The premium came to fall on social facts of an empirical sort, as judgment from the new point of view is rendered in terms of the effects, in fact, of changes in legal norms. Thus, experience rather than speculation came to be seen as the heart of the legal process. "The life of the law," said Holmes in a famous passage, "has not been the life of logic: it has been the life of experience." [37]

Social facts or experience were to provide guidelines against which the effects of legal prescription could be checked to indicate to lawmakers, judges, and the society at large what could be expected as a result of legal enactments or interpretations. It did not mean abandonment of legal precedent but supplementation of the slippery substance of precedent with concern for the empirical impact of legal fiat on the social structure. This "sociological" approach had a notable impact on its introduction into the legal system. In the famous "Brandeis brief," for example, Mr. Brandeis, later to be Associate Justice of the Supreme Court, introduced "social science" materials into argumentation on social reform legislation. In *Muller* v. *Oregon*, 1908, Brandeis, urging the constitutionality of a 10-hour law for women, presented to the Court extensive evidence from diverse

---

[37] O. W. Holmes, Jr., *The Common Law* (Boston: Little, Brown & Co., 1881), p. 1.

sources about adverse effects of overlong work hours on the health, social, and moral well-being of women. The point he attempted to make was that the ill effects of such work were sufficient to justify exercise of the state's police power. Brandeis won his case, with Mr. Justice Brewer commenting in the majority opinion that "We take judicial cognizance of all matters of general knowledge." [38] The introduction of systematic accounts of social experience has not by any means been a universal practice since the development of the Brandeis approach, nor has its use by any means been as persuasive as Brandeis apparently made it in the Muller case. Its use has, however, been widespread, not only in litigation on social welfare narrowly defined but also on other kinds of problems, as the school segregation cases (*Brown* v. *Board of Education,* etc.) and state reapportionment cases (*Baker* v. *Carr,* etc.) recently have illustrated. [39]

"It is true, I think, today in every department of the law that the social value of a rule has become a test of growing power and importance," wrote Benjamin Cardozo in 1921. Quoting Pound, he continued, "Perhaps the most significant advance in the modern science of law is the change from the analytical to the functional attitude." And again, quoting Pound, "The emphasis has changed from the content of the precept and the existence of the remedy to the effect of the precept and the availability and efficiency of the remedy to attain the ends for which the precept was devised." [40] Again, in Cardozo's words, "All departments of the law have been touched and elevated by this spirit." [41] Beyond such generalizations as these, it is difficult to specify what if anything has held together the views of those who have participated in the reorientation of American jurisprudence. In an essay directed chiefly to the breadth and diversity of what he called the ferment of realism, the late Karl Llewellyn enumerated the following as "common points of departure":

(1) The conception of law in flux, of moving law, and of judicial creation of law.

(2) The conception of law as a means to social ends and not as an end in itself; so that any part needs constantly to be examined for its purpose, and for its effect, and to be judged in the light of both and of their relation to each other.

---

[38] *Muller* v. *Oregon,* 208 U.S. 412, 421 (1908).

[39] *Brown* v. *Board of Education of Topeka,* 347 U.S. 483 (1954); *Baker* v. *Carr,* 369 U.S. 186 (1962).

[40] Benjamin N. Cardozo, *The Nature of the Judicial Process* (New Haven: Yale University Press, 1921), p. 73.

[41] *Ibid.,* p. 75.

(3) The conception of society in flux, and in flux typically faster than the law, so that the probability is always given that any portion of law needs reexamination to determine how far it fits the society it purports to serve.

(4) The *temporary* divorce of Is and Ought for purposes of study. By this I mean that whereas value judgments must always be appealed to in order to set objectives for inquiry, yet during the inquiry itself into what Is, the observation, the description, and the establishment of relations between the things described are to remain *as largely as possible* uncontaminated by the desires of the observer or by what he wishes or thinks ought (ethically) to be. . . . .

(5) Distrust of traditional legal rules and concepts insofar as they purport to *describe* what either courts or people are actually doing. . . . .

(6) Hand in hand with this distrust of traditional rules (on the descriptive side) goes a distrust of the theory that traditional prescriptive rule-formulations are *the* heavily operative factor in producing court decisions. . . . .

(7) The belief in the worthwhileness of grouping cases and legal situations into narrower categories than has been the practice in the past. . . . .

(8) An insistence on evaluation of any part of law in terms of its effects, and an insistence on the worthwhileness of trying to find these effects.

(9) Insistence on *sustained and programmatic attack* on the problems of law along any of these lines.[42]

The principal political perspectives of this jurisprudence can be summarized in three comments on the substance of the paragraphs above. In the first place, it was, like pragmatism, a declaration of war on political theories of absolutes. It attacked that view which saw in law the earthly embodiment of transcendental values, particularly, in the circumstances, those values that would limit the sphere of activity of the state. While not denying the quality of justice, it viewed and attempted to interpret law as an experiential outgrowth of the relationships embodied in a social system.

Second, it stressed the dynamic role of law in the creation of change in social conditions. This perspective is, in a sense, the complement of the one preceding, for it suggests that the law is to be seen not as an abstracted rule but as a rule in social context, a rule with a social function to fulfill. Thus, the conflicts that constitute the subject matter of legal activity would be decided in terms of the "realities" of

---

[42] Karl N. Llewellyn, "Some Realism about Realism—Responding to Dean Pound," *Harvard Law Review*, Vol. XLIV (June, 1931), pp. 1222–64, quoted from pp. 1236–38. Copyright 1931 by the Harvard Law Review Association. See also Karl N. Llewellyn, *The Common Law Tradition* (Boston: Little, Brown & Co., 1960).

societal needs and societal relationships. Hence, the premium on knowledge, on command of the social facts.[43]

Third, this perspective raises questions about the nature of political institutions, the locus of the power to make legal decisions, in short, about where and by what criteria legal rules are made and legal conflicts judged. Though the matter is certainly not solved this simply, there are pervasive majoritarian political implications in this attitude toward law. To say that disputes are to be decided in terms of a realistic view of social needs and relationships leaves open the question of which needs and the question how those needs are to be assayed. These questions can be answered in two ways, not necessarily mutually exclusive, and the new jurisprudence drew on both types of answers. In the first place, they can be answered from the Aristotelian –conservative position that institutions and policies which have flourished in a given society are representative of that society's persistent need patterns and preferred modes of problem solution. In its mildest application, this prescription may be interpreted as merely demanding respect for the "realities" of the social situation; in another range of application, it can yield a Burkean perspective which prescribes a politics controlled by the longer-run "organic" aspects of community life; in its extreme application, it may yield to the classic "force" position that "whatever is, is right."

The second answer to the questions posed above is that policy must be made and conflicts resolved in the final analysis by that institution most likely to reflect ongoing social needs accurately. From the perspective of the democratic tradition, informed by philosophical radicalism, that institution would be the legislature. For the legislature is seen by classical theory as a microcosmic representation of the pattern and interplay of interests in the community. It is the sounding board on which social needs are expected to make themselves heard. Insofar as jurisprudence frames its question in these terms, it tends to state a case for legislative supremacy, and in doing so, it comes to share an institutional perspective with analytic jurisprudence.

The new jurisprudence thus tended to make available a range of complementary and interchangeable orientations toward the institutions of the legal system. Describing one as dominant is as difficult as finding a satisfactory common label or assuming a common set of commitments. As Llewellyn's comments suggest, we are not dealing here

---

[43] From this viewpoint, social science might become an intimate contributor to judicial decision-making and to the legal process in general. See Victor G. Rosenblum, *Law as a Political Instrument* (New York: Random House, 1955).

with an integrated "school" but with an unintegrated "movement."
Its overall effect was to call attention to social needs and policy implications. More particularly, it prepared the ground for introduction
of new kinds of materials on social relationships into the process of
making legal decisions.

The impact of these new perspectives on jurisprudence has been
great and lasting, though they have neither driven competitive viewpoints from the field nor really dominated the American legal systems. They did clearly have detectable manifestations in the work of
the courts, particularly the Supreme Court of the United States. Here,
the effects were most obvious in the treatment of economic issues
such as those reviewed in the chapter on social Darwinism and in the
comments of the current chapter on the Brandeis brief. The reader
might be reminded again of the famous dissent of Mr. Justice Holmes
in the Lochner case. The import of Holmes' position was that it was
not up to the Court to impose absolute standards that it assumed to
render untenable the policy of the legislative body. The Court,
Holmes suggested, could not defensibly become the guardian of
property rights without regard to the social implications of those
rights or the wishes of the people expressed through legislative policy.
Thus, he would have honored the judgment of the New York legislature in passing the 10-hour law, and he opposed the Court's interposing itself to declare the policy invalid.

As we have already suggested, until the middle of the 1930's, this
position was most often unavailing on the high bench as far as economic matters were concerned. On occasion it prevailed, more often
it did not. It is dubious to say that with the ascendance of the Court's
liberal majority, in itself a very tentative thing, the new jurisprudence
became the Court's predominant position. However, it may be suggested that with the passing of the hegemony of the property-oriented
conservatives, the outcomes of the Court's conduct of its business
were more congenial to the sociological point of view. The expansion
of federal power, the development of commerce clause and tax clause,
the finding of ways to rationalize the development of protective and
regulatory legislation in the economic and social fields were products
of an approach to law sensitive to the needs of an expanding and interdependent "Great Society." Since the mid-1930's, the Court has
become much less inclined to interpose its power into economic regulations, and has accordingly tended to allow legislatures, both state
and federal, more freedom in dealing with economic relationships.
Thus, some commentators have felt that the Supreme Court has

virtually abdicated its participation in policy-making in these fields.

The Court's attitude toward its own power and its relationship with legislative policy can also be illustrated by reference to its treatment of civil liberties problems since about the time of the First World War. The best-known device in this field was the clear and present danger test first enunciated by Holmes in the Schenck case.[44] While the test can be seen as restrictive of legislative freedom to deal with threats to community stability, it may also be used as a legislative tool for restriction of rights. Thus, it has been applied so as to hold that if the legislature believes certain speech, press, religious, or assembly activities are clearly and presently threats to the stability and security of the society, it is free to deal with them without regard to the First Amendment protection. Clear and present danger, bad tendency, and clear and probable danger are tests of social effect or function. They are tests divorced from absolute standards of governmental behavior, tests framed in response to what some may think are the realities of the social situation. It is in the field of civil liberties that the sociologically oriented jurisprudence has been most effectively challenged in recent years and a new doctrine of absolutes developed. The new absolutism has been promoted, interestingly enough, by some of those on the Court most inclined to be permissive of government action in economic affairs, e.g., Rutledge, Murphy, Black, and Douglas.

The general tendency of pragmatic jurisprudence, in sum, has probably been to restrict the sphere of the Courts and to leave legislatures more freedom to deal with a wide range of social problems. This tendency was probably most consistently and profoundly represented on the Court in recent years by the leading inheritor of the Holmes tradition, Mr. Justice Frankfurter, who more than anything else may be noted for his propensity to respect and, therefore, to uphold legislative judgment on policy matters.[45] Thus, from his point of view as from others we have discussed in this chapter, community could be sought and change rationalized through dynamic social policy.

---

[44] *Schenck* v. *United States,* 249 U.S. 47 (1919). See above, pp. 135, 141, for discussion of Schenck and the clear and present danger doctrine.

[45] For commentary on Holmes, see Yosal Rogat, "Mr. Justice Holmes: a Dissenting Opinion," *Stanford Law Review,* Vol. XV (December, 1962), pp. 3–44; Vol. XV (March, 1963), pp. 254–308.

XII

AMERICAN THOUGHT AND INSTITUTIONS TODAY

It would be easy to end our account here and suggest that there has been no significant political thought in America from World War II forward. Other preoccupations, it might be suggested, have lured Americans away from political philosophy and left the nation content with the manipulation of symbols inherited from earlier times. There is doubtless some truth to this proposition, although it probably suffers from the myopia common in attempts to deal with contemporary ideas and events. We will not attempt to support or refute it at this point. In this chapter, we will be concerned with two things relevant to a broader consideration of the relationship between ideas and practice. One is the shape of the institutions, practices, and processes of American politics as they have developed out of the accumulated experience of the nation. The second is the interpretations and perspectives, the ideologies and "sciences" that are visible forces today in the intellectual setting of American political life.

THE PROBLEM SETTING OF AMERICAN POLITICS IN THE MIDDLE DECADES OF THE TWENTIETH CENTURY

It has been our premise throughout the foregoing analysis that there is a close relationship between the political thought of a given period and its context of social problems. In the contemporary world, the relevance of the social setting to modes of thought and action is overwhelming. It seems wise to take note, if only briefly, of some of the contextual elements that seem most influential in giving shape to political ideas and, in turn, to institutions and processes. We will not attempt to fill in the details, since these are familiar or thoroughly discussed elsewhere. All that is attempted here is to provide a general indication of the types of social forces that seem most influential and the direction of their influence.[1]

Easily the most apparent and probably the most important element in the problem setting of the American polity during this period has been the international situation. The presence of this factor needs no documentation or explanation. Like other major social forces, it is something that took shape over a long period of years but seemed to explode to crucial dimensions at about the opening of World War II. The story of American response to international forces in World War I and the subsequent retrenchment of isolationism in the 1920's is well known, as is the story of her reaction to international challenges in the hot war of the 1940's and the cold war of the late forties and the fifties and sixties. America conditioned herself over the course of this period to participate on the international scene. This entailed a revision of popular beliefs and an alteration of leadership postures, changes doubtless made easier by dramas of ideological confrontation and weaponry development. While on one level, the growth of an international system may appear to be no more than the product of ideological conflict and changes in the scale and techniques of warfare, these in themselves are but manifestations of the growth of a world society increasingly interdependent and, therefore, increasingly sensitive in all its reaches. The coming of "internationalism" has been not only a military but also a political, economic, and social phenomenon.

The impact of this phenomenon has extended to all reaches of American life. Politically, it has been felt in the specific demands it has put on policy and the allocation of resources, in its impact on the shape of institutions and policies, and indirectly through the conditioning to which it has subjected the culture and social structure. In the conditioning sense, the effects of the world's intrusion into the center of the American political scene can be summarized in the concepts of tension and involvement. Both at the level of individual behavior and at the level of institutions, American society

---

[1] The potential bibliography on American society and culture is as broad as the topic itself. Various aspects of the subject are touched by many volumes of scholarly and popular writings. In the circumstances, it is difficult to select a few for special reference. Among general sources, see Robin Williams, *American Society*, (rev. ed.; New York: A. A. Knopf, 1960); Max Lerner, *America as a Civilization* (New York: Simon and Schuster, 1957); David Reisman, *The Lonely Crowd* (New Haven: Yale University Press, 1950) is an interesting and widely read analysis of American society and American character. For statistical information, consult especially the annual editions of the *Statistical Abstract of the United States* and *Historical Statistics of the United States* (Washington, D.C.: Bureau of the Census, 1960).

shows deeply the imprint of threat, particularly the threat of nuclear war and of a seemingly inescapable entanglement in the affairs of a complex world. Thus, military considerations have helped make the world's problems in reality the problems of American society, as have enhanced communication and commercial intercourse. The subjective accommodation to change, both in political institutions and in individual attitudes, is manifest in a variety of kinds of evidence. This is not to say that tension and involvement have been met with rational or undifferentiated response, but only that an international situation has presented the American political society with forces which have made tension and involvement ever-present parts of the problem setting within which the American political system now functions. There seems to be little if any prospect that the tension level and problematic character of international relations will ever be eliminated, short of a nuclear catastrophe that would "solve" nearly all the problems of the human race.

A variety of other social forces of the past few decades have had direct effects on the political ideas and practices of contemporary American society. Among these, we might stress the interlaced effects of accelerating technological development, urbanization, and affluence. All these have been mentioned earlier for their impact on the American political structure, particularly with the development of industrial society in the late nineteenth century. With all three, the trends of earlier periods have continued at increasing rates.[2] Technological advancement has presented the political system with problems of regulation and control and with opportunities for heightened social and political interaction. In many cases, technology has forced the hand of the polity. The construction of the transcontinental railroad, for example, created the conditions for federal regulation that penetrates deep into the transportation system. The railroads fell under the regulation of the national government at an early date (1886) and were the beneficiaries of its promotional largesse even earlier. It is conceivable that a national railway network could function without the overall regulative hand of the national govern-

---

[2] One of the most suggestive works on the relationship of technology and social life is W. F. Cottrell, *Energy and Society* (New York: McGraw-Hill Book Co., Inc., 1955); see also Lerner, *op. cit.*, chap. 4. On economic considerations more generally, see J. Frederick Dewhurst and Associates, *America's Needs and Resources* (New York: Twentieth Century Fund, 1955); Editors of Fortune, *America in the Sixties: the Economy and the Society* (New York: Harper and Row, 1960). A very comprehensive treatment is Merle Fainsod, Lincoln Gordon, and J. C. Palamountain, Jr., *Government and the American Economy* (3d ed.; New York: W. W. Norton & Co., Inc., 1959), esp. chaps. 1 and 3.

ment. But it is unlikely that the development of competing transportation systems in a highly interdependent society could long remain free once growth was technically feasible.[3] It is even less likely that airborne transportation, given the logistical and safety problems involved, would not be the subject of federal regulatory activity, and it is almost unthinkable that a widespread network of radio and television communications could operate satisfactorily without some rationalization imposed by federal authority. In the last case, some aspects of effective regulation are now international rather than national in scale, technology thus pushing political response even beyond the limits of the national structure.

Examples of the pressures for regulation and control arising from the advance of means of production, distribution, and communication could be multiplied almost endlessly. Any reflection on the functions of government in the contemporary United States illustrates the point and suggests the breadth of political response. The political–social effects of advancing technology should not be seen, however, merely in terms of pressures for regulation. It is also reflected in a variety of secondary effects, including changes in the structure of dependency, heightened individual vulnerability to social and economic change, and the expansion of social opportunities. In gross terms, for example, the society has witnessed a shift from a predominantly agricultural work force to one much more heavily weighted toward industrial production activities. With automation and associated developments, a further rapid shift toward emphasis on professional and technical skills as well as distributive and service occupations is underway. Far-reaching effects on the political system must ensue from such social changes, for the horizons of men are broadened, the sites and types of their interactions are changed, and with complexity, their efforts to understand and control their environments become ever more difficult.

Many of the same effects and some of the same causes are associated with the urbanization of American society. In 1850, 15 percent of the American people lived in urban places; by 1900, this figure had grown to 40 percent; by 1960, to 70 percent.[4] Furthermore, within the urbanized category, a similar change has come about with the compacting of more people into small areas. According to the 1960

---

[3] See Joseph C. Palamountain, Jr., *The Politics of Distribution* (Cambridge: Harvard University Press, 1955).

[4] Bureau of the Census, *Statistical Abstract of the United States, 1963* (Washington, D.C.: U.S. Government Printing Office, 1963).

census, 61 percent of the American population lived in the 212 "standard metropolitan areas."[5] In that year, 70 percent of the American people lived in only 6 percent of the space. This urbanization in part illustrates the impact of new economic patterns, but it is also in itself important as a social phenomenon, for with the growth of the city come mass changes in life style, in the complexity of daily life, in types of services needed, and in types of problems faced.[6] The growth of the city itself has been a source of social problems and social outlooks that are characteristic of America in the middle of the twentieth century.

Another dimension of the contemporary American social situation is what has come to be called affluence, a term referring to the level and distribution of necessities and amenities in American society.[7] America has always been a nation of relative plenty, but particularly since the advent of the 1940's, the availability of goods and services to wide categories of the populace has been notable. Pockets of deprivation, of course, remain, particularly among the highly visible "new minorities." But statistics on such things as ownership of cars and houses, money spent on fringe and luxury items, and the growth and popularity of expensive diversions and recreations, suggest the extent to which affluence has run. One can only speculate on the sociopolitical effects of this phenomenon. One certain result, however, is change in the need–demand structure and consequent shifts in grounds for social tension. More specifically, economic opportunity has for many segments of the population become something to be taken for granted—an impossible attitude in an earlier period. With the scramble for opportunity allayed by relatively full employment at high levels of remuneration, attention is shifted to other matters, some of which may in themselves become sources of social friction. Thus, perhaps it is the development of the "affluent society" that has made possible sustained and more effective attempts to deal with interracial relations. The growth of affluence has probably also altered the position of such economic institutions as the trade union, as achievement has cast some of the unions' traditional aims and demands into obsolescence.

Thus, changes in the positions and relationships of both institu-

---

[5] *Loc. cit.*

[6] Scott Greer, *The Emerging City* (New York: Free Press, 1962); Editors of Fortune, *The Exploding Metropolis* (New York: Doubleday Anchor Books, 1958).

[7] J. K. Galbraith, *The Affluent Society* (Boston: Houghton Mifflin Co., 1958); David M. Potter, *People of Plenty: Economic Abundance and the American Character* (Chicago: University of Chicago Press, 1954).

tions and individuals in contemporary American society have had effects on the ideational and structural characteristics of the political system. As the distribution of resources and social power has changed, new problems have taken the place of old ones. The problems of war, peace, and defense, for example, have utterly changed shape in the last few years. In a subjective way, many of the ideological and theoretical components persist and will continue to persist, but the technological, economic, and political considerations surrounding relationships among nations have promoted the whole question to a primary and pervasive place. The same sort of movement of priorities has also gone on with what are usually called domestic issues. For example, in the sphere of economic relationships, the problems used to be almost problems of subsistence, now they are for the most part long-run problems of security. It is significant that trade unions' demands and collective bargaining in the 1950's have been more concerned with what are called "fringe benefits" than with wage levels themselves; that the 40-hour week is almost a universal achievement; and that insofar as hours of work are part of organized labor's goal, many unions now seek reduction far below the long-sought 40-hour standard.

What we are saying is that social change, in good part itself brought about by the redistributive effects of political power, has revised long-standing priorities on the social agenda. Some goals have been achieved, some problems have disappeared—as the problems of the industrial worker, for example, may "disappear" with the advance of automation—and new problems have arisen to take their places. New social tensions have also replaced old ones. Here, we may illustrate by reference to what is commonly called the race problem, which most commentators would identify as the primary source of internal disadjustment in the society today.[8] In many ways, the tensions that formerly surrounded economic relationships seem to have been transferred to relationships seen fundamentally in racial terms. The most dramatic and most divisive of domestic social issues in the past few years are those surrounding the movement to desegregate public schools and other public facilities as well as those to raise the level of Negro participation in the political process. The social tensions that now surround urbanization—the problems of the city—tend to restructure themselves as "race problems." Housing,

[8] On this subject, one is faced again with a flood of current literature. The classic work is Gunnar Myrdal, *An American Dilemma* (New York: Harper & Bros, 1944). Also Alan P. Grimes, *Equality in America: Religion, Race, and the Urban Majority* (New York: Oxford University Press, 1964).

levels of public service, and levels of political power, take their shapes from the presence in the city of large and growing numbers of the visible minority groups. Thus, where the distribution of values in the city setting was once a problem of tension between rich and poor, it now tends to be closely linked with race. It would be grossly in error, of course, to suggest that ethnicity has been irrelevant to the social and political structure of the American city in the past hundred years. What we are suggesting is that in terms of relative emphasis, ethnic relationships have become more prominent, and that at least to a degree, the character of social questions changes as the minorities of the city become more visible because of skin color and other physical attributes. It should be emphasized that on the contemporary American scene the race problem and economic problems are not inseparable. Indeed, there is reason to believe that many questions commonly identified with race are economic in root when they are looked at carefully. Our major point, however, is merely that new items have assumed new prominence on the agenda of important social problems, and race is one of the most pressing.

Our interest in the changed social setting of American politics runs basically in two directions—first, to its impact on political institutions and, second, to its impact on political thought. Here, as at most points in our analysis, it is much easier to assert relationships than to demonstrate cause and effect, and for the most part, we must be content with doing the first. For the present, it may be sufficient to say that the shifting character of the American society has imposed new demands on social thought both as analysis and as ideology. Just as established ways of doing things have been shaken to their roots by new technologies, so have established ways of understanding and structuring the world. The situation may be most clearly illustrated, perhaps, by reference to the country's relationship to the rest of the world. On the level of ideology, the American people have been "required" by the social situation to accustom themselves to the idea of their nation's living as an actor on the international scene, an actor whose role is of such proportion as to make even the smallest move vital to the course of international relations and perhaps to the survival of the human race. The American people have also been "required" to face the prospect of involvement as combatants in a new kind of war that may be precipitated and perhaps finished in little more than a moment, and to adjust to the identification of new friends and new enemies, sometimes over short periods of time. On the level of analytic social thought, similar new requirements are imposed and the adequacies of old frameworks questioned. Such concepts as power, bipolarization, coexistence, and deterrence enter the vocabulary of those whose function it is to try to make an orderly intellectual structure out of what sometimes seems to be chaos. Whether these demands on ideas are being met adequately is a matter of application of standards of judgment. It is at least clear that the demands are high. Description, explanation, understanding, or evaluation—it may be doubted whether traditional formulations are adequate to the task and whether new concepts and theories have developed at the pace of the changing social world.

The preceding paragraphs suggest that this is a highly sensitive, interdependent, and changing scene. They suggest, as many aspects of daily life must suggest, that this is a highly different setting from that of a few years ago, though some of the outward appearances might induce one to think otherwise. Problems of loyalty, freedom, and community, for example, force themselves on the attention of those who must or who choose to think about sociopolitical conditions; to a degree they even force themselves on the minds of all men. Perhaps in part because of the tendency to cling to established ways of understanding the world, perhaps in part because of the very technical difficulty of the task, social thought at best responds only slowly and partially to the world with which it deals. Consider, for example, the new demands put on the concept of community. Community traditionally has referred not only to a space but to a space in which meaningful social and political interaction took place. The community, in other words, was both a site of common residence and a political–social thing based on propinquity and common interests. With expanding social scale, the basis of community has changed and perhaps even disappeared. It may be suggested, for example, that what was formerly a community is no longer a basis for meaningful or important interaction and that much of life that once went on in limited space now knows no geographic confines. Whether old concepts about the fundamental importance of community to political life are any longer relevant or, if they are, what problems for political life are posed by empirical changes in community are kinds of questions that social thought must face if it is to "keep up with the world."

THE CONDITION OF AMERICAN POLITICAL INSTITUTIONS

Our approach has assumed that institutions and political structure both reflect and condition social thought. It seems wise at this point, therefore, to offer a summary sketch of the present situation of American political institutions. Since institutional change has been a major focus of our entire discussion, it seems unnecessary, even if possible, to offer any but the briefest comment on the subject at this point. As we do so, it should be kept in mind that our interests are both general and directed to relationships between the three broad variables of social structure, institutions, and ideas.

Before we proceed to the discussion of structures and processes, we might take passing note of the breadth of governmental activity in present-day America. Since 1900, and particularly since the early 1930's, the functional role of American political power has spread in dramatic fashion; vastly more things are now done under political authority than was formerly the case. Thinking back to the Hamiltonian economic programs, it is difficult to put any historical limits on the functional expansion of governmental activity. One of the most significant thrusts toward expansion of function came with the growth of public enterprise in elementary, secondary, and higher educational systems.[9] Beyond education, probably the most notable expansions of government power have occurred in the fields of welfare, economic regulation, and defense. In all of these fields, government has acted through a variety of structural mechanisms to fill functional vacuums. Many were initiated during periods of social crisis, particularly depressions and wars, and inertia combined with prolonged and newly discovered needs has tended to sustain governmental activities in fields opened during periods of crisis. These activities have not ordinarily been maintained at crisis levels or in crisis styles, but often they have been maintained. On such problems as labor relations and housing, for example, where both the Great Depression and World War II stimulated public authority, policy has changed content but the subjects continued to be considered appropriate ones for governmental action. Except in the case of the purely defense functions, and perhaps even to some extent there, the role of crisis has ordinarily been to intensify and call to attention frictions and disadjustments that have long existed in the society.

The major point is that such items now are "assumed" to have an appropriate place on the agenda for public action. Both in particular and in general, the functional orientation of American government has come to be active rather than passive. Governmental "intervention," not its converse, is what is expected, and policy-makers are

---

[9] For a history of American education, see Lawrence A. Cremin, *The Transformation of the School* (New York: A. A. Knopf, 1961).

sensitive to these expectations. The history of the Eisenhower administration in this respect is enlightening. General Eisenhower came into the presidential office proclaiming that the activities of the national government must be contracted. Except in minor ways, they were not. Total federal expenditures grew, as did federal expenditures for many specific programs—for example, grants-in-aid to state and local governments. The Social Security program was expanded, and government intervention in labor–management relations penetrated deeper than it ever had during periods of peace. While the pace of expansion of government activities doubtless slackened during the period, modest expansion and little contraction were its general characteristics. Thus, even with the change of party in control of the executive, policy tended to retain the floor already established, even if not all the furniture was preserved. Consideration of the condition of American public policy suggests at least that, objectively speaking, American government now operates at a very high level of functional activity, however we might speculate about the underlying causes. This is not to insist on the inevitability of maintaining policy activism at its present level, though such a hypothesis is not in itself implausible (although literally, of course, inevitability cannot be tested). The difficulties of reversing the process and moving to lower levels of policy activity are patently immense, perhaps even insurmountable, given the condition of the society and the self-sustaining propensities of organization.

On the matter of distribution of governmental functions and powers as distinguished from their scope, the general outline of the contemporary situation is likewise familiar. The question is really two; it pertains both to distribution among levels of government and to distribution among the functional elements within various governments. Classically, the first problem is the problem of federalism, which we have broached several times before. In general terms, expansion of federal power has been disproportionate to expansion of state and local governmental power, and thus the power of the national government has gained relatively.[10] Some of this expansion has occurred in fields where no political activity had been exercised. In others, the power of the national government has expanded at the expense of state power, the national government's moving into fields—for example, the regulation of child labor—where state power

---

[10] Among works on federalism in the United States, see esp. Commission on Intergovernmental Relations, *A Report to the President for Transmittal to the Congress* (Washington, D.C.; U.S. Government Printing Office, 1955).

had acted before. In such cases, a kind of preemption has occurred, sometimes enforced by the courts and sometimes the practical result of substantive federal programs. In other fields, state and federal power coexists in dual or cooperative arrangements, without either being shut out of the functional picture. There is little room for doubt, however, that the most important single fact here has been the broadened role of national authority.

Thus, the substance of federalism in the United States has undergone very substantial change. Programs that once were the causes of great controversy on the federal level have now come to be accepted in almost routine fashion as subjects of federal activity, and the most controversial problems of federalism today are not those of yesterday. Whereas in former periods, particularly from the 1890's to World War II, these controversies centered around the distribution of power over economic affairs, they now tend to involve problems of civil rights and political relationships such as segregation in public facilities, voting, and legislative apportionment. That is to say, these, along with the ideologically unique function of education, form the substance of the current controversy about the proper extent of federal activity. Hence, the advancement of federal power continues, neither steadily nor inevitably, but haltingly and pragmatically, as relationships in some fields come to be regarded as settled and new problems move up the agenda and gain federal priority. In a very gross way, the phenomena we have been describing here can readily be explained as products of the recent social forces described above —heightened international tension, increase in social scale, and relative decline in economic deprivation and tension.

These phenomena can be treated in terms of the concept of community. With the growth in scale, meaningful social interaction tends to move to broader geographic grounds, particularly as means of rapid transportation and communication are improved. One of the consequences has been the shifting of social problems to higher levels when these come to be problems appropriate for political action. Thus, the level of "community" is shifted with respect to social loyalty, attention, and expectations, and as to positive manifestations in the exercise of political power. In a sense, America has moved ever further toward the tightening of the long-developing national community.

In a peculiar way, the states have been caught in the middle of this movement of functions. As we pointed out before, state power has undergone absolute growth but relative decline. More important in many respects, it has suffered a kind of obsolescence and disjunction from the most crucial problems of the day. In part this may be traced to the rural focus of many state institutions and functions, in part to the ineffectiveness of those institutions themselves. In another part, it may be laid to the forces which keep local government alive and strong: the considerable American ideological attachment to the idea of locality, and the immediacy to locality of the social and economic problems of the complex society. The state, in other words, seems to be lost in a world that is internationalizing on the one hand and urbanizing on the other hand. This picture of state government is, without doubt, unduly one-sided. State functions continue to be important and state problems real, as do the problems of the nonmetropolitan areas of America. However, in many of its functions, the state seems to be playing increasingly an agent's role, either as agent for national power or as agent for local demands. This is spectacularly true with respect to the three largest objects of state expenditure—highways, education, and public welfare. Even politically, it may be suggested, the state's power has come to be such that it can mainly be troublemaker rather than veto power or initiator in vital public areas.

Because of the uneven diffusion of problems and political responses, it is both difficult and dangerous to generalize about the condition of American local government. The prime phenomena have already been mentioned: urbanization, the concentration of population, technical and social complexity, and the growth of the metropolitan area. In many ways, the problem of local government in the United States has come to rest with its inability to keep up with the pace of social and physical change. In the blooming metropolitan area, for example, the established patterns of political power have in many ways been irrelevant to or inadequate to developing social needs. The difficulties of political change are borne home as problems lop over political boundaries and growth splashes haphazardly ahead.[11] Certainly, the modes of political power at the local level have undergone revision, as have institutions of authority. The presumed decline of the old-type political machine and the development of the city manager plan are two of the most notable changes. What has been said here is not meant to suggest that the political "solution" for the problems created by the

---

[11] Scott Greer, *Governing the Metropolis* (New York: John Wiley & Sons, Inc., 1962); Raymond Vernon, *Metropolis 1985* (Cambridge: Harvard University Press, 1960); Robert C. Wood, *1400 Governments* (Cambridge: Harvard University Press, 1961); David W. Minar and Scott Greer, "Metropolis and Its Problems," in J. W. Peltason (ed.), *American Government Annual: 1963–1964* (New York: Holt, Rinehart, and Winston, 1963), pp. 106–30.

metropolitan phenomenon are of a certain type. Political integration through "metro," for example, is only one of a range of possible alternatives for dealing with the politics of the metropolis.[12] The point is that the sociopolitical problems of local government today are overwhelming and in some cases actually seem to have overwhelmed established political practices.

We may now turn to relationships among the "functional" institutions of government, that is to say, relationships among executive, legislative, and judicial branches on a single governmental level. For this purpose, our focus will fall mainly on the condition of the national government, although many of the problems and developments are shared by American government at state and local levels. As in our discussion of the federal system just completed, our interest here is substantially in the relative distribution of power and functions among institutions. Practically, however, we will focus on the questions concerning who seems to have the initiative in national affairs and why. The discussion of initiative should yield us a gross assessment of the condition of institutions on the contemporary scene.

The basic tendency in the distribution of initiative in American national government would seem to have been the gradual and relative enhancement of the position of the Presidency. If the trend were described graphically, it would take the form of a wavering line whose general direction of movement is upward, the relative power of the President being the area below the curve, the power of Congress the area above. In other words, while there have been fluctuations of development, the power of the President over the long term has gained. A plausible argument can also be made that given the conditions of the twentieth century, in all likelihood the curve will not again descend very far, for the social and political situation is now such that decline in presidential initiative seems highly unlikely.[13]

The sources of change that have led to this redistribution are many, but four factors appear to have been central. One is the high priority and persistent intrusion of foreign affairs in the contemporary world. The President has historically been recognized as the nation's leader in foreign relations. With the Great Wars, the cold war, the development of the system of free world alliances, the pressures of develop-

---

[12] Scott Greer, *Metropolitics* (New York: John Wiley & Sons, Inc., 1963).

[13] On the Presidency generally, see Richard Neustadt, *Presidential Power: the Politics of Leadership* (New York: John Wiley & Sons, Inc., 1960); Clinton Rossiter, *The American Presidency* (New York: Harcourt, Brace Co., 1956); E. S. Corwin, *The President: Office and Powers* (4th ed.; New York: New York University Press, 1957). For history, see Wilfred Binkley, *The Man in the White House* (New York: A. A. Knopf, 1959).

ment in formerly colonial areas, and other aspects of persistent international interaction, this function has assumed ever greater proportions in the overall picture of power in the American government. The hegemony of international affairs is illustrated in the budget, where the defense factor alone accounts for more than half the total while other expenditures related to international interaction add a further substantial piece. Although the Congress is not entirely excluded from participation in the conduct of foreign policy, the role of the executive branch in the total picture is heightened by the necessities of constant attention to relations with other parts of the world.

The second factor is the advantage of the executive in commanding expertise. With the growth of an ever more complex world and with government performing ever more complex functions, the ability to understand and articulate social, economic, and technological phenomena is crucial to the ability to propose and control public policy. The very nature of the executive branch as the employer of more than 2 million people makes it a more likely repository of these abilities than the Congress. While in some sense the bureaucracy is in the employ of the Congress as well as the executive, the President has the advantage of immediate command and coordination. Thus, the initiative in developing programs to keep up with the world is more likely to lie with the President than with the Congress. Furthermore, it may be suggested that to a degree the mode of selection of the President is more likely to yield a man more representative of the broad panoply of forces at work in the contemporary world, for congressmen at least in part represent local and factional interests whose composite is not necessarily representative of the overall thrust of society. This very relationship is in itself an argument for the separation of powers, but it does, at the same time, suggest causes of executive advantage.

The third factor conducing to the advantage of the Presidency is its inbuilt unity and cohesion as well as the initiative that unity is likely to yield. Over the past few years, students of public administration have been inclined to emphasize unity in the executive as a high-priority structural goal. It is, however, not only a goal but also a fact with empirical implications. The unity of command and purpose on which the President may draw would seem to equip him with many of the attributes of organizational success unavailable to a Congress in which, by necessity, structure is loose and authority is dispersed. The ways in which the President takes advantage of the unity of his office are, to be sure, affected by his own personality, style, the demands of the time, and his political situation, but recent Presidents have without exception capitalized in one way or another on this factor. The President thus has at his command a variety of tools, formal, informal, and political, that he may use in varying degrees and varying combinations to make advantage out of the peculiar situation and power of his office and the institution he heads. The fourth factor in the accretion of greater power to the Presidency is the personality contribution of some of the office's past occupants. Without drawing on a "personality theory" of politics, it seems plain that the succession of politically active and often astute men who have held the Presidency in recent years has left much with the institution. The styles, tools, and attitudes developed by Jefferson, Jackson, Lincoln, the Roosevelts, and some others in the White House have in many ways been bequeathed to the use of successors for the tasks of policy development and direction.[14]

Thus, the American Presidency is now an office of institutionalized leadership and initiative. This development may pose a threat to some established values; it has also been a weapon of political warfare. From the standpoint of explanation and analysis, however, it is more vital to understand the extent to which social pressures have brought it about. To a considerable degree, the position of the President is such that he must do most of what he does, because problems refuse to disappear and cannot be handled by default. In many fields, the exercise of presidential power once thought extraordinary has become expected and routine. Witness, for example, the President's role as economic reporter and planner for the nation, developed in good part for the executive in the 1930's and now required by the terms of the Full Employment Act of 1946. Even a Whiggish President cannot pretend that such responsibilities do not exist. The powers and patterns of authority that have developed around the President, of course, are by no means fixed. Each of the recent Presidents has changed the character of his office to suit particular needs and tastes. But these changes chiefly reflect ways of meeting problems; the problems themselves persist, as does the ever-elaborating network of expectations and roles into which a President is thrust.[15]

Much of what may be said about the Congress is implicit in the foregoing discussion of the Presidency.[16] In view of the broad develop-

---

[14] See Rossiter, *op. cit.*, pp. 142–81.

[15] Cf. Neustadt, *op. cit.*, esp. pp. 5–8.

[16] On Congress generally, see Roland Young, *The American Congress* (New York: Harper & Bros., 1958).

ment of national power, it is probably rather meaningless to say that the powers of Congress have declined in any absolute terms, for, indeed, every exercise of presidential power is heavily conditioned by the attitudes and relationships of the legislative branch. At the same time, the role of Congress has undergone changes in substance. In most circumstances, its initiative in the large and vital fields of national action is slight. In foreign affairs, defense, and fiscal matters, in economic problems, and to a fair extent in the fields of welfare and civil rights, the executive branch has assumed the role of prime initiator.

Individually, congressmen still serve as ambassadors and mediators for their constituencies and constituency interests. The collective role of Congress, its general role in the structure of national government, would seem to fall into two parts—that of validator and that of watchdog. As validator, Congress grants or withholds its approval of the policy that comes to it in the form of legislation and presidential appointments. Congress must put its stamp of officiality on many kinds of governmental acts. The exercise of this authority gives Congress a sort of veto over much of the policy that emanates from the executive branch. Its existence impels the President to take account of congressional power, even in those fields where direct validation is not formally required, as in, for example, some acts in the field of foreign negotiations. Thus, the Congress is in a bargaining position, with validation as its final tool but with powers somewhat broader than the term validation may suggest. The power to appropriate or withhold money is probably the key to much of the effectiveness of Congress' validating role. More than ever before, national policy is dependent on a supply of funds; more things cost more money than ever before. For this reason, the President is heavily dependent on Congress' willingness to appropriate the moneys his program requires, and the appropriation power is a constant leverage on executive activity. This power has historically been a chief weapon in the arsenal of legislative bodies.

Congress' role as watchdog is also a historically important aspect of the legislative function. In this role, the Congress checks on the execution of laws and the spending of public funds by the bureaucracy, using its investigative power, its impact on public opinion, and the leverage of its validation power and power of the purse as sanctions. This is probably the most important and effective tool the legislative body exercises in this day of bureaucratic complexity and executive initiative. The Congress is also in a position to serve as watcher over the condition of the nation, to identify needs and political demands and place them on the public agenda. The extensive and often spectacular use of investigating committees in recent years helps illustrate the magnitude of this congressional role. It should also be noted, however, that though Congress has improved its techniques for fiscal control, most students of the subject still seem to regard these as wanting.

This is perhaps the appropriate place to mention the very important functions of the administrative agencies in American national government, particularly those so-called independent commissions with regulatory responsibilities in economic fields. These are the product of the advancing technology of the past 75 years and the growing disposition of the American people to seek government intervention in the adjustment of economic relationships. Some of them are direct outgrowths of the Progressive era. We will not attempt to deal here with the many problems of procedure and organization that surround the exercise of the regulatory functions. It should be noted, however, that in rule-making and adjudication the discretion of the agencies is broad and they have primary responsibilities in many of the most important phases of governmental activity. These agencies, with their peculiar relationships both to Congress and to the executive branch, pose unique problems in public responsibility, control, and clientele relationships, problems of both empirical and normative sorts.

As a final item in this discussion of distribution of functions and powers, we will turn to the role of the courts in the governmental system. The subject is a very complex one, difficult to deal with despite the fact that the courts are self-conscious and systematically articulate about the roles they play and the actions that grow out of them. The massive body of legal literature as well as the evidence of written opinions provide perspectives on what the courts are doing when they exercise their "judicial" functions. Traditions of legal scholarship are such, however, that these sources do not by any means provide clear and unexceptionable interpretations of role. Differences of opinion are many, and there is much tendency, perhaps more than elsewhere, for prescription and description to merge and positions to be clouded. What follows is not in any way intended to be more than a review of some of the questions that can be asked about the subject.

One point on which there is a fair measure of agreement is that the focus of the courts' work, and especially the work of the Supreme Court in judicial review, has shifted considerably in the period of the past 50 years. Where once most of the notable conflicts that came before the high Court were economic in substance, a greater proportion of its business now involves individual civil, political, and procedural rights. Thus, in considerable extent the Court has read itself out of the function of adjusting economic relationships. A moment's reflection will suggest that this change is in itself a reflection of a change in the outlook of the society on political issues. As the courts came to look more kindly on the exercise of federal and state power for economic control, they progressively narrowed the area open to litigation in this field. The enormous scope now conceded to the commerce power, for example, restricts the ability of interests to claim that a given regulation falls beyond the legitimate scope of national authority. Thus, the courts, by their own doctrine and under social and political pressure, have left behind a subject matter that once provided its most notable and controversial business.

Meanwhile, as economic relationships have become more settled, social tensions have shifted into other fields, and these have come to preempt the attention of the judiciary as they have the attentions of the other branches of government. The most spectacular are the fields of race relations and/or relationships between individual rights and subversive activities. Such matters as the right to vote and legislative apportionment have also been more notably subject to court attention in recent years. The point is not to be seen so much in terms of the volume of court activity as it is in terms of the significant areas of decision, that is to say, those areas where court decisions have altered existing relationships in important ways.

Another aspect of the same set of problems is the function of the courts among the organs of government. This is a question with deep-running normative and political implications. It is also a question with which we have dealt several times at earlier points in our account, and for this reason we will attempt only to touch its more general aspects here. The major questions are what contributions the courts do and should make to the American political process.

In substance, responses to this problem from both legal scholarship and the bench itself continue to draw heavily on long-established traditions. Thus, differences of opinion continue to flourish, particularly on the normative side, falling along a continuum running from those who would have the Court be a more active participant in policy-making to those who would have it be less.[17] There are, too, those who would have the Court differentiate its functions according to the type of business before it.

Three principal points of view, by now familiar, merit our sum-

---

[17] See the discussions of judicial power in chaps. 4 and 11, above.

mary attention. One is the position that the courts should restrict themselves, as far as participation in the policy process is concerned, to examination of the procedures by which policy is made and carried out by the other branches. This position is close to that of Mr. Justice Holmes, and its most articulate devotee in recent years has been Mr. Justice Frankfurter. Its major premise is the majoritarian democratic prescription that policy should be settled by those directly responsible to the people through electoral processes. Thus, its result is legislative supremacy as far as the substance of decisions is concerned, accompanied by a corollary judicial self-restraint.

At the other extreme is the position that it is the proper role of the Court to participate actively in the policy process by making judgments guided by its own insights into the nature of civic morality. This activist viewpoint is based ultimately on assumptions about the absolute nature of goodness and the peculiar fitness of the judicial system to discover and apply it. Hence, it affords a basis on which the courts have cut down actions of legislative and executive bodies on all levels of government. The substantive results of the activist position vary with the predominant ideology of the Court, as we have already had occasion to observe. At some points, they have been manifested in decisions striking down the use of state and national power in the welfare and economic fields, as during the era of Darwinian individualism. More recently, they have led to the use of Court power on behalf of civil liberties, particularly during the late 1930's and 1950's.

Between these two positions one finds another, this placing its emphasis on "balance," i.e., on the role of the courts as seekers of balance in public policy. This position, too, has found favor in some civil liberties litigations of recent years. In these, the Court has often spoken of its efforts to find a balance between the claims of the individual to freedom of thought and action and the claims of the community to stability and security. In a sense, the Court as balancer sees itself as mediating among the various centers of power in a pluralistic world. In another sense, it attempts to mediate between the absolute ideas of natural law and the relativistic ideas of majoritarianism. The strengths of this point of view would seem also to be its weaknesses. It comes to appear to see moderation as an end in itself. While it seeks the appealing middle ground, it does not offer very firm guidelines for the development of future policy; it casts the Court in the role of conservator and provides but little for innovation.

Despite persistent attacks on their role and some of their substantive decisions, particularly from the far right of American politics, the courts—especially the high Court—have continued to exercise substantial power in the policy process. In such vital fields as civil rights they have often (e.g., in matters of voting and segregation in public facilities) led the legislative and executive branches in creating policy in response to social change. In general terms, it may be suggested that though its participation is circumscribed by institutional characteristics and by tradition, the judiciary is now and probably always has been an active political force in the American system. Despite the various claims that it is an organ of deliberation on a plane above politics, the political quality of its work seems unquestionable.[18]

One final comment on contemporary institutions concerns the American political party. At various points above, the politico-constitutional role of parties in the system has been mentioned. The parties continue, haltingly, to fulfill functions as mobilizers of interests, channels of communication, and links among the diverse structures of American government. Whatever descriptive terms might be applied to them, they persist in their loose, ideologically incoherent way, yet they persist in contributing in important ways to binding the system together. The parties as institutions can hardly be thought to have changed much, even through the social and political trauma of the Great Depression. Their "condition" remains diffuse and irresponsible, despite occasional outbursts of reform. Their presence on the scene probably has little to do with innovation, much to do with stability, and everything to do with democratic choice in the American political scene.

THE IDEOLOGIES OF AMERICAN POLITICS: CONTEMPORARY LIBERALISM AND CONSERVATISM

Having sketched a general picture of the condition of American society and its political institutions, we may now turn to the social thought of the contemporary period. What sorts of political ideas have come out of the social situation described above? In what ways have political problems stimulated intellectual response? What impacts on institutions and policy have new modes of thought had? Some answers to such questions may be found by taking stock of the ideologies of American politics. The treatment of this subject so traditionally revolves around the symbols of conservatism and liberalism that we may fruitfully use these as focal points for our discussion.

The problem is, however, far from an easy one to treat, and we

---

[18] Victor G. Rosenblum, *Law as a Political Instrument* (New York: Random House, 1955).

should probably begin by entering some caveats, qualifications, and explanations. We face, for one thing, the general difficulty of treating objectively the world of ideas in which we live, a world that inevitably takes on value-loading for anyone in it. Not only our bias but the narrow range of our vision makes it hard for us to give our intellectual environment adequate treatment. Hence, we must approach the task with substantial reservations that grow out of the very nature of what we are trying to do.

One supposed corrective to these failures of objectivity and perspective—one sometimes used in commentaries on current thought—is to treat everything equally. Hence, one might, confronted with the task at hand, undertake to touch the entire range of relevant literature. The problems with this approach are quite obvious. Not only does it pose an almost impossible burden of volume of material, it also mixes the significant with the insignificant. Thus, unless it is to be interminable, such a discussion is likely to take on the characteristics of rather indiscriminate name-dropping. Since our aim heretofore has been to select by the criterion of contribution to the shaping of an action-related tradition of ideas, such a procedure hardly seems satisfactory. What follows will be, instead, a selective and impressionistic discussion of the general outlines of political thought in America today. It is presented as a set of cues and propositions, not as a comprehensive report on the state of American ideology.

Speaking first in general terms, the most notable aspect of the situation is perhaps the barrenness of political ideology in America today.[19] Probably no literate culture is without its public pronouncements of political ideas; America is certainly not an exception to this rule. But on a scale of originality, or one of notability, or one of rhetorical power, there is little of significance in the nation's recent ideological product. Such an observation is, to be sure, highly judgmental and impossible to verify. But because we are dealing here with the present and near-present, it is a judgment that can be checked against the reader's own experience and impression. What we are suggesting is simply that there has been nothing interesting contributed to the ideological dimension of the American political tradition since pragmatism.

The causes of this situation can be treated only casually, for they scarcely present the ingredients for systematic empirical proof. It may be proposed, however, that it reflects the demands put on the Ameri-

---

[19] On a similar theme, see the "Epilogue" in Daniel Bell, *The End of Ideology* (Glencoe, Ill.: The Free Press, 1960), pp. 369–75.

can intellect during the recent period, the distribution of societal values, and the heritage of solid, durable traditions and institutions. Much has been written along these lines; there seems no need to retrace them in detail. The crux condition would seem to be a period of affluence since World War II that despite threats from abroad has given the society the "feel" of stability. Attention has gone to technological development, an aspect of "way of life" given tremendous impetus by the technical demands of war. Social action has been directed mainly toward cleaning up pockets of deprivation left over from depression days and detected by New Deal standards. Hence, the stimulus to and the valuation of social thought have been slight, except, as we shall have occasion to observe below, for the development of technically inspired social science. In a sense, then, it is technology that has diverted the culture from ideology, and, fittingly enough, it is technology that will bring us our next ideological crisis. But that, too, is a matter for further discussion at a later point.

Two aspects of the postwar situation might have been expected to modify the effect; these are the cold war challenge and the ferment in race relations. Neither, however, has had the impact of forcing creativity in political ideas. The external threat posed by the cold war, the spread of communism, and the development of nationalism has destroyed established systems of expectation. These are, nonetheless, movements that have inspired as much contraction as innovation in American outlooks. The defensive posture into which changes in the world have cast the nation has had the general effect of throwing it back on its established and internalized values and perspectives. Insofar as that is not true, the changes have been easy to accommodate within preexisting ideological frames of reference. The spreading of an "internationalist" point of view to certain segments of American society, for example, need not take one far from the rationalist themes of eighteenth-century thought that have never been lost to the American tradition.

The case of race relations is somewhat different, but with similar overall results. The pressure exerted in this instance is a pressure clearly bringing about institutional reforms. Its ideological appeal, however, except at the extreme fringes, is an appeal for the reassertion and instrumentalization of long-established and fundamental values—equality, liberty, and democracy. As in the Jacksonian movement for democratization and in abolitionism, the symbols involved are largely those long ago received by the system in a formal way. There is no doubt that changes in individual values of a fundamental sort are required in the situation; the point is that the rationalization for such changes is ready-made in the culture. This is not to argue that the process of change in race relations is in any way simple. It is traumatic to many of the individuals, groups, and institutions involved. It requires, as some of the work of James Baldwin suggests, a rethinking of many of the deepest questions of meaning.[20] Still, as a public problem it does not evoke new basic symbols but questions people's relationships to the old ones.

Thus, if our estimate and analysis of the situation are correct, even these most extraordinary pressures of the postwar period have not excited the production of new political ideas. This observation suggests something about the condition of contemporary liberalism and conservatism. These continue, at least in degree, to be symbols around which pictures of the political world are commonly organized, and in an individual sense, they are widely supposed to describe "real" commitments (e.g., party-free commitments) to meaningful ideological positions. It is commonplace, however, to comment that liberalism and conservatism are less than distinct nowadays; from this popular doubt, one may move to more sophisticated analysis of philosophy and polemic. The results, however, seem likely to be much the same: Liberalism and conservatism today are both confused by and bound to outmoded pasts. At that, their situation merits some slightly fuller exploration.

The initial difficulty in discussing today's liberalism is the difficulty of identifying its spokesmen. This is not to say, of course, that there are no liberals in America; quite the contrary, it may be the very popularity of liberalism that makes it look diluted and diffuse. Among figures active in public life, liberals abound, if one is to take self-identification as the criterion of ideological commitment. Philosophical or semi-philosophical statements of liberal doctrine, however, are surprisingly rare. Thus, it seems deceptive to attach the liberal label to any single person or group of persons or piece of writing.[21]

Some of the causes of this situation have been suggested above, but others more particular to liberalism may be added. The liberalism of the current period seems to be largely a holdover from the days of

[20] See esp. *The Fire Next Time* (New York: The Dial Press, Inc., 1963).

[21] Among recent works of a liberal orientation, see James Roosevelt (ed.), *The Liberal Papers* (Garden City, N.Y.: Doubleday Anchor Books, 1962); Arthur M. Schlesinger, Jr., *The Vital Center: the Politics of Freedom* (Boston: Houghton Mifflin Co., 1949). Commentaries include Louis Hartz, *The Liberal Tradition in America* (New York: Harcourt, Brace & Co., 1955); J. Roland Pennock, *Liberal Democracy: Its Merits and Prospects* (New York: Rinehart & Co., Inc., 1950); Arthur A. Ekrich, Jr., *The Decline of American Liberalism* (New York: Longmans, Green & Co., Inc., 1955).

the New Deal, both in aim and to considerable degree in personnel. At the same time, the needs of the age are not the needs of the depression era. By no means are all social problems solved. Pockets of deprivation remain; unemployment persists; internal freedom is not entirely secure; human equality is far from complete realization. Yet the character and magnitude of these difficulties are not the same as they were three decades ago. Hence, it may be proposed that liberalism has lost much of its cutting edge as the goals to which it was directed have slipped away from under it. Furthermore, the New Deal itself was sufficiently pragmatic, at least in a loose sense of the term, that its tradition has more to do with specific aims and general postures than with an integrated approach to politics. Despite the claims of its adherents and detractors, the heritage of Franklin Roosevelt provides less than a coherent guide to political thought and action.

The situation of liberalism is further confused by the long-term doctrinal ambivalence of its own tradition. A typical undergraduate reaction today is to ask what liberalism and conservatism "really are." The question itself may be epistemologically pointless, but it reveals a quite understandable confusion induced by the equivocal histories of the terms. Liberalism has probably been most clearly identified throughout the modern period with the view that the individual person is both morally and empirically prior to all other social entities. It is in this sense that Machiavelli, Hobbes, and Locke developed systems of ideas that distinguished modern liberalism from the organicism of the Middle Ages; indeed, it is in the development of this idea that liberalism became the distinctively modern perspective on social life and social morality.

Two periods of "revision," however, have obscured many of the implications of the doctrine. One came with the blooming of democracy as a political form, particularly at the time of the French Revolution.[22] While democracy has usually been identified with liberalism, mass democracy may have quite illiberal implications. Majority rule, the crux democratic idea, is at least not identical with the notion of the priority of the individual, as the political theory of Rousseau may be seen to reveal. The point is not that democracy and liberalism are antithetical, but that democracy does not necessarily imply liberalism. This is one of the main premises of Tocqueville's concern with the consequences of democratic institutions. The resultant for ideology has been a large

---

[22] See esp. Guido de Ruggiero, *The History of European Liberalism*, trans. R. G. Collingwood (Boston: Beacon Press, 1959); J. Talmon, *The Origins of Totalitarian Democracy* (London: Secker and Warburg, 1952).

measure of uncertainty about what is liberal and what is not liberal.

A second development that has worked against clarity in the liberal symbol came out of doctrinal divisions over the implications of liberalism for public policy. The split over these problems grew in the nineteenth century, particularly taking shape in the development of English liberalism around laissez faire on the one hand and welfare policy on the other. The question of the policy that ethical individualism requires is nowhere more clearly revealed than in the divergence between the Spencer–Sumner position and the position of its detractors. Put in simple terms, the problem is whether the well-being of the individual is to be sought by letting him alone to make his own way as he will or by supporting and assisting him through common social action. Adherents of both points of view lay claim to the liberal title today. Thus, the same label is used by those who defend the welfare state and by some of its most vehement enemies.

In this way, liberalism of all sorts is troubled by the seemingly contrary pulls of responsibility to individual and community, by the divergent demands of absolute adherence to the doctrine of individual integrity and the needs and potentials of the common life. Answers have been sought through attempts to separate economic concerns from concerns for personal liberty of action in other spheres, as in the "preferred position" accorded Bill of Rights freedoms.[23] They have also been sought in the ideas of pluralism, in the position that essential freedom is to be found in the maintenance of a society of institutionalized diversity. The freedom that has flourished in America is probably to be explained in the juxtaposition of points of view, and in the operation of institutions which have encouraged their interplay. Still, one result, whether good or ill, has been the frustration of liberalism as a clearly defined symbol for ideological attachment.

Turning to today's American conservatism, one confronts a similar but not identical situation. There is considerable ambivalence and discrepancy of view among the many people in the contemporary society who think of themselves as conservatives. Generally speaking, however, there is probably more focus and identity here than on the liberal side of the spectrum.[24] Since the Second World War, conservatism has undergone an interesting if not spectacular revival, and a substantial number of people and publications have participated in efforts to refurbish the conservative image. Though there may not be a unique

---

[23] See above, chap. 4, p. 146.

[24] See the interesting comments on this question by Frank S. Meyer in Frank S. Meyer (ed.), *What Is Conservatism?* (New York: Holt, Rinehart, and Winston, 1964), pp. 229–32.

conservative ideology in the nation today, there are discernable foci
of interest clustering around the label and some of its traditional doctrines.[25]

Before we look at the conservatism of the postwar period, it would
be well to note that it was preceded by some interesting examples of
conservative orientation to social life. Here we have in mind not the
semiconservatism of the social Darwinists but the ideas of such men as
Henry Adams, Irving Babbitt, and Paul Elmer More.[26] These were
people skeptical of individualism, doubtful of the capacities of individual men, and strongly oriented toward the mystical qualities of an
elevated community life. They attacked equality and doubted the
ability of democracy to create the conditions in which virtue might
flourish. In terms of descent, they owed more to the irrationalist European conservatives of the nineteenth century than to the tradition of
Aristotle and Burke.

The "new conservatives" of the postwar era, however, have not
drawn primarily on the conservatism of the Brooks Adams or the Babbitt varieties. The group identified here and there by the "new" label
is large and diverse, and any attempt to treat it in terms of a common
short description is bound to do injustices. For the most part, it has
been dominated by two kinds of voices—those that are strongly
Burkean in flavor and those that have attempted to fix the conservative
label on extreme laissez-faire individualism. On neither side does one
find much theoretical innovation, though some of the conservatives'
work has been highly stimulative and some has been aesthetically
significant. Perspectives at this point in time are altogether too short
to permit a fair evaluation of the theories of the new conservatives and
their impact on American ideology. Reflection on their ideas, however, suggests there is little in these formulations that is likely to contribute in an original sense either to politics or to thought. They have
been chiefly occupied with warming over the doctrines of earlier days.

---

[25] For representative writings, see Peter Viereck, *Conservatism Revisited* (Rev. and enl.;
New York: Collier Books, 1962); Russell Kirk, *The Conservative Mind from Burke to
Santayana* (Chicago: Henry Regnery Co., 1953); William Buckley, *Up from Liberalism*
(New York: McDowell, Obolensky, 1959). A recent collection of essays is Meyer, *op. cit.*
For the viewpoint and program of a prominent political actor, see Barry Goldwater, *The
Conscience of a Conservative* (Shepherdsville, Ky.: Victor Publishing Co., 1960).

[26] Irving Babbitt, *Democracy and Leadership* (Boston: Houghton Mifflin Co., 1925),
and *Rousseau and Romanticism* (Boston: Houghton Mifflin Co., 1919); Henry Adams,
Democracy, an American Novel (New York: Henry Holt & Co., 1880), *The Education of
Henry Adams* (Boston: Houghton Mifflin Co., 1918); Paul Elmer More, *Aristocracy and
Justice* (Boston: Houghton Mifflin Co., 1915). See also Brooks Adams, *The Law of Civili-
zation and Decay* (New York: A. A. Knopf, 1943).

Like liberalism, contemporary conservatism has labored under the weight of a confused tradition, and it has also been faced with a largely unreceptive culture. On the former point, it has found itself pulled at least four ways, for conservatives commonly borrow not only from the main stem of the Burke tradition, from Spencerian individualism, and from romanticism, but also from the nation- and community-oriented aspects of populism. Again, it is fruitless to talk about what the ideology "really is"; there is no eternal form or essence of conservatism any more than of liberalism. In its classic usage, however, conservatism ordinarily attached to the idea that the community was prior to the individual. Thus, Aristotle and Burke found social reality in the persistent relationships of obligation and complementarity among men. From this assumption, they drew the premise that the social nexus must be preserved and stability cherished. The life of people is the life of a people, an organic entity with a present, a past, and a future. Policy gains legitimacy through its contribution to this common, shared life.

Such a view in contemporary American society is far from the view that the laissez-faire economic system embodies absolute good. It is also antithetical to the view that the path to goodness is to be found by returning to some supposed social system of the past. Both the second and the first positions involve a sort of selective retention through which the "real" qualities of the society are discovered. This process relies, in turn, on the imposition of ulterior standards which may or may not be shared widely by the people who profess the conservative ideology. Here again, then, there is much latitude for difference among those who are presumably united by a symbol, this time the symbol of conservatism. The diffuseness of usage has probably helped blunt the effectiveness of conservatism as a creative and potent force in society.

The situation may be illustrated by reference to some of the strange labeling found among today's conservatives. Many of those who call themselves conservatives—for example, those on the extreme right —are labeled "radical" by their opponents, and their perspectives often show an admixture of populistic adherence to the "folk life" and "folk" standards.[27] On the other hand, one of the purest of Burkean conservatives on the current scene, Walter Lippmann, is widely regarded as a "liberal," and in policy and candidate preferences he is

---

[27] See the collection of essays in Daniel Bell (ed.), *The Radical Right* (Garden City, N.Y.: Doubleday Co., Inc., 1963).

often found on the side of people and groups with "liberal" reputa-
tions.[28]

Perhaps the main drawback to contemporary conservatism relates
to its inability to accommodate theoretically and coherently to change.
Here we must enter the realm of even more far-reaching speculation
about the failure of contemporary ideology. The point is not that classic conservatism is intrinsically opposed to change, for it seems a fairer
reading of Burke to say that his theory was a theory of how change
could be handled. Political conservatism today, however, must deal
with a society in which change is vast, rapid, and self-propelling, a society in which technical innovation and its attendant social problems
do not wait. Contemporary conservatism has not been, by-and-large,
a change-oriented conservatism. Its public image has most usually
been defensive of selected aspects of the status quo, and it has often appeared to be concerned chiefly with the rationalization of certain particular interests. In an age when the crucial internal political need may
have been the development of a constructive image of the community,
conservatism has not been able to fulfill this task to which by tradition
it might have been so well-suited.

CONTEMPORARY POLITICAL SCIENCE
AS POLITICAL THOUGHT

The foregoing discussion suggests that contemporary ideology provides little in the way of constructive, innovative theoretical answers
to the day's sociopolitical problems. In a surface sense, the reason may
be that there are no problems to be answered. Yet, certainly it is clear
that there are tensions, disadjustments, and challenges in the American situation, some apparent and some bubbling just beneath the surface. The world does not stand still; indeed, it is ever increasing the
pace of its change. On the level of political ideas, the question is
whether some mode or modes of thinking will move into the vacuum.
It is too much to assert that such a thing will inevitably happen, and
also too much to say that if it does not, some sort of social breakdown
will ensue. Nonetheless, the question is sufficiently threatening and
sufficiently intriguing to merit speculation.

Before we present some final comments on it, however, we should
give passing attention to one further kind of thinking about political
matters—that found in the scholarly activities of current political sci-

---

[28] Lippmann has written much that is worth reading. Perhaps his most comprehensive
recent statement of political belief is *Essays in the Public Philosophy* (Boston: Little,
Brown & Co., 1955).

ence. We have reference here not just to that portion of the discipline that deals with political thought as its subject matter, but to the whole range of investigation, analysis, and speculation that political science produces. The study of politics now has a secure place in college curricula, and it is carried forward by a lively, vital, and dynamic discipline. Our problem is whether it can be considered as the center of political thought today, whether it is filling or partially filling the void left by the deficiencies of current ideology.

For several reasons, what follows will not attempt to provide an answer to this question, nor will it attempt to describe comprehensively the characteristics of political science. We will be content, instead, to suggest some main themes and possibilities. Again, perspectives are too short to permit confident evaluation; furthermore, changes in orientation and method that have come over portions of the political science field since about the close of the war have only recently begun to settle down and show results. With the development of new foci of interest has come a disciplinary self-consciousness that has stimulated writing about the nature and potential of the field. Thus, there is a literature of political science itself, available to those who wish to look at it in a more exhaustive way.[29]

The political science of today grew in great part out of the scholarship of progressivism. While German and English influences were felt in the early development of the discipline, much of it was founded on indigenous perspectives and stimulated by interests in the creation and restructuring of political institutions. American preoccupation with political institutions perhaps reflects the conditions of the founding and expansion of the nation, conditions that required frequent attention to the building of institutions *de novo*. At any rate, it was during the Progressive era that political science took shape as a field of study, and much of its early growth came in conjunction with institutional critique and movements for reform.

We have already had occasion to discuss, if briefly, the work of Beard and Smith.[30] In some ways, their approaches, interests, and sub-

---

[29] Roland Young (ed.), *Approaches to the Study of Politics* (Evanston: Northwestern University Press, 1958); Charles S. Hyneman, *The Study of Politics: the Present State of American Political Science* (Urbana: University of Illinois Press, 1959); David Easton, *The Political System* (New York: A. A. Knopf, 1953); Heinz Eulau, *The Behavioral Persuasion in Politics* (New York: Random House, 1963); Harold P. Lasswell, *The Future of Political Science* (New York: Atherton Press, 1963). Critical analyses of recent trends are found in Bernard Crick, *The American Science of Politics* (Berkeley: University of California Press, 1959); Herbert J. Storing (ed.), *Essays on the Scientific Study of Politics* (New York: Holt, Rinehart, and Winston, 1962).

[30] See above, pp. 352–54.

ject matters were representative. They wrote from a set of values, chiefly the values of Progressive democracy. They did not hesitate to attack tradition, as witness the constitutional polemics of both, and they had faith in the ability of man to reconstruct the social conditions of his life in important ways. But most significantly, they were "realists"; they sought to grasp what went on behind the appearances of politics. They wished, in the words of A. Lawrence Lowell, to "look through forms to the vital forces behind them." They also began their efforts with practical problems for which they tried to find practical solutions.

Thus, the early political scientists of this century were pragmatic in motivation and scope, if not always in world view. They wished above all to reform American political society, to cut the ground from under corruption and privilege. To do so, they felt, depended on "real" understanding, and this was to be had by going to the hard facts. In this way, the field early took on a coloration of empiricism, a bent toward the gathering of data about the way the world appears to the senses. There were, to be sure, limitations to this approach; by present standards it was atheoretical, piecemeal, often biased, confused about concepts and units, and so on. Nonetheless, it was an empirical political science with heavy ideological and practical overtones. In greater or lesser degree, these were the intellectual conditions that inspired the constitutional studies of Beard, Smith, Ford, and others, the comparative studies of Bryce and Lowell, Wilson's institutional critiques, Bentley's group approach and the several studies growing out of it, the administrative commentaries of Goodnow and Willoughby, and others. The list is long, and it includes nearly all the political science greats of yesterday; what we have said by no means exhausts what might be said about these developments.[31]

Out of the Progressive scholarship of politics also grew an interest in the psychological basis of politics, in a sense, an interest taken a step deeper into human life than the organizational and economic formulations of those mentioned above. Notable among those who contributed to this trend were Graham Wallas, an Englishman, and Walter Lippmann (neither of them a political scientist in the strictest sense of the term); Charles E. Merriam, one of the greatest single forces in drawing the discipline toward its new focus; and Harold Lasswell. The work of Merriam and Lasswell typified many of the developmental aspects of political science: interest in detailed empirical

---

[31] Perhaps the best discussion of this early scholarship is in Crick, *op. cit.*

investigation and quantification, concern with power as a central concept, invigoration of interest in systematic theory, and attention to the policy consequences of the advancement of political knowledge.

This brings us face to face with the question what political science is like today. Brave indeed is the political scientist who would offer a categoric answer. That the field has been in flux would be a matter of universal agreement; where it is, where it is going, and where it should go are much more problematic questions. We will be content here merely to point to some broad characteristics and comment on their implications for political thought. What follows is by no means an attempt to describe the condition of the field.

Much of political science remains what it has been, devoted chiefly to rather loose institutional description and speculative generalization. Some, too, continues the Progressive tradition of reformist evaluation, with assumptions sometimes explicit and sometimes not. The most significant developments in the field, however, would seem to be those that have pushed beyond the piecemeal empiricism of the realist Progressives to the more systematic approaches sometimes called behavioral. Precisely what this label means and how useful it is may be matters for doubt; unfortunately, it has as often served as a symbol of division as it has as a symbol of progress in the discipline. But whatever name is put on it, there has been an influential reorientation of much work in political science toward approaches which take their cues from the established "natural" sciences. Some of the hallmarks of this movement are these:

1. Emphasis on the strict separation of facts and values. This demand stems from the influence of logical positivism, though its intellectual lineage goes back at least as far as David Hume. It is based on the view that statements of fact and statements of value are different in reference, and that those of fact are subject to verification ultimately through operations of the senses. The problems of logic and epistemology involved are vast—too much so to try to handle them here. But the principal point is the insistence that this view puts on the separation of propositions that are verifiable through publicly reported and replicable procedures from propositions that are not.

2. Following from the point just stated, the assumption that scientific methods are applicable to the materials of social science. This point proceeds from the premise that there are observable regularities in human social behavior that can be defined so that statements about them are susceptible to testing through sense-based operations. In turn, it gives rise to the use of quantitative methods in social research,

though only in a loose sense does verification *require* quantitative measurement.

3. Attention to the use of precise units, levels, and concepts of analysis. This is a requirement that grows out of the needs of verification, i.e., the reproducibility of research efforts.

4. Emphasis on systematic theory with ultimate reference to the empirical world. Contemporary political science is experiencing a revivification of theory in the sense that it seeks generalizations that will tie together into bigger packages of reliable knowledge the results of its empirical discoveries. In theory and in research operations, it has borrowed considerably from other disciplines, including psychology, sociology, economics, and mathematics.[32]

While much more might be said in qualification and elaboration, these seem to be the main points around which innovation in political science moves. They are much more like goals than like standards of present-day work, for little of contemporary research meets the high criteria they imply. Nonetheless, they make themselves felt in all segments of the discipline: in more systematic efforts at comparison of political systems, in survey investigation of electoral behavior, in the infusion of organization theory, social psychology, and anthropological questions into public administration studies, in quantitative analyses of judicial business, in new questions put to old systems of political theory.

It was pointed out above that the modes of science do not completely dominate the field of political studies. Perhaps the most interesting and notable countermovement has been that centering around Leo Strauss and his students.[33] Their position is founded on natural law assumptions, i.e., on the idea of a rationally discoverable set of standards of right. They attack the separation of value and empirical statements, asserting the fusion of the two realms, and they reject the idea that the function of political science can be understood without reference to an evaluative role. The study of politics has as its purpose the finding of means to virtue and justice, the development along many lines of a neoclassical interpretation of and approach to the current character of American society. In their emphasis on wisdom and

---

[32] Discussions of the problems of methodology in social science are many. For a comprehensive but nontechnical summary, Vernon Van Dyke, *Political Science: a Philosophical Analysis* (Stanford: Stanford University Press, 1960) is recommended. A more detailed treatment is Abraham Kaplan, *The Conduct of Inquiry* (San Francisco: Chandler Publishing Co., 1964). See also the excellent chapters in Ernest Nagel, *The Structure of Science* (New York: Harcourt, Brace & World, Inc., 1961), pp. 447–546.

[33] Leo Strauss, *What Is Political Philosophy* (Glencoe, Ill.: The Free Press, 1959), particularly the title essay, pp. 9–55. Also Storing, *op. cit.*, and other of Strauss's works.

prudence, on interdependency among men, and on the suffusion of the world with ultimate values, people of this persuasion tend to look at social life much as classical conservatives do.

Others, too, have attacked the premises and consequences of positivistic political science, variously on grounds that it is morally corrupt, that it misconstrues the character of science, that it denies free will, and that it subverts the mission of the discipline to attend to the entire sweep of social and political life. It is not our intention here to review the arguments over the proper orientation of political science; that is a question beyond our scope. What we should attempt, however, is an assessment of the field in terms of its character as political thought, and in this connection, we should take account of the potential contributions of political science to public policy.

The positivistic thrust of today's political science carries with it some implications for the role of scholarship in public life.[34] These probably indicate the limits and qualifications that must be recognized for all political science research, not only for that explicitly positivistic in basic assumptions. Insofar as the positivists are correct in saying that value statements cannot be verified or disverified by empirical scientific procedures or the evidence of the existential world, they indicate the potentials of the discipline for policy-making. Policy at some stage must involve choices made with reference to values, decisions about ultimate standards. In fact, of course, these values need not be explicit; many, perhaps most, decisions are made without conscious consideration of all their value assumptions. The choice among values to be sought is beyond the range of scientific procedure. Short of that element of the decision process, however, there are contributions social science can make. One of these is to raise to the level of consciousness the nature of the decision-making process itself. The development of frameworks for analysis of the process and the accumulation of empirical evidence about how it works will presumably clarify for those involved what it is they are doing. In this sense, social science can contribute to the making of "rational" decisions about public policy.[35]

A second contribution of political science lies in demonstration of the consequences of one choice as compared with another. That is to

---

[34] Probably the most influential writing on political science and public policy has been that done by Harold D. Lasswell. See especially *The Future of Political Science, op. cit.,* and Harold Lasswell and Daniel Lerner (eds.), *The Policy Sciences* (Stanford: Stanford University Press, 1951).

[35] A very comprehensive analytical review of the literature of decision-making is Richard C. Snyder and James A. Robinson, *National and International Decision-Making* (New York: Institute for International Order, n.d.).

say, it is within the power of a developed science to show what it will cost to follow various alternatives. In this way, too, the findings of political study may be put at the disposal of those in positions of responsibility. A third potential of political science is to accumulate relevant, reliable evidence about the state of the environment of decision-making. This function might produce information about such things as social "needs," tensions, and demands—information about how the people are living and what they want.

Given these possibilities, the contributions of political science to the society may be significant, perhaps critically significant. In a number of ways, the field has already pumped such information into the political system. It did so in its early, reformist period as respects a variety of questions of governmental organization. It does so now in such diverse fields as defense policy and strategic problems, opinion and attitude research, organization, and even, to an increasing degree, in the work of the judiciary and legal profession. The potentials are much greater than current activities would suggest. There are some who think that in social science lies the key to a decent and effective public life in the future. The forces of social change, as we pointed out earlier, have brought an ever more complicated environment into being, and control over the environment becomes ever more difficult for both individuals and the polity as a result. One answer to the problems of the age may lie with more effective use of the fruits of a more relevant and comprehensive social science.

There are also grounds for fear of social science; many think its potential for ill outweighs its potential for good. These fears are often expressed as fear of "manipulation," fear of loss of freedom, fear that social science will obliterate the values and processes of liberal democracy. Whether such fears are well-founded, we will not attempt to settle. Social science could probably make freedom either a higher reality or a vestigial memory, depending on the structure of civic values in which it is embedded.

As political thought, as ideational stimulant to action, political science may thus have much to say, but much of a specialized sort. Under the impact of a technological age, it has developed into a semi-technical tool for exploration of the facts of social life. Perhaps, however, it has leaned too far toward isolating itself from the ethical dimensions of political life; this, at least, is a charge sometimes brought against it. Insofar as it focuses entirely on the empirical, it may have forgotten to give adequate attention both to its own responsibilities and to the responsibilities of the society and its people. If this is true, political science might bring the culture new potentials for the development and use of political ideas and, at the same time, obscure a vital part of the whole human common life. At best, political science on its present course thus promises only part of the answer to our search for ideas to guide the action of the future.[36]

POLITICAL THOUGHT AND THE POLITICAL FUTURE

Thus, we have a picture of American social problems and political responses. On the basis of a projection of the past, we might suppose that the institutions of American politics, prodded and channeled by political ideas, will adapt to new needs as they arise, will continue the steady accommodations that have marked the experience of the past. There are, however, some reasons for concern, if not for fear. For there are reasons to suspect that the future will in many ways be even more different from the present than the present is from the past. We have already commented on the accelerating rate of change. Some of the conditions likely to be wrought by change promise to confront political and social thought with challenges of massive magnitude. In the face of these, we now have a society where creative, imaginative political ideas are rare.

For example, the automation of industry proceeds apace, redistributing needs for man's most basic pursuit—work. Before many years, it may be that work in the present sense will become obsolete. Much of the labor now done by man will certainly fall into the grip of the machine. What, then, of our social problems? By what means will we distribute wealth, if not as a reward for work? What kinds of activities will be honored, what kinds valued? What of the moral fiber of such a society, what of its capacity for creativity? How will people use their time? And what of the relationship of this nation to the rest of the world, particularly to the parts that may take decades or centuries to "catch up?"

It may seem bizarre or ridiculous to talk of work as obsolete. But the measure to which it seems so may be the measure by which we will fail to equip ourselves to meet the future. There are deeply embedded reasons—reasons of ideology in the general sense—for our rejecting

---

[36] Several people in contemporary political science have in one way or another approached problems of theory with considerable breadth. Besides the sources mentioned above, particularly those by Merriam and Lasswell, the reader might consult Robert A. Dahl, *A Preface to Democratic Theory* (Chicago: University of Chicago Press, 1956); Henry D. Mayo, *An Introduction to Democratic Theory* (New York: Oxford University Press, 1960); Neal Riemer, *The Revival of Democratic Theory* (New York: Appleton-Century-Crofts, Inc., 1962); Thomas D. Thorson, *The Logic of Democracy* (New York: Holt, Rinehart, and Winston, 1962).

the suggestion that work could disappear. It has long been the center of the American man's universe, its centrality affirmed and reinforced by the Puritan ethic. Now to be told that our relationships to productive enterprise must change jars the entire perspective through which we understand the world. The reluctance of the society to accept the virtual disappearance of the farmer, illustrated by a variety of public policies designed to hide the fact, demonstrates how tenacious a cultural grip on the past can be.

The situation of work is only an example, albeit a fundamental one, of the kinds of demands the future will put on political ideas and actions. A further example, closely related, might be drawn with the concept of community. The cruciality of community to political system has several times been discussed above, as have the impacts of change on community in its classic form. What kind of community will we have in the future? Must community come to be seen in national or even transnational terms? If so, what psychological and sociological adjustments will this require, and what political innovations? And what does all this portend for political responsibility? Perhaps the community of the future must be envisaged as a spatial gathering of the "unemployed," its main "industry" being the production of education and leisure activities, both enterprises that do not create troublesome physical surpluses. How will this be brought about, and what political problems will it produce?

All these questions are acute. They are not, to be sure, the sort that press for answers, as, for example, the question where tomorrow's meal will come from must press people in less fortunate societies. But they are there, and it seems likely that the need to find new approaches will grow more and more nagging. The questions mentioned above are in some way, at least, identifiable. But what of other questions not thought of, needs not yet imagined? The problems briefly discussed above seem to call for new ideology, new policy, and new political organization. And experience suggests that these will go only if they articulate with the major established patterns of the culture. Thus, whole new perspectives must grow out of old ones.

What we have, then, is a challenge to political ideas and to those who like to work with them. The dreary failures of communism argue strongly that there are no ready-tailored answers. The American experience argues that the challenge can only be met through the difficult path of piecemeal adjustment of a going system. The times call for measured innovation, for responsible creativity. At present, the call is not being answered at the level of new thought. Social science may help save us, but vision and evaluation may also be required. The field seems quite open to those brave enough to try.

INDEX

429

This book has been set on the Linotype in 11 and 10 point Baskerville, leaded 2 points. Chapter numbers and chapter titles are in 18 point Deepdene caps. The size of the type pages is 27 by 46½ picas.